Portrait of Johnny

Portrait of Johnny

The Life of John Herndon Mercer

 Pantheon Books, New York **GENE LEES**

All rights reserved under International and Pan-American Copyright
Conventions. Published in the United States by Pantheon Books, a division of
Random House, Inc., New York, and simultaneously in Canada by
Random House of Canada Limited, Toronto.

Pantheon Books and colophon are registered
trademarks of Random House, Inc.

Due to limitations of space, permissions to reprint previously
published material can be found following the index.

Library of Congress Cataloging-in-Publication Data
Lees, Gene.
Portrait of Johnny : the life of John Herndon Mercer / Gene Lees.
p. cm.
Includes index.
ISBN 0-375-42060-6
1. Mercer, Johnny, 1909– 2. Lyricists—United States—Biography. I. Title.
ML423.M446L44   2004
782.42164'092—dc22
[B]   2003060859

www.pantheonbooks.com

Book design by Soonyoung Kwon

Printed in the United States of America
First Edition
2 4 6 8 9 7 5 3 1

To Janet

It's quarter to three.
There's no one in the place
    except you and me,
So, set 'em up, Joe,
I've got a little story
you oughta know. . . .
                    —Johnny Mercer

Acknowledgments

I owe much to many persons for help in the making of this book.

Howard S. (Howie) Richmond, whose TRO (The Richmond Organization) published many of John's songs, as well as my own, was the first to urge me to undertake the project, and it was he who told me that John wanted me to do it. John's daughter, Amanda Mercer Neder, also let me know that John wanted me to do it. Mandy opened the doors to the Mercer relatives for me.

The late Steve Allen, who did so many things well that it was often overlooked that he was a fine songwriter, was a major impetus. It saddens me that he did not live to see the book finished. Alan Bergman, who, with his wife, Marilyn, has written some of the loveliest lyrics of our time, also urged me to undertake the book.

I owe thanks to current and past members of the staff of the Pullen Library Special Collections section at Georgia State University, where many of Mercer's papers repose, and especially to Charlene S. Hurt and Laura Botts.

Certain materials, including Johnny's letters to his wife, Ginger, and the quotations from his unpublished autobiography, are among the Johnny Mercer Papers, Popular Music Collection, Special Collections Department, University Library, copyright owned by Georgia State

Acknowledgments

University, a unit of the Board of Regents of the University System of Georgia.

I thank the staff of the Georgia Historical Society in Savannah. Chuck Haddix of the University of Missouri–Kansas City provided material pertaining to the late Dave Dexter. My late friend Willis Conover did a superb interview with Mercer for his Voice of America program, *Music USA*. The tape of it is in the National Archives in College Park, Maryland.

In 2002, the British Broadcasting Corporation (BBC) did a four-part radio series titled *Johnny Mercer: Accentuate the Positive,* for which many of John's associates, including me, were interviewed. The producer drew on past interviews with John and various of his colleagues, including Harry Warren and Hoagy Carmichael. This archive material is invaluable.

Johnny Mercer began an autobiography. After his death, his widow, Ginger, brought it to me. It was sporadic and fragmented, and its chronology was confused. She asked me whether I could edit it into some kind of coherence, which I did. A copy of my edited manuscript was left to Johnny's daughter, Amanda, and another remained in my hands. I have drawn on this manuscript. At times I wanted to keep the feeling of John's vocabulary and flavor of speech. Where I have incorporated these passages into my text, they have been set in italics.

Over a period of years I interviewed Johnny several times, either for magazine articles or, in one instance, a program for the Canadian Broadcasting Corporation. I have drawn on these articles, and a tape of the CBC broadcast, and of course our many informal conversations.

The late Jimmy Hancock, a friend of John's and nephew of one of the close friends of John's youth, was my first guide to Savannah and the Mercer relatives. As I worked on the book, Jimmy left us, but he lived long enough to read and advise me on an early draft. I thank the late Jimmy McIntire and his wife, Barbara, and John's niece, Libby Hammond.

I especially thank Rose Gilbert of Rancho Mirage, California, widow of John's friend and fellow lyricist Wolfe Gilbert, and herself John's friend of many years.

John was often in my conversations with his friends and professional colleagues, among them Johnny Mandel, David Raksin, the late Henry Mancini, and the late Les Brown. Though I did not foresee using

Acknowledgments

this "material," these conversations were valuable indeed. I especially cite my gratitude to the late Peggy Lee; the late Jay Livingston; the late Paul Weston and his widow, Jo Stafford; the late Harry Warren; and the late Harold Arlen.

And I especially thank Nancy Keith Gerard, for reasons that will become abundantly clear.

For reading the manuscript in whole or in part, I thank Nancy; my wife, Janet; Jo Stafford; Mickey Goldsen; Howie Richmond; Rose Gilbert; Mandy Mercer Neder; the late Jimmy Hancock; and Phil and Jill Woods.

Formally or informally, I interviewed over a period of years Steve Allen, Jean Bach, Betty Bennett, Alan and Marilyn Bergman, Oscar Brand, Les Brown, Bob Corwin, James Corwin, John Corwin, Ray Evans, Nancy Keith Gerard, Rose Gilbert, Mickey Goldsen, Bill Goodwin, Jill Goodwin, Jimmy Hancock, William Harbach, Dwight Hemion, Gilbert Keith, Alan Livingston, Jay Livingston, James T. Maher, Nick Mamalakis, Henry Mancini, Jeff Mercer, Amanda Mercer Neder, David Oppenheim, Howie Richmond, André Previn, Arthur Schwartz, Carl Sigman, Harry Warren, Jo Stafford Weston, Paul Weston, and Margaret Whiting. I interviewed one of John's physicians, Dr. Michael R. Kadin, who treated him after his surgery. I gained insight into his condition from interviews with three neurologists: Dr. Barry Little, radio neurologist Roméo Éthier, and neurosurgeon Albert MacDade.

I thank Matthew Haskins, lecturer in the American Studies Department at California State University, Fullerton, for providing me with a complete set of copies of *The Capitol News* from March 1943 to December 1951.

I am not enamored of footnotes, and so I have identified the sources of quotations in the text itself. Wherever there is a quotation without attribution, the comments were made to me.

Johnny's friends tended to call him John. He signed his letters to his mother "John," "Johnny," once or twice "Jawnnny," and occasionally "Bubba." I think Johnny was the public figure, but John was the private friend. Both names are used throughout the book.

Portrait of Johnny

One

It is often difficult to remember exactly where and when you met some-one, but in the case of Johnny Mercer I remember that first encounter almost to the minute. I had come out to Los Angeles from New York, where I then lived, to write the lyrics for some songs in a movie. I called a friend, the wonderful singer Betty Bennett, and asked if she might be free for dinner that night. She said she would be attending a birthday party, and then added, "Do you want to go with me?" I asked her whose birth-day it was and she said it was that of the composer John Williams.

I said, "Since today is also my birthday, I'd love to go."

We went to the Williams house. As we entered, I saw three men stand-ing at the top of a little stairway from the foyer into the living room. The one on the left was a friend of several years, Henry Mancini. The one on the right I did not recognize, although I soon learned he was Dave Cavanaugh, one of the most important producers at Capitol Records. The one in the middle, the man with a space between his incisors when he smiled, was Johnny Mercer. I knew that face from countless photographs in *Down Beat* and other publications, including one called *The Capitol News,* which was distributed free through record stores throughout the United States. And because it was my thirty-eighth birthday, and John Williams's thirty-fifth, I can date this meeting exactly: February 8, 1966, shortly after eight p.m.

I had the most immense respect for Johnny Mercer. Every American lyricist I have known considers, or considered, him the best of them all, and the volume of his output of great lyrics, at all levels, from the outright commercial ("Goody Goody") to the reaches of high art ("Once Upon a Summertime," "One for My Baby"), over four decades, is awesome. In 1942 alone he wrote for motion pictures twelve major standard songs that are still performed around the world.

In addition to that, he was the man who founded Capitol Records, an upstart company that had a huge impact on American—and, by extension, world—culture. The company began in 1942, in the midst of World War II, under conditions that would have halted a lesser man, including a major shortage of the shellac on which discs were pressed and a pending musicians' strike. Capitol was a fresh wind in popular music and jazz, and its artistic direction, as I would eventually learn, was set almost completely by Mercer.

Even its black label with silver lettering and an outline of the Capitol building in Washington, D.C., seemed special. But above all it was the music that came out on Capitol, produced either directly by Mercer or indirectly by his close collaborators. Suddenly we were presented with an array of new artists, most of them of the highest quality, in those middle and latter years of the war: the King Cole Trio, Jo Stafford, Freddie Slack, Stan Kenton, Andy Russell, Bobby Sherwood, Ella Mae Morse, Peggy Lee, and so many more, including Mercer himself. He was a singer of distinctive, rough-hewn, vaguely bucolic insouciance and charm whose humor shone through such of his songs as "The Strip Polka," one of Capitol's first important hits. Mercer's roots were in jazz, and his vocals had a wonderful and unpretentious swing. Later came his recordings of such poignant works as "Any Place I Hang My Hat Is Home," which he wrote (with Harold Arlen) for the musical St. Louis Woman. That was another thing about Capitol: a lot of its records were just plain funny, including such Betty Hutton hits as "My Rocking Horse Ran Away."

When I was growing up in Canada, you couldn't get those records there: Capitol had no out-of-country distribution during the war. So I used to buy them in Niagara Falls, New York, at a favorite record store and smuggle them home, along with the latest issue of The Capitol News, under the seat of an intercities bus. I remember feeling tremors of apprehension as the bus went through Immigration and Customs and a uniformed inspector would ask what I was bringing into Canada; I'd say, "Nothing," hoping he would not see through my lie. I wondered if for my transgression I might be hustled off to, if not jail, perhaps reform school. I never got caught, but certainly my venture into small-time smuggling lent those records a certain special glamour—because they were *illegal,* they were *contraband.* And, furthermore, few other kids where I lived had them.

I did not foresee that I would follow Mercer into the craft of song-writing. It was not on my list of uncertain aspirations; I just liked great songs, and I recognized that his were among the finest. And by then I was an avid observer of the writers' credits under the song titles on those heavy and breakable old 78 rpm records. The late Alan Jay Lerner thought that Mercer was the greatest lyricist in the history of the English language, which essentially means the American language, since the body of good songs from England is limited. Paul Weston, the arranger who worked closely with Mercer, said, "John did more things well than any other lyricist. John had genius." Jimmy Van Heusen, with whom Mercer wrote "I Thought About You," also applied the word *genius* to Mercer. "As far as lyric writers are concerned," he said, "I don't think there's any-body near him."

One of John's friends, the television producer William Harbach—son of another great lyricist, Otto Harbach (who, with Jerome Kern, wrote "Smoke Gets in Your Eyes")—recalled a luncheon with his father and Oscar Hammerstein II. Harbach said, "My father and Oscar Hammerstein were very close friends. They wrote a lot of shows together—*Rose Marie, Sonny,* and about four other shows. I asked Oscar how he felt about Johnny Mercer. He said, 'Johnny Mercer is the greatest American lyricist alive. I could no more write a lyric like one of his than fly. It's so Americana.' "

Alan Bergman, of the lyric-writing team of Alan and Marilyn Bergman, said, "He was the most versatile, the best of those we study and appreciate. He could write anything. He could be very funny, yet he wrote a lot about lost youth. The images and the metaphors are just marvelous. I'm amazed every time I hear his work."

What is it that was so great about Mercer's work?

The late Boris Vian, a gifted French musician, author, and songwriter, once said in an interview that he was far more proud of his song lyrics than of his novels. There are good reasons why he felt so.

The song is unique among literary forms, and by far the most exact-ing. It has the function of retarding emotional time, so that the listener can experience the feelings it is attempting to convey with an intensity compa-rable to the effect of watching the wings of a hummingbird in slow-motion cinematography. This is one reason a song can move you to tears.

It has been said that poetry can communicate before it is understood.

This is questionable. Language is structured specifically to convey information, and you can be moved only by words in a language with which you are familiar. If you do not understand what is being said, you won't be moved. Furthermore, one's own language has a power that no acquired language can probably ever have. Emotion, however, is conveyed by pitch and inflection and sonority. You can hear it even in the cries and yelps and whimpers of animals. Hearing is our early-warning system. We are designed so that we respond instantly to sounds: it is a survival mechanism. And *that* is what music is made of.

Music, therefore, *can* communicate before it is understood. It need not be understood at all, ever. It doesn't matter whether you have a technical knowledge of the art when you are being moved by, say, a Rachmaninoff concerto or a jazz solo by Dizzy Gillespie. Music is the only art that works directly on the nervous system. Much has been written, and continues to be written, about how music achieves its effects, but in the end even neurologists seem to be baffled. They can describe some of the mechanics of the process, but they cannot tell you why the process *works*.

In these observations one catches a glimpse, though only a glimpse, of the power of song. The words must be slowed to the pace of the music, which gives them time to have their emotional effect, while the music has its own direct emotional effect. There is nothing in literature to compare to this form.

Modern free verse (*vers libre*) is all but useless as musical material, since it lacks recurrent pattern, essential to the structure of a song. And poetry in meter has little to do with the nature of the song lyric. For the syllables of a song lyric, wedded to music, must be long or short, to match the note. You need long vowels on long notes, short vowels on short notes, and always there is the problem of articulation: the words must not so much fall trippingly from the tongue, as Shakespeare put it, as move smoothly in and through and from the mouth of the singer. And if the singer is confronted by a rapid-patter song, such as Stephen Sondheim's brilliant and difficult "I'm Not Getting Married Today" in the musical *Company,* the flow of the consonants becomes only the more important.

Thus, as a result of this emphasis on length of vowel and consonant, the modern song lyric has more in common with Latin poetry than later European metered poetry. (A trace of this still exists in Italian.)

There is yet another critical factor in good lyric writing: the intervals of the melody line must be close to the intervals that would occur in natural speech, an idea and ideal abandoned in the rock age. English and

French are far more tonal languages than is generally recognized. For example, in the opening song of *Company,* which is based on the name of its principal character, Bobby, Sondheim (who also wrote the music) employed a falling minor third, which is the way you ordinarily say that name. In *My Fair Lady,* the song "I've Grown Accustomed to Her Face" begins with the title phrase set (in C) to the notes CDEGD. That is the way you would say it. The falling fourth, from G to D (". . . her face"), has an uncertain, sighing quality about it, expressing the protagonist's bafflement at discovering how much he has come to need her. Whether Lerner set the words to Loewe's music or Loewe set the music to Lerner's words I don't know. Probably they worked the way Cole Porter did: he would find the title, build his melody from it, and then fit the rest of the lyric to the music. Johnny Mercer was reluctant to write lyrics first, believing that a song's musical flow is more natural, more lyrical, when the music is written first. In general, good lyricists are better at hearing the words in music than composers are at hearing the music in words.

If you *do* write the lyric before the music, you are forced to set up some sort of metric structure to accommodate music's need for repeats, particularly the first, second, and final eight bars in an AABA song form. And this forces you into a metrical scheme, which, when the composer attempts to solve the problem, often results in a sort of *recitativo* chanting effect.

There is another problem specific to lyric writing: you should try to avoid beginning a word with the same consonant that ends the previous word. If you don't, they run together, causing a confusion in the ear. (Americans still seem unable to decide whether the stuff is called *duct tape* or *duck tape.*)

Long notes tend to occur at the end of musical phrases. For this reason, long open vowels—those not terminated by a consonant—are ideal at the ends of such lines. The most singable vowel sounds in the English language are *oo* and *oh.* But of course you cannot count on open vowels to end every line; there aren't enough words containing them. Next best are the liquid consonants, sometimes called semivowels, of which there are four in English: *m, n, l,* and *r.* Technically *f* and *s* qualify as well, but if you sustain them they sound odd. M, *n, l,* and *r* can be sustained in singing. You can sing "Dream" (one of Johnny's most successful songs), and sustain that *m,* singing *Dreammm.* Conversely, you cannot sing *upppp.* That word would best be used on a short note.

Mercer wrote a deceptively simple song (music by Victor Schertzinger) called "I Remember You." He built the entire lyric out of the *oo* and *oh* sounds and the liquid consonant *l*, with brief appearances by *m* and *n*.

Furthermore, in the second eight bars—the repeat of what song-writers call the front strain—he manages a deft character sketch of shy humility.

> *I remember you.*
> *You're the one*
> *who made my dreams*
> *come true*
> *a few*
> *kisses ago.*
>
> *I remember you.*
> *You're the one*
> *who said: "I love you, too."*
> *I do.*
> *Didn't you know?*
>
> *I remember, too,*
> *a distant bell*
> *and stars that fell*
> *like rain,*
> *out of the blue.*
>
> *When my life is through*
> *and the angels*
> *ask me to recall*
> *the thrill of them all,*
> *then I shall tell them*
> *I remember you.*

It sounds so simple, but it is stunning in its technical virtuosity.

Finally, it must be said that English is a very poor language for rhyme. Every lyricist hears (and inwardly sighs) repeatedly, "Is it true that there is no rhyme for *orange?*" Yes, it is. But there is no rhyme for *April*, either, and for a rhyming dictionary I wrote some years ago, I compiled a list of more than three hundred words that have no rhymes, among them *charcoal, culprit, envy,* and *fondle.* But beyond that, there are many words for which the rhymes are few, including the word *love.* It has only four rhymes, *above, dove, glove,* and *shove. Of* is often used, although it properly rhymes with *suave.* That's why you get so much stuff about the *stars above* and *dreaming of.* Only occasionally does someone use these rhymes brilliantly, as in Alan Jay Lerner's quatrain in *My Fair Lady:*

> *You want to talk of Keats and Shelley.*
> *She only wants to talk of love.*
> *You go to see a play or ballet*
> *and end up searching for her glove.*

These are some, but by no means all, of the technical problems of writing good lyrics, most of which, of course, have been largely abandoned in the period after the golden age of American songwriting, that time when a lot of popular music was good and a lot of good music was popular, that epoch of American High Culture.

Obviously I was not thinking all this, but I certainly appreciated Mercer's mastery of the craft when I saw him standing there with Henry Mancini in John Williams's living room. I approached them and said, "Hello, Hank."

He greeted me and said, "Gene, this is Johnny Mercer." Hank and Johnny had collaborated on such songs as "Moon River," "Days of Wine and Roses," "The Sweetheart Tree," "Charade," and more. "John, this is Gene Lees. He's a writer from the East." And Dave Cavanaugh, whose identity I did not yet know, added, "He's also one hell of a lyricist."

Well. To have that said in front of a man whose body of work I revered—from "Jeepers Creepers" to the songs with Mancini—produced the most confused conflict of emotions in me. To have that said in front of my hero thrilled and embarrassed me at the same time. In that discomfort, I managed to blurt, "Well, Mr. Mercer, if I know anything about writing lyrics, I learned it from Cole Porter, you, and Charles Trenet."

At which he flashed that gap-toothed grin I knew from so long ago and said, "How'd I get in there between two queens?"

I don't remember anything more of that evening.

Two days later, I got a letter at my hotel from Mercer. He had telephoned Mancini—whose office at Sunset and Vine I used as home base when I was in Los Angeles—who told him where he could find me. The typed letter read:

> *What a coincidence, after meeting you. I was driving in*
> *my car when I heard a song on the radio called "Someone to*

*Light Up My Life." I pulled over and phoned the radio station to
find out who had written that lyric. And it was you.*

*That sure is some elegant lyric. It made me cry. I wish I had
written it. Please give me a call. Perhaps we can have dinner.*

A day or so later I had dinner with Mercer and his wife, Ginger. Having been a newspaper reporter before I was ever a songwriter, I questioned him about the nature of the craft. One of the tricks I picked up during my newspaper days was that of doing interviews without taking notes. The moment you pull out a notepad and pencil or, in later years, a recording device, you remind the subject that he or she is under interrogation, and this tends to produce a certain stiffness in the responses. But if you take no notes and scrupulously memorize what is told you, you can get a lot more out of the subject. Back at my hotel, I wrote that conversation up as a magazine article for *High Fidelity,* for which I was then a contributing editor. I later learned that John had a thousand copies of that piece printed and gave them to friends and colleagues, telling them (I have been advised) with amazement and almost paternal pride that I had taken no notes. He didn't know he'd been suckered.

His full name was John Herndon Mercer. He was born November 18, 1909, the direct descendant of a certain Hugh Mercer of Aberdeen, who, as a young physician just out of medical school, attended the Scottish wounded at the Battle of Culloden on April 16, 1746. The battle was an attempt by the feckless Charles Edward Stuart, known as Bonnie Prince Charlie, to put himself on the throne of England. A much larger, and certainly more disciplined, English army defeated the Stuart forces decisively and proceeded to bayonet the wounded. They even killed the doctors. After that they hunted down all those they could find who had anything to do with the battle and killed them, often along with their wives, children, and livestock. (These were actions worthy, in a later time, of the Nazi butcher Reinhard Heydrich.) Hugh Mercer managed to hide on a farm, and in March of 1747 was able to board a ship to Philadelphia. He settled in due course near Greencastle, just north of the Maryland border in central Pennsylvania, where he accepted command of the local militia, which was assembled in defense against the Indians.

He carried on two professions in America, that of soldier and that of physician. He fought in the French and Indian Wars, then resigned his commission and moved to Fredericksburg, Virginia, to resume his practice as a physician. In the early 1770s, Mercer was an habitué of the Rising

Sun Tavern, among whose other patrons were Spencer Monroe, father of the future president James Monroe; John Marshall, who would become Chief Justice of the Supreme Court; Patrick Henry; George Washington; and John Paul Jones, a fellow Scotsman whose past, rumor held, included piracy and murder.

The owner of the tavern was George Weedon, a colonel in the Continental Army. Hugh Mercer married Weedon's sister-in-law, Isabella Gordon, who bore him five children, among them Ann Gordon Mercer in 1765, and in 1775 or '76, the youngest of them, Hugh Tennant Weedon Mercer. It was from this line of the family that Johnny Mercer was descended. John was well aware of this ancestry, and proud of it.

Among the regulars of the Rising Sun Tavern was a man who was in fact a wanted criminal in Scotland, with a price of five hundred pounds on his head. And so he took a name that was common among Scots immigrants, Patton. To his dying day, Robert Patton never told his children his real name.

Hugh Mercer took up his military career once again in the American Revolution, becoming a brigadier general, an aide and close confidant of George Washington. His brilliance, some historians believed, would have made him the first president of the United States had he not been wounded in the Battle of Princeton—a statue to him now stands there—and died.

Robert Patton turns up again in historical records in 1793 as superintendent of the Fredericksburg Bank. In his late forties at the time, he married Hugh Mercer's eldest child, Ann Gordon Mercer, then twenty-eight. They had six children, among them John Mercer Patton, the foundation of a distinguished family line. I am pressed to wonder if General George S. Patton III ever knew that the lyrics of many of the songs his soldiers heard on the radio and from jukeboxes, including that most poignant of all World War II going-away songs, "My Shining Hour," were written by a man who drew his descent from Hugh Mercer, survivor of Culloden. And to this day I do not know if Johnny Mercer knew that Patton was his distant cousin.

I began research on this book with meetings and telephone conversations with Mercer's daughter, Mandy, who urged me to talk to her cousin, Nancy Keith Gerard, daughter of Johnny's sister Juliana. She said that Nancy was keeper of the family flame, its true historian.

"To understand my Uncle Johnny," Nancy said, "you have to know Savannah, and Georgia, and you have to know about his mother and father. I grew up in the same house on Gwinnett Street that he did. His mother raised me as her own. You really must come to Savannah and stay with us."

I told her that I didn't want to impose; I could take a hotel room. She thought that this would be unsatisfactory, saying we would need to spend long stretches of time together: she had cartons of letters, photos, and memorabilia that I would need to examine. It would be far easier if I stayed with her and her husband, Steve. And so I agreed.

I drove up to their house, a beautiful new home on the very edge of a great stretch of tidewater marsh. As I walked toward it, she and Steve came out to greet me. A thought flashed: *She looks like somebody I know.*

Of course! She resembled Johnny remarkably.

Two

The state of South Carolina is roughly an equilateral triangle standing on one of its points. Its eastern boundary is the Atlantic Ocean, the western the state of Georgia. The city of Savannah lies just over the Georgia state line at the bottom point of that triangle, the two states being separated there by the Savannah River. The land is low: the entire coastal area is known locally as the Low Country, and the regional cuisine reflects the geography, with a certain emphasis on rice, which is readily grown in its wetlands. The great marshes, mile on mile on mile of saw grass sharp enough to slash you—green in the spring, yellow-brown in the fall, intricately intercut by meandering saltwater channels—dominate the land, and the waters yield what the people call "coon oysters," since the raccoons love them. The folks say these are the tastiest oysters in the world, and once there were, along these estuaries, countless factories where the oysters were shucked and packed in ice and shipped off to canneries. The shells were spread on the dirt roads to be crushed beneath the wheels of wagons and under the hooves of horses and, later, the tires of automobiles. On moonlit nights they still make ghostly blue-white paths among the black shadows of trees. John talked to me about that land, always poetically and often, it seems now in memory, with a certain yearning.

The dominant flora are palmetto and great live oak trees and tall conifers, pines mostly, with long needles or short, and all these trees are hung with gray beards of Spanish moss, an epiphytic plant almost universal in this region. Even without the history of slavery that always shadows this land, these trees and this moss would lend the region a distinct melancholy.

The fauna include Virginia deer; 79 species of reptiles, among them 23 of turtles, 13 of lizards, and 3 of crocodilians, as well as rattlesnakes and water moccasins; and 160 species of birds, including dove, blue heron, white ibis, and snowy egret, wading birds whose sudden flight can make the heart leap, and the bobwhite, subject of one of Johnny's several bird songs. The swarms of mosquitoes compounded the torment of the slaves who toiled here.

In fact, Georgia forbade slavery when it was founded in 1733 by James Edward Oglethorpe, a young English idealist, military officer, and Member of Parliament. He landed his small colony of settlers on a bluff that rises the height of a two-story house above the Savannah River, and established a friendship with the chief of the local Creek Indian tribe, who gave the settlers considerable help, a friendship that lasted as long as Oglethorpe remained in the New World. In time, however, the greater prosperity of the surrounding slaveholding states drew off population from Georgia until it declined, and the prohibition of slavery was rescinded.

Oglethorpe laid out Savannah in a grid of streets that lie in tidy right angles on a north-northwestern slant that follows the course of the river. His precise plan established open squares every third street on the north-south lie, every fourth on the east-west lie, to be used for defense in times of hostility, as markets in peacetime. These have become small parks. The largest of them, Forsyth Park, one of the loveliest in America, was laid out by Governor John Forsyth ten years before the Civil War; its fountain was added in 1868.

John Herndon Mercer grew up two blocks from Forsyth Park in a large white clapboard house at the intersection of Lincoln and Gwinnett Streets. Street names in Savannah predate the Civil War: the Lincoln in question is not Abraham, and Button Gwinnett was Georgia's delegate to the Continental Congress and a signer of the Declaration of Independence. John was born at a women's hospital called Telfair. According to the baby book kept by his mother, he had his first outing by automobile on December 8, 1909, when he was taken home to an apartment at 118 Hall Street. When he was two, according to the book, the family moved to the house at 226 Gwinnett. Four brick steps rise to its front porch, the roof of which is upheld by four white round pillars.

John's father, George Anderson Mercer, was the second in the family line to bear that name. Successful in banking and real estate, he was beloved in Savannah, and above all trusted. His intimates, though no one else, knew that he was in the custom of slipping a ten-dollar bill into a plain envelope, without return address, and sending it to someone he thought was in need. His first wife, Mary Ellis Walter of Savannah, gave birth to three sons, dying after the birth of the third. John was born of his second wife, Lillian Ciucevich.

If John made much of his Scottish lineage, according to his daughter, Mandy, he hardly if ever mentioned that on his mother's side he was a mixture of Croatian and Irish.

In the summer of 2000, the Bonaventure Historical Society published a paper by Glenn T. Eskew of the Department of History at Georgia State University in Atlanta on the subject of the Mercers and their relatives. Eskew noted that "The Ciuceviches first appeared in Savannah when two Croatian brothers left the Austrian Empire in the 1870s. Born in Dalmatia in 1834, John Ciucevich married Julia Merritt, a native of North Carolina. His brother Frank Ciucevich married Sarah, a native of Ireland. The Ciucevich families developed truck farms outside Savannah at the Five Mile Bend on August Road. They sold produce in town and supplies and liquor to folks in the country."

According to Eskew's narrative, Frank Ciucevich—brother of John's maternal grandfather—was murdered by a sharecropper in 1897. No further information about the incident seems to have survived.

A family friend described Lillian Ciucevich, John's mother, as having skin as white as a lily. She was born on September 22, 1881, one of eleven children, two of whom died in infancy. In her older years she was called, in keeping with Southern custom, Miss Lillian. I never met her, but once Johnny phoned me from Savannah, and when I returned his call I spoke for a short time to her and to Johnny's sister, Juliana. If Miss Lillian was Irish through her mother, Croatian on her father's side, no one ever sounded more richly Tidewater Georgia than she.

In 1978, and again in 1984, her younger sister, Katherine Ciucevich O'Leary, dictated memoirs of the family. In the first she described her mother and father, Johnny's maternal grandparents. Her mother, she related, was Julia Ann Merritt, an Irish girl born in Charlotte, North Carolina, on May 10, 1856. She died in Savannah on April 26, 1929.

Her father, John Joseph Ciucevich, was born in Lagosta, an island in the Adriatic off the coast of Yugoslavia, near Dubrovnik. The country was then a possession of the Austro-Hungarian Empire, under the rule of the emperor Franz Joseph.

Katherine said: "At the age of fourteen, my father went as a cabin boy on a sailing vessel on which his uncle was a crew member. A year after leaving home, at Christmastime, his boat passed within sight of Lagosta, and he could see smoke arising from the chimney of his house. He never returned home, but corresponded with his family until his death.

"In time he became a first mate, and later left his boat to live in Charleston, South Carolina, in the United States, where he became a naturalized citizen. Being a skilled seaman, it was only natural that he became involved in the business of the fast-growing port. He purchased a sloop for river operations and short outside trips, being of particular use in the rice trade and standing high in the esteem of the planters and commission merchants. The saying went, 'If Captain John handles it, one can count on proper care and full delivery.'

"In 1871 my parents were married. Mother was living in Charleston with an older sister, Nora Ivanovitz. There were other sisters living in Charlotte, North Carolina. When my parents first came to Savannah, they rented living space on East Broad Street, north of Oglethorpe Avenue. Several children were born. Two little brothers, John and Vincent, died young. They are buried in our family lot in the old Catholic Cemetery. Then Mary and Lillian were born. About this time father sold his sloop and bought forty acres of cleared land and some wooded and swamp land back of our house on Pipe Maker Creek. There was a wooden, two-story house surrounded by a white picket fence. Later, Mother had a lovely flower garden.

"I went down to see the swamp one time and I stood on the edge and saw all this muddy water, the trees growing up through it, with no people around, and it scared me to death."

Captain John Ciucevich died of pneumonia, leaving eight children and an estate consisting of the farm, a house in Savannah, and an insurance policy worth $4,000. His widow decided to stay on the farm and work it with the help of her son Frank.

"Education and our Catholic faith," Katherine said, "were of the most importance in my mother's eyes. She was of the Methodist faith but joined the Catholic Church before her death. Mother was the kindest, most loving and generous person I ever knew. She was always ready to help anyone in need.

"According to Mother, our father was equally kind and ready to help others."

. . .

Portrait of Johnny

On Saturday, December 8, 1906, the *Savannah Press* printed a small item as the lead story on its society page. It read:

NOON WEDDING

Today at noon at Christ church Mr. George A. Mercer, Jr., and Miss Lilly Ciucevich were quietly married by Rev. Francis Allan Brown in the presence of immediate friends and family. Mr. and Mrs. Mercer left this afternoon on the Atlantic Coast Line for a Northern trip.

The next day, the *Savannah Morning News* carried this item:

MARRIAGE AT CHRIST CHURCH
Interesting Wedding Which Took Place Quietly at Noon Yesterday

Miss Lillian Barbara Ciucevich and Mr. G. A. Mercer, Jr., were very quietly married yesterday at half past twelve o'clock in Christ Church by the Rev. Francis A. Brown. Only the immediate relatives and close friends of the contracting parties were present.

Miss Ciucevich is the daughter of the late Capt. John Ciucevich, an honored and respected merchant here for years. She is of Austrian descent and has all the charm and sparkling vivacity of that nationality and is of a very lovable and unselfish nature.

Mr. Mercer is one of Savannah's young professional and business men, being engaged in the practice of law and the real estate business. Mr. and Mrs. Mercer left on the midday train for New York. On their return they will live at No. 210 Taylor Street.

Note that one paper said they left by train, the other that they went by boat. What is odd about the two items is the emphasis both papers put on how quiet the wedding was. And the *Savannah Morning News* added what seems a gratuitous comment on the character of the bride. Puzzling. Note, too, that she is identified as Austrian, rather than Bosnian, although as Bosnia was at that time part of the Austro-Hungarian Empire, this was technically correct. "Austrian," of course, has more class.

Lillian became an Episcopalian. "Her siblings were staunch Roman

Catholics," recalled Nancy Gerard, "and I am sure they were certain she was going to Hell, especially my Aunt Nora. Aunt Nora used to take me to Mass after I got home from Sunday School at my Episcopal church."

The Ciucevich family lived near what was known as Five Mile Bend, where the trains turned around. Nancy, who was trained as both a singer and an occupational therapist, says her grandmother Miss Lillian always remembered the lonesome sound of the train whistles. "I think she told me the same things she told Johnny, because she raised me and she raised him. I think 'Blues in the Night' came from that."

And of course it opens with "My mama done tol' me . . ."

Nancy Gerard continued: "Granny told me she didn't get beyond a fourth-grade education. However, she was very smart and read constantly. She was generous almost to a fault and expected others, especially Johnny, to be as generous. She had gone to work for Mercer Insurance, and that's where she met my grandfather. She raised his three sons, George, Walter, and Hugh, by his first wife, Mary Walter. He was so upset and distressed by her death, and maybe angry at Hugh for her death, that Hugh stayed with an aunt and didn't come to live with him until he was eight years old, when my grandfather and grandmother got married. I know that Hugh never felt confident, never had self-esteem, never got it together. Johnny helped him a lot over the years. He even bought a house out at what is now Moon River so that Hugh could live in it.

"Hugh was the youngest. He was about eight. Then there was Walter, who was about twelve, and George was probably fourteen or fifteen, maybe sixteen. Johnny loved his brothers, and especially loved Hugh, who was closest in age. When Johnny was born, Lillian was disappointed that it was a boy. But she loved him to death. A year or two later, a little sister, Nancy Herndon Mercer, was born."

In the second of her two memoirs, Katherine Ciucevich recalled: "Lillian worked in George Mercer's office and he was a widower. I don't think Lillian was interested in him, because she was romantic. She had lots of boy friends. She was pretty. But Mr. Mercer had position. His family had a little background. . . . He courted her for a good many years before she decided to marry him."

The date of their wedding was December 8, 1906, according to Eskew's account. George A. Mercer was born in 1868. Eskew gives her birth year as 1881, which would have made her thirteen years his junior, but family accounts give the difference as twenty-two years.

"They were married in the Christ Episcopal Church," Katherine wrote. "I think Lillian went to the Christ Episcopal Church but she was not a religious person. She was a good person, sound, but religion didn't mean anything to her. When she and [my sister] Mary were small children, they went to church and Papa used to see that they went to the Catholic school. Mary became a good Catholic, but Lillian didn't; she was superficial. I don't think anything appealed to her except she would like to have lived in a lovely home, in nice surroundings and around cultured people, and she didn't accept not having it.

"Mr. Mercer was a wonderful man. He certainly was a God's blessing to Mother. He was wonderful to her."

John was adored by his parents and by his older half brothers, and he returned their affection. He was called Bubba by his mother and other relatives. The prejudices of the North have attached a pejorative connotation to that nickname, but in the South it is not unusual and means simply "brother."

"Granny used to tell me stories about my Uncle Bubba," Nancy said. "When he was five or six years old, he said, 'Muvva, is there some job I can do?' He couldn't say *mother*. 'I need to earn some money.' She let him do some jobs, and he got a quarter or something. He was gone for a little while, and then he came back with this droopin' old lily. It was a Mother's Day gift for her. So even very early, he cared about that. She was so touched. She never forgot that.

"She would tell stories about how he would be missing and she would call over to the east side of town, which is where the colored theaters were. We said 'colored' in those days. She knew them. They'd say, 'That you, Mrs. Mercer? Yes, John's here. Shall I send him home?' He followed all the bands."

"My father was a religious man," John told an interviewer for a *Reader's Digest* article published in February 1956. "He lived his religion with everybody he knew, rich and poor, Negro and white. He was a gentle, humane man. I admired him."

Nancy said, "I was always taught how honest and generous my grandfather was, how he had friends from all walks of life, how he kept a collection of dimes in his pocket to give to the little boys or girls on the street, and how he paid his bills every month exactly on time. I'm certain Johnny got the same impression, especially since he actually knew his father. I didn't."

Johnny's father, like his mother, was a music lover. John remembered that when he was a very small boy, perhaps three or four, his father would sit in a rocking chair in front of the fireplace and sing old songs, among them "Genevieve, Sweet Genevieve"; "In the Gloaming"; and "When You and I Were Young, Maggie." In his uncompleted memoirs John wrote:

Maybe I was a product of the Roaring Twenties, but a lot of songs I have written over the intervening years were probably due to those peaceful moments in his arms. Secure and warm, I would drift off to dreams, just as, later on, out on the starlit veranda, I would lie on the hammock and, lulled by the night sounds, the cricket sounds, safe in the buzz of grown-up talk and laughter, or the sounds of far-off singing, my eyelids would grow heavy; the sandman was not someone to steal you away but a friend to take you to the land of dreams and another day, there to find another glorious adventure to be lived, experienced, and cherished, and— maybe someday—put into a song.

George Anderson Mercer was a small man who wore high, stiff shirt collars. In keeping with formal Southern practice, he wore them even in hot weather, and Savannah in summer can be suffocating. Because of the crushing, humid heat, the family maintained a summer home at Vernon View, a grouping of about eight such homes overlooking one of the great littoral estuaries, where a sea breeze was an estival luxury. A small spur railway line ran from the city. A long wooden pier stretched out over the marsh to the water line; at its end was a small sheltering gazebo. Such piers were, and still are, a characteristic feature of this coastal terrain. They were everywhere. Wrote John:

It was a sweet, indolent background for a boy to grow up in. Savannah was smaller then, and sleepy. Trees and azaleas filled the parks, and as we drove out to our place in the country at Vernon View, there was hardly a scene without vistas of marsh grass and long stretches of salt water.

Punctured tires on the Model T made the trips long at times. When the family arrived finally, there were many things to be done: get sawdust to pack the ground bin where we kept the ice, fill the lamps with kerosene, put up the mosquito netting on the beds, and have "Man'well" walk the cow out from the commercial dairy farm, so that we'd have our own milk all summer long. The ice cream was homemade, the living generally rural. The twelve miles into Savannah might have been a hundred. Father made the trip in his Ford every day to go to the real estate office.

The help, the colored people who worked for the family, lived over at Back Island, but there was a small cottage just out back of our place where they could sleep over. Between that and the big house we kept the cow and a few chickens, and there was always a dog or two roaming around. The second-floor kitchen was over the garage, which had lattice-

work sides and was connected to the house by a breezeway. This elimi-
nated the cooking odors, but necessitated that the food be brought in
to the table in covered dishes and on trays. And for that, you had to have
servants.

They were plentiful then, and glad to get work as, over on the back of
the island, they lived by fishing and what they grew in small gardens. So
four or five would come over to work at "reddus"—Red House, so-called
from one of the early large homes there, or the roofs. They would do the
cooking, cleaning, baby-tending, and all the other things required in a
summer household out "on the water." This does not mean we were living
in plantation times, but as they received only from two or three to maybe
seven dollars a week, plus food, we could afford to live like landed gentry.
To get home at night, Manuel and the others would have to go through
narrow paths in the "bresh" where rattlesnakes and black moccasins were
a constant danger.

The cook was a woman named Bertha Hall; John was especially close
to her. The "help" prepared and served the family three meals a day at the
formal dining table or on the screened veranda overlooking the river.

John always remembered the wind, soft and comforting in the summer, or sad, or even threatening when hurricanes hovered off the coast.
Sometimes heat lightning would illumine great white cumulus clouds with
a pink shimmer, and often John would watch the rain beginning miles
away across the coastal marshland, then "like silver bayonets, come racing in from the horizon until it thudded on the tin roof like little horses'
hooves." Nothing has changed: the huge summer clouds are astonishing,
the summer storms spectacularly beautiful. The composer Alec Wilder
described lyricist Lorenz Hart as an indoor writer and John as an out-
door writer. Images of Georgia inhabit all his work, even the most urbane
pieces.

The summer wind
came blowing in
across the sea.
It lingered there
to touch your hair
and walk with me.

All summer long,
we sang a song
and strolled

the golden sand,
two sweethearts and
the summer wind.

Like painted kites
the days and nights
went drifting by.
The world was new
beneath a blue
umbrella sky.

Then, softer than
a piper man
one day it called to you.
I lost you to
the summer wind.

Johnny's mother used to take him to visit his grandmother Julia Ciucevich and his aunts Annie, Hattie, Nora, and Kate. John said that his Aunt Hattie used to swear that he hummed back at her when he was only six months old. Annie Ciucevich was the first public nurse in Chatham County. She had been married to Paul Rivers, who died in 1909—the year Johnny was born—and left her with a son, Walter Rivers. The four sisters, young Walter, and Johnny's grandmother lived at 301 East Charlton Street. Walter, somewhat Johnny's senior, became one of his closest friends, and they would remain so for life. According to Eskew's chronicle:

"The two of them watched the annual return of Daddy Grace to his followers in Savannah as the Bishop led his people down Iguacu Road and into the House of Prayer For All People. Likewise the boys looked forward to the black Easter Parade down West Broad Street (now Martin Luther King Boulevard), when, during the early years of the century, white people watched black people promenade on Easter afternoon. The two boys spent summer days playing on Burnside Island where, when not swimming in the brackish river water near the Atlantic Ocean, they hunted huckleberries in the island's interior."

Asked about the term "huckleberry friend" by television producer Bob Bach, John's cousin Walter Rivers wrote:

"John and I and three black boys, Caesar, Eli and Tommie, in early summer, June or July, went picking these berries. We each had a quart measure—a small pail from which the hucksters sold a quart of okra, peas, beans, or whatever.

"John looked forward to these safaris with great pleasure. The black boys knew mainly the best places for finding the berries, and I think now of the brambles, briers and *snakes* which we encountered. I wouldn't dare go into some of these places now!

"We would spend several hours to fill our pails and trudge homeward on the oyster-shell roads of Vernon View.

"I remember vividly Walter Mercer, John's half brother, making ice cream for Sunday dinner—huckleberry ice cream. It turned out pretty bad and no one would eat it. I think huckleberries are the same as blueberries—look and taste the same but grew wild in our area.

"Shortly after 'Moon River' became a hit, I called Johnny and told him I loved the line 'my huckleberry friend.' He laughed and said, 'Hell! You ought to know—you were there!' "

Walter and Johnny were friendly with a brother and sister named Jimmy and Cornelia McIntire. In 1997, Jimmy McIntire told me:

"I was a little younger than Johnny. My family lived on Hall Street, and we had what we called the Hall Street Gang, young people around my age; and on Johnny's street they had the Gwinnett Street Gang. One of them was Alec Lawrence, who later became a federal judge in Savannah. When I would try to go to Amy Hopkins's store, to get chewing gum or whatever I had enough money to buy, if I went down Gwinnett Street, they'd grab me and tie me to a tree. So I learned to come up the lane. And they wouldn't come to Hall Street, either. The Hall Street Gang would grab *them,* too.

"That went on for years, until we got a little older and got much more sense."

One is forced to reflect on these tyrannies and petty bullyings, the territorial imperatives of little boys that seem to go on all over the world. Is it all a matter of rehearsal for war?

In due course, Walter and Johnny grew close to the McIntires. Walter married Cornelia McIntire, and Johnny was best man at their wedding.

And an echo of those frightened moments of boyhood would turn up in "Whistling Away the Dark," one of John's most haunting lyrics, written near the end of his career.

Three

"I think I *always* liked music," John once told an interviewer for a magazine published by the American Society of Composers, Authors, and Publishers (ASCAP), "and probably wanted to be a tune writer rather than a lyricist." His lack of technical command of music bothered him all his life. And that comment reminds me of something he said in one of our many conversations: "I think writing music takes more talent, but writing lyrics takes more courage."

John told the ASCAP interviewer: "I can remember as a little tiny fellow—I think I still had dresses—we used to have cylindrical records, and I loved them.

"And I loved all songs. Always listened to records. And when they got to be the big thick Edison records, I had those, and then when they got to be regular 78s, we had all those. By the time I was ten or eleven years old, I wanted to know who wrote the songs. Somebody told me Berlin was a big writer—I can remember that—and by the time I was twelve I knew about Walter Donaldson and Victor Herbert."

His cousin Walter Rivers, in that letter to Bob Bach, wrote:

"Another memory was West Broad Street in Savannah. This was totally black, stores, houses, R.R. station, churches, everything for blacks.

"John and I frequently slipped off from our families and went over to the record shop called Mary's Records or Mamie's Records. There we would listen for hours to Bessie Smith, Armstrong, Joe Pat Sullivan, and many people I can't recall. . . .

"John loved to imitate Bessie Smith's record of 'Go Back Where You Stayed Last Night.' We were good customers, so we were allowed to listen for hours. A real Victrola, with a horn on top! His Master's Voice. This, I believe, is where Mercer picked up his beat and phrasing."

John was steeped in black culture, and it can be heard in his adult singing. One example: he could crack his voice, a little like a yodel, into octave leaps. He was the only white singer I ever heard who could do it.

John and his mother spoke Gullah, that all but impenetrable black dialect of the Tidewater area and the Sea Islands; the Georgia variety was known as Geechee, from the Ogeechee River. A lot of white children in those days knew the dialect, and to a large extent John's niece Nancy still does. And from a time before memory he heard the traditional black lullabies and work songs. His Aunt Hattie took him to see the minstrel shows, which were still immensely popular, both in the North and the South.

There was no segregation for small children. John and other white children played with black children. They played roly-poly, marbles, and what they called "one-o-cat"—softball. He always remembered the young black men playing softball after church, wearing hand-me-down uniforms from the Woodberry and Episcopal High Church schools. He remembered and loved the colorful names they bore: Maybud (for Maybird); Ol' Yar (for Old Year, because he was born on December 31); Buh Dayday (Brother David); and Pompey, who, John said, pitched in the manner of Satchel Paige, and with all the flamboyance of Meadowlark Lemon.

A friend of his Aunt Katherine came to Vernon View to interview children for the purpose of compiling a book of stories by children. These included the black children John played with, for, as he—and others—attested, no difference was implied or imposed until about the age of fourteen, the time of puberty. This visitor took down the children's flights of fancy in longhand. Long afterwards, John thought about her. He believed this experience had given him the confidence to create and perform.

What was left of the Mammy tradition of plantation days we found in our cook or laundress or nurse. I vividly remember taking a quail I had swiped from a neighbor over to Rachel who, neither knowing nor caring that it was ill-gotten, cooked it deliciously and entertained me in her news-wall-papered shanty with the warmth and friendliness she always had for children.

. . .

John appears to have been accident-prone in childhood. He ran his veloci-pede off a high curb and put his teeth through his tongue. His nurse had to hold it in her hand as she took him to a hospital, where it was stitched. When he was about four, he pulled a pot of water in which a ham was boiling off a stove and scalded his feet. At about six, he tried to crank one of the family's cars, something that wasn't easy for a grown man to do. The apparatus snapped back and hit him, scarring his forehead. About two years after that, while they were playing softball, his cousin slid into him at second base and broke John's leg. He spent six weeks in a wheel-chair and then on crutches. When the cast was removed, it was discovered that the leg had not been set properly and had to be broken and set again. While he was immobilized, his mother paid his young black friend Caesar twenty-five cents a week to keep him company. Returning to the house at Vernon View one day, she saw Caesar trudging homeward down the road. She stopped to ask what had happened.

"Mistuh Johnny done fire me," Caesar said.

"Why should he do that, Caesar?"

"I ain' know, Mis' Mercer, but we duh play fish, and I hollah 'e is fish, and 'e fire me!"

Caesar was reinstated in his job, his quarter restored, and John was admonished to hold his temper in future. Caesar presumably was one of the boys with whom John and Walter Rivers went searching for huckleberries.

Nancy Gerard told me: "Johnny went to Massie School, a few blocks away from the house on Gwinnett Street. He came home and said, 'Father, Father, I'm the number-two boy in my class.' And his dad said, 'Well, John, how many boys are there in the class?" He said, 'Two, Father.' From what they told me, Johnny wasn't a great scholar. I guess he was dreaming all the time, thinking of things."

In an interview with *Crescendo International* of London, published in February 1974, Johnny said: "I always was drawn to music and once fol-lowed a band around the town when I was six, which my mother must have found difficult to understand. And of course songs always fascinated me more than anything."

It was at that age that he began singing in the boys' choir at Christ Episcopal Church, a large, white, handsome, unadorned structure that overlooks one of the city's many parks. John sang in that church for eleven years, indeed for the rest of his years in Savannah. He entertained relatives and anyone else he could capture as audience. "Maybe I was a natural-born ham, even at that age," he said. The songs he learned included "The Goat That Flagged the Train" and "Mr. Donnerbeck." He was six in 1915; the Great War had already begun in Europe. The film *Birth of a Nation* had its premiere at the Palace Theater in New York that year, with a full orchestra playing the musical background. Among the big songs that year were "Are You from Dixie?", "Memories," "Paper Doll," "There's a Broken Heart for Every Light on Broadway," "Pack Up Your Troubles in Your Old Kit Bag," "Fascination," "I Love a Piano," "Keep the Home Fires Burning," and "I Didn't Raise My Boy to Be a Soldier."

On the "graffola," as one of the servants called it, John heard the songs of Harry Lauder, all of which he memorized; songs by Crumit and Sanderson; and songs from Broadway shows. He told a BBC interviewer: "When I was a little guy, I listened to Harry Lauder, colored singers in the South, sang in the choir by the time I was six, Episcopalian hymns. I went to minstrel shows when I was seven or eight years old, watched blackface comedians. We'd go to John Philip Sousa concerts in the park. I would hear all the popular songs that came out at the time, especially around the time of the First World War, when I was an impressionable age, around eight or nine. 'Poor Butterfly' always made me cry. All those war songs, those postwar songs, influenced me, and I was soon writing little poems, then soon trying my fledgling wings out, writing melodies, even though they sounded familiar, they sounded like other things. At least I had nerve enough to write 'em myself. Hardly *anybody* did that back in those days. Now everybody does it."

He devoured music wherever he could find it—in the church choir or in the singing of a black church within walking distance from the house in Vernon View. He and one of his friends, Dick Hancock, would stand outside and listen, or sometimes venture inside, their white faces conspicuous in the congregation. Another boy who accompanied him to these churches was Jimmy Downey, who would remain his friend long into their adult years.

This absorption of lyrics and tunes from records and minstrel shows and church services unquestionably constituted an informal kind of training for his life's work. The spirit of the music of that black church clearly infuses, for example, "Accentuate the Positive." John knew in his deepest being the rhythm of black Southern preaching.

Amateur singing was a favorite form of entertainment in America in that time, before talkies or radio. Brass bands played in the parks all over the continent, and the ability to play piano or a brass instrument was common. Especially at Christmas, John remembered, "as the flowing bowl got to flowing," men attending the parties around Savannah would form into quartets to sing old songs. John did a lot of that kind of singing, his ear absorbing the elements of harmony.

As remarkable as his ear would prove to be, John was unable to learn a musical instrument. He tried the trumpet but never could develop an embouchure. At various times in his later life he tried to learn the piano, but without success, and he could never read music properly, although he developed an idiosyncratic notational system of his own. He admitted, "I would like very much to have become more fluent in the techniques of music, so that I could have written more tunes of my own."

The joy inspired by the end of World War I in 1918 was overshadowed for many families by the Great Influenza Epidemic of that same year. Ranking with the Black Death as one of the most lethal pandemics in history, the disease killed an estimated twenty million people in a few months, 548,000 in the United States—one of them John's sister Nancy, who was two years younger than he. His niece Nancy, who was named for his sister, thinks her death contributed to Johnny's melancholy in later life. There exists a family photo in which John, about five at the time, can be seen gazing at her with utter adoration. Another younger sister, Juliana, survived, and became the mother of Nancy Keith (now Gerard).

Nancy said, "The other Nancy's death was a horrible tragedy for my grandmother. Even when I was ten or twelve and I would ask her about that little girl, she could never talk to me about it. She said it was just too painful. But I knew that I had been named for her, and when I got older, I always felt that I was sort of a replacement."

Nancy's mother and father divorced when she was less than six months old.

"My grandmother raised me because my mother wasn't capable, or wasn't allowed to," Nancy said. "It's like a Tennessee Williams story. My grandmother was entirely permissive and entirely possessive with me. My mother was named Juliana after the queen of the Netherlands. She was always different. People said she was strange. She never did well in school. She was never really self-sufficient, and Johnny helped her. She had a beautiful voice. She was trained by Addie May Jackson, the choir mistress and organist at Christ Church; later, Johnny sent my mother to Juilliard.

"My grandmother was always listening to music. She would almost swoon to music. She was very artistic. She could make a twig look like a beautiful flower arrangement, and was known for that. I remember her getting up on her knees on the altar at Christ Church, arranging flowers. And every Sunday after church—it was a Southern custom—we went out to the graveyard and brushed off the graves and watered the flowers. She rocked me and she sang to me and she helped me do my homework and I slept in the same bed with her for years and years and years. And she would get short-tempered with anyone who wasn't generous and wouldn't help others. She gave a lot and she expected a lot. She was quite a lady. At the same time she was always conscious of what Savannah society would think, and that's probably because she knew she wasn't [a part of it]. She didn't ever say this to me, but just from conversations we had, I think it was a while before she began ever really to feel accepted.

"The house always had to be spotless and neat, and I had to write thank-you notes, because otherwise what would people think? It's normal and natural for girls growing up to want to go into the kitchen and help, but I was not allowed to go into the kitchen and wash dishes and help. I was encouraged to sit in the parlor, and I always sat at the grown-up table and ate with the right silver from the time I was two or three years old. When I went to college, I had never even made a bed before."

John was surrounded by loving family, including his three half brothers and his Uncle Walter. This was Walter Mercer, and he had a home in Bluffton, a small community just across the state line in South Carolina. Bluffton is on the water, and faces on the ubiquitous marshes and wooden piers. John would spend parts of his summers there. He would fish and swim—he was a good swimmer all his life—and, along with the other boys, leap off the jetties and piers into the water. He said later that he was a happy boy in a happy family, loving his brothers and aspiring to be like them.

There is a vivid passage in a lined notebook—or "scribbler"—of John's that dates, as closely as Nancy and I can determine, from the time he was seventeen. In it John described the surroundings of his family's summer house at Vernon View:

"Vernon was a very small, very beautiful, island—not beautiful in the sense of blue transparent waters and pebble-flecked beaches but of sturdy solidity, of dark salt-smelling marsh grass, narrow, blinding white ribbon-roads of crushed oyster shell, and gray moss hanging low on old oaks. Of a group of [islands], it was easily the most picturesque. At the front, so-called, there were a few low rambling houses, some of board and shingle, white and green, some of plaster and slate, white, red-topped. The Vernon

River flowed below a semi-high bluff, a steady slow green blanket, murky in contrast to the light green of the endless marsh; past these the horizon showed in jagged relief the pine tops, like pin points, of the far distance."

Reading these lines now, can anyone question what that boy's destiny would be? In the same notebook there is a full page of possible song titles: "Don't Baby Me," "Don't Be an Ostrich," "My Place in the Sun," "Over the Weekend," "Let's Put Love to Work," "Things Are Looking Up," "Out of the Right Side of the Bed," "Have It Your Way," "If I Were in Your Shoes," "Roses in My Cheeks," "Take My Word for It," "Carrying the Torch," "First Last and Always," "There's a Word for That—It's Love," "In the Years to Come," "Love at First Sight," "High and Dry," "A Lot of Good That Does," "Alone with the Stars," "Full Moon," "All I Need to Know," "In the Same Old Way," "Another Moon," "The Time Has Come," "I'll Never Forgive Myself," and more . . . every one of them workable. And they already manifest one of John's favorite tricks (and that of many songwriters, for that matter): the use of everyday expressions for titles.

Many years later, John told Max Wilk, who quotes him in his 1973 book *They're Playing Our Song,* "I guess I just gravitated to songwriting. I think I absorbed it. I don't think I actually studied it consciously."

His friend Robert Emmett Dolan, the composer with whom he wrote two Broadway musicals, *Texas, Li'l Darlin'* and *Foxy,* had a very different view. He told Wilk, "Johnny *studied.* He listened and he learned the basics. He absorbed everything, and then transformed it with his own style. Believe me, it's no accident that he's been able to work with so many great composers."

Dolan is surely right, and his corroboration is in that early scribbler. As John told Wilk, "I get a lyric idea from anywhere. Maybe from a billboard on the street, or something I read. An idea will hit me and I jot it down. I'm an inside-the-matchcover type of writer." And he was doing it very early in his life.

When the summer heat became insupportable even in Vernon View, the family would repair to Asheville, North Carolina, where George Anderson Mercer had real estate holdings and was building a hotel. Asheville, which is in the Appalachian Mountains, rests on a plateau that averages 2,200 feet above sea level. The altitude relieved George Mercer's asthma, from which he suffered severely at times.

John found friends there, too, boys with whom he could look for buckeyes—the seeds of shrubs and trees in the horse chestnut family. Carried in the pocket, rubbed by the thumb, they were used like worry stones or Greek worry beads; they would, over time, take on a soft gloss and become objects of real beauty. In the South, the buckeye was considered a good-luck charm, most effective if given to you by a friend. This use of the nut eventually spread to the West, and many cowboys carry buckeyes, even today. John developed his leg muscles walking the steep streets of Asheville, and riding his bicycle there.

While his father's hotel was under construction, the Mercers resided in an Asheville home. John remembered a neighborhood girl who could play on the piano "Georgette," "Leave Me with a Smile," and other now-forgotten hits of the time. Two other, older girls, both of whom could play the piano and sing, arrived from New York—New York!—and from them John learned some of the latest songs. It was the year, John remembered, of Ted Lewis's big recording of "When My Baby Smiles at Me" and of Warren G. Harding's defeat of James M. Cox for the presidency. It was 1920.

Thomas Wolfe was born in Asheville on October 3, 1900. He would portray the city (which he called Altamont) and its people vividly, if not always to their liking, in his novels. He entered Harvard University that autumn, but he was in Asheville that summer, and no doubt during the summers before it. He would turn twenty that October; John would turn eleven in November. The temptation is irresistible—imagine them passing in the streets of this quiet resort town, neither knowing who the other was, neither dreaming of the poetic mirror each would hold up to the South and to the country at large. Wolfe would write: ". . . of a stone, a leaf, an unfound door. And of all the forgotten faces." John would write: ". . . through the meadowland toward a closing door, / a door marked 'Nevermore' / that wasn't there before." Wolfe died in 1938. He could not have helped, even if he had tried, knowing some of Johnny's songs, because by then some of them, such as "Lazy Bones" and "Jeepers Creepers," had become immensely popular.

John encountered Arthur Murray teaching Asheville debutantes the fox-trot, which preceded the Charleston, at the Princess Anne Hotel, where by now the Mercers were living. Long afterwards, in 1942, John would write "Arthur Murray Taught Me Dancing in a Hurry."

He remembered, too, a young itinerant black pianist playing a piece called "Bee's Knees" over and over. John was particularly impressed by the fact that the young man, like himself, couldn't read music; it encouraged him. When he was fifteen or sixteen, he heard the Jan Garber orchestra at various locales around Asheville, and was thrilled by it.

John had a taste for girls even then, despite his deep shyness.

My nurse used to say I had a girlfriend when she took me out to the park at age three or four. And I remember giving away my pencils and erasers to girls in grammar school, and going to my first dance in my Boy Scout suit.

The second dance was in a girl's school gymnasium and I can still see us little bloods, at age eleven or twelve, some of us smoking outside the gym, talking about some of the girls we heard you could kiss and one who had "gone further" than that. At that point I didn't smoke, and I really didn't want to know if the girl in question was a woman of the world or not. I thought she was too pretty that night, looking all gossamer and spun sugar in her voile or organdy or whatever it was girls wore in the age before blue jeans. Like an angel.

I was determined to get in on the fun, so I manfully went back inside and began dancing. The first time is like swimming: you just have to jump in, and luckily I asked the cutest girl there (and the best dancer), for she was amused and she encouraged me to keep trying. Once started, I wouldn't stop, and my enjoyment was topped only by my nerve. I can remember the feeling of elation as I lay in bed that night, feeling that I had really accomplished something. I had learned to dance! And I was good; at least, that's what the one girl had said!

Southern girls are terrible flirts with that "Hiya, sugar!" and "Come back soon, y'hear?" and all that ante bellum jazz, but they're the greatest dancers in the world, bar none. Talk about feeling like a feather in the breeze! You hardly know you've got one in your arms—unless she wants you to know.

Just before he turned thirteen, John was sent to Woodberry Forest School near Orange, Virginia. His father and his Uncle Walter had also gone to Woodberry Forest. The school was located on a property that had once been called Woodberry Forest Estate, a farm founded by James Madison's brother. At Woodberry, John studied European, ancient, and English history; the New Testament, the Old Testament, Caesar, Cicero, mathematics and sciences; *Treasure Island, Robinson Crusoe, Gulliver's Travels, Silas Marner;* Irving, Macaulay, Emerson, Tennyson, Franklin, Milton, and Shakespeare; and three years of English grammar and two of composition.

It was at Woodberry Forest that John wrote his first song. Or so he said. Written one night when he was fifteen, it was titled "Sister Susie, Strut Your Stuff." The lyric went:

Portrait of Johnny

Sister Susie, Strut your stuff.
Show these babies you're no bluff.
Let these fellows see you step,
Do that dance with lots o' pep.
Toss your toe and kick your heel.
This ain't no Virginia reel.
Do your walk—and your strut.
Shake that thing—you know what.
Ain't she hot, boys?
That's my gal!
Sister Susie Brown.

When he sang it the next day for some of the other boys, several said it was plagiarized. In later years, amused, John granted that it was indeed looted from other songs of the day. The style and form were drawn from two big hits, "Red Hot Mama" and "Flamin' Mama." The name, he thought, was probably derived from "If You Knew Susie" and "Strut, Miss Lizzie." The music he had contrived for this little wonder was drawn from all these songs, as well as from another of the period, "Sweet Georgia Brown." But for all its obvious derivative qualities, the song reveals even at that early age one of the defining characteristics of John's work: his ear for the current vernacular and an ability to use it in lyrics.

Like everyone else, John had been steeped in the songs of World War I. Of course, the war to end all wars was not yet known by that name. It was simply the Great War, and the music industry mobilized to inspire a victorious spirit in the American public, and to make a little money at it, too.

The classic American song of World War I was "Over There" (1917), by George M. Cohan, a shout of naïve and earnest confidence that the doughboys would end it all forthwith when they arrived in Europe. Cohan received a Congressional Medal of Honor for his patriotic songs, which included "You're a Grand Old Flag," "(I Am) the Yankee Doodle Boy," "There's Something About a Uniform," and "Stand Up and Fight Like H——."

Close behind "Over There" in popularity were "K-K-K-Katy," "When the Boys Come Home," and Berlin's "Oh How I Hate to Get Up in the Morning," which had the virtue of taking a certain realistic complaint about military life and making it an object of amusement. Johnny would echo its sentiment during the next war in a song called "G.I. Jive."

Two interesting trends occurred during this period. A number of songs based on Negro spirituals came to the fore, including, in 1918, "Deep River," "Go Down, Moses," "Nobody Knows the Trouble I've Seen," and "Swing Low, Sweet Chariot," and, in 1919, "Oh Peter, Go Ring Dem Bells," "Sometimes I Feel Like a Motherless Child," and "Standin' in the Need of Prayer." Also on the hit list of 1918 one finds "Clarinet Marmalade," "Original Dixieland One Step," and "Ostrich Walk." The Original Dixieland Jazz Band, a white group, had played Reisenweber's Restaurant in New York in January 1917, and had become the first jazz group to make records. They were thus instrumental in launching a fascination with jazz in the United States and, eventually, Europe. Those three tunes were the most prominent in their repertoire. And the year produced a song called "Swanee," a hit for Al Jolson with words by Irving Caesar and music by an unknown twenty-one-year-old composer named George Gershwin. Jolson sang it in blackface.

In the wake of the flu epidemic of 1918 came another calamity, this one called the Volstead Act, aka Prohibition. During the war, a temporary Prohibition Act had been passed to save grain for use as food, but now the ban was made permanent. Prohibiting the manufacture, transportation, and sale of alcoholic beverages—which our species had been making since before the misty beginnings of recorded history—the Eighteenth Amendment was ratified on January 16, 1919, and went into effect on January 16, 1920. The result, of course, was the same as with all unpopular prohibitions: it corrupted the forces of law enforcement and made criminals rich and powerful.

Prohibition launched what F. Scott Fitzgerald, rightly or not, called the Jazz Age, and Johnny was one of its creations. He was eleven when the Eighteenth Amendment took effect, and he looked up, as boys at that age always do, to those just a few years older than he. They danced the Castle Walk; the girls bobbed their hair and rolled their silk stockings down to a point just above the knee, which was revealed by their short skirts; the boys carried hip flasks of illegal liquor; and a favorite pastime was necking under the stars in the rumble seats of roadsters. There was, of course, a dark side to this cocktail of alcohol, automobiles, and youth. John wrote: "You would come home from a dance or some other event and learn that two beautiful young people not out of their teens had been in a wreck, and might not live, and if they did live could be disfigured or crippled for life."

Portrait of Johnny

A child of the age, Johnny acquired a taste for the automobile races. He recalled:

Cars were fewer and mechanically not so advanced then. One of the wondrous things to me was the Vanderbilt Cup race, which for a time was staged on a track which curved within five miles of our summer place.

All we young boys—cousins and friends—would pile into the back of a pick-up truck or a Ford touring car and go with a picnic lunch to watch the daredevils of the day put the snorting steel monsters through their paces. Ralph DePalma, Barney Oldfield, Louis Chevrolet, and the unlucky Bruce Brown, killed within a year, would careen around the steeply banked but imperfectly engineered turns at the unheard-of speed of sixty miles an hour—a mile a minute!—and down the straightaways in clouds of swirling dust or the dry fine powder stirred up from the oyster-shell-surfaced road until they and the spectators were covered from head to foot.

I was enthralled. I can still see Barney Oldfield, with his racing cap pushed back on his forehead, his face grimy with oil and grease except where his goggles had been, smoking a long black cigar, his linen duster flapping in the breeze as he leaned over his noisy engine to see if its parts were working harmoniously. How our blood pounded as they came, specks in the distance, roaring toward us, then kicking up rocks and gravel as they took the sharp turn. It's no wonder we little fellows were cautious as we peered from behind a tree. We were no more than five or ten yards away.

Whenever a band came to play in the area—at a school, in a pavilion, sometimes out at the nearby resort area on Tybee Island—Johnny would be there. In later embarrassed memory, he would see himself as he stood close to the band, hands raised in front of him, playing an imaginary trumpet. His behavior was no different from that of young rock fans more than half a century later, fingering and flailing away on an unseen instrument, playing "air guitar," as they came to call it.

Encouraged by his first timid efforts at dancing, he continued, feeling that he could try anything. One of the memorable moments in his youthful dancing career occurred at the De Soto Hotel near central Savannah. (This edifice did not survive into the time when Savannah took stock of its architectural treasures and moved to preserve them. It was torn down a few years ago.)

Johnny entered a Charleston contest. His dancing partner at the De

Soto was a buxom girl named Fanny, with round cheeks, a blush, and ready musical laughter. In her short skirt and rolled stockings, she swirled around him and, he remembered, they held the audience enthralled. He gave her the credit for their prizes—a scarf, a bottle of perfume, and the bantamweight championship of Savannah's Charleston dancers. *Ah, Fanny, merci, mademoiselle, for an evening to remember, you playing Ginger Rogers to my bumbling Fred Astaire. If I was not becoming famous musically, I was becoming notorious as a fellow who would try anything.*

Not every dancing experience was a joy, however. The first time Johnny heard the song "Coquette," written by Johnny Green, Gus Kahn, and Carmen Lombardo, he was drunk. . . . *While my pretty little date was dancing with all the other fellows, I was outside weeping the maudlin tears of my first crying jag as I listened to that beautiful tune with its simple little lesson about youthful promiscuity. Music can still make me cry. More so than really sad things. I'm inured to those, expecting death and taxes, and taking them as a matter of course.*

By that time, Johnny was actively exploring the art of the lyric. His early scribbler contains sketches and explored rhymes, including some that are almost bizarre. English is a language poor in rhyme compared to French or Italian, and lyricists overcome the problem by devising compound rhymes of two or more words. Here are some from the Mercer scribbler, written when he was at most seventeen: *rationed / fashioned, dachshund / impassioned, deadhead / redhead, deadpan / bedpan, dough-boy / in-the-know-boy, double quick / trouble quick, drama / pyjama / llama / mamma / charmer* (which of course would work with a Southern accent), *orchid / for kid, colombo / some beau.*

Most of these would be useless, but they show us how his mind was already working and presage some of the ingenious rhymes he would later employ in such songs as "Hooray for Hollywood," lines such as: "where any barmaid / can be a star maid . . ." Some of John's rhymes were pretty extreme, but they almost always work.

The scribbler also contains a number of complete lyrics. They are a little naïve, perhaps, but they foreshadow what's coming. For example, this one:

> *Spring is coming to my heart again.*
> *Soon happy songs will start again.*
> *Spring is coming to my heart again.*
> *You are coming back to me.*

Portrait of Johnny

Nights were dark as nights could be.
Now the morning shines for me,
for I know that soon I'll see
all the lonely days that I am spending
ending.

I'll be going down the lane with you,
laughing at the April rain with you.
We shall never be apart again.
Spring is in my heart again.

Note the grammatical precision of "we shall." For a kid of, at most, seventeen, that lyric is pretty promising.

In later years, John was wont to say, "I tried to be a cartoonist and failed. I tried to be an actor and failed. I tried to be a singer and failed. So I just naturally drifted into songwriting." He said it to me, he said it to Bob Thomas of the Associated Press, and no doubt he said it to others. And it's aw-shucks nonsense.

Four

One of John's closest friends, who would remain so for life, was a boy named Dick Hancock. Three miles away, across the water from Vernon View, "as the red-wing blackbird flies," just beyond Pettigaw and opposite Skidaway, lies Montgomery. The Hancock family lived there. All of them were musical, all of them played guitar, and, Johnny said, harmony came naturally to them.

John said the Hancock boys were seven of the most talented boys you ever met. He described Dick Hancock, who was close to his own age, as a red-haired, freckle-faced fan of the pioneering jazz guitarist Eddie Lang and of Cliff Edwards, who went under the stage name Ukulele Ike.

Dick and Johnny probably first heard Lang (born Salvatore Massaro in Pittsburgh in 1902) on his recordings with the Mound City Blue Blowers in 1924, though he is best known for his later association with violinist Joe Venuti. Johnny was then fifteen. Lang was an original musician whose place in jazz history has been too casually slighted. He was one of the great formative influences on the instrument, and Johnny always said Dick Hancock played like him. In fact, Johnny said, "Dick could play as good as anybody on the records." Tapes of Dick Hancock, made in later years, indicate that Johnny was not wrong. Dick Hancock was a very good musician.

Johnny and Dick were also enamored of the playing of Bix Beiderbecke and Frank Trumbauer, whose early recordings they collected. They were avid, too, for the Paul Whiteman band. History has not been kind to Whiteman, partly because of the sobriquet "King of Jazz," attached to him by publicists. But Whiteman's recordings were often of high caliber, particularly when they featured the jazz musicians he admired, Beiderbecke among them. Johnny and Dick liked Whiteman's Rhythm Boys, a group that included Al Rinker and Bing Crosby, who before he became known as a romantic singer of ballads was a skilled ensemble singer of brisk rhythmic novelties. Johnny and Dick listened to new records in shops in the black neighborhoods of Savannah. In that era, even records were segregated: those made by black performers were known as "race records" and were not available in the stores of white neighborhoods. In fact, there were few record stores as such in either white or black neighborhoods; phonograph records were usually sold in furniture stores, the phonograph machines themselves being considered pieces of furniture. When Johnny and Dick would enter these stores in black neighborhoods, they felt obliged to buy at least one record, since the white owners had posted signs intended to be read by blacks: NO FREE RIDERS and BUY OR DON'T LISTEN.

When the weather was good, Johnny and Dick would go by canoe or outboard motorboat to one of the innumerable docks along the river to attend summer parties, where they would sing, accompanied by Dick or his older brother on the guitar. The boys claimed to know all the new summer songs.

In the last analysis:

If you should ask me what makes me tick, I would say that it is that I am from Savannah. Savannah really is about all that's left of the Deep South. Two or three more wars, high-speed transportation, "progress" and social change have altered almost unendurably the old way of life. I am aware that a lot of people like *the change. Materially there has been vast improvement. But so much has been lost. I miss so many of the old ways, the old days. Maybe it's just being a kid I miss. But I remember Savannah in the old times, and I am overcome by a nostalgia nearly too strong to bear.*

The scribbler containing some of John's early writing gives us some idea of his perception of himself during that period. It contains what I can only believe is a fragment of autobiographical fiction. Probably every would-be writer in his chrysalis phase attempts this, and the theme of a lost youthful love recurs even in the later years. The notebook is inscribed

"Early Writings" and bears a date: 1924. Perhaps it began then, but on the basis of internal evidence, it was probably written mostly in 1926 or '27. In such experiments, young writers are careful in their choice of the names for fictional protagonists, and John calls his young man Don. Don, which rhymes with John—get it? The story starts with a description of a boy being awakened by a railway porter. In places the handwriting is illegible, but this is what it says:

> Donald Reeves Trevier, gentleman of leisure and Savannah, Ga., slowly rose up to a sitting position [illegible] looked into the vertical strip of mirror between the two windows on either side. Hair awry, one eye closed, the other nearly so, and his pyjama collar standing perpendicular to one ear, Donald looked once at the blurred scenery. He laughed sarcastically, as if the very action were an effort.
>
> "You're a fine-looking egg this morning, eh?" he said to the image in the glass, making a grimace as if to say, "Say something back." To tell you the truth, Donald Trevier was quite disgusted with himself and the world. Everything had gone wrong. Little things not important enough alone to make a difference in the usual routine had piled up on him, irking and [illegible] his poor soul so much.
>
> His last year at school gone, his girl gone, his money gone, and his self-control gone. Donald, for the last 48 hours, had behaved himself disreputably—quite. The idea of looking forward all year to the close as the only thing that he really wanted, then to cry, like a baby, before J.C., that big hypocritical fathead. Having started, nothing could stop him. And there after, like a distant cousin at a near relative's funeral, he cried quite promiscuously. Well that damn girl had started it any way. If she hadn't been so damn indifferent, not to mention a few remarks she made, he might never have lost his composure. Given over to self-pity, he brooded over his [illegible] and wondered if he would ever get a square deal.
>
> Donald Trevier had been so spoiled all his life that he thought nothing was a square deal unless it was entirely suited to his wishes. Adored by his mother, he had been given "everything a child could want," which of course classified him no more or less with the others of well-to-do people. He had had a better bicycle than the little Boyd boy or, later on, no worse than Mary Hen-

dricks' son. The really spoiled part had entered when older girls had thought him nice-looking and "such a cute little kid." At first, he had been embarrassed with this praise but gradually he had accepted it as a matter of course, and then become rather bored with it all. Consequently, his first year at boarding school embarked upon at the tender age of 11, he had been lonely and tear-filled when the older boys discovered the [boredness?] of praise and the younger [illegible] had analyzed it as conceit. Two years of this and the pictured popularity not even seen in the distance [sentence incomplete].

Donald's letters home then were few and very unsatisfactory. Pride kept him from telling of the situation to anyone and pride kept him from capitulating to the unspoken custom of school life and thereby became a "good fella." He stuck and soon other boys began to respect him. He was always nice to the first-formers, remembering his own plight, and in return he got their enthusiastic young support. His lessons were always well-done, thus gaining the teachers' respect and confidence.

His third-year acquaintances were made much more easily and lasted long. When he'd walk in on a "bull session," the hitherto nod and cool glance followed by resume of talk had changed to a smile and "Hi, Don, how's the kid?" It was that year that he had gotten a place on The Lynx, and had started building up a following.

There the narrative ends. I find this passage fascinating for several reasons. First, the boy could write—and well. To the extent that Don is a thinly veiled reflection of John, we see that when he was sent off to the Woodberry Forest School, he did not sleep in an upper or lower berth: he had a private compartment. He was well aware that he enjoyed the privileges of a highly prosperous family. His apparent conceit is more a matter, I think, of covering up adolescent self-doubt. He was very interested in girls and craved their attention. He was anxious to be popular. And after a few false starts, he was obviously successful in his efforts.

The Fir Tree, one of the publications at Woodberry Forest, notes that in his final year there he was Football Squad '26; *Oracle* Board '26; *Oracle* '27; Daily Dope Editor, *Fir Tree* '27; Hop Committee '27; Vice President Madison Literary Society '27; Censor Madison Literary Society '26; Choir '23, '24, '27; German Club '24, '25, '26, '27.

The entry notes that he answered to both John and Johnny and the nickname Doo. The origin of that name remains unknown, but I have seen it in several Woodberry Forest publications.

Under the heading "Wit Is Thy Attribute," one item reads:

"John has been with us since the fall of 1922; and during his five-year-sojourn has grown not only in stature, but has become an embodiment and example of true Woodberry Spirit. His willingness and desire to work in the interest of others and his unfailing brightness of personality and humor have made him one of the most outstandingly popular boys in the school.

"John's untiring efforts culminated this year in the attainment of enviable positions among the school activities. His work as an editor both of the *Oracle* and *The Fir Tree* has been superb, and his performance has contributed largely to the success of both these publications.

"Among Doo's hobbies and accomplishments there is one which eclipses all others, his love for music. The symphony of Johnny's fancy can best be described with his own adjective 'hot.' No orchestra or new production can be authoritatively termed as 'good' until Johnny's stamp of approval has been placed upon it. His ability to 'get hot' under all conditions and at all times is uncanny. The best explanation we can offer is that we do not properly appreciate melody at its best.

"John is yet uncertain where he will turn for the future, but whether it be to college or to business, the friends he leaves behind are confident of his success and wish him every joy and happiness wherever he may go."

There had been talk in the family of his attending Princeton University, as his father's father had done. John knew there was a statue there of his ancestor who had died in the American Revolution, but he didn't think he would be able to pass the Princeton entrance exams. And then his father experienced a disastrous financial reversal.

George Anderson Mercer had founded the G.A. Mercer Company to invest the savings of working people. For some time the company did well, but in 1927 land values in Georgia and Florida, which had been rising rapidly, suddenly dropped. Within weeks George Mercer was out of business and more than a million dollars in debt to seven hundred investors. Most of them were sympathetic to him; recriminations were rare. But he could not reconcile the failure with the principles of responsibility by which he had always lived. He declined the option of declaring bankruptcy, and the Chatham Savings Bank, acting as his liquidating agent, took over his company while George Mercer gave all the money he had, a total of $73,500, to his certificate holders. He was penniless. Yet his reputation remained untarnished, and the bank even lent him money to open a private real estate office to support his family. Despite such emotional and financial support, the failure turned a warm, ebullient man into a resigned and silent and self-doubting one.

When Johnny received a letter at Woodberry Forest from his mother, telling him of his father's business failure, he wrote to her: "The news is a severe blow, but I don't care, except for Father. I only hope and pray that I can be of some service to him."

The family could no longer afford Woodberry Forest. John dropped out of school. His formal education was over. He told his father, "Don't worry about that money. I'll pay those people back." George Mercer quietly told him, "Son, you don't realize how much it was. You won't ever have that amount of money."

The late Lucy Chapman, who was George Mercer's personal secretary, told the story in greater detail:

"Johnny was back from Woodberry Forest. He came to the office to bum some money to go to the theater. His daddy said, 'What time is the next show?' Johnny said, 'Eleven o'clock.' His father said, 'Come with me to the bank. I've got to sign some papers. And you'll still have plenty of time to go to the theater.'

"Johnny listened to his father and George Hunt, who was president of the bank. They were talking, two and a half million, one and a half, whatever it was."

One can only imagine—or try to—the sinking feeling in the stomach of the boy who fashioned himself in fiction as Donald Reeves Trevier. According to Lucy Chapman, he said to George Hunt, "Mr. Hunt, what would it take to keep Daddy's company from being broke?" To which the broker replied, "Well, Johnny, the company isn't broke. We're going to put it into an orderly disposition of assets."

"Johnny said, 'Well, I'd like to know.'

"And George Hunt said, 'Can you raise me a quick million and three-quarters today?'

"And Johnny said, 'Well, someday, if I make it big, anybody who bet on my daddy ain't gonna lose five cents.' "

Nancy Gerard said: "I was going through some old things, and I found an old wallet of my grandmother's. In it was an envelope. I knew that it was there, but I had forgotten about it. In pencil, in her handwriting, it says, 'Johnny's two dollars he gave Pop after the liquidation.' And these two dollar bills are those great big ones. Those are the original bills that he sent his father to help."

John bore a scar from his father's 1927 business failure for the rest of his life. And something else happened that year that may have caused him—and the family—embarrassment: the arrest of his Uncle Eddie Ciucevich.

On Sunday, May 8, 1927, not long after John had to drop out of Woodberry Forest, the *Savannah Morning News* carried an item headlined FINE ASSORTMENT OF LIQUORS TAKEN. FEDERAL OFFICERS MAKE HAUL IN TYBEE INLET. ARREST E. J. CIUCEVICH. The reporter clearly enjoyed himself in writing the story:

> A collection of liquors, of a kind which makes some people jump up and down in ecstasy, and makes others find their throats growing excessively parched and thirsty, was seized by federal agents and deputy marshals on Tybee Island in the inlet yesterday morning.
>
> E. J. Ciucevich is charged with receiving, concealing, and smuggling into the country 400 cases of assorted liquors, ranging from choice champagne to choice gin, and including Scotch and rye whiskey. There was also found by the officers some beer of particularly appetizing appearance, and, according to their declaration, of a kind which seldom touches the Georgia shore.
>
> Of more than ordinary interest was the discovery by the federal men of little sample bottles, holding just one drink, and which few people see now-a-days in Savannah environs, though they used to be prolific at a cost of fifteen cents. The little rye bottles used to be shaped like a miniature regular quart bottle, and those filled with Scotch used to be like a tiny decanter, each holding just one drink. . . . The gin bottles found yesterday were of a square shape, the first yet found in these regions since the prohibition law went into effect. . . .
>
> The estimated value of the seizure, rated at the lowest cost across the water, would be approximately $6,000, allowing for each case to average $25 in cost. At retail, such an assignment of liquors would triple and some-

times quadruple in price, the grade of those seized being declared by the officers to have been of an exceptional kind. The raiding party left Savannah just before midnight Friday and made the seizure Saturday morning. They returned to Savannah at 3 o'clock yesterday afternoon.

Mr. Ciucevich was released under $5,000 bond after a hearing before United States Commissioner G. Noble Jones.

No one seems to know what happened to Eddie Ciucevich after this— or, for that matter, to all that high-class hooch.

Unable to continue his education, John went to work as an office boy in his father's real estate business. He was seventeen that summer. He would later say he was delighted to be finished with school, to have a job with a salary, and to be able to drive a car, but that may have been rationalization.

He said that it was in the course of that summer of 1927 that he took his first drink, during an intermission at a country-club dance. "I had previously resisted temptation," he said, "but this one night, a girl took one too! What else could a self-respecting young man do? Promises to my Dad chug-a-lugged away with that drink. I was in for a lot of unsteady legs, retching in the bushes, and reeling beds and ceilings, before I would truly enjoy alcohol."

John was taking a night-school course in typing during this period. Although I can find no documentation for this, somewhere in the shadows of memory I recall, from a conversation we once had about typing, that he told me he'd won a state championship in some contest. Certainly he became an excellent typist, and all his friends remember letters from him written on a portable typewriter, now among his memorabilia at Georgia State University in Atlanta. The last typewriter he owned had a cursive font, and anyone who knew John recognized the type instantly. His letters were almost devoid of typing errors and corrections.

At night, when I wasn't going to typing school, and on weekends, I was free and there was a lot to do in Savannah in the '20s. Blue Steele played at the Tybresa Pavilion and, a step up the beach and the social scale, you could go dancing at the Hotel Pavilion, where your friends were, or drive to the Saturday night dances at Barbee's, where the pretty girls were, or the Yacht Club, and a beautiful old place with a circular porch running around it called the Casino. Every one of these places is gone now, lost to fire, to creditors, and—some—to progress. Sad.

Going to these places required a date and, more than that, a car. I was always in big demand for double-dating as, from age eleven—no driver's licenses were required then—I had a car to drive. Dad's or Mom's, but a car. According to the ritual, by about age sixteen, you'd make a date, get your linen suit from the cleaners, go by the bootleggers for a pint of corn whisky—or peach brandy, if you were just beginning to drink—then pick up the girls and drive to the dance.

Stagging it was even more fun, as all the dances were cut-ins. Besides, afterwards you and your friends were free to do a little singing, cruising around looking for trouble, and winding up at the railroad station or a roadhouse drive-in—drive-ins were rare in those days—for some food. It was all very innocent by today's standards, but it was exciting and danger-ous enough then.

We sang so many quartet songs that I was constantly hoarse. None of us had heard of keys, and, as my boyhood soprano was just changing, I was forever straining for some high trumpet effect on "Behind the Clouds" or taxing it to the limit on the top tenor part of "You Tell Me Your Dream." It was always two octaves out of sight.

The summers flew, the tunes and the times changed, and my friends all went in different directions, though not before setting me on the royal road to Tin Pan Alley.

Why me, of all the quartet singers under the South Georgia moon? Why should I be the one to draw the lucky musical number?

Charlie wound up selling paint in Florida, Walter at Reynolds Metal in Birmingham. Cliff married a girl in Paris. But I, the poorest singer of all in that "old quartet that sang Sweet Adeline," got my wish to sing for my supper. Dick Whittington's cat went to London to look at the queen.

I went to Gotham to look for a job.

In an interview published in *Crescendo International* in London in 1974, Johnny was asked why he made the risky move to New York. "I had to," he replied, "because there was just nothing I wanted to do back home. My brothers went into the family real estate business and I would probably have followed suit, but in those days I had a notion I wanted to become an actor. And I must say that I might easily have had parental opposition to overcome. My father was really marvelous. He helped me and encouraged me and kept me in a little money—not much, for he hadn't much, but enough."

Portrait of Johnny

Johnny had moved from his job in his father's office to another in a brokerage house. His friend Dick Hancock got a job in a band on the *City of Chattanooga,* one of four boats owned by the Savannah Line, which sailed to New York and back.

John, like so many of us, would associate songs with events in his life. The hits of 1927 included, as he always remembered, "Blue Skies" and "Russian Lullaby" (both by Irving Berlin, whose name John held in awe—they would one day be friends); "At Sundown, Rain," "Back in Your Own Back Yard," "Chloe"; "Funny Face," "S'Wonderful," and "Strike Up the Band" (these three by George and Ira Gershwin); "Girl of My Dreams," "Just a Memory," "Let a Smile Be Your Umbrella," "Lucky in Love"; "Can't Help Lovin' Dat Man," "Why Do I Love You?", "Make Believe," and "Ol' Man River" (these four from *Show Boat,* lyrics by Oscar Hammerstein II, music by Jerome Kern, with whom John would one day write); and "Thou Swell" and "My Heart Stood Still," both by Richard Rodgers and Lorenz Hart (Hart was to be one of John's idols among lyricists). Another hit of that year was "The Best Things in Life Are Free," by Ray Henderson, Lew Brown, and B. G. (Buddy) DeSylva. John would one day join in partnership with DeSylva in founding Capitol, which would grow into one of the world's major record companies.

Another hit that year was "Ramona," music by Mabel Wayne and lyrics by Wolfe (always pronounced "Wolfie") Gilbert, who had also written "Waiting for the *Robert E. Lee.*" Wolfe Gilbert, sixteen years John's senior, would be one of the closest friends of his lifetime.

But it was "Sometimes I'm Happy" that John especially associated with that summer of '27. He had one of his recurring crushes, this time on a girl from New York with whom he'd danced at the Hotel Pavilion. The next evening he saw her off on a ship of the Savannah Line for her trip back to New York, and he promised her he would come to see her before the summer ended.

Now, if Nancy and I are dating that scribbler of sketched lyrics correctly, 1927 would be the year he wrote this one:

> *Wanderlust still haunts me.*
> *The open road wants me.*
> *I hear its call and I must start,*
> *start to travel on.*

I feel summer dying,
or see a wild bird flying,
and there's no peace in my heart
until I have gone.

Restless hands that search the sky,
what things will you find?
Will they meet your restless eye?
Are they left behind?

Though my journey's aimless
and every path is nameless,
when wanderlust is in my heart,
follow it I must,
endless wanderlust.

This is surprisingly deft work for a boy of seventeen. Note the AABA structure, with the release, or B section, a rhythmic departure from the front strain. Apart from that, this lyric (if he wrote music for it, it has not survived) suggests that John was getting ready to leave Savannah.

Dick Hancock was on deck the evening John saw his young lady off for New York. John discussed the situation with him and together they planned John's first trip to the Big Apple. Nor was the girl the only attraction in Manhattan. The Paul Whiteman band was working at the Paramount, and Dick—whose job on the shipping line had taken him there and who had heard them in person—so praised the ensemble that John was determined to make the trip and hear them live. He wanted to hear the Beiderbecke solos, for Bix by now was with Whiteman, along with Bing Crosby and Al Rinker, members of the Rhythm Boys. Another hit of that summer was a Whiteman recording, featuring the voices of Crosby and Rinker, called "Mississippi Mud." Its lyric, with its flagrantly racist condescension, makes any rational person squirm today, but it apparently raised no eyebrows then.

With Dick Hancock's connivance, John planned to stow away on the SS *Savannah*, hiding in Dick's cabin for the trip to New York. John made the mistake, if such it was, of confiding in his mother about the plan. For she discussed it with her brother, Morgan Ciucevich, who was a purser on the ship and knew the owner—as, for that matter, did John's father, who would have been embarrassed by the scheme.

John, as planned, stayed in Dick Hancock's cabin through the calls of

Portrait of Johnny

"All ashore that's going ashore." Music played, the whistle blew, the ship shuddered and began to move. Only when it was past the Savannah Light and well out on the ocean, heading north, did John emerge from the cabin for a look around the deck.

A ship's officer approached and asked for his ticket.

Five

John was put to work. He soon realized that his uncle had "betrayed" him, informing his superiors of the boy's scheme, "so that I could safely work my way to New York without being clapped in irons or having to walk the plank. Looking back, I'm grateful."

The crew comprised Poles, Canadians, Swedes, and a few Greeks; crew members were never allowed on the passenger decks except to wash them. That was one of John's jobs, along with scraping off old paint, repainting metal, and coiling rope. The crew's sleeping quarters were dirty, and no bed was ever made. The toilet was filthy and John didn't use it once in the three-day trip.

Because mingling with passengers was forbidden, John never got a chance even to speak to Dick Hancock and his other musician friends. Nor did he have a smoke or a drink. It was undoubtedly his first, and last, experience of hard physical labor. And then came the reward.

It was about five a.m. He was on deck, leaning on a rail as the chill wind from the ship's forward progress whipped his gray flannel shirt. The sun was rising behind the skyscrapers. The first view of Manhattan is something one never forgets. *Ready or not, New York, here I come!*

John helped the crew secure the boat, waited until all the passengers had departed, bade his farewells, and, suitcase in hand, descended the gangway. This new arrival, however, made his way not to some cheap hotel in the Bowery, like so many who had come to New York before him, but to a luxury duplex in the Fifties. Relatives of his Aunt Katherine, who was in Europe for the summer, had allowed his cousin Joe and his parents to stay there in their absence, and they welcomed John warmly. *And I was indeed glad to see them, though not half as glad as I was to see that bathroom!*

But the two main goals of his journey were no longer attainable. The girl he had come to visit was away. He thought afterwards that she might have been frightened of someone so madly impetuous, or embarrassed, or merely indifferent. And the Paul Whiteman band had left the Paramount.

John found himself with nothing left to love but New York itself:

The steam coming up out of the manholes, the noise of the traffic and the subways, the kaleidoscopic anonymity of the faces in the crowd, more than fulfilled any dreams I had had of it, and I wandered around for a few days like a peasant in Baghdad, or like Alice, fallen down a rabbit hole and finding so much to explore.

His cousin Joe Mercer was studying sculpture with Daniel Chester French, the great American sculptor famous for the statue *The Minute Man* in Concord, Massachusetts, and many more, including his masterpiece, the grave and awesome seated figure of Abraham Lincoln in the Lincoln Memorial in Washington, D.C. Joe was busy most evenings, as well as during the days. John was alone for two weeks, exploring music stores and theaters, small restaurants and athletic events and great rococo movie houses with huge pipe organs and awesome stages. It seemed, he said, "like a fairyland to a stagestruck youngster from the sticks." He stared up at the buildings, walked in Central Park, gazed at the Hudson River, with its great ships landing and departing, and at the myriad windows, glowing with reflected gloaming light as the day ended, then lit bright in the enclosing darkness.

One of the shows he saw was *Hit the Deck.* He was enchanted by its songs, among them "Hallelujah!" and "Sometimes I'm Happy," by Irving Caesar and Vincent Youmans. At the Paramount he heard the Williams Sisters, one of whose songs, *Sweet Sue,* was a new one. The composer was Victor Young, and after the show, in a shop on Broadway, John bought a copy of the sheet music, never imagining that he would one day not only know Young but write with him.

John knew another girl in the vicinity. She lived in New Jersey. John called her and was invited to come over for the weekend. Her family was gracious to him, and their kindness, he remembered, restored a little of his self-confidence.

He knew he had to come back to New York to stay and, consciously or otherwise, had begun to formulate plans for the move. The city had destroyed "any tolerance I might ever have had for the real estate or brokerage business, or for anything except something that had to do with music and the theater."

And so he went home, to work again for his father in the reduced circumstances brought on by the Florida and Georgia land bust. Along with two of his brothers he ran errands, collected rents, answered the telephone, and typed. And he listened to records, including one by Paul Whiteman that he found "modern and haunting." It was "Sugar." Among the other tunes he ever afterwards associated with that pivotal summer were "China Boy" and "Clementine," and Walter Donaldson's "Changes." And then came a small role in a little-theater play. "One day," John said, "two cute girls, both older than I, drove up to my house and honked their automobile horn, *aaa-OOO-gah, aaa-OOO-gah*. I thought they were there to see my mother. I was surprised and delighted when it turned out that they were looking for me."

One of the girls, Peggy Stoddard, told him she would be playing a role for the local group called the Town Theatre. Would he be interested in playing her younger brother, a boy of fifteen? Could he act that age? John was seventeen. "In about two seconds, I said I could. I would have done *anything* for her."

He became accustomed for the first time to stage makeup, struggled through rehearsals and the near paralysis known as stage fright, and went on. The play was a success, and shortly after its premiere, a local paper reported:

O. W. Burroughs, who plays the lead in the Town Theatre production of "Hero Worship" in the Little Theatre tournament, will leave today for New York.

Mrs. Annot Willingham, director, accompanied by Mrs. Mabel DeLorme, left for New York yesterday. The others in the company are Mrs. Frank McIntire, who plays the part of the wife, Mrs. Heyward Lynah, who plays the part of the daughter, and John Mercer, who plays the part of the grandson. Mrs. McIntire will leave for New York tomorrow, accompanied by Mrs. Craig Barrow.

The Towne Theatre will present the play at a performance Friday night at the Frolic Theater. If selected as one of the prize winners, it will be repeated Saturday afternoon and Saturday night. The four plays considered best by the judges will be given at a matinee Saturday, and from these four the judges will select the one to receive the Belasco cup. This is awarded after the performance Saturday night. . . .

The Georgia Society in New York will show their interest in the performance by buying seats for the Friday night performance.

The clipping is faded and tattered. It is impossible to date it precisely, and part of it is missing. And it is a little confusing. These final performances, according to John, were presented by David Belasco in New York "at the roof of the old New Amsterdam Theatre on Forty-second Street. It's now a porn film house." A group from Edinburgh, Scotland, took the prize with a performance of James Barrie's *The Old Lady Shows Her Medals,* but the Savannah group won second prize, and John got some good reviews for his acting, none of which survive.

James W. (Jimmy) McIntire, the son of Mrs. Frank McIntire, offered some clarification in a November 1997 conversation: "Whoever chose the people to act for little Town Theatre, they picked Mother. She played the mother of the group. And Johnny and his cousin Walter Rivers were in it. They won the first prize for Georgia, then they were sent to New York to compete with some other state's winner.

"I was up at Phillips Exeter Academy, and of course my mother sent me a ticket and I came down to New York to see it. I was sixteen years old, two years younger than Johnny. And my mother came on the stage and I burst into tears, because she was gray, and when I left home she had very blond hair and looked very young. And I thought, *Oh my God, look how my mother's aged! Aaaah! Six months! She's dying.* So I was very unhappy seeing that damn play.

"Johnny and Walter stayed in New York and Mother came home. Johnny was eighteen or nineteen. Walter and he both thought they were going to be actors. They were young and they had won this prize and they *knew* they were going to Hollywood."

For his part, John received many gracious compliments—one from a handsome English actor with a regimental mustache. The man was friendly and told John he admired his acting, offering his counsel and assistance should John ever need them. John, who was seventeen, felt as if he were walking above the floor. And as he was leaving the theater lobby, Elsie Ferguson—a major theater star of the time—kissed him. His face still greasy with makeup, he was embarrassed but thrilled. And then back to reality.

He returned by train to Savannah and a job at the brokerage firm

Hentz and Company, putting up stock quotations. Two summers later, he was invited by friends to Lake Mahopac, New York. Savannah by now bored him. There was no music, no acting, and little if any fun, for the pleasures of childhood had lost their magic. A fellow employee at Hentz and Company said something that offended him—what, we do not know—and John saw no reason to compound boredom with insult.

Mahopac lies twenty or thirty miles north-northeast of New York City, not far from Brewster, just shy of the Connecticut border. The countryside is rolling, the old farm fields alternating with deciduous woodlots. There are old homes, some of them pre–Revolutionary War, and it is altogether pretty country, New England in its general ambience. John spent two pleasant weeks there before he and his friends went into New York one afternoon to buy tickets for *Rain or Shine,* whose title phrase would later turn up in one of the songs he wrote with Harold Arlen. The show starred Joe Cook and Dave Chasen. Music was by Lewis Gensler, a successful composer for musical theater who today is all but forgotten, along with his songs. For John, the major thrill came from the presence in the pit orchestra of guitarist Eddie Lang and violinist Joe Venuti, childhood friends from Philadelphia whose duo recordings had made them major jazz stars.

The next day, John saw his two friends off on the train to Savannah, and then moved into a midtown boardinghouse recommended by an uncle who was living in New York. Sustained by the modest amounts of money sent by his father, he began knocking on doors. He planned on staying in the Big Apple two months, after which, if he failed to find a path into his dream world, he would return to Savannah and the dull life he envisioned there. He encountered the English actor Tony Brown and confessed his desire to stay in New York to try to establish himself as an actor. Brown urged John to call him, promising to show him the ropes.

He waited in outer offices. He talked to secretaries. He met producers and managers. Ultimately, Brown directed him to a team of theatrical agents—two elderly women—who operated from a shabby one-room office over the National Theater and Gray's Ticket Counter, where one was able to buy for half-price seats for shows that were limping along. The two women must have been living hand-to-mouth, John thought, and the job they sent him for, which he got, was a walk-on in a Theatre Guild play that paid him $30 a week, of which $3 went to the ladies as their commission. *It certainly didn't pay their rent, but maybe it bought them stamps.*

Informed that he had gotten the part, John went home to his boardinghouse and told his landlady, whose daughter was an actress. The latter's advice was that given since time immemorial by disillusioned denizens of the theatrical professions: she told him to go home and forget it. His landlady, a Mrs. Drake, was not quite so discouraging. As they celebrated with beer—quite illegal in those Prohibition times—and pretzels, she gave him only this advice: "Always pay your bills, keep your collar and wristbands clean, and buy your clothes at Brooks Brothers."

It was then that John met Cheryl Crawford, later an important theater producer in New York who, at that time, was a casting director. "Due to her kindness," John said, "I learned a lot—not so much about acting but about actors."

Almost all the small parts, which would have gone to chorus boys had it been a musical, were filled by homosexuals. They had, like all good fairies, their water wings on at all times and it was a footrace to get back to the dressing room or pass them in the halls without being handled. But I had been to a boys' prep school, so I knew how to dodge, and how to take the advances in the manner in which they were presented—lightly and casually, that is—and not act as if I were insulted.

John got small parts in two plays. One was an adaptation by Stefan Zweig of Ben Jonson's *Volpone,* in which he played a Venetian policeman at a salary of thirty dollars a week. (In time he would write the lyrics for a musical based on this play, starring Bert Lahr.) The other was Eugene O'Neill's *Marco Millions,* in which he played a Chinese coolie. The others in the company included Imogene Coca, Margalo Gilmore, Dudley Digges, Claude Rains, Hiran Sherman, and H. C. Potter, all of whom became prominent on stage or in film. The tour lasted six months, following the established Theatre Guild subscription circuit. But, John remembered, some of the friendships formed "lasted all our lives." And some of the girls married some of the older actors.

The company played in Chicago in early 1929, and John remembered the city for a bitter whistling cold that no overcoat could shut out as he and his fellow cast members walked home at night. The winter was cold in New York that year, too. When John returned to his boardinghouse, expecting a hero's welcome from the landlady who had been kind to him, she told him that her actress daughter—John remembered her only as "Miss Drake"—had died of pneumonia while he was away. She also told John she had decided to give up her boardinghouse and marry a long-patient suitor.

John took a small basement apartment in the West Eighties with a young member of the company named Sidney Mansfield, who had also attended a Southern prep school. All of John's clothes were stolen from the apartment, and not long afterwards a man on the street tried to sell him his own clothes out of a trunk. He judiciously chose not to press the issue.

One night John came home to find his roommate in bed with another boy.

I'm not a prude and I wasn't a prude then, but I couldn't see living in a ménage à trois unless the third member were a girl. So, as pleasantly as I could, I packed, left, and went home with three other guys in a five-flight walk-up on 72nd Street behind a big electric sign that flashed Coca-Cola in red neon all night long.

We had a good time. One of them played piano, and that was enough of a bond for me. The other two were great guys and went on to become prominent.

My first roommate, Sidney, I heard years later, was found bludgeoned to death on an Army post. His presence there was questionable, as he was a civilian. I guess he always did pick the wrong people. But what a tragedy. He was a sensitive man.

John was determined to succeed in New York, and there can be little doubt that his father's business reverses and consequent sense of humiliation acted as a goad. He was making the rounds of casting offices and chorus calls, and going to parties in Greenwich Village with other young people who were likewise striving to get a foothold.

His brokerage background got him a job in a Wall Street company, running errands, punching holes in stock certificates, running between banks, after which he would descend into the roaring subway and, for a nickel, take the ride back uptown, climb the five flights of stairs to the apartment he was sharing, soak in a bath, and, later, down some bathtub gin.

Prohibition was still very much with us, and we knew a few bootleggers and a few cheap speakeasies. I was trying to learn to drink like a gentleman. There have been rumors that I never succeeded at that study.

We had as much fun as we could. We were young. We did a lot of our own cooking, we scrounged free meals from visiting relatives and friends, and now and then got a little money from home. Two of my roommates got work again in a touring Guild play. My third roommate had a job with Squibb, and I couldn't afford the rent for the four-roomer. I got a job in The Black Crook, *a play by Dion Boucicault that was being revived in Hoboken, New Jersey. I took the ferry or the subway every day.*

That revival bombed in record time—two weeks without pay.

But he made a new friend in one of the members of the cast, Buddy Dill, who taught John a lot about living on little. He could, John said, do more with a dollar than anyone he had ever met. But he insisted on the importance of a good address, and so he and John moved into the Whitby, "haven of vaudevillians," and for the first week lived on oatmeal. They washed their shirts in a sink and ironed the collars and cuffs with the bottom of an aluminum pot that had been warmed on their hot plate.

Then Buddy and John got parts in a play called *Houseparty*. Produced by George Tyler, it was a murder mystery with a college-campus setting. Buddy got a fairly large part, but John's role was limited to running around the fraternity house with a tennis racket in hand. Buddy took John to a small Eighth Avenue restaurant called Ye Eat Shoppe, where they were able to get a dinner—including excellent pie—for thirty-five cents. "Buddy was really smart about money," John said.

What a marvelous guy. A marvelously natural actor too. A great fan of S.J. Perelman and a devotee of the Palace, where every week we'd climb (we did a lot of climbing in those days) to the top gallery to see Ted Healy and the Stooges (his favorite act) or Clayton, Jackson and Durante (mine) and other unforgettables, like Frank Fay, Herb Williams—"Hark! Them bells!"—Professor Joe Brown, Herbert Timbery, Burns and Allen, Block and Sully, Jimmy Barton—the greatest drunk I ever saw: "with the swif'ness of the wind, I whirled aroun' "—Van and Schenck, Will Mahoney, the McCarthy Sisters, and so many more that I'd have to find some old bills to remember them all. The big acts, like Jolson and the Marx Brothers and Joe E. Brown, were already in Hollywood, playing in their own musicals. But the last gasp of vaudeville was like a fireworks display, most dazzling just before the end. We learned a lot. And we loved it all.

John became friends with *Houseparty*'s assistant stage manager, Everett Miller, on the basis of a mutual interest in music, particularly their admiration for Venuti and Lang. The friendship grew still warmer when Miller learned that John wrote songs. *Houseparty* ran six months on "the subway circuit" in New York, and over the course of the run John's salary fell from $55 to $35 to $25 to $15. During this time, Miller showed him eight bars of a tune, for which John was moved to write words. With the show's closing, John and Buddy Dill moved into another hotel of faded distinction but with a good address. And John kept looking at Miller's tune, which he thought was "cute"—one of John's favorite words for something he liked, or, when an almost imperceptible sarcasm informed his tone, didn't like.

Johnny had nerve, what denizens of the theater world called moxie. That becomes quickly apparent in any examination of his early life. Yet this nerve contradicted a general insecurity to which every friend of his later years would attest. He was plagued by doubt; his self-effacement was no affectation. But he never let it stop him.

One evening, while walking past the New Amsterdam Theatre, where Eddie Cantor, one of the biggest stars of the period, was playing in *Whoopee* (he played a hypochondriac who goes out to the Wild West for his health), John suddenly said to Buddy, "I think I'll go in and play him some of my comedy songs." And Buddy, laughing, said, "Why not?" A few nights later, with his material neatly written by hand—he had no type-writer, then, he later remembered—he went to the stage door of the New Amsterdam and announced he was there to see Mr. Cantor. He speculated later that the doorman must have thought he was a relative.

John stepped into a tiny backstage elevator "with a lot of ladies who looked like Aphrodites and were just as naked." He found the language of these unclad goddesses lurid. Knocking on Cantor's dressing room door, he was told to enter. There, sitting in a flannel dressing gown, talking to a few friends and his wife, Ida, whom he had celebrated in a song of that name, was Eddie Cantor, the Broadway star. Cantor was known for his big round eyes, and they opened even wider when he learned John had got past the doorman and come up in the elevator with the half-naked "Indian" girls. Suppressing his surprise, Cantor asked John to show him a song. John sang it for him, a putatively comic number called "Every Time I Shave I Cut My Adam's Apple."

"Well, the poor man was petrified," John recalled. "He told me, 'You're afraid of me?' because I had told him I was. 'Well, I'm afraid of *you.*' "

Cantor may well have sensed the scope of the talent confronting him: some professionals are uncanny at detecting it in its early stages of devel-opment. He told John he was about to leave on tour, but, John told a BBC interviewer, "he said, 'I'll tell you what you do, young man. Go home and write six or seven choruses, and bring me the song again.' So I did go home, and I wrote fifteen or twenty choruses! And I mailed them to him. And he never used the song, but he kept corresponding with me. He encouraged me. He said, 'They're very good, and I'm gonna put them in the show.' And he really gave me confidence to keep going. Years later we used to laugh about it, when I met him in Hollywood. Nice man, Eddie Cantor. He was one of the biggest influences on my life."

Christmas approached, and John was desperately homesick. Two years in a row his mother sent him train fare, and he went home by coach. No one knew how discouraged he was. He was turning twenty and had nothing to show for his time in New York except a third-floor walk-up apartment on Jones Street in Greenwich Village, where his clothes were piled in a corner. He maintained a brave front, sufficient to deceive the local newspaper, which ran a short item about him (and got his father's name wrong).

JOHNNY MERCER
Actor, Visitor
Savannahian Is Enthusiastic Over Theatrical Outlook

Johnny Mercer, son of Mr. and Mrs. George A. Mercer Jr., returned this morning from New York, where he has just concluded an engagement with Eugene O'Neill's Marco Millions and Ben Jonson's Volpone. Mr. Mercer will spend several weeks with his parents, returning in the spring to New York, where he expects to enter stock.

He is extremely enthusiastic over his new vocation and has optimistic things to say about the theater world, which he says recently reached the peak of the season. He admits there is an influx of bad productions, but speaks very encouragingly about the number of hits of the year and of theatrical conditions in general.

John remembered this as the darkest period of his life: "While the hometown talk was about how well young Mercer is doing on the stage, I was just about to go back on oatmeal."

Six

The Depression was at its deepest. Men and women sold apples on street corners, and in New York City men were sleeping in doorways. John was scraping by on the largesse of friends and relatives with jobs.

He was studying drama with an actress named Arnot Willingham, who, as John did, lived in the Village. "She always had a kind word for me," John said, "or a bathtub-gin Tom Collins. It was to her apartment I often went to get free meals and to listen to Louis Armstrong records. All Mrs. Willingham's children were working, two daughters and a son, and when I had anything to offer, I'd bring it along—food, records, or a funny joke. It was years before I was in the chips enough to try and repay their kindness and hospitality.

"On warm nights we'd go up on the roof, and in the winter we'd go out to one of the little Italian bistros so numerous in Greenwich Village in those days."

An actor friend named Tom Rutherford told John they were casting at the Theatre Guild for a third edition of the revue known as *The Garrick Gaieties,* but he was told that there was no need for more actors; what the producers needed were "songs and pretty girls." John phoned a friend, Cynthia Rogers, the prettiest girl he knew in New York, who was out of work. And he completed a lyric to the tune his friend Everett Miller had written. The next day he took Cynthia and the song to the Guild, and both made it into the show. Cynthia sang the song on opening night.

"And," John told an ASCAP interviewer, "I met other guys who had songs in the show, like Yip Harburg and Vernon Duke. Later on, Harburg was very instrumental in helping me."

His friend Everett Miller had failed to tell John something important, namely that his father was Charlie Miller, who wrote arrangements for Jerome Kern, Sigmund Romberg, and other major Broadway composers. He was also an executive at T.B. Harms, the music publishing company, and through this connection Johnny soon had his first published song, "Out of Breath and Scared to Death of You."

And a girl in the *Gaieties* chorus attracted his attention—a dancer from Brooklyn named Ginger Meehan. Born Elizabeth Meltzer on June 25, 1909, she was five months older than John, a granddaughter of Russian Jewish immigrants Anna and Joseph Meltzer. Her sisters were Claire, the eldest, and Rose. All three received a measure of musical education, and Elizabeth was given acrobatic dancing lessons.

Joseph Meltzer committed suicide, leaving Anna to raise their three girls. As a child in Russia, she had worked in a ribbon shop, and to support herself and her daughters she took up sewing high-quality children's clothes, eventually overseeing several employees.

In time Elizabeth Meltzer went to work as a Broadway chorus girl, touring with a show called *Honeymoon Lane*. One of the cast members was Mary Meehan. In that period of American history, "foreign" and especially Jewish names invited opprobrium and closed doors. Elizabeth Meltzer changed her name to Ginger Meehan—it had a sprightly sound. She roomed with Dolores Reade, who married Bob Hope and became Ginger's lifelong friend. Even in her eighties, Dolores Hope was a fine singer.

When the show played Philadelphia, Ginger and Dolores met Bing Crosby, then one of the featured acts with the Paul Whiteman band. Crosby was already known as a womanizer and a drunk. His toping companion was Bix Beiderbecke, but, Gary Giddins notes in his biography *Bing Crosby: A Pocketful of Dreams*, "Bix held his liquor better than Bing, who frequently fell into a stupor." A little later, Giddins says, "Bing could be cantankerous and was becoming unreliable. Some nights he was so green from drink that he had to be held up at the mike; on other nights he did not show at all. . . . The women they saw were chorus girls, of which there was a limitless supply." One of whom was Ginger.

One night, when Ginger was staying at Philadelphia's Emerson Hotel, Crosby sent her a wire from New York: ACCORDING TO US STATISTICS THERE ARE 7 MILLION PEOPLE HERE BUT WITHAL IM A STRANGER AND MIS-

ERABLY ALONE BECAUSE YOURE NOT ALONG LOVE UNDYING BEST REGARDS TO DOLORES AND STUFF. BING. Note that the wire contains a hint of the affectation of erudition (the word *withal*) that would become a part of Crosby's humor in his later years.

Giddins writes, "The affair continued on and off through the summer [of 1927]. When Whiteman pulled into Chicago in July Ginger was already there, in the road company of *Good News*. Bing wired her at the Selwyn Theater: WOULD YOU LIKE TO SAY HELLO THIS EVE AFTER YOUR PERFORMANCE SAY AT ELEVEN FIFTEEN. BING. Six days later he wired her a few minutes before she went onstage: WOULD LIKE TO CALL YOU TONIGHT. IF BUSY SUE ME. BING. Ginger didn't sue, but the romance fizzled, possibly because Bing became enamored of another *Good News* cast member, the star, Peggy Bernier. . . . Bing's infatuation with Peggy, who could keep up with his late-night carousing, lasted several months, unlike most of his romances, which were as fleeting as stops on a vaudeville circuit."

Having been one of his girls, Ginger now became one of his castoffs. After the cool of Crosby, Johnny must have seemed pretty naïve. *The Garrick Gaieties* was Ginger's fourth show. John would bring ice cream and Coca-Cola and hot dogs to her dressing room and take her to movies. He said she had eyes that crinkled when she smiled. Many of those who knew John and Ginger in their later years wondered what he saw in her; she was withdrawn and remote, and his friends found conversation with her difficult.

John kept writing and trying to sell his songs, waiting days on end in outer offices for appointments with publishers, traveling long distances on subways to meet some obscure melody writer who perhaps had a tune that could be developed into a hit.

When I had money, I'd take Ginger home to Brooklyn in a cab, and when I didn't, we'd take the subway. She never had any false pride or false values, thank God, and she knew what it was to work for a living. We didn't have much to talk about at first except Bing Crosby, whom she had known and whom I admired.

This passage is telling in two ways. Even then John could not find much to discuss with Ginger. And he does not say he "liked" Bing Crosby, only that he admired him.

John became an habitué of Walgreen's drugstore in Times Square and the English Tea Room in the Fifties. There he met Morgan (Buddy) Lewis, a composer who in 1940 would have his only hit, "How High the Moon," a favorite of jazz musicians for its modulating major-to-minor chord patterns; Richard Lewine, who would succeed on Broadway as a composer and producer; actors Gene Raymond and Robert Montgomery; and other young people looking for a big break in theater. They would remain among John's friends a few years later in Hollywood.

The publication of "Out of Breath" by Harms gave John entrée to that company, and there he would catch fleeting views of George Gershwin, Vincent Youmans, Jerome Kern, Sigmund Romberg, Oscar Levant, Oscar Hammerstein II, Brian Hooker (a former assistant professor of English at Columbia University and lecturer on rhetoric at Yale who wrote the lyrics for the Rudolf Friml operetta *The Vagabond King*), and Harry B. Smith (who had been a music critic for the *Chicago Daily News* and drama critic of the *Chicago Tribune* and had become lyricist to Victor Herbert, among others). Smith is all but forgotten today, but his lyrics include "Yours Is My Heart Alone" and "The Sheik of Araby," written at a time when the Rudolph Valentino silent film *The Sheik* had set off a fad for songs about the deserts and all things Arabian.

Harms was at that time ruled over by the Dreyfus brothers, Max and Louis. Louis was the businessman, Max the creative member of the team. Max Dreyfus had an incredible ear for talent, and he was responsible for launching the careers of a great many major composers and lyricists in American popular music, among them Cole Porter and all those writers John saw whisking in and out of the offices at Harms. It is hard to estimate Max's influence in the development of classic American song; harder still to overestimate it.

John also met Herman Hupfeld, who wrote words and music for "As Time Goes By" and "Let's Put Out the Lights and Go to Sleep." John would write a few songs with him, none of which is known today. Most significantly at this time, he met composer Arthur Schwartz.

Schwartz, the son of a lawyer, graduated Phi Beta Kappa from New York University with a B.A. and went on, pressured by his family, to take a law degree at Columbia. He practiced law for several years and, like Yip Harburg and Cole Porter, didn't take up songwriting professionally until his late twenties. His primary partner, lyricist Howard Dietz, was a graduate of the Columbia School of Journalism. Dietz, who had a simultaneous second career as head of advertising and publicity at MGM, was one of the most scintillating of all American lyricists. His command of language exceeded in precision and surprise that of all but a few. The songs of Howard Dietz and Arthur Schwartz include "I Guess I'll Have to Change My Plan," "Something to Remember You By," "Dancing in the Dark," "Alone Together," "A Shine on Your Shoes," "If There Is Someone Lovelier Than You," "You and the Night and the Music," "By Myself," "I See

Your Face Before Me," "Haunted Heart," "Make the Man Love Me," and the ingenious "That's Entertainment."

And so when Johnny says in that casually dismissive way of his that Arthur Schwartz listened with a critical ear to his early work, it is not to be taken lightly. His advice to John goes unrecorded, but that this connection was ever made is significant.

Schwartz was born into a comfortable situation. So, indeed, was Johnny Mercer, but in John's case the money had evaporated with his father's reverses and John had to struggle in New York. In this he was different from most of those composers and lyricists who overawed him when he encountered them in the Harms and other publishing offices.

None of the composers and lyricists John was meeting had to wonder, as he did, where the next meal was coming from, and they knew their way around Manhattan. Most were college educated, grew up with New York City street smarts, and had every advantage over this Savannah boy with soft Southern manners and naïve ideals. Considering the odds and the nature of the business, John shouldn't have "made it" at all. But he was there, and he was making contacts. In time, he would write with many of these composers, including Harry Warren, Hoagy Carmichael, Jerome Kern, and Harold Arlen.

He also met Louis MacLoon and his wife, well-respected theatrical producers in California. They were on their way back there after a trip to Europe, where they had bought an operetta from the Hungarian composer and symphony conductor Emmerich Kálmán, who wrote *Love's Own Sweet Song* and *Play Gypsies, Dance Gypsies*. MacLoon's wife, who worked under the professional name Lillian Albertson, would write the book for an American adaptation of this operetta, and the MacLoons were looking for a young American to write the lyrics.

A week later, the MacLoons, with John in tow, were aboard a train to Los Angeles. During the three days of the trip, John pored over a translation of the Kálmán operetta, offered suggestions, and began looking for titles.

There had been a girl in John's life in Savannah. A fragment of a news clipping from a Savannah paper quotes him:

"My memory was of a girl who meant very much to me when I was at college." He presumably referred to Woodberry Forest. Either that or, faintly embarrassed by the limitation of his formal education, he was embellishing it a little. "We had dreams of a life together. And we probably would have married. But I also was dreaming of writing songs, and the impulse to compose made me restless. I loved a girl and I loved an ambition, and I was divided between the two.

"The girl could see that. She could see that I could not yield myself fully to any love until I had also yielded myself, in part at least, to my ambition. And so she allowed herself to drift away from me, and I threw myself more completely into my work. The girl heard less of me."

It is clear from this clipping, and from his own comments, that John still had this girl on his mind in the months after he met Ginger. Apparently she was Savannah socialite Elizabeth Cummins, whose coming-out party at the city's DeSoto Hotel John had attended on New Year's Day, 1930. In John's absence she married Edward Bubier Wulbern of Charleston, and one of John's friends sent him a newspaper clipping announcing the marriage. He doesn't seem to have been shattered by it, and there is even a certain insouciance in his references to her.

He told the newspaper reporter:

"All this ran through my mind now as I walked through the trees to the Lovers' Wall. And then a melody seemed to flow out of my thoughts; a melody and some words. When I reached the wall, the song was formed."

There the clipping ends. We do not learn what the song was.

Writers inevitably—there is no other way—draw on personal experience. It has been said that there is no more autobiographical novel than Swift's *Gulliver's Travels*. Balzac said that the characters in his novels were made up of bits and pieces of persons he had known, but, he added, the soul of a Balzac character is always Balzac. John was always at the top of his form when he was writing from his own memories and experience. And lyricists are ruthless in their retention of early wistful memories for later resurrection and cold-blooded use as "material."

Is the girl in Savannah the fox fire figure that haunts John's lyrics? Is she the "Laura" of the song, footsteps that you hear down the hall, the laugh that floats on a summer night that you can never quite recall?

Transplanted from Savannah to Paris, is she the girl of whom he writes in "Once Upon a Summertime"?

> *But I remember, when the vespers chime,*
> *you loved me, once upon a summertime.*

John wrote: *When I departed Savannah, I left* [her] *with the understanding that we would somewhere, someday (like the lyric of the Carl Fischer song) be together again. So even though Ginger and I had formed an attachment, we were not really engaged. I got a clipping in the mail saying that my Savannah inamorata had announced her engagement to a Carolina boy. I think that made up my mind for me, if I ever had any doubts. . . . Fortunately for me, Ginger had made some changes too, sending a few of her old beaux packing.*

Well, maybe.

Seven

Though John was a prolific letter writer, few of his letters survive. Some of them he wrote in pencil, many others he typed, but apparently he never kept carbon copies. However, a striking series of letters to Ginger, which John began to write on the train to California in that autumn of 1930, survive because she kept them all her life, along with her telegrams from Bing Crosby. They are preserved in a folio in the Special Collections section of the Pullen Library at Georgia State University. They are almost eerily informative, particularly about the character of Ginger Meehan during their courtship.

I must caution you about these letters—you may find them embarrassing; I did. For one thing, you will get the feeling that we are eavesdropping on the most tender secrets of someone else's life—and so we are. Beyond that, Johnny's utter sexual subservience is really quite disturbing. You will also find evidence that Bing Crosby was hardly Ginger's only paramour. Furthermore, there are clues that Ginger must have been an adept sexual technician; note the reference to Wednesday night.

In later years, John's friends would sometimes wonder what hold she had over him because her personality was so vapid. The answer is in these letters, and she had it very early in the relationship. It is one of the oldest tricks in the catalogue of feminine wiles: a combination of promise and threat. She never let him feel secure in the relationship, telling him that there were other men standing by. She kept him perpetually off balance, lonely and pleading for letters from her, and vows of affection, which apparently were rare. We do not have her letters from this period, but Johnny's are their mirror: we often can deduce the approximate contents of her letters from his.

Another point before you read on: had any woman treated me the way she treated him, she'd have heard, as we say nowadays, "I'm outta here." But Johnny was fresh out of the South, and very naïve. And he was, God help him, only twenty-one.

The earliest of these letters was written on the stationery of the Santa Fe Chief as John was on his way to California. After some humorous divagation on the origin of the name Hollywood, he suddenly bursts out:

> *I love you. Can you stand it? Ginger, every minute I've been thinking about you. I adore you and think what the hell I would do if you ever stopped loving me. What would I do? And how did I live before I met you?*
>
> *The trip has been lousy so far. So damned hot that I yearn for the Paramount balcony. All of which is very incoherent but then that's how I feel about you. You didn't know I was so silly, did you? Anyway, the Chief is giving this letter hell with his rocking about. So I'm going to stop. Maybe I'll do better next time. Write me soon, my precious, and tell me you love me. I can never hear it enough.*
>
> *Johnny*

Another letter written aboard the Chief, in September 1930, reads in part:

> *I would like to tell you that I am being awed tremendously by the landscape but at the present moment I'm not. The only thing I can think, Ginger, I never will forget Wednesday. I have never had anything so sweet happen to me before. I'm sure it never will or could with any one else. Someday, I hope you find out how real and sincere my love is for you—you can't possibly know by anything I say, because if I try to, I could never approach the real feeling. And, dearest, if it's got to end sometime, please tell me and don't let it happen gradually. I couldn't stand it that way.*

Portrait of Johnny

*I've just finished reading 'Queer People', a very amusing
story of Hollywood. Read it, you'll get some laughs.*
*Write Johnny soon and tell him how everything is and how
much you love him, because there's never been anyone who loves
you as much as he does.*

The Colonel

A postcard written soon after his arrival in Beverly Hills ends: "Rhythm Boys next day. I'll say hello to Bing for you. I adore you, Sweet. —J."

John at first fell in love with the California sunshine, with the oleander, bougainvillea, and royal palms, and with the roofs of half-round red Mediterranean tiles on Beverly Hills "cottages." The MacLoon home had once belonged to Greta Garbo, and they joked that they hadn't washed the ring out of the bathtub.

The MacLoons' son, Eddie Albertson, who himself aspired to songwriting, introduced John to the miniature golf courses that were already a fad in California, as well as to the temple of Aimee Semple McPherson, whose name would turn up in a Mercer lyric, and to the Brown Derby. He took him to the Cotton Club, where Louis Armstrong was performing, and to the Coconut Grove, where the Rhythm Boys were singing with Gus Arnheim's band.

John introduced himself to Bing Crosby, who was already popular with young people but not yet the national idol he was to become. John said later that he was "impressed . . . by those opaque, China-blue eyes, and his manner and talk, at once warm and hip with a touch of aloofness that was always there." John was on his best behavior when he wrote that, but you can catch the feeling behind the description. Though they would eventually record together, he did not particularly care for Crosby. John took note of "his lack of hair."

He was only a few years older than I . . . but he was practically bald. After our talk backstage, I watched the act again and had only one fault to find. It wasn't long enough. Jazz was still a rare commodity in 1931 but all the kids were hungry for the music that the trio was putting down. Only a few seemed to understand it. The Williams Sisters, Roger Wolfe Kahn, Ray Miller, Red Nichols, and quite a few instrumentalists, but hardly any singers. That's why I wanted to hear more. I knew [the Rhythm Boys'] records by heart, but wasn't interested in "Surrender, Dear," I wanted to hear more "Wistful and and Blue" more "Old Man River," more "Because My Baby Don't Mean Maybe Now."

The great Louis Armstrong was at his youthful peak, his prime, but those dumb customers at the Cotton Club didn't want to hear "Struttin' with Some Barbecue" or the "Heebie Jeebies" or "Knockin' a Jug" or "Monday Date." What they loved was the suggestive "Golfin' Papa, You Got the Nicest Niblick in Town."

In a letter to Ginger postmarked Beverly Hills, September 22, 1930, John says:

> It seems rather futile to keep writing if you're not going to answer. I think I'd better give it up as a bad job. Far be it from me to let you know my real feelings (ha) but can't you guess how much I love you? Ah, but you little glad rag dolls, what do you care how many hearts you break as long as you achieve your dastardly ends? Woe is me for ever setting eyes upon those two cherry lips that are luring my heart straight to Hell! Incidentally, I may as well apologize now for this typewriting.
>
>> The day is breaking
>> My heart's awaking
>> Run to the gate
>> The postman is late
>> But who can tell
>> What the hell
>> He's bringing anyhow
>> Chorus: a letter edged in black!
>
> And that's the way you affect me, my little Ninon. You see, Ginger, I'm forced to write such silly (?) nonsense which isn't even funny and isn't meant to be because other wise I'd only be saying I love you all the time. You'll have to stand it until you answer one of my letters and tell me something to say (I've already apologized for that mistake).
>
> Would you like to hear about the corny tunes and lyrics that are going in this opera? One thing I promise is that I'll try not to bore you with business when we're married. . . .
>
> For God's sake, write me, baby; it's no fun hoping to get a letter every day and never getting it.
>
> I adore you, I adore you.
>
> *Johnny*

Portrait of Johnny

On October 4, 1930, he wrote:

Ginger, love:

 Your letter was the most welcome thing in my life. I really had begun to think that you had forgotten me all together. I was so sorry to hear of your ligament. My land sakes alive, girl, you must be more careful of your ligaments; they might stand you in good stead some day. Anyway, you'll have to keep yourself perfect for your little Johnny. . . .

 I've got a week left to finish three quarters of the show so pray for me, baby. Old Madame Mercer isn't used to operettas. . . .

 Ginger, don't ever worry about Johnny being your own. As long as you want him he can't help himself. I adore you, my precious, and always will as long as you'll let me. So don't ever let anybody even make an impression on you that will make you change your mind about me.

 I've got to try and do a little work now, honey. I love you and just wait for your letters so write and tell me you love me.

Early in October, he apparently learned that Ginger was going out with a road version of *Garrick Gaieties*. Why this disturbed him, I do not know, but on October 6 he wrote to her:

 A mood of ever increasing depression has set in since I got your letter and, as the writers have it, I feel a foreboding of evil. Maybe you won't go after all, but I have a strange fear that our short interval is over.

 I've never been much at expressing thoughts in a grand manner, Ginger, because I hardly think it lends itself to my type. Then too, I may lose the goal in "fearing to attempt"—but anyway, I'll try. Before I say anything, my dearest, please believe that everything I say is honest—and no kidding about even a single word.

 I've been around a lot—although not as much as most— but I've had the experiences that everyone has, and maybe I know the facts—maybe not. There's never been anyone who's meant as much to me as you, Ginger, and I don't think anyone ever can hold the position you do. Because no one could. You see, precious, you're "my first love" in the real meaning

*of the word—And no one else can hardly be that, can
they?*

*It's been short but terribly sweet—and it always will be to
me. And I don't want you to think you were just one of the
others. (This all sounds a little somber but I feel it, darling, and
I've got to say it—whether it's a type you don't like or not.) So
this letter is really to thank you for coming into my life—as
'twere. I'm so glad it was you and not someone else, because
you're pretty perfect to me—and I adore you.*

On October 11, he sent her a wire at her mother's home—1103 Sterling Place, Brooklyn. It read: THANKS FOR YOUR WIRE SWEET MAYBE IT'S
NOT HOPELESS. JOHNNY

Two days later he wrote her a letter:

Ginger, my darling:

*Of course I would say that your letter was a disappointment
to me but I was sure you would go. Old man Pessimism himself.
You were really too sweet to last my dearest; combined with this
lousy business we're in. I say were because even if I do come to
see you in Pittsburgh or where ever you [are] when I leave this
dump, what's after that? This show is practically finished and
although I don't think I've done any Hammerstein or De Sylva
job on it, there's talk of doing another in a couple of months. In
the interval I want to go home for a month or so and if you're on
the road there is nothing to prevent me from doing so. God,
Ginger, I hate to even think of it. I must sound like a baby in
these maudlin letters I've been writing, but, my darling, I'm so
crazy about you. I don't believe you know how much (for the
50th time). . . .*

*Well, Ginger mine, drop a line—with your first few stops and
length of stay indicated—maybe I will come to see you and find
that you've fallen for some mug in the company.*

I LOVE YOU

Oscar

On October 14, he wrote:

*You're really treating me too well in this letter writing racket.
Your last one was marvelous. . . .*

Portrait of Johnny

So I haven't been telling you much about myself? I've a hunch it would be terribly boring. I haven't done one interesting thing since I've been out here. But I'll try: The show looks fair. . . . The music is pretty, most of the corny things having been kicked out—after I had written lyrics too. They are all right too—so don't say it. . . . The engagement for me has been one of grief—I can't stand the producers, but what the hell.

I heard the other day that Bing had gotten married to Dorothy Lee—thought you might like to know. I wish you were here so we could go to these "dance palaces" together and appreciate the music, for unlike you, I have yet to find a kindred soul.

Ginger, won't it be marvelous . . . if we can be with each other in Chicago? Darling, will you stay by yourself there so I can have you all for my own? Please do. Just think of all the crazy things we can do. We can go to the zoo, and have more fun just being together every minute. (That might sound funny, but then I go a little mad when I think of how wonderful it could be.) Even if you play Vancouver I'm coming to see you, sweet. I do love you so, Ginger; I even dream about you—and every night, which is a pretty good average. As long as there is even a doubt in your mind that you still love me don't ever stop, Dearest; I'd probably die. . . .

The land of sunshine! Praise God! I'll soon be leaving it. I've never seen a bigger hick town than this one. And the blondes— I've never seen as many. And hope I never see another one. It would be all right if they were naturals but they haven't even that excuse.

Maybe I'd better stop if all I can think to talk of is that. Remember, I love you, my own Ginger, and can hardly wait until I see you again. I've been keeping myself for you, and, oh, will it be worth it. I adore you.

Your Johnny

On October 26, he sent her a Postal Telegraph wire at the Blackstone Theater in Chicago: PROBABLY LEAVE ABOUT NOVEMBER FIFTH. I MISS YOU SO MUCH.

Then, on November 6, he wrote:

My precious:

Everything seems to happen to keep you away from me. I had my reservation to leave tonight and these bastards decided to rewrite the second act finale. My heart is about to break, Ginger. Sometimes I wish I'd never even met you, if I must be away from you so long. Darling, I hope you don't miss me as badly as I do you, because it's hell. Right now I feel so disgusted that I feel like saying let's quit. There doesn't seem to be any chance of seeing you. God knows when I'll leave—And I do adore you so. I swear I think I'll do something awful—like committing a murder—or something equally as bad—If I ever do see you again, I'll never leave you.

I feel too badly to write any more, darling—please forgive me—Remember I adore you—more than anything in this whole lousy world—

I love you so.

Johnny

On November 10, he wrote from San Francisco to say, among other things:

I'm so anxious for this show to close and for everyone to forget I ever wrote it—It will never be in condition to reach New York—if it does, God help it. . . .

Do you remember [Bob Knickerbocker] from Good News? *Always be good, Gin, because your sins will find you out. Can you imagine how I felt when he showed me a picture of you? I guess I'm not the highest rating boy in the world with you after all. I'll certainly have to eat those words I spoke to you by the old pagoda in Brooklyn that night, won't I?*

I got a wire from Charlie Miller not long ago, telling me to see him when I get back—and this week I saw in Variety *that he is opening a publishing company of his own—so maybe I'll have a decent job when I get back—up the stairs to fame & fortune for my Ginger—even though the medium is that of a lyricist, a lonely profession—really.*

Charlie Miller, with whose son John had written "Out of Breath . . . ," had left T.B. Harms to set up his own publishing company in partnership with the president of the American Locomotive Company, Charles

Woodin, later to become Franklin Delano Roosevelt's secretary of finance. Miller put John on a drawing account of twenty-five dollars a week. Under the terms of such contracts, these were advances, to be recouped from future royalties.

In reply to a letter from John's father, Miller urged George Mercer to continue sending John fifty dollars a month. He called John a literary genius and said that someday he would hit his stride.

Paris in the Spring had a successful opening in San Francisco on November 3, 1930. John wrote to Ginger: "The fanfare of trumpets have ended, the grief is over, and out of the dust strode—who do you think—a fair-sized hit—not a smash and not for New York—but a hit just the same." It ran for three weeks, closing on November 22, and by that time he was aware of its shortcomings. It was the first of many disappointments he would suffer in writing for theater.

During this period, Walter Rivers had a small part in a show called *Schoolgirl,* which John went to see. He wrote to Ginger:

"All evening I thought of us. The play dealing with adolescent love is trite, but so many times the girl character reminded me of you. She saw so much more clearly her way about than the boy, who was rather much of a jellyfish. I'm not that, am I, sweet?"

He asks: "Do you feel that you'd like to marry me but that it would be unwise and you'd rather wait? But that if we wait something will happen and then you won't want to?"

He adds: "I really do want to—and I'm only afraid I can't make you happy enough."

The letters are all of a tone: Johnny is a desperate supplicant, pleading for her acceptance. I never heard Ginger express ardor for anything or anybody—or even heard *of* her doing so—with a single exception: a gigolo she met after Johnny's death. She was a bland woman, and those who knew her during their courtship were puzzled by their relationship even then.

In any generation of show business, coteries of ambitious girls encircle the rising young men of the profession. It is a constant. Some of them are in the business, dancers and minor starlets; others are mere satellites. But they seem to have an eye on the main chance and a sixth sense about who is going to "make it" big. When Ginger's friend Dolores Reade married Bob Hope, she set out upon a lifetime of tolerating his ill-concealed marathon affairs with other women.

There is no record of Ginger's expressing affection, much less passion, for Johnny. Even his own letters show no evidence of it; there is nothing in them that seems to be in response to some gentle or affectionate thing she has written or said to him. Even in *his* letters, she comes across as devoid of personality, which is how acquaintances found her in the later years. I do not recall one interesting thing she ever said.

Perhaps because his friends were baffled by his infatuation with her, a story went into circulation. It held that Johnny, drunk, got into an automobile accident in which Ginger's face was badly marked. As she supposedly lay bleeding, she told Johnny that now he would *have* to marry her. I first heard the tale from Artie Shaw, and it's still in circulation. I don't believe it, for several reasons. It is unlikely that John would have been driving a car in New York City in that era. Whose car? Certainly not his own. There is no evidence that John was then the drinker he became in later years. Also, Ginger had no major scarring on her face. There was only a small scar from an accident that occurred in Los Angeles many years later.

And no one could believe that fairy tale after reading his letters to her. Indeed, his desire to marry her caused a conflict with his parents.

Nancy Gerard uncovered some letters from John to his parents, together with a note from Miss Lillian to Nancy, telling her to destroy them. Nancy disobeyed. These letters are in response to some he received from his parents, none of which seems to have survived; chances are that John destroyed them. But there is much that we can deduce from John's letters. They were written in March and April of 1931—four months after his work on *Paris in the Spring*—according to the cancellation stamps on the envelopes, but the exact dates cannot be determined. Evidently his parents learned of the coming nuptials from a newspaper before he had had a chance to discuss the matter with them. A letter typed on the stationery of Miller Music Incorporated, located at 62 West Forty-ninth Street—in the heart of Tin Pan Alley—reads:

> *Dear Mother and Father:*
>
> *I can easily understand your surprise, reproach, and grief over the unfortunate discovery of the announcement in the paper. Again I apologize for it. It would be perfectly useless to write you and tell you every thing that I had in mind when I took such a step. Believe me I thought of you though, and would never have done anything without your knowledge, had I not thought that I would be the first one to inform you.*
>
> *I have listened to all your views, but they are nothing new. I really think that you think I am still a baby in mind. You ought*

to know such is not the case, and that I have never thought out anything so carefully in my life. My only feeling about the matter is one of disappointment that you should make Ginger feel so unwelcome. She is a lovely, sensitive girl and naturally feels keenly the hostility which you have unconsciously shown. I know how much you love me, but I regret that you don't respect my judgment more.

I know every reason why we shouldn't get married, but we are both eager to make a success of it and will. I can't talk to you by letter, so I will come home and speak to you about it. But I won't come without her. You needn't be afraid to send me money. I have promised not to get married without seeing you, and I keep my promises.

Above all, it is not just sex. Don't think for a moment that it is.

All these letters get us nowhere, so send me the money to journey homeward. Remember, she's coming with me. The doctor says that a trip south would be swell for my sinus, so I think I can come right away.

Remember, I love you both dearly.

Johnny

The next letter is to Miss Lillian alone; apparently his parents had told him *not* to bring Ginger to Savannah, and he in turn stopped them from visiting him and Ginger in New York:

Mother sweet:

I don't know exactly what to say in this letter, they all seem so unsatisfactory, don't they? I won't take the tone of an outraged son any more though. I can't begin to tell you what you have done to Ginger. Maybe you don't mean to have that effect but you do. What would you think if you were her? Naturally you would feel hurt and who wouldn't?

I want you to know that I didn't even see her from the time I got your wire to the time I phoned you. The objection to the projected visit was entirely mine, simply because if we need money as much as you say we do that would be an awful waste of it. It isn't because I don't love you or that I don't want to see you, but I think it unwise. You couldn't possibly make me see anything I don't already see. I know all about Juliana's education, etc. but that can't stop me from wanting to get married. I'm no vulture who wants to drain you of all the capital you have. I merely want to borrow enough to get started. Naturally, I will be making more than 25 dollars most of the time. As soon as I get even one song in a show, that will be doubled. If I get a successful one, I will probably have an income of several hundred dollars a week. And it isn't likely that I won't soon. I've had two already, and one is sure to be successful. This thing won't go on forever, you know. I only wanted a little help until I could get firmly planted, which can't be long. If Ginger's willing to marry me, knowing all these things, please don't make it seem so hard. After all, I've got to get married sometime and it will be just as hard on you whenever I do. She will have to work if she doesn't marry me, and she might have to go away if she does. Can't you see what might happen? You know what absence can do to people, even though they're terribly in love. And if this ever causes a separation between us, I'll never forgive you. But I'm sure it won't, she's got too much sense to let it.

Naturally, when you asked her to come to Savannah she told her mother, had clothes made, and broke off all relations with every one else. It was hardly decent of you to change your mind about it. Because now she thinks you don't want her, and of course, wouldn't come for anything. She couldn't be comfortable with all the undercurrent that there would be.

I thought I would get a little support in this, but it seems that I will just have to do everything on my own hook. After all I don't plan on getting married every year and I expected this would be a little easier for me. Because my mind is made up.

I love you all very dearly.

Bubba

It is the harshest exchange between John and his mother I have encountered. In another (probably the next) letter, this one to his father, handwritten in pencil and for once bearing a date (April 22, 1931), his tone has softened almost to the point of the unctuous. But we suspect the reason for the family's objection to Ginger: they had apparently learned that her real name was Meltzer, and that she was Jewish. We may also speculate that they may have learned by then how she was leading him around on a string.

Portrait of Johnny

Dear Pop:

Your letter received and I've never really felt quite like it made me feel before. When you and mother tell me how much you love me, I feel like such a dog. Not that I'm a bad boy—but no matter how wonderful I am, it could never justify the things that you both have done for me, and the opinions you hold of your boy. I'm sure that you're the best parents anywhere.

As to your questions, here are the answers.

1. *Miss Morris thanked you for the candy but wouldn't accept it.*
2. *Elizabeth Meltzer changed it to Meehan for the stage, Ginger to her friends. Ginger Meehan to me.*
3. *At a church probably—but no reception.* [His father had apparently asked John where they planned to marry, perhaps wondering if it would be in a synagogue.]
4. *Only her mother is living, her father having been dead about 5 years.*
5. *Do I love you. I could never tell you how much. I think you're swell. I wish I could tell you how proud I am of you. Pop, you're just grand.*

I'll let you know about the money. I don't want to take it if I don't absolutely need it. But thanks so much—I know you all need it.

Things are dull—but looking up, as they say. I hope for the best. I know I'll get there, Pop—and I am considered good by contemporaries, which is something. Although I haven't definitely come through—I hope I shall—and will work hard towards that aim. You've set me a wonderful example to follow and your character is a goal for me to aim at. If I half succeed, I'll be happy.

Lots of love to you, dear father; I'll write again soon. Kiss mother for me and convince her that I adore [heavily underlined] *her. And that no one can take the place she fills in my life.*

My love to my darling family—hoping that I can make them all really proud of me and my wife.

> *Your black sheep,*
> *Johnny*

His parents apparently relented, for it is evident from John's next letter that they have invited him and Ginger to come to Savannah after all. But this time John puts it off with excuses that may be a little disingenuous.

Mother sweet:

Your sweet letters came intact, and I feel like an old pot for not writing you sooner. But you know this delinquent. I'm not mad at all darling, nor am I hurt. And I hope you're not. I love you so much. And I only wish you could have known more about it if it would have made you feel better.

Ginger and I both want to come home so much, but I'm afraid there's not much chance to do so soon. I talked to Mr. Miller yesterday and he said that this was the most unpropitious time to leave and there would probably be a great deal of opportunity to do some work during the next month or two. And of course, as that is the thing I am most interested in— making money—I had better stay. We have pretty definitely decided to get married, probably in the next month or two. When we do I will send you a picture of Gin to put in the Sunday News. *I'll probably stay at her house until we come to Savannah and then get an apartment when we get back. Which gives us a chance to save some money, as we will have about four or five months free rent. Then too, the outlook is pretty bright on my selling some of those original and unique songs for which old Massa Mercer is noted.*

Darling, the only reason I didn't want you to come was that I thought it would be a waste of money. I don't want you to feel badly about that, so please don't. I love you terribly.

My nose is much better since spring has set in and I'm actually going out without my top coat.

Lots of love to my darling family. You mustn't think I've deserted you.

I love you so.

Bubs

These pledges of love are more than submissive—they border on the abject, and all his life his letters home would have that same tone.

Eight

During this time, John worked on a show called *Jazz City*, which contained sketches written by a New York native just eleven days older than John named Norman Krasna, later a successful Broadway and Hollywood writer and producer. *Jazz City*, however, went unproduced. Nonetheless:

On the strength of this . . . Ginger and I, one day in the Spring, walked with my boss Charlie Miller the few blocks to St. Thomas' Church. Ginger and I were just twenty-one at the time. Charlie Miller had tears in his eyes, because, he said, we were so young.

The wedding took place on June 8, 1931, in the Chantry Chapel of St. Thomas Episcopal Church on Fifth Avenue. Walter Rivers was John's best man. One wonders about the tears in Charlie Miller's eyes. Were they only because John and Ginger were so young? John's parents were not present, and seen from here, it seems such a forlorn little wedding. Shortly thereafter John at last took Ginger to Savannah to meet his family. Several persons have attested that Ginger was not made comfortable. But she and Miss Lillian must have reached some sort of accommodation, for she made the somewhat plaintive confession, "Mrs. Mercer, I can't even cook."

And Miss Lillian, in her thick Southern accent, said airily, "Never learn, darlin', never learn." Nancy Gerard believes the story. (Growing up in the home with Miss Lillian as her surrogate mother, she was never *allowed* to learn to cook.)

John's new friendship with Yip Harburg would soon get him an assignment. Harburg was in charge of assembling the score for a Shubert revue
called *New Americana,* set to open in early October of 1932. In that era, it
was not always the practice to entrust an entire score to one composer
working with one lyricist. Several teams might contribute to a show.
Whatever discontinuity of style this produced apparently didn't bother
anyone. The "integrated" musical lay in the future.

John was aware of the work of a gifted young composer and pianist
named Harold Arlen, who had been contributing, with lyricist Ted
Koehler, to the revues at the fancy Harlem speakeasy called the Cotton
Club, owned by gangster Owney Madden. (It was the hypocrisy of a later
time to bruit it about that Frank Sinatra "associated with gangsters." So
did everyone who ever worked at the Cotton Club, including Duke Ellington and Cab Calloway, and the same was true of Las Vegas as well.) The
song Mercer and Arlen wrote for *New Americana,* "Satan's Little Lamb,"
was their first piece together, and it appears to have been John's first
recorded song: Ethel Merman recorded it a week before the show opened,
backing it with an Arlen-Koehler collaboration, "I Gotta Right to Sing
the Blues." Edward Jablonski, in his biography *Harold Arlen: Rhythm,
Rainbows and Blues,* points out that "Satan's Little Lamb" united Arlen
"for the first time with two of his most gifted lyricists, E.Y. Harburg and
John H. Mercer, who would soon be better known as Johnny Mercer."
At the time of *New Americana,* Arlen, born in Buffalo, New York, was
twenty-seven, John not quite twenty-three. And Harburg was thirty-six.

Yip Harburg, John said, gave him assignments and encouragement
and work when he badly needed them. "More than that, in making me a
kind of assistant during the formation of the *New Americana* score, he
taught me how to *work at* lyric writing. I had been a dilettante at it, trying
hard but very undisciplined, waiting for the muse to smile. Yip taught me
to go seeking her, never letting a day or a work session go by without
something to show for it. Often the songs went unpublished, but there
were *songs.* Finished. Complete. Work done."

After a trip back home to Savannah, John wrote his mother a letter. He
had the unfortunate habit of never dating his letters, and one can determine the date of one of them only if one has the envelope and its postmark.
This envelope is dated 8 p.m., January 29, 1933, postmarked in Brooklyn.

Portrait of Johnny

Mother darling:

Here is your chile—up before the judge again.
Procrastination is the charge and as this is the 50th offense, I
guess it makes me a lifer at hard labor: to wit, writing letters.

The trip back was swell but how I hate this place. So dirty
and noisy and whatnot. I can hardly wait until I make enough
dough to leave it all—and come back to Savannah for good. It's
[the] hardest thing, getting adjusted. Especially if getting adjusted
is unpleasant. Ain't it the truth now? Enty?

Everybody says I look wonderful. I certainly feel wonderful.
I have started right to work again. Not with what you could call
a bang—but I have started and everything seems to be going
smoothly. "Spring Is in My Heart" and "Little Old Crossroad
Store" look like hits—and of course, if they are, it won't hurt
at all.

Steamy Brunswick Stew ala Ginger is being put on the table
now—so I'm gonna eat. I just wanted to write and tell you that I
love you dearly and miss you like the devil, my precious
sweetheart—Ginger sends love—Kiss Dad and Julie for me and
do write again soon.

Your own
Mistuh Jawnny
"Tide High, Eli"

Here is an early piece of evidence that Johnny's heart never left Savannah. (*Enty,* by the way, is Gullah for "isn't it.") It turns up often in Johnny's letters. The letter was written at the time of his new friendship with the late Carl Sigman. John and Ginger by now had their own apartment, and Sigman was a neighbor. He was another Brooklyn boy, born there in 1909, two months older than John, and he was yet another lawyer by training. He had a B.L. degree from New York University Law School.

Carl told me in August 1998:

"I was playing some songs for Henry Spitzer, when he was with Harms." (Henry Spitzer was a "professional manager"—the industry euphemism for song-plugger.) "One of the best in the business, he moved from Harms to Chappell. Estimates vary on how much he earned, but it was between five hundred dollars and one thousand dollars a week, a considerable amount in that era. But he was a gambler, liked to go to Las

Vegas, and got fifty thousand dollars into debt to The Boys. He committed suicide."

Spitzer told Sigman, "Well, I can put you with somebody. There's a guy named Johnny Mercer who's going to be on the radio on Monday night." The show was a semiprofessional contest. Spitzer said, "Why don't you listen in, and I'll give you his phone number and you can call him. He's an up-and-coming songwriter and maybe he can help you."

Carl said, "So I called him the next day after the performance. He lived just a few blocks around the corner from me in Brooklyn. He walked to my house. We talked and I played a few tunes for him. He sat there like a lyric writer. Then we established a relationship. We wrote a few songs. They weren't very good, but they were professional. I was a beginner, but he liked my melodies—some of them."

Johnny said of this relationship: "After playing softball together in the Brooklyn schoolyards, we'd spend long nights writing what seemed to me Isham Jones–type songs." A prominent bandleader of the time, composer Isham Jones wrote "On the Alamo," "I'll See You in My Dreams," "The One I Love Belongs to Somebody Else," and "There Is No Greater Love." His name is largely forgotten; his songs are not.

Sometimes, John said, "I would go over to write at Carl's, and his little, round, attractive mother would fill me up with blintzes or chopped liver on rye bread. I wished I could have laid some turnip greens or artichoke pickles and divinity fudge on her. Still, I doubt that she would have dug my Southern reciprocity as much as I did her smoked sturgeon."

"We were living in Crown Heights, a couple of blocks from Ebbets Field," Carl said. "Johnny and Ginger lived around the corner in a little apartment on Carroll Street, I was on Crown Street. I think Ginger's mother, Mrs. Meltzer, was on St. John's Place.

"We all smoked. And I'd play tune after tune after tune. Every once in a while he'd stop me and say, 'That's a nice tune.' And once in a while I had a title.

"That's how it started. A song I wrote with him was called 'Just Remember.' Southern Music published it but never released it in this country. But it was a modest noisemaker in England, and I didn't even know about it. It was never a hit, but that was my first published song.

"Not too long after that he drifted out to Hollywood and became very important. I was struggling. He would see me every now and then. I would call him, push myself on him and pick his brains. Every once in a while I'd play some tunes for him.

"I was a counselor at a boys' camp, and I called him when I learned he was going to be in New York. I insisted on having an appointment with him. He was so busy. He had songs everywhere. He'd write a song here, he'd write a song there. I was at Camp Lenox in East Lehigh, Massachusetts, in the Berkshires. I took a day off and took a train into New York. I met him at one of the publishing offices.

"I sat down and played a tune for him. He liked it very much, and I mentioned a title—not for that tune, just a title I had, 'Come Out of Your Dream and Into My Arms.' That was my little catchphrase. About two minutes later, he put both of those together. 'Please come out of your dream . . .' In about ten minutes we finished the lyric, most of which was his.

"Now when I left, he said, 'Good luck with your song.'

"I said, 'What do you mean, my song? It's *our* song.'

"He said, 'No, it's your song. It was your title, it's your tune. I just helped you. I had nothing to do with it.' I fought with him, but he insisted, and he wouldn't put his name on the song. He was that kind of man.

"I got it published. Guy Lombardo introduced it. In those days that was important. It almost made it. It was the first really noisy song I had in the country.

"But still I couldn't get rolling, I couldn't break through. One day Johnny said, 'Look, you write nice melodies, you've got a flair for lyrics. We need lyric writers. There are fifteen tune writers to every lyric writer. Every band has a couple of guys who can write a couple of tunes a day.'

"That was my clue. And I started to write lyrics seriously. I started to take assignments of foreign melodies like 'Arrivederci, Roma' and 'What Now, My Love?' So I became a lyric writer and more in demand, and I started to get songs published. That was one of the great things he did for me. He steered me into it."

Carl would eventually write "Dream Along with Me" (Perry Como's television theme song), "Dance Ballerina Dance," "Crazy She Calls Me," "Where Do I Begin?", "It's All in the Game," "Ebb Tide," "My Heart Cries for You," and "A Day in the Life of a Fool." He was the first of many lyricists whom John would encourage, and whose careers he advanced.

"I *worshiped* him," Carl told me, "because I was learning about writing. He really helped me a lot. There was real goodness in the man. We *all* worshiped him. He was, to me, the hippest, coolest person that I ever met. And he was so good. And he was so talented. It was unbelievable. He would sit there and thoughts would come pouring out of him."

Carl Sigman died in early 2001, aged ninety-one.

With his drawing account from Miller Music, and having the company's office from which to work, John felt a certain measure of security. He wrote with a number of composers, but the most fecund of these collaborations was with Bernard (Bernie) Hanighen, a native of Omaha, Nebraska, a graduate of Harvard who gained his first songwriting experience writing for that university's Hasty Pudding shows, training camp for so many important songwriters in those days. A love of jazz made them regular clients of the Onyx Club and the Famous Door, two speakeasies that became legitimate nightclubs when the Volstead Act was at last repealed in 1933. Johnny felt that he and Hanighen and Arlen were far ahead of their time in the influence that jazz had on their work.

With Hanighen, John wrote "Bob White," "Dixieland Band," "Weekend of a Private Secretary," "Show Your Linen, Miss Richardson," "Calling All Squares," "The Air-Minded Executive," and "The Blues Sneaked in Every Time."

All these songs, and indeed most of Mercer's output up to that time, exploited his gift for the quick, the clever, the witty, the flippant. The exploration of his own demons, his darkly and magnificently melancholy lyrics, had not yet begun.

Every day John would take the subway into Manhattan from Brooklyn and make the rounds of the publishers' offices in what was known as Tin Pan Alley. Mitchell Parish, who wrote the words to Hoagy Carmichael's "Star Dust," one of the most magnificent lyrics in the English language, once described to me the thrill of Tin Pan Alley on a warm day, when you could walk down the street and hear the composers and song-pluggers sending their piano music out through open windows and over the cobblestones—most of the streets were not yet paved with asphalt.

John remembered an afternoon sitting around at Harms when a "rather scrawny girl from the South, with her hair in twin ponytails, came in and sat down and played." Dana Suesse was a twenty-two-year-old from Kansas City, Missouri. Among the melodies she played that day were two that became, with words added, "My Silent Love" and "Have You Forgotten?" Her catalogue would eventually include "You Ought to Be in Pictures" and "The Night Is Young and You're So Beautiful." Yet another large talent who gave lie to the myth of a separation between jazz and classical music, jazz and popular music, she had trained as a concert composer, studying with Nadia Boulanger in France, and indeed had given her first piano recital at the age of eight.

"If we were lucky," John said, "we might bump into Jerome Kern or Otto Harbach in the lobby, or get a nod from Sigmund Romberg or Rudolf Friml, while Oscar Hammerstein—that tall, shy Abe Lincoln of a librettist—was quietly padding around the corridors, working out his assignments with most of the great composers then under contract to Harms."

There seems to have been a conspiracy of fellowship, of mutual sympathy, rather than competition among the writers. They would introduce each other to someone who might be of use—a producer assembling a revue, a comedian looking for jokes. "We covered all fields, picking up experience and learning all the while," John said.

We younger ones were content to sit around and kibbitz among ourselves, trying out our wares on each other, or lapsing into discreet silence if one of our more famous brethren dropped into the conversation for a few bars. Some of the older, more established, writers might place a song, get an advance, and hurry back to the bar to celebrate—or off to the track to try and double their money.

In that milieu, playing the ponies was apparently as endemic as drinking. It was a world celebrated in the short stories of Damon Runyon and Ring Lardner.

John used to tell a story about two big Broadway songwriters who went to the Shapiro-Bernstein publishing office about an hour before post time and sang this song:

> *With a C and an O*
> *and an L and an O*
> *and an R and an O*
> *and a D and an O—*
> *That's how you spell Colorado!*

They got a five-hundred-dollar advance on the song from one of the partners, who called the other partner and said, "Listen to this, Elliott," and sang the refrain.

"Fine, Louis," his partner said. "But unless you change the next-to-last O to an A, you won't sell many copies in Colorado."

The song-pluggers hung around Lindy's restaurant (the Mindy's of the Damon Runyan stories). John loved these people, men like Broadway Rose, Chuck the Jeweler, and Swifty Morgan.

Elmore White, who called everybody "Pally," and who had always just gotten a letter from Bing, would fumble for his glasses while reaching for his plug sheet, telling the waiter to "fill it up, Pally," indicating his coffee cup for the tenth time, and getting ready to do battle with the office drop-ins—fellows with songs to sell, or a hard-luck story—before he went out on his nightly round of the bands. Because of his false teeth, his wrist bands and knee bands, his double truss and his arch supports, he had a look of leaning into the wind. So it was only natural for his confreres to speak of him as "the man who walks uphill." He always had a joke or an anecdote to amuse you. He always had "one in the third," which usually ran out. And he was a good music man. He got his songs played.

Harry Link was another one-of-a-kind. He was reputedly a compulsive bender of the truth. It was no more possible for him to tell a straight story than it was to fly. They used to refer to one of the songs he worked on as "It's a Sin to Tell a Link," and it was said that when they buried him his tombstone should read merely "Here lies."

But he was a powerful music man, a high-pressure salesman of the first rank. In a more lucrative business he probably would have wound up a very rich man. However, he too suffered from the occupational weakness for the horses, and had to switch job affiliations more than once to get out from under the loan sharks who had him in durance, to put it mildly.

It was Harry who pestered Joe Venuti to play his song "An Old Spinning Wheel in the Parlor" so many times that Joe, who was working the Silver Slipper, finally said, "Awright, Harry. You wanna hear the song, tune in tonight from ten to eleven." Harry did, of course, and happily heard Joe play "An Old Spinning Wheel" for an hour straight. No breaks, no commercials, no other songs. Just "An Old Spinning Wheel" for one hour.

John never lost his affection for the old song-pluggers, or his nostalgia for their era, and when he would talk to me about them, I would listen in rapt attention. Their profession had begun years before the development of microphones and phonographs.

They used to be as close to an entertainer as those small birds on rhinos or elephants or the pilot fish that accompany whales, but their original function was entertaining also. They would demonstrate a new song to whomever would listen, much in the manner of the buskers outside London theaters, and try to get the public to buy or sing the song they were promoting. . . . All over the country, not only at the side show in the Savannah Park extension, men were working—on the boardwalk at Atlantic City, at vaudeville houses in Chillicothe, in basements, at the music counters in dime stores—all plugging away at new songs each one hoped would sweep the country and make him rich. Hence the attendance on and solicitude shown a star. If Jolie-baby [Al Jolson] sang your song, it was an immediate sensation, while any leading headliners such as Van and Schenck, Sophie Tucker, or Jimmy Barton could lift one from obscurity to a permanent place in the hearts of any unsuspecting public who thought all songs just happened because they had "a catchy melody."

Little did they dream of the skullduggery that went on backstage to knock one guy's song out of an act and get your own in; of the payola that those sweeter-than-light vaudeville stars got; or of the cut-ins, the kickback of the music business where a big entertainer got his or her name on a song as co-writer and—forever thereafter—a share of the royalties "either now in existence or yet to be invented." The lawyers had every contingency covered, then as now.

If, as they say, a cynic is a disillusioned idealist, then maybe Mercer was becoming one. We see here for the first time his dawning awareness of the corruption of the business. When, later, he founded his own record company with backing from fellow songwriter Buddy DeSylva, it would become known for its infrangible integrity.

Hanging around stars the way they did, like satellites around planets, the pluggers always had a place to congregate and have a "cup o' jav'," some lox on a bagel, or a short beer while they bemoaned their luck or lack of it with their latest "dog."

"Hey, Mouse! What ever happened to that song you were working on last month, 'Everything You Said Came True'?"

" 'Everything You Said Came True' came back!"

Meaning that the dealers had sent back the copies, and the publisher was stuck with a lot of returns.

They used to gather every day for lunch and the morning line. Most pluggers are inveterate horse players and nothing pleases them more in life than horse talk, except song talk. Coming to the restaurant, they would stop on the pavement outside to make their daily bet with Libby the bookie. This particular stretch of pavement on Broadway was known as Libby's Beach, as the sun occasionally shone there between tall buildings. Then they'd go in to gossip about the happenings of the night before, who won the fight at the Garden or the fourth at Aqueduct, or what band leader was making it with what vocalist—usually female, but not necessarily. . . .

When I worked in bands I'd sit with them between sets and when I wasn't working I'd go along to catch the various openings or closings, often as far as Philadelphia or Washington. Without realizing it, I too was a plug, in a small way, since I might record or sing one of their songs on a [radio] guest shot. So I often tagged along and got to know them all, and became fast friends with most of them.

Sad, but most of them are gone now, along with almost everything else.

Nine

One night in New York, probably in Jim and Andy's, a bar that catered to musicians, or in Charlie O's, John was telling me about the early days in Manhattan, when he met so many of his idols. Along with Arlen and Harburg, he met Rube Bloom, J. Fred Coots, Walter Donaldson, Fats Waller and his lyricist partner Andy Razaf, Harry Woods, Sammy Fain, Willard Robison, and Harry Warren, with whom he would eventually write some important songs. He still had that glow of discovery, all these years later. I have discovered that most people who become stars were starstruck in their youth, and the sense of wonder stays with them.

"You have no idea what New York was like in the 1930s," John told me. "It wasn't crowded then. You could walk down the street with ten cents in your pocket and feel like a millionaire—just because you were in New York." John, in fact, had a budget of twenty-five cents a day. He would take the subway from Brooklyn into Manhattan for five cents, for lunch buy two hot dogs and an orange drink for fifteen cents, and return home at night on the remaining nickel. Ginger, who was a skilled seamstress, was sewing buttons on leather gloves to augment their income.

But their world was about to change: John was about to meet Paul Whiteman.

Bandleader Paul Whiteman's position in American cultural history has been obscured by jazz criticism, which has been notable from its earliest days for its partisanship. (The late Grover Sales once observed that "the average jazz critic would rather catch another jazz critic in an error than bring Bix back from the dead.")

When John met Whiteman, Bix Beiderbecke, one of John's heroes, was already dead, despite Whiteman's best efforts to keep him alive. Beiderbecke's life later "inspired" the novel *Young Man with a Horn,* by Dorothy Baker, who derived most of her knowledge of jazz from her position as the girlfriend of one of the first writers about jazz, Otis Ferguson, Beiderbecke's champion. The novel (and the subsequent movie, starring Kirk Douglas) presents an idealistic young man working against his best aesthetic instincts in a "commercial band," the torture of which leads him into alcoholism and his own destruction. With this inaccurate portrayal, Baker did Whiteman more than a disservice. She did him grave damage.

He was, to be sure, an easy target for satire. Big, rotund, with a pencil mustache and a pretentious approach to staging, he lent himself to caricature. By his own admission, Whiteman did not know much about jazz, but he had a keen appreciation of its masters. He hired them, and he featured them—Joe Venuti, Red Norvo, Jack Teagarden, Frank Trumbauer, and Bix among them. He also employed such pioneering orchestrators and arrangers as Bill Challis and Ferde Grofé. When Beiderbecke's alcoholism reached the point at which he could no longer play, Whiteman put him on a train to his hometown and kept him on full salary while he was gone. Bix admired and loved Whiteman. I never met a musician who'd worked for him who didn't; when, years later, John was head of his own record company, one of the first people he signed was Paul Whiteman. Joe Venuti once said to me, "Pops"—Whiteman's universal nickname—"got jazz up out of the sewer. We'd been playing in toilets. He put it in the concert hall."

Whiteman was *big,* both physically and commercially. He was the most important bandleader of the 1920s, so successful that he had to establish farm-team bands to fill the engagement offers inundating him. In 1924, he staged the Carnegie Hall concert that introduced Gershwin's *Rhapsody in Blue* to the world and forced even the *New York Times* to pay attention to jazz. That the piece (which even now is often undervalued) was not jazz per se gave ammunition to later jazz critics, but the composition was heavily influenced by jazz and thus helped along a process the jazz critics themselves were calling for: freeing the music from its cultural confinement.

Whiteman had passed through career highs and lows, and he had been in a low when Mercer met him. Now he was on a comeback.

Portrait of Johnny

Network radio, which dated only from 1928, had in a few years become a major force in American culture. In January 1932, Whiteman began to broadcast "coast to coast," as a phrase of the time put it, under the advertising sponsorship of the Pontiac division of General Motors. At the Edgewater Beach Hotel in Chicago, an important broadcasting locale for bands, Whiteman had begun a search for new talent that attracted aspiring performers from throughout the region, with consequent large audiences, even at this nadir of the Great Depression. The success of this venture caused Whiteman to expand the project to his radio broadcasts. Local radio stations would screen young talent just before the Whiteman band's arrival in their cities and call back the finalists to audition for Whiteman himself. After a tour, the band reached New York for an engagement at the Palace, on a bill with singer Russ Columbo and the comic team of Weber and Fields (father of lyricist Dorothy Fields).

The New York auditions were held at the New Amsterdam, the Times Square theater where John had appeared with his theater group from Savannah. There were three hundred contestants that week; the winner of the contest would be given a single booking on Whiteman's network Pontiac broadcast.

Ginger urged John to try his luck. Auditions are always traumatic, both for those who submit to them and who feel like cattle being judged, and for those who must make the judgments, well aware that it is in their power to change an aspirant's life or to dash his hopes forever. John vividly remembered the hellish day of the Whiteman audition. He was with a new acquaintance, Archie Bleyer, an established arranger and, later, a producer who was important to the careers of a good many performers.

I wandered into the New Amsterdam theater—this was back in the days when it housed the Ziegfeld shows and was the nicest theater in New York—to find all types of men and women waiting to try out for the Paul Whiteman vocal contest. Cab drivers, truck drivers, porters, maids, waitresses, bus boys, college boys, young people both white and black (though not so many then) and older people too. As each one of them in turn would get up and sing, "All of me, why not take all of me," or maybe "Just friends, lovers no more," a voice would come over the intercom from somewhere up near the roof of the darkened theater: "Thank you very much. Next contestant, please."

It wasn't that the management was rude. It was just that there were so many AWFUL singers trying out for that one shot on the Pontiac radio program. Well, Archie Bleyer had graciously consented to accompany me.

And as he was a busy man, and I didn't want to waste his time, when our turn came and my name was called, we jumped up on the stage. He seated himself at the piano, I grabbed the mike, and we hit a tempo lickety-split! I mean, we were going so fast and so rhythmically that no one could have interrupted our chorus. No one did, in any event, and we were held for the finals, which meant the great Paul Whiteman himself would hear us the following day.

Well, he did, and I won a Pontiac Youth of America contest as a New York contestant. The prize was one air shot, singing with Whiteman. And no money. So what good was it?

A few days later, on March 29, 1932, the *Brooklyn-Queens Journal,* a branch of the *New York Evening Journal,* which has long since disappeared, carried a story under the headline JOHN MERCER CAN SING IN HIS BATHTUB, which is revealing in several ways:

> There's one housewife in Brooklyn who doesn't voice any objection when her husband begins to sing in the bathtub.
>
> In fact, Mrs. John Mercer urges her husband to sing in the bathtub, the shower, the rain or any other places he wants to.
>
> But, then, John Mercer does not emit a raucous, ear-splitting howl when he vocalizes. For Johnny Mercer, although he's "just turned 22," has acquired the art of singing heart-rending ballads with the pathos of one who has loved and lost innumerable times.
>
> And John has that art down to such perfection that out of the half a hundred crooners, warblers, torch singers and mammy wanters [*sic*] who tried to convince Paul Whiteman that they were the greatest young singers in all America, John Mercer was selected as the winner.
>
> As for the singing in the bathtub angle:
>
> "Why, that's how Johnny happened to try out in the competition," Mrs. Mercer explained in her home at 932 Carroll street, Brooklyn, today. "You see, when I married him about a year ago he wasn't a singer."
>
> "And I'm not now, either," he broke in.
>
> But his wife overlooked the interruption.
>
> "Aw, don't be so modest. I married him under the

impression that he was a song writer. And he was—and is. But he used to go about the house and the office and the streets always singing to himself. And gradually I began to notice that he did have a beautiful voice.

"So when I read that Paul Whiteman was running an elimination contest in the N.B.C. studios for young singers I made John fill out an application blank. And that's all there is."

But that isn't all there is. Mrs. John Mercer is more modest about her husband than he is about himself. But that's probably because she's a new bride. She's only been married about a year, having first met John at a party at her home on Sterling Place.

This newspaper story is factually wrong in almost every way. First of all, John always said he met Ginger when he tried out for *The Garrick Gaieties*. And then there's the business about John having to wait for Ginger to inform him that he had a voice. He had been singing all his life, in his Episcopal church choir, in barbershop quartets, with black play-mates, as a soloist with Dick Hancock's guitar accompaniment—indeed, just about anywhere he could. And given his intense ambition, it's hard to believe that he had not picked up from his friends among the song-pluggers and songwriters the intelligence that Whiteman would be hold-ing these auditions.

Thomas A. De Long, in a generally scrupulous 1983 biography titled *Pops: Paul Whiteman, King of Jazz,* writes: "The greatest talent to emerge in the New York auditions was . . . Johnny Mercer. He had just written 'Lazy Bones' with Hoagy Carmichael. Paul signed him at $75 a week to write special song material and comedy sketches."

This is not in accord with John's recollection, which is supported by that of Red Norvo. According to John, a friend of Archie Bleyer's, a com-poser and arranger named Eddie Wood, offered to introduce John to Carmichael, who had already written "Washboard Blues" and "River-boat Shuffle"; Mitchell Parish was just attaching his remarkable lyrics to "Star Dust."

In a BBC interview, John remembered their first encounter this way:

"One of my favorite collaborators, and one of my closest friends, is Hoagy Carmichael. I admired him as a singer when he sang 'Washboard Blues' and some things with Paul Whiteman. Ten years after that, when I got to New York, I met him. And a fellow said there was a chance to write a song with him. I said, 'You don't mean it! Could it really be possible?' And he arranged this interview."

Carmichael recalled: "He walked in one day and I was sitting in the chair, the door was open, summertime. He knocked, and I said, 'Come in!' and I'm sitting in the chair, half-dozing. This is the absolute truth. I said, 'What's on your mind?' He said, 'Well, I thought we might try to write a song.' I said, 'Have you got any idea?' He said, 'I thought I'd like to write a song called "Lazy Bones." What do you think of that title?' I said, 'With this kind of summer we're having in New York, and what with the Depression, and nobody working, it sounds mighty logical.' "

John said, "We had a great big song with it, and it changed my life. It got me a job singing with Paul Whiteman, it got me respect. Irving Berlin came into a little demo room to meet me, 'cause he loved the lyric so much. I was just a kid, you must remember, about twenty-two or -three. It just meant a great deal to me. And Hoagy and I began to write songs. And over the years we have written together intermittently and occasionally."

John said that Carmichael was one of his most important teachers. He wrote: "I leapt at the chance to write with Hoagy. He proved an understanding friend and teacher. . . . When I say teacher, I mean just that; he broadened my ability with his knowledge and experience." But John later also recalled Carmichael as a stern taskmaster: "He is such a gifted lyric writer on his own that I felt intimidated and tightened up too much to do my best work." This is one of the signs of a relationship that seems often to have been an uneasy one. But it was a fruitful one.

The affinity between Carmichael and Mercer was a natural thing. Both were outsiders, exceptions among all the New York–born composers, lyricists, and publishers. Carmichael was born in Bloomington, Indiana, on November 22, 1899, which made him just four days short of being ten years John's elder. Both were admirers of Willard Robison, now known only for a handful of songs he wrote, among them "A Cottage for Sale," "Guess I'll Go Back Home," "A Woman Alone with the Blues," "Don't Smoke in Bed," and "Old Folks." But Robison was an enormous presence in the music world back then. Born in Shelbina, Missouri, in 1894, Robison carried over into his music a certain rural folk quality, though the music itself was sophisticated. He made many recordings and was constantly heard on radio in those days with his Deep River Orchestra.

Another thing Mercer and Carmichael had in common was an adulation of Beiderbecke. Carmichael so idolized Bix that he had acquired his mouthpiece—Carmichael also played cornet. He carried it in his pocket all his life, and after his own death, it passed to John, who kept it for years. Bud Freeman, one of the dominant saxophonists of that era, told me that "Star Dust" was not only like a Bix solo, it *was* a Bix solo. Others have refuted this, but certainly the melody reflects Carmichael's admiration for Bix, as does a song he would later write with John, "Skylark."

When John auditioned for the Whiteman band and did his one broadcast for Pontiac, a member of the band was Red Norvo, the great xylophone player who was married to the brilliant singer Mildred Bailey. Bailey liked "Lazy Bones" and sang it on a nationwide broadcast. Within a week, it seemed—according to Red—just about every singer in America was performing the song. It became one of the major hits of the Depression years, and won for Hoagy and John an award of $1,250 each from the American Society of Composers, Authors, and Publishers (ASCAP), the performing rights society that collects and distributes royalties to songwriters and publishers for radio and other exposures of their works.

This was a significant sum in those days.

"Mildred and I were living in Queens at the time," Red said. "Johnny phoned me on a Friday. He said he'd just got this check from ASCAP and couldn't cash it. We told him to come out to our apartment. When he got there, Mildred told him to call Ginger and tell her to take a cab. She said we'd pay for it. Ginger came and we spent the weekend with them and on Monday morning, Mildred went to her bank and got the check cashed for him."

In John's recollection it was the success of "Lazy Bones" that got him his contract with Whiteman a year *after* the Pontiac radio-show audition. Whiteman heard it and asked John to form a new group along the lines of the Rhythm Boys, who had long since left his band. (Crosby was by then a star.)

John assembled a trio that included a fine pianist named Jack Thompson and Harold Arlen's brother Jerry, who sang rhythm songs well. After a week with the band, they were given two weeks' notice. Present when the trio got fired was the respected guitarist Dick McDonough, who suggested to Whiteman that he keep Mercer on to sing duets with Jack Teagarden, who was in the band at the time. Texas-born Teagarden was a breakthrough trombonist. He had explored a style of execution on the trombone that gave it almost the fluency of trumpet, and he intimidated other trombonists. Glenn Miller and Tommy Dorsey, both young studio trombonists at the time, were in awe of him. Whiteman took McDonough's advice, and John went on staff with Whiteman for eighty-five dollars a week.

John sang duets with Teagarden and the other singers and wrote songs with Matty Malneck, who played violin in the band and wrote arrangements for it as well. Between sets one night, in what they later estimated was about fifteen minutes, they wrote "Goody Goody," which became a huge hit in 1936. John also wrote parody material for Whiteman broadcasts on a show called *The Kraft Music Hall*. (The FCC had not yet imposed its prohibition of the use of a sponsor's name in the title of a program.)

He recalled: "I worked with [Whiteman] for a couple of years. I went on the road with him. We played theaters, we played concerts, we played nightclubs, we had radio programs. And I was just one of a big organization, about twenty-five or thirty people. I was kind of like a utility ball player. I would write lyrics, or I would sing songs; I'd go to the store for sandwiches, whatever. I gradually got to sing a little bit more and more. I wrote things for the radio programs. I met people like Al Jolson."

On the strength of his Whiteman salary, John and Ginger moved into a better apartment in Manhattan. This enabled them to entertain friends more easily and, since they did not face the long trek to Brooklyn, they could spend more time where the music was being played after hours.

Although John's relationship with Hoagy Carmichael would remain sporadic, in 1934 they wrote "Moon Country," which Richard Sudhalter described (in his Hoagy bio *Stardust Melody*) as being "in every sense a union of two compatible and complementary sensibilities.

"A hymn to home, it casts a longing glance back at an age already vanishing when Hoagland Carmichael and John Mercer were boys, and an America still largely agrarian in character. The Industrial Revolution had not yet touched this imaginary landscape or its people. No matter that the composer had grown up in Indiana, the lyricist in Georgia, or that the lyric refers to a 'sycamore heaven back South,' a heaven that may have never existed in this form for either man. This idealized Elysium transcends geography and hard reality; it is what singer Barbara Lea, a faithful interpreter of both writers, wisely calls 'generic home,' immune to time or despoilment. . . . Every image in Mercer's lyric evokes some idealized home. The gray mare grazes peacefully, and the land affords sustenance and contentment. Moonlight through the pines, lazy river flowing serenely by. A rocking chair, emblem of solace and peace of mind, waiting on some shady veranda, as an old hymn, played on the parlor piano, wafts across a breeze at dusk. . . .

"Both Carmichael and Mercer, of course, went on to write successfully with other collaborators, and Mercer's adaptability and eloquence soon proclaimed him a poet laureate among American lyricists. But it's hard to resist Indiana historian Duncan Schiedt when he reflects, 'It would be interesting to see the output of these two men had they remained full partners in music, in the manner of Rodgers and Hart, or the Gershwins.'

"Carmichael agreed. With guidance and diligent work, he wrote, 'Johnny and I could have flooded the market with hit songs. We were atune and he "knew" and he knew I "knew." But the chips didn't fall right. Probably my fault because I didn't handle them gently.' "

That is probably true. Sudhalter interviewed Amanda (Mandy) Mercer, John's daughter, who said the two men had a special respect for each other. "My Dad thought Hoagy was above everyone. He had this natural thing, very intuitive, that placed him above the others as far as Dad was concerned. They both had fast minds; things would go through with my Dad click-click. That fast, and if he thought of something he'd get on the phone and call Hoagy right away. They both had these fast minds. He got such a kick out of Hoagy. He'd say, 'How can a boy from Indiana write about the South?' "

I notice that Mandy speaks of respect, but there is no mention of affection.

I met Hoagy only once—in Indiana, appropriately enough. It was in the resort town of French Lick, where as part of a jazz festival on Labor Day weekend in 1957, a tribute to his songs was mounted. Someone introduced us in the bar of the hotel, and a moment later I had to step back. I have no idea how much he'd had to drink, but I observed as he insulted everyone who came within range one of the nastiest drunks in my experience. Johnny could be that way, too, but Johnny had other redeeming qualities, among them warmth and generosity (consider all the careers he launched or abetted) and a capacity for remorse and apology.

John once mentioned something about Hoagy to Johnny Mandel, with whom he collaborated on the song "Emily." He said, "Hoagy was a very big talent but a very small man."

In his biography of Carmichael, Richard Sudhalter observes that " 'Moon Country' remains a musical still life, a captured moment, a summing-up; idealization and artifact, it resists age, mortality, attrition. For Hoagy Carmichael especially, it defines home, and he returned there—as he returned to his beloved Indiana—for the rest of his life."

So it was with Johnny, always returning to Savannah. Often his visits were unannounced. He would just turn up. James McIntire said, "Every time he did, he'd come over and see us, spend a day with us. He loved Savannah. He was a wonderful person, you know."

He made one of his many trips home to be best man at the wedding of his cousin and almost-brother, Walter Rivers, to James McIntire's sister Cornelia. They had all known each other since childhood, and the marriage linked the McIntire family to the Ciuceviches, and thus to the Mercers. As Nancy Gerard put it, "Down here we're all more or less cousins."

Cornelia was known, even in her own family, as an eccentric. She was small and thin, with curly brown hair. She was not a great beauty, but was strikingly attractive in her own way. "She was full of wound-up energy," a niece said of her. She was a painter, and not your polite Sunday lady-with-a-hobby painter, either. Her painting, though representational, was remarkably varied, with works ranging from landscapes to portraiture. There exists a haunting, large portrait of Johnny, painted by Cornelia.

Jimmy McIntire's wife, Betty, told me: "Cornelia almost set our house on fire. We went out to hear Johnny sing. We came back. She had chucked a lighted cigarette in a wastepaper basket when she was high. There was a very valuable secretary we had that was about to catch on fire, and it was about to blister. Flames were coming up from the goddamn thing. I called the fire department, naturally, and Jimmy grabbed that wastepaper basket and threw it in the bathtub. The heat had already burned through the bottom and burned the floor.

"That painting over there," Betty said, pointing to one of several of Cornelia's works on her living room wall, "it caught on fire, too." And then, she made one of the funniest remarks I heard in my visits to Savannah: "You see, we all smoked a lot, and drank a lot. So there was a good deal of fire."

Recalling the wedding of Walter and Cornelia, Betty said: "Johnny was going to be the best man. The organ kept repeating the same thing over and over and over again, and everybody kept looking down the aisle, and nothing was going on. Walter and John had been in the back of the cathedral, drinking. At last they came in and Walter and Cornelia got married."

Jimmy added: "When the wedding was over and they went on their honeymoon, guess who went with them? Johnny. He said, 'You all look like you're going to have fun. I think I'll come with you.'

"Whenever he decided to do something like that, he did it, irrespective of what else he was supposed to be doing. Once in Grand Central Station in New York, he met Wingy Manone. He said, 'I'm going to Savannah. You wanna come?' And Wingy Manone said, 'I haven't got any clothes.' Johnny said, 'That doesn't matter, we'll buy some. Come on, go with me.' They arrived in Savannah higher than two kites."

Ten

It was Paul Whiteman's idea, or so John thought, to present him and Jack Teagarden as a kind of musical Amos and Andy. But Johnny had to admit that Whiteman's use of him and Teagarden in that way worked to his benefit in the long run, when an assistant director in Hollywood who heard the band's broadcasts (and was, indeed, a fan of *Amos and Andy*) thought John might be a suitable writer for a low-budget college musical to be made at RKO. John, suffering from a case of jaundice, had left the band during a booking in Pittsburgh and was spending most of his time in bed when the call from Hollywood came in.

So it was goodbye to my new-found musician friends and all the side men who were to turn into leaders, Benny Goodman, Jimmy and Tommy Dorsey, Artie Shaw, Glenn Miller, Claude Thornhill; to Dick McDonough and Jerry Colonna. Farewell to the Spirits of Rhythm, Dick Wells, and Pod and Jerry's, the Stork, 21, and all the celebrities I had begun to meet, Cole Porter and Buddy DeSylva, Lew Brown, Billy Rose, Joe Bushkin, Willie the Lion, and especially Irving Berlin.

It's all such a montage of work and drinking and nightclubbing and publishing rooms, writing all day and calling Ginger to tell her I'd be home late; or meeting her at some little pad where a few of our old friends were waiting to introduce us to new ones, that I can't get the sequence of events right.

Portrait of Johnny

Did Wingy and Bob Bach come up to the Biltmore roof or did we all meet at a recording session where George Simon was writing a story for Metronome? *It was a time of youth and excitement and the long shadows falling as I'd hurry home from Broadway, stopping to have a drink with some cats on my way to dinner before changing into my band costume for the night shift. Always writing, writing, writing. . . .*

California seemed a land of distant glamour in those days before the 747. Back when it took a four-day train trip to cross the continent, California was almost a nation unto itself. Indeed, its immigrant population sent exotic gifts back East—boxes of dates packed in beautiful redwood boxes and pictures of cars driving through a tunnel that had been cut in a giant redwood or Douglas fir. It seemed a soft, benign, sunny land of ocean shore and palm trees and deserts and mountains, infinitely attractive—which of course is just how the slick land developers wanted it to appear. And there was the music that came from California. John had, like so many young men of his generation, listened through the hard Bakelite earphones of a crystal set to the San Francisco band of Art Hickman, to Harry Owens, to the California Ramblers; to "Whispering," "Avalon," "California, Here I Come," "Home in Pasadena," "Orange Grove in California," and "Linger Awhile." They seemed to embody that distant, lovely place.

The Super Chief had a number of celebrities aboard on that trip, most notably Joe Schenck and Al Jolson. Johnny remembered the two of them having the waiters bring for their inspection a brace of dressed ducks, or pheasants, before ordering them cooked. This kind of affectation was in bad taste, John thought, and it bothered him. He would impale this sort of pretension later in the song "Hooray for Hollywood," but for the time being, "I kept my eyes and ears open and my mouth shut, for Ginger and I were heading for a chance of a lifetime, and I wanted to be as big as my small talent might allow."

He always remembered passing through orange groves and gardens filled with enormous cabbage roses, and, coming into San Bernardino, the big blue mountains—the land of Lake Arrowhead and Big Bear—with snow in their crevices. It was an experience he would have many times in his life, for he always crossed the country by train even after air travel became the accepted way to go.

In Pasadena, he met the producer who had sent for him, Zion Myers. Whatever images of movieland power John carried in his head were promptly dashed by his meeting with Myers, who turned out to be a very small man—John guessed he weighed about 130 pounds—with a gray pallor. And the movie John was to write would have a pathetically small budget. The story revolved around a man who decides late in his life to get the college education he'd always missed. The film, *Old Man Rhythm,* sank under the weight of Hollywood cliché and dubious taste. The lead role was played by George Barbier, supported by Buddy Rogers, Dave Chasen (a young pantomimist who gave up performing for the restaurant business), and Johnny himself. The costumes and sets were trite, the music inadequate.

Yet John liked Zion Myers, who was always patient, courteous, and seemingly unperturbed. "The studio," John said, "gave him only left-overs, and, suffering multitudinous setbacks in every department, he still kept cheerful while he watched his staff putting together one of the most old-fashioned college movies ever made. This in spite of the fact that he, or somebody, had been smart enough to have among the bit players and extras running around the campus both Lucille Ball and Betty Grable.

"Hollywood was like a boom city in those days, and even I got better offers from other producers on the same lot the day after the picture opened. But if Zion wanted me, I wouldn't desert him, and we did another picture right away before my RKO contract ran out." (Loyalty is another of John's characteristics.)

John may not have liked the picture, but his hometown newspaper did. It ran a snappy one-column story under the headline

JOHNNY MERCER,
SAVANNAH'S OWN,
ON SCREEN HERE

Tune tickles and just plain old Southern pride will course with quickened pace the veins of Savannah's music lovers and cinema addicts next week when Savannah's own Johnny Mercer—of "Lazy Bones" and "Pardon My Southern Accent" fame—makes his screen debut in the city of his birth.

For Johnny is coming to the Lucas not a full-fledged star, but nevertheless a featured player in the summer's hottest musical comedy number, "Old Man Rhythm." It's headlined for three days, starting Monday, at the deluxe house with the mountain air.

> Johnny achieves double distinction in his first appearance on screen. With charming little Evelyn Poe, he renders a number you'll be whistling when you leave, "Comes the Revolution, Baby." That's not all, either, for Johnny wrote the lyrics for the entire show, which seethes with campus romance and rhythm.
>
> This sparkling, collegiate picture, which is full of catchy songs and humorous situations, will replace that "down-in-the-dumps" feeling with a giddy lightness of heart, it is declared.

This sounds as if it were a press agent's plant, but whoever wrote it, the item must have made John squirm. And read it he assuredly did; it's inconceivable that Dick Hancock or Walter Rivers or another of his friends and relatives would not have sent it to him.

He went to work on another B production, another college picture—such films were common at the time, perhaps because college education was still something of a novelty, and the studio executives, little educated themselves, saw it as something romantic and wonderful. But some A-grade musicals had been and continued to be made at RKO, including, of course, the Astaire-Rogers films.

While John was in residence at RKO, Fred Astaire showed him a tune he had written. Celebrated as a dancer, Astaire was regarded by some as a dilettante when he ventured into composition. In fact, he was a more than passable pianist, and quite a few songwriters have cited him as their favorite singer: he sang a song as written, invariably giving it an intelligent and sensitive interpretation. John took the tune away and returned with a lyric titled "I'm Building Up to an Awful Let Down"; published in 1935, it became a moderate hit.

John had been away from Savannah for a longer period than he ever had before, and he was overdue for a visit home. A Savannah newspaper carried the story:

MERCER, GENIUS OF MUSIC, AT HOME
Author "Lazy Bones" and Other Big Successes Visits Parents

> Johnny Mercer, author of "Lazy Bones," "Here Come the British," "Pardon My Southern Accent," and scores

of other popular songs published recently, returned for the first time in two years yesterday to be with his parents, Mr. and Mrs. George A. Mercer. He lives in New York.

He is still the likable, modest chap that he was when he left Savannah in 1928 . . . despite the fact that he has become noted as a lyric writer at the age of 25.

Christened John Herndon Mercer, he is not likely to be called "Mr. Mercer" more than once by anyone, for his charming manner soon prompts even a stranger to call him "Johnny."

Confessing that he loved Savannah and wanted to return here when he made enough money, Johnny declared "it was easy for a Southerner" to write "Lazy Bones," his biggest hit by far.

He exploded the popular opinion that one makes enough on a single "hit" to retire. "The best writers can hope for is approximately $5,000 or $6,000," he said, and mentioned a few songs which had probably netted their authors this figure. The composer and the lyrics writer split two ways, he explained.

Johnny wasn't able to explain what had prompted him to write the lyrics of some of his favorites. "You see, a word somewhere which suggests a title, or just think it up," he declared.

Of the songs which he has written, he likes "P.S. I Love You" best. "Lazy Bones" brought him in the most money, but it wasn't as much as the average person thinks, according to Johnny.

He works with several composers because so far he hasn't found a single person who writes tunes fast enough for the number of lyrics he turns out.

Johnny has an average of one song published each month, but he writes about four times this number. Usually the words are written by him after someone else has completed the tune, although the process is sometimes reversed, it was learned. . . .

Some day Johnny hopes to write a novel, and his "pet ambition" is to write a movie story and then act in it. Like a good many other young men, he likes to play golf, fish, and read, although his present routine doesn't allow much time for such activities.

He is under contract with Paul Whiteman. . . .

The rest of the clipping is missing.

In December 1939 he looked back on this period of his life in a guest column for the music magazine *Swing,* long since vanished. He described the writing of "P.S. I Love You":

"I recall one time when my wife Ginger was away on a trip and I naturally desired to write to her. Taking pen in hand, ol' massa Mercer wrote a long letter dealing with just the sort of trivia that occurs to one lonely for another. There it was, completed. I'd written many a love song, and I read it over. I'd left out the real reason I started the letter. So below the great message, I scrawled 'P.S. I Love You.' Immediately, the thought of that phrase as a song title struck me and I dashed off what later, thanks to forgetful me and lucky fate, became a hit tune."

John described the writing of his next important song in an interview. "Between movie assignments, Ginger and I took a trip down to Savannah in a little car," he said, obviously referring to the sojourn noted by the newspaper. After that they headed for California.

"We took three days out of six just to cross Texas, and I saw all those guys down there in those spurs and ten-gallon hats driving cars around. They struck me as kind of funny and so I thought maybe I should put it all in a song."

The song, "I'm an Old Cowhand," is noteworthy for several reasons, quite apart from the ingenuity of the writing. John had, from the beginning, a flair for incorporating the current vernacular into his lyrics, but in this song we first encounter his capacity for wry and sly comment on the society around him. And America was changing quickly. Asphalt was covering the gravel of city streets and country roads, rural electrification was well under way, network radio had in a few short years become a pervasive medium of entertainment and of cultural education, and old ways were dying out. The lyric is worth examining at length. After the verse, each chorus is in AB form.

VERSE

> *Step aside, you ornery tenderfeet.*
> *Let a big bad buckeroo past.*
> *I'm the toughest hombre you'll ever meet,*
> *tho' I may be the last.*

Yesirree we're a vanishing race.
Nosirree can't last long.
Step aside, you ornery tenderfeet
while I sing my song.

CHORUS

I'm an old cowhand
from the Rio Grande,
but my legs ain't bowed
and my cheeks ain't tanned.
I'm a cowboy who never saw a cow,
never roped a steer 'cause I don't know how,
and I sho' ain't fixin' to start in now.
Yippy-I-O-Ki-Ay.
Yippy-I-O-Ki-Ay.

I'm an old cowhand
from the Rio Grande,
and I learned to ride
'fore I learned to stand.
I'm a ridin' fool who is up to date,
I know ev'ry trail in the Lone Star State,
'cause I ride the range in a Ford V-Eight,
Yippy-I-O-Ki-Ay.
Yippy-I-O-Ki-Ay.

I'm an old cowhand
from the Rio Grande,
and I come to town
just to hear the band.
I know all the songs that the cowboys know
'bout the big corral where the doagies go,
'cause I learned them all on the radio.
Yippy-I-O-Ki-Ay.
Yippy-I-O-Ki-Ay.

I'm an old cowhand
from the Rio Grande,
where the West is wild
'round the Borderland,

Portrait of Johnny

where the buffalo roam around the zoo
and the Indians make you a rug or two
and the old Bar X is a bar-b-cue,
Yippy-I-O-Ki-Ay.
Yippy-I-O-Ki-Ay.

The music to the song is Mercer's own. It is clever, catchy, and per-fectly suited to the material. And there are several more choruses of lyric.

In the Paul Whiteman band, John had become friends with tenor sax-ophonist and arranger Fud Livingston. Through his offices, John said, he was able to get the song to Bing Crosby. Crosby by now was a big star, and though they had met, John wasn't able to approach him directly. The timing was good, because Crosby was about to make a light comedy film called *Rhythm on the Range* with Martha Raye, Frances Farmer, and the now-forgotten comedian Bob Burns.

John said: "I met Crosby after I got to Hollywood. I admired Crosby and knew all about him before I joined the Whiteman band. While I was with the band, I heard a lot of stories about Bing, and so one of the first things that happened when I got to Hollywood was that he asked me out to his house—Ginger and I. And we got to be friends, and then we made some records. He sang one of my first big songs in a movie, 'I'm an Old Cowhand from the Rio Grande,' and got me off to a good fine start in Hollywood. . . . I really think he saved my Hollywood career, because I began to get some more offers after that. Another thing I did out there was make some of my own recordings away from the Whiteman band."

In the same year that "I'm an Old Cowhand" came out, 1936, a song written with Matty Malneck, "Goody Goody," became a hit, though it had been written earlier. Nor was it a lean year for great songs; the com-petition in '36 included "Easy to Love," "The Glory of Love," "I Wished on the Moon," "Is It True What They Say about Dixie?", "It's D'lovely," "I've Got You Under My Skin," "Let Yourself Go," "Let's Face the Music and Dance," "The Night Is Young and You're So Beautiful," "No Greater Love," "Pennies from Heaven," "Poincianna," "There's a Small Hotel," "These Foolish Things," "The Touch of Your Lips," "Until the Real Thing Comes Along," and "The Way You Look Tonight."

John told the BBC: "I made a few records with Bing. One was 'Mr. Gallagher and Mr. Sheen,' [rewritten as] 'Mr. Crosby and Mr. Mercer.' We did 'Mister Meadowlark,' 'On Behalf of the Visiting Firemen,' and a few others. Well, I was very scared, and very much in awe of him, because he was a little bit older, and much more experienced, and a first-class rhythm singer, besides being a great ballad singer. But what was better than that is Bing's rapport, Bing's talk, his slang, and his sort of theatrical experience. He made you feel at home, his ad-libs were so great."

By now, thanks to radio broadcasts, Mercer, too, was becoming a national figure. Lyricists for the most part pass their lives in anonymity, but because he was a performer, John was already something of a hero with the college crowd. In Philadelphia, a young man from Long Island named Howard Richmond was studying business at the University of Pennsylvania. "I thought Johnny Mercer was the hippest, coolest thing of our time," he said. "I responded to all the things kids did who listened to records, and I followed everything Johnny Mercer did. Everything he did, I knew." Richmond, whose father was in the music publishing business, had a desire to write, and one of his professors encouraged him to pursue it.

"Toward the end of 1936," Howie (as he has always been called) recalled many years later, "I was in New York on a break. It was between Thanksgiving and Christmas. I remember it had snowed and there was slush on the sidewalks. I went to see Uncle Jack Bregman, who was manager of the Leo Feist publishing company. I called him Uncle Jack because he had worked for my father, and I had known him since childhood. I wanted to leave school at the end of the term and get a job on a newspaper.

"I walked into Jack's office. Within a few minutes, in walked Johnny Mercer. He'd just gotten off the Super Chief from Los Angeles. He was in Hollywood clothes with French, Shriner, and Urner white crepe-soled shoes that had the style of the young people. You saved up for *them*. And we already had snow. I couldn't believe it! Here was Johnny Mercer!

"Jack got busy, and Johnny asked me if I wanted to come down with him and listen to some records at O. Saporta, a store on Broadway around Forty-sixth Street. They played records over loudspeakers. I walked down there with Johnny, and he was like my big brother.

"We stood there in the street and listened to records. He wanted to know everything I thought about songs and records. And that never changed. We were friends for the rest of his life."

There's an image that sticks in my mind: Mercer, at five foot eight, deferential to a gangly six-foot-two college student he had just met. He was like that his whole life, devoid of pretense, a man with what used to be called the common touch. It was one of his most admirable, indeed endearing, traits.

Portrait of Johnny

Howie Richmond, unable to get a job at a newspaper, became a publicist whose clients would include Larry Clinton, Glenn Miller, Gene Krupa, Woody Herman, and, later, Frank Sinatra. Still later he became a prominent and highly successful music publisher who published some of John's lyrics, including "Early Autumn."

Eleven

It was at about this period that John met and first collaborated with a new melody writer. He said, "There was a new young fellow who was playing piano in the professional rooms of the music publishers named Jimmy Van Heusen. He hadn't had many songs. And Harry Warren's brother, Charlie Warren, . . . touted Jimmy very highly. He said, 'You've gotta write some songs with this kid, he's great.' "

Van Heusen, born Chester Babcock in Syracuse, New York, in 1913, recalled his first encounter with Mercer in a BBC interview:

"He was friends with Buddy Morris—Edwin H. Morris—who was running the Music Publishers Holding Corporation, the Warner brothers' publishing companies. Buddy Morris was fired, even though his father was a big executive at Warner Bros., and went into business with Mercer. The firm was called Mercer-Morris. Johnny and I wrote the first catalogue that they went in business on, and we wrote three songs. Actually we wrote about five songs, but the three songs that they published and worked on, one song was called 'Blue Rain,' and another was called 'Make with the Kisses,' and then 'I Thought About You.' Of course 'I Thought About You' has survived the years, and the others you don't hear too much. But that music publishing company had a life of seven, eight, nine years."

John said of "I Thought About You":

"I can remember the afternoon that we wrote it. He played me the melody. I didn't have any idea, but I had to go to Chicago that night. I think I was on the Benny Goodman program. And I got to thinking about it on the train. I was awake, I couldn't sleep. The tune was running through my mind, and that's when I wrote the song. On the train, *really* going to Chicago. And it was nothing exceptional, except that Jimmy had a great tune, and of course Jimmy is very famous now.

"I think that's the essence of lyric writing, to paint pictures, especially before television. You had only the radio. And you transport people to someplace that they don't know. I never was happy with the ending [of "I Thought About You"]. I know it could be better. I don't know why, but I just have a feeling about it. I think it's because I used 'you' twice." And he laughed. What he was complaining about is a very fine point of songwriting: to use the same word twice does not constitute a rhyme; it's referred to as an "identity," and in the era of American high culture it was considered to be something of a cheat. But John was the only one I ever knew who was bothered by the ending of that vivid song.

What he wrote was exactly what he saw from his train window—stars, parked cars, moonlight—and what he heard. Consider the onomatopoeic evocation of the sound of train wheels near the end: "I peeked through the crack and looked at the track, the one going back to you . . ." I can think of no other song that was written this way, as if it were a painting drawn from observation.

Back in California, John heard about a Shirley Temple movie that was about to go into production. He urgently wanted the assignment to do the lyric writing, but it went to Ted Koehler, Harold Arlen's frequent collaborator. Meanwhile, composer Rube Bloom had been set to do a stage project with Koehler for producer Lew Leslie, but the Shirley Temple assignment was obviously more lucrative, and Bloom was stuck without a lyricist. He took Johnny on. The show, to be produced in London, had an all-black cast. Bloom and the Mercers embarked on a ten-day trip aboard a Cunard Line ship. John wrote, "Leslie, a good hearted man with a desedem-and-dose way of speaking, affected a beret and French phrases, which he must have made up, as I've never found anyone who could translate the words he used to lay on us."

The cast included the unbelievably gifted young dancers the Nicholas Brothers, one of whom, Harold, was in John's estimate about ten years old. Leslie, it turned out, had conned almost everyone into working on a shoestring, but by the time Rube Bloom realized this, they were already halfway across the Atlantic. They worked incessantly on the songs, all the way across, producing about half the score during those ten days. What little capital Leslie had on hand came from two New York gamblers, and only when the company had settled into London's Savoy Hotel did they learn that most of the money had yet to be raised. John and Rube Bloom continued to work in their hotel rooms.

"Ginger saw the Tower, the Abbey, the Thames, and something every day," John wrote, "but Rube and I saw the four walls of that hotel room. Even a dummy catches on eventually, however, and when by the third week there was no money forthcoming, I informed Lew and his two backers that no lyrics were either."

With a tour of Manchester and a theater in London already booked, Leslie somehow scraped together the money. Rube Bloom and John finished the score, and, their job done, went about the sightseeing thus far denied them. Though the show, *Lew Leslie's Blackbirds of 1939*, was not, in John's opinion, very good, it ran six months in Britain. (A New York production was mounted later. The cast included Lena Horne in her first appearance other than as a band singer.)

John wrote: "After the black-tie first night, I couldn't wait to get to Scotland, where I had been invited to visit a relative who lived just outside of Edinburgh. Nell Blackie was my father's cousin, but we called her Aunt Nell, as she was older. She was blind and her husband, who had been a prominent publisher, in London, had died, leaving her a nice estate on the water in Scotland.

"It was a lovely chance to unwind and a total change from the room-service life we had been living. Now it was three or four meals a day, countless teas, from low to high, and plenty of backgammon and Monopoly before we switched to auction bridge. . . . Croquet on the lawn, perhaps a ride through the lochs before a bath, a couple of sherries, and dinner. Then the radio news, which was already full of Hitler and the Nazi Party, before we climbed up to our big bed with the stoneware hot-water bottle.

"I sopped up my Scotch and my Scottish forebears, dug the moors, the lochs, and the castles, the heather and the gorse. It was a sweet, peaceful interlude that ended when we got a wire saying that Warner Bros. was interested in signing me to a writing contract. Was I interested? Was I!

"We were lucky enough to get on one of the first of the *Queen Mary*'s return trips. She was a magnificent boat, and Ginger and I lived it up, walking the decks, playing shuffleboard, and dancing to the four-piece college band."

On another occasion, he recounted: "So when we got back to America, [Rube] said, 'I've got a few ballads I'd like you to hear.' I think he was disappointed in not having a hit show. I said, 'Well, play 'em for me.' I was busy then. By now I'm on the radio, I'm maybe working with Benny Goodman or something. And he played me these two or three songs in one afternoon—'Fools Rush In,' 'Day In—Day Out.' I picked the ones I liked and I said, 'I can't write these for a week or so. But if you play 'em for anybody else, I'll never talk to you again.' So fortunately he saved them for me, and I wrote the right lyrics, because they all happened."

John was under contract to Paul Whiteman from March 1, 1934, to March 1, 1938, with options renewed during that period. Warner Bros. made a deal with Whiteman to pay him $120 a week for Mercer's services, with $630 a week to go directly to John. On August 30, 1937, Warner Bros. bought out his contract with Whiteman for $6,160, according to files still extant at the company. John was thenceforth paid $850 a week by the company, and he signed with them again in 1941 for $1,000 a week, a formidable sum in those days.

And John loved Hollywood in those years.

Hollywood was funny, really idyllically so, with lots of people in the same business all making big money and living in that gorgeous country with nothing to do between pictures but play tennis and golf and look at all the pretty girls passing by.

I suppose the fellows back in Savannah thought we picked the oranges off the trees and threw them at passing Indians, but it was even better than that, because in the commissary at lunch or walking down the studio streets, you could see Carole Lombard or Claudette Colbert. Sylvia Sidney lived right around the corner. Ann Sheridan, Martha Raye, and dozens of other beautiful girls might be having a drink in Lucey's or going in full makeup to the Vendome, or maybe getting up in some little supper club and singing.

Hollywood was never much of a night town. Everybody had to get up too early. Musicians always had some little pad they could fall by late at night to see each other or sit in, and to introduce some new player or vocalist to the crowd. But the movie people were in bed with the chickens (or each other) long before curfew. Sebastian's Cotton Club and the Coconut Grove were about the only two places you could hear any big musical acts until later, when the Palomar opened, and still later the Palladium.

The miniature golf craze was still with us, and on almost every corner there were fad buildings built in the shape of something or other: a hot dog on a roll, a bottle of milk, a puppy, a boat, all patterned, I presume, after the Brown Derby, which was the superstar of Hollywood gimmick buildings. . . .

What is now one huge town was then only little villages, and we'd drive from one to the other to catch a sneak preview. And what a thrill when a "biggie"—not just one of the B pictures—opened. Since each of the major studios made about twenty big ones and sixty run-of-the-mill pictures a year, there was hardly a night when something wasn't being previewed somewhere, in Glendale or Inglewood or Cucamonga or Tarzana. Then maybe a snack at the Beverly Hills Derby or Armstrong Schroeder's for the indigestion special—something light, like a Limburger and raw onion sandwich.

Everybody was young and vital and interested in their work. Talented people from all walks of life and from every nation in the world, all there to get the gold at the end of the rainbow and the fame spilling off the silver screen—there for the taking, only needing a beautiful or a funny face, a parlor trick, or a sexy body to catapult its owner to riches and notoriety.

If Johnny was himself perennially starstruck—he wrote these observations when he was more than sixty years old—he was also skeptical of the sham and shabbiness of the movie industry, the unabashed mendacity of the great dream machine by the Pacific. This would eventuate in one of his keenest social observations in the lyric form, the immensely clever "Hooray for Hollywood," which he would write a little later with composer Richard Whiting for the film *Hollywood Hotel.* The song should be done—should *only* be done—as a fast vaudeville two-beat, like Berlin's "There's No Business Like Show Business" and the Dietz and Schwartz masterpiece "That's Entertainment."

Aside from its sardonic observation, the song is notable for another reason: John's capacity to write very long grammatical lines in song form without losing clarity or the listener's understanding. "Days of Wine and Roses," which of course came much later in his career, consists of only two sentences. "Hooray for Hollywood" is much more complex, yet it contains only four, and the first stanza comprises only one.

> *Hooray for Hollywood,*
> *that screwy*
> *ballyhoo-y*
> *Hollywood,*
> *where any office boy*
> *or young mechanic*
> *can be a panic*
> *with just a good-looking pan,*
> *and any barmaid*

can be a star maid,
if she dances with or without a fan.

Hooray for Hollywood,
where you're terrific
if you're
even good,
where anyone at all
from Shirley Temple
to Aimee Semple
is equally understood.
Go out and try your luck—
you may be Donald Duck.
Hooray for Hollywood!

Shirley Temple was then at the zenith of her childhood career, and Aimee Semple McPherson's evangelist crusade had ended a decade earlier in a personal scandal. Sally Rand, whose performances were decorous and even modest by today's standards, covered herself as she danced with huge feathery fans, behind which, the audience was expected to believe, she was nude. *Pan* was commonplace argot for the face; and it flows naturally out of the word *panic. Ballyhoo* here means inflated and noisy publicity and advertising, but John extends the word by making it an adjective, and, in the process, achieves a Joycean elision with the word *hooey,* a term for which in our own scatalogically inarticulate time we use a harsher word. To find a use of sound like what Mercer shows here, one must look to the French lyrics of Charles Trenet.

The song is, in language and content, very much of its period, again showing John's capacity to capture the language of the time he was passing through, its zeitgeist, if you can put up with that word.

For *Hollywood Hotel*'s "Hooray for Hollywood" sequence, choreographer Busby Berkeley wanted to have dancers wearing face masks of famous film stars. John wrote lyrics for them, including these:

TOM MIX

Hooray for Hollywood,
that bully wild and wooly Hollywood.
Some big producers came and bought my ranch out
and made me branch out.
I left my ten-acre tract.

And I am thankful.
I've got a bankful.
Shows what you can do if your horse can act.

JOHNNY WEISSMULLER
    Hooray for Hollywood.
    In the Olympics I was fairly good.
    Then someone said I was the perfect shape man
    to be an ape man
    and they convinced me I should.
    So now I grunt and yell
    and people think I'm swell.
    Hooray for Hollywood.

It was at some point during this period that Johnny made one of the last-ing friendships of his life—with Wolfe Gilbert. If he wondered, in speak-ing of Hoagy Carmichael, how a boy born in Indiana could write about the South, what about a man born in Odessa, Russia—in 1886—writing "Waiting for the Robert E. Lee"? The song was published in 1912. Later Gilbert wrote "Ramona" (1915), which became the theme song of Arthur Tracy; "The Street Singer" (1931); and "Green Eyes," a big hit in 1941. A particularly interesting witness to Johnny's life is Rose Gilbert, Wolfe's second wife. When Rose was twelve, her family moved from Chicago to Los Angeles. There, years later, Rosie met Wolfe at a party. She told me the age difference of twenty-seven years between them meant nothing to her. She must have been a stunningly beautiful young woman; she was still beautiful when I first met her in 1998, when she was eighty-five, and one of the most vital and intelligent persons I've ever known.

"I was mad about Wolfe," she said. "I still am. My daughter said to me at one time, 'Mother, why don't you remarry?' I said, 'Your father was a hard act to follow.' "

Another of Johnny's friends was Abe Olman, composer, pianist, and publisher, born in Cincinnati in 1888. Abe and Rosie Gilbert were with Johnny and Ginger in England when John wrote his last musical.

Howie Richmond said: "When Rosie and Wolfe and Johnny and Gin-ger and Abe and Peggy, the six of them, were together, there was a kind of harmony between them.

"Wolfe was somewhat of an idol to Johnny. He was a very successful lyric writer before Johnny. Wolfe and Abe and Johnny complemented and supplemented each other. And the girls had a harmony. Peggy Olman had her own personality needs. Peggy was a vaudevillian who had worked with a pretty good act called Parker and Buzzell.

"Guys like Harold Arlen and Jack Yellen were on the perimeter of the group, and this little group of the six of them were the nucleus. Abe Olman was one of my heroes. It was the best of ASCAP and Broadway. Rosie was the buddy of the girls and the harmonizer of the differences. And the men had this friendship. And Johnny was always a pleasure to be with."

In his own memory of the early days in Hollywood, John had this to say in an interview for the BBC:

"I was so crazy about songs so early, I knew them all—and I didn't do it on purpose. I knew verses and second choruses. And when I met these gentlemen out in Hollywood, we'd go to a nightclub or a saloon, and we'd sit around, and I'd sing songs that they'd forgotten they wrote. And I'd sing the verses and the choruses. I didn't put them on. I didn't go home and study those songs, I *knew* them. So when I'd do these songs, I think they were really impressed about my love for the craft of songwriting. That's what impressed them. And I think that's how I got to write with a lot of them."

In another BBC interview, he said: "Of course I've had great luck in my writing career. I've gotten to work with all the great guys. . . . Well, I guess just about everybody, except maybe Richard Rodgers and Frederick Loewe."

Twelve

John found that Warner Bros. was run more or less like a stock company, the studio using its stars as repertory players. During the casting of *Gone With the Wind*, one of the parlor games in the movie business was casting the film as it would be if made at Warners: James Cagney as Rhett Butler, Dick Powell as Ashley Wilkes, Ruby Keeler as Scarlett O'Hara, Joan Blondell as Melanie, and Edward G. Robinson as the father. Those who were under contract at Warners envied those at MGM, whose stable of great stars was large, and where films seemed to be made at a leisurely pace.

John, with his prodigious memory for lyrics, recalled a novelty piece Harry Warren would perform at parties to the amusement of other denizens of the industry. The lyric is probably by Warren's frequent songwriting partner Al Dubin. Harry would begin the music very *agitato* and sing:

> *Warner Brothers, you're late, you're late!*
> *Check with the cop at the gate!*
> *Hurry up, Mr. Warren, you're late!*
> *Have you got the song finished yet?*
> *Mr. Warner says you're using too many Dixie cups!*
> *Efficiency, efficiency, hurry up, hurry up!*

Portrait of Johnny

[Slow, serene music]
But at Metro, birds are singing.
The sun is shining at Metro.
See the beautiful stars.
Everybody has the book of the month under his arm.

[Music *agitato* again]
But at Warners, get the song written,
we need it by noon!
Get a hot dog for lunch! Back to the piano!
Write the score, play some more, write the score!

But at Metro, take your time.
Come to the commissary for lunch with L.B.
Are you having the chicken noodle soup?
It's famous, you know. Have another helping.
We don't start shooting till a year from August.

But at Warners, check the gate for Warren!
Where's Dubin?
Did he drive in yet? Go directly to the set!
Busby Berkeley needs you! The song! The lyric!
Where is it? We're shooting at noon!
We're shooting, we're shooting, it's shot, it's shot!
And it's shit!

Though I saw Southern California for the first time years after John's arrival there, I looked with wonder at all the beautiful people, and then realized that the movie industry had long attracted pretty girls and handsome young men who, if they failed to get into pictures, stayed on and found other employment and bred beautiful children. Even the cars were good-looking. A man from Michigan—where the salt from winter streets rots out the underparts of automobiles—visiting Los Angeles for the first time said, "I couldn't figure out at first what was wrong. And then I realized. I have never seen so many old cars in good condition." And Johnny found California almost overwhelming.

First, there is the size of it. If you leave Milan, Italy, at noon on a train going north, by midnight you're in Denmark. If you leave San Diego, California, at noon on a northbound train, by midnight you're not even out of the state.

California is a land of wildly disparate topography, from the grim desert below sea level called Death Valley to the magnificent snow-peaked mountains, from the agricultural valleys of incomparable fertility to the Mojave Desert. The men who grew rich in the great California gold rush looked with contempt on Southern California, which they called the "Cow Counties," bald and arid land on which it was thought that little but scrub could grow. When the gold rush finally played out, these men looked around for places to put their earnings. Some took their money and experience to Nevada and began silver mining. Others took another look at the Cow Counties.

The ground was baked hard by the sun. Someone wondered if orange trees could be grown here, and a few were imported from North Africa. Dynamite was used to blast holes in the ground to permit their planting. And, oh yes, Southern California could indeed grow oranges—all that was needed was water. And if there was one thing the old placer miners knew, it was hydrology: they had used water under pressure to tear the gold from the earth. They took water from the Owens Valley, from the Colorado River, from anywhere it could be found. Vast irrigation channels were constructed, and great real estate scams were set in motion in the Los Angeles basin. And the flora was brought in: *Crassula argentea* (the jade plant) from Argentina and all sorts of succulents from Africa, pepper trees from Brazil, the jacaranda trees from Brazil with their startling purple flowers, royal palms and fan palms and date palms, and various kinds of eucalyptus from Australia. They say in Southern California that even the weeds were imported, and it's probably true.

And all this imported plant life, nourished by plundered waters, grew into fantasy foliage, incomparable gardens of outsize roses and walls of climbing bougainvillea. It became, even before the movie industry, a fantasyland of con men and shysters and just plain crooks whose descendants were already assuming the manners and mantle of aristocracy by the time Mercer arrived.

It is a folly and a fantasy, Southern California. And it is real; in the movie industry that Johnny was becoming part of, fantasy *was* the reality.

Meaning no disrespect, Hollywood had its share of religious nuts, too. All the faith healers and Heaven-on-Earth sects seemed to gravitate there, to set up some sort of Nirvana or Valhalla in the euphoric climate that was free for all and surrounded by the beautiful mountains, deserts, trees, and hills that rolled down toward the ocean. They had plenty of followers, too, for it seems all God's children, like love, come in many strange shapes and sizes.

Portrait of Johnny

There, in strange shapes and sizes too, were the tragedy that life seems to hand out impartially to the swimmers who can't buck the tide— Paul Bern, Ross Alexander, Jean Harlow—sandwiched in between old tragedies, like the Fatty Arbuckle and William Desmond Taylor debacles, and the more recent Marilyn Monroe suicide and Sharon Tate horror story. Senseless. Terrifying. The ultimate dramatic catastrophes in the most dramatic of all towns.

But life went on as the make-believe went on. Even if it touched you personally, you would leave the cemetery of a friend and, before the ride back to town was completed, you were thinking, talking life's business again, planning the next move in your career. Not that anyone was cold-blooded or cold-hearted about it all. Show people don't like to be sad. They know the risks and they take them. There's no use dwelling on them. They prefer to laugh.

And they know the value of a laugh and a tear. After all, that's what the rest of the world pays them for.

Contrary to later impression, the music for silent films was not all performed by little old ladies in print dresses and flowered hats seated in front of battered upright pianos, or, in the major cities, by organists on what used to be called the Mighty Wurlitzer. Some of it was, to be sure, but major motion pictures were often accompanied by full symphonic scores played by the large pit orchestras hired by the exhibitors. The coming of sound movies in 1928 brought that to an end. Scores could now be recorded and printed on the edge of the film itself. This bit of progress put a lot of musicians out of work, not only in America but around the world; however, it also created considerable employment for those who could get in to the Hollywood recording studios.

Since music had been performed almost without interruption in the silents, it was only natural that talking pictures would use music in much the same way. Large orchestras of superb musicians were assembled to record the scores of the early talking pictures. And what do you do when you have throngs of musicians sitting around on staff and on salary? You make musicals, and in the 1930s, the studios ground them out like sausages—the Astaire and Rogers movies, the bizarre Busby Berkeley extravaganzas, and the sort of college musicals that gave Mercer his baptism of writing for the screen. Good or bad, these musical films required songs, and the studio executives began importing songwriters from New York as fast as the Super Chief could carry them.

Rodgers and Hart had made the move to the Coast. So had the Gershwin brothers. Cole Porter was writing for movies. Most of these composers and lyricists, to be sure, retained their Broadway affiliations, but a few, among them Harry Warren, moved west and stayed. In 1937, he and John contributed the title song to a Dick Powell movie called *Night over Shanghai*. The song has achieved a resounding obscurity.

And then, as John told Max Wilk, "Buddy Morris at Warners asked me who I'd like to write with, and I said, 'I'd rather work with Dick Whiting than anybody.' Another one of my idols. I had heard all his songs. I loved them. 'Japanese Sandman,' 'Till We Meet Again,' 'My Ideal,' 'Sleepy Time Gal,' and those songs he'd done with Leo Robin for Chevalier, 'Louise' and 'One Hour with You.' He had a lot of quality, and he was an original. A dear fellow, too. Modest and sweet, and not at all pushy like a lot of New York writers are. He came from Detroit, and he was kind of a shy man. He wasn't too well by that time, but we were really good friends. We went to work at Warners, did a couple of pictures together. We did *Hollywood Hotel* and *Varsity Show*, and a picture called *Ready, Willing and Able*."

Richard Whiting, born in Peoria, Illinois, in 1891, was eighteen years John's senior, and already an established composer. In 1916, Whiting wrote "It's Tulip Time in Holland," which sold a million and a half copies in sheet music. Then he met Raymond Egan, a bank teller, who told him, "I write lyrics." They wrote "Japanese Sandman." There was a contest for a war song in 1918. Their entry, "Till We Meet Again," won the contest and ultimately sold eleven million copies, reputedly the largest sheet-music sale ever.

The next year Whiting wrote a song based on a sarcastic catchphrase common among the American soldiers in the trenches of France: "Ain't We Got Fun," with lyrics by Egan and Gus Kahn. He continued collaborating with Egan, who wrote the lyrics for "Sleepy Time Gal" and "Some Sunday Morning," as well as with Gus Kahn. Raymond Egan never went back to a bank, except to make deposits.

Whiting's daughter, the singer Margaret Whiting, told me: "My father was a very gentle, generous, very funny guy—delightful. Not a pusher. One of his close friends was Buddy DeSylva, with whom he worked on Broadway. Later on Buddy came out to Hollywood, to Paramount.

"So, we're in Hollywood. My father writes all these things with Leo Robin for Paramount. Then he went to Twentieth Century Fox. He wrote for several pictures there, including the song for Shirley Temple, 'On the Good Ship Lollipop,' for which I was the inspiration.

"The great thrill of my life was to come home from school and go into the living room and he would play songs that he had written or had gotten. That's how I first heard 'My Funny Valentine.' He said, 'This is Dick and Larry's new song.' Every day I'd come home and hear something new, whether he wrote it or Jerome Kern wrote it or whoever it was. . . .

"Johnny Mercer came into the picture 1934, 1935. He was asked by Buddy Morris, who was head of Harms, Witmark and Remick, to come out to write for pictures. He was asked who he wanted to write with, Harry Warren or Dick Whiting. He said, 'Dick Whiting first. I know he's a good golfer and he'll help me with my game.'

"They wrote songs for a picture at Warner Bros. called *Ready, Willing and Able*. The producer told my father and Johnny that they had to write a song about a man who's sending a letter to a woman, and then the woman is going to read it to her girlfriends. Then Busby Berkeley, the choreographer, had this idea where the women were going to be typewriter keys. Daddy said, 'How're we going to write a song describing all the words that she is? We're going to have to go through the damn dictionary.' He and Johnny were going through the dictionary together, and laughing about it. Mercer said, 'I'll probably go for every word in the dictionary. She's beautiful, she's wonderful, she's glorious.' Eventually they came up with the title 'Too Marvelous for Words.' "

Johnny worked on five pictures with Richard Whiting. Some of the songs are now forgotten, but *Hollywood Hotel*, which dates from the same year as *Ready, Willing and Able* (1937), produced "Silhouetted in the Moonlight," "Hooray for Hollywood," and "Have You Got Any Castles, Baby?", while *Varsity Show* (also 1937) produced "Love Is in the Air Tonight" and "We're Working Our Way Through College." All three pictures starred Dick Powell. The next year, they wrote songs for *Cowboy from Brooklyn*, also starring Powell. Its best-known song was "Ride, Tenderfoot, Ride." Their last picture together was *The Dude Rancher*, a film so obscure that it isn't listed in most movie guides. Their one song in it was "Howdy, Stranger."

Richard Whiting wrote songs for twenty-seven movies and four stage musicals. Johnny wrote:

Richard Whiting was like Peck's bad boy. Though he was in his middle forties when I met him, he liked to set off firecrackers, chase away the blackbirds with a slingshot, and play practical jokes on his friends. Dick had tact to a marked degree, and would go through long, tortured, roundabout evasions to protect your feelings if he thought a line of lyrics should be changed.

He was a gentle, loving man, a great golfer, and father of two darling girls, but he was naughty, and nothing gave him more pleasure than to get his friends pleasantly zonked. He couldn't drink much but he would chortle merrily whenever he saw us getting more and more tiddly.

He tried to steer me right. We spent a lot of time in his studio and around his pool. He got me a guest card at the Bel Air golf club, and generally tried to initiate me into the studio mystique, which he had lived through so successfully at Fox and Paramount. That mystique consisted of smiling at the right people, staying away from certain starlets, playing politics, being at the right place at the right time to get the good assignments, and generally being aware of how to get along with your fellow workers, and especially the producers, the powers of the lot.

In any studio, we'd receive our assignment and we were free for four, five, or six weeks until we had to turn in the finished score. When this happened, Dick would get more nervous than usual as the day approached when we had to play for those great stone faces, the producers. They were no dummies, but they were not very musical either. After I sang one score for Sam Bischoff, he looked at me incredulously and said, "You sang with Paul Whiteman? Phooey!"

Come to think of it, Dick must have been more ill than even he knew, as he was always feeling the veins behind his ears, and would get terribly nervous over little things. We only had a year or two of writing together before he lapsed into the illness which finally ended his melodious career.

Richard Whiting died in February 1938. He was forty-six years old. John was devastated. He returned to writing with Harry Warren, with whom he had worked on *The Singing Marine* in 1937.

Harry Warren was a magnificent melody writer and one of Johnny's most effective collaborators. He had his first hit in 1922, "Rose of the Rio Grande." In 1938, he and John wrote three songs together: "The Girl Friend of the Whirling Dervish," "Jeepers Creepers," and "You Must Have Been a Beautiful Baby." In 1945, they wrote one of John's many train songs, "On the Atchison, Topeka and the Santa Fe." Harry (one of the many songwriters to whom John introduced me) was a keen observer, especially of the music and movie industries.

He was born in Brooklyn, the son of a bootmaker from Italy named Antonio Guaragna. Harry grew up in Columbia Heights, near the Brooklyn Bridge.

"My father changed the family name to Warren," he told me. "We never lived in an Italian neighborhood. We were a very Americanized family. We didn't like being Italian in the old days, because they were picked on a lot, like they pick on the Mexicans now. They thought we just smelled of garlic, and that's all.

"I always wanted to write songs, I guess, as far back as I can remember. I learned to play piano by myself; I had no formal education. At first I was a drummer. My godfather had a band, and I used to go on tours with him in the summer. We worked with a carnival show up and down the Hudson River, into Connecticut and Massachusetts. I picked up the piano, and got to like to play the piano much more than drums. And I finally got a job playing piano in Sheepshead Bay. I was also an assistant director for Vitagraph [the movie studio]. I had so many jobs. I found out they needed a baritone singer for the Vitagraph Quartet. I went down and applied for the job and I got it.

"Then I got a job as a property man, and then as an assistant director. I used to play the piano for scenes there.

"The war [World War I] came along and I went in the navy. When I came out, I tried to get into the music business. I met two fellows who were music publishers. One of them said, 'Do you want a job here?' I said, 'Yeah.' He said, 'Twenty dollars a week.' That's how I got in the music business.

"I did the first show of Billy Rose, *Sweet and Low,* which had 'Cheerful Little Earful' and 'Would You Like to Take a Walk.' That was a revue. And I did a show for Ed Wynn called *The Laugh Parade,* which had 'You're My Everything.' And I did another show for Billy Rose called *Crazy Quilt.* That had 'I Found a Million Dollar Baby in a Five and Ten Cent Store.' "

Harry was extremely disparaging of Hollywood executives. "Since you're not enamored of these people," I said, "tell me, Harry, how a good New York boy got sandbagged into Hollywood and the movie industry."

"It was easy," he replied. "I was a staff writer at Remick Music Company. Remick guaranteed me, which I had never heard of before, two hundred dollars a week from a drawing account. I had been making forty-five dollars a week. I couldn't turn that down. That was about 1924, or '25. It was all against royalties, which I never earned, by the way.

"Warner Bros. bought Remick, as well as Harms and Witmark, and paid something like four million dollars, which in those days was a lot of money. Then my contract expired, and Max Dreyfus, who had been the owner of Remick, sent for me. He always liked me, I don't know why. I liked him, too. He was responsible for developing Kern, Gershwin, everybody.

"Max said to me, 'Your contract's up. What do you want to do about it?' (Uncle Max, I used to call him.) I said, 'What do *I* want to do about it? What do *you* want to do about it?' He said, 'We'll re-sign you.' I said, 'At the same money?' He said, 'Do you know you're overdrawn forty thousand dollars already?' Then he whispered to me, 'I don't care about the Warner brothers. I'm going to re-sign you for five hundred dollars a week on a drawing account.'

"I said, 'How about going out to California?' He said, 'I'll put that in the contract, that you'll have to be in California for six months a year, and while you're out there you'll have to get a thousand dollars a week.'

"I said, 'Fine.' And I signed the contract.

"And that's how I came to California. And I *hated* it. I couldn't stand this place. It was corny then. It was nothing like New York. At least now it's a cosmopolitan city. You know, you couldn't get a good meal out here! The coffee was like black soup. Bernstein's Grotto and Victor Hugo's in downtown Los Angeles were the two best restaurants. But there wasn't anyplace to eat. Gus Kahn and I went to a restaurant one night and ordered a steak and we couldn't cut it. I asked the guy for a sharp knife; he brought another—we *still* couldn't cut it. We went hysterical; we went berserk. Even the hamburgers were lousy. There were no delis out here. When we worked at the Warner studio in Burbank that summer, 1932, when I came out, there wasn't a soul on the lot, except two guys writing the script for *42nd Street*. We looked out our window, you couldn't see a thing for miles—there wasn't a building."

In the twenty-five years from 1932 to 1957, Harry turned out songs for movies at Warner Bros., Twentieth Century Fox, Metro-Goldwyn-Mayer, and Paramount. He wrote something like two hundred fifty songs in that period, fifty of which became standards. He was the songwriter on a number of Busby Berkeley musicals, including *Gold Diggers of 1933* and *Footlight Parade*.

Harry's lyricist for many of his movie assignments was Al Dubin. Their songs included "42nd Street," "Shuffle Off to Buffalo," "You're Getting to Be a Habit with Me" (which, I once told Harry, was an obvious dope song, and he admitted it), "Shadow Waltz," "We're in the Money," "The Boulevard of Broken Dreams," "I'll String Along with You," "I Only Have Eyes for You," "Lullaby of Broadway," "About a Quarter to Nine," "She's a Latin from Manhattan," "Lulu's Back in Town," "With Plenty of Money and You" (one of the true Great Depression songs), "Remember Me?", and many more, including an oddity titled "Flagenheim's Odorless Cheese."

Harry Warren's is an estimable body of work, and a lot of it was created in partnership with Al Dubin. Dubin, who was born in Zurich, Switzerland, in 1891, was an excellent lyricist, a round, heavyset man with thinning, swept-back hair. But he had some peculiar work habits.

John told *Crescendo International* magazine in London in 1974: "Al Dubin was a real character. He'd often disappear for long periods and come back with his pockets stuffed full of lyrics scribbled down on tickets and dirty scraps of paper, all spilling out all over the place. Harry Warren wrote some of his greatest songs with Al, but there was one occasion when Harry was out on a job and Al couldn't be found. As usual, he'd temporarily gone out of circulation. So I was brought in to take his place. That was in 1937 for *The Singing Marine;* some of the songs were Al's, the rest mine."

Harry recalled his first meeting with Mercer in a BBC interview:

"He just rang my doorbell. He said, 'My name is Johnny Mercer. I've been singing with Paul Whiteman.' I said, 'Yeah, I know who you are.' And so we got acquainted. He was writing with Dick Whiting at Warner Bros. And then when Dick Whiting died, they had Johnny under contract. He and Al Dubin were writing lyrics to my music. Then when Al quit, to do a show with Carmen Miranda in New York, Johnny and I, in '39, I think, something like that, we wrote 'Beautiful Baby,' things like that. 'Jeepers Creepers.' "

John recalled: "My wife and I went to see a movie one night at the Grauman's Chinese [Theater] and Henry Fonda played a farm boy in it. And you know how he is, he's got that wonderful kind of slow delivery, genuine, real, homespun. And in the movie he saw something, something impressed him, and he said, 'Jeepers creepers,' and that just rang a little bell in my head, and I wrote it down when I got out of the movie. 'Cause, you know, 'jeepers creepers' in America in those days was kind of a polite way, I think, of saying 'Jesus Christ!'

"I think you're halfway home if you've got a phrase that everybody knows. As a matter of fact, if it becomes well known, it's *ripe* to be a song, and I've done a lot of those. 'Goody goody' of course was a famous expression. And there are many of them like that."

Harry told me: "The people in the picture business didn't know anything about songs or show business. Most of them were dressmakers. Coat cutters.

"Johnny Mercer and I did a picture for one producer who was a horse player. He had a list on his desk of all the tracks in the United States, and he'd call up his bookmaker. He'd tell you to stop playing or singing until he called up his bookmaker. In New York, it was later than here.

He'd get the New York results first. In between these calls he said to me, 'You're the lousiest piano player I ever heard.' I said, 'If I played good piano, do you think I'd be writing songs? I'd play with an orchestra.' And he said to Mercer, 'You really stink as a singer!' "

Welcome to Hollywood.

Harry Warren calls me Cloud Boy and tells a story to explain why. One day he came into the studio bungalow where we were working and said, "How's Ginger?" He says that I stared at the ceiling without answering, thinking about the lyric I was working on. He played a few tunes, lit a cigar, went to lunch, stopped by the producer's office, went back to the commissary for more coffee, and finally came back to the bungalow in time to hear me answer, still looking at the ceiling, "She's fine, thank you."

Since he tells that on me, let's begin with him. Harry is a professional hit writer. By that I mean, like Irving Berlin and Walter Donaldson and a few others, he thinks writing anything less than a hit is wasting time, and he knows how to write hits. Not everybody does. It's easier writing with men like that, because they don't waste time on obviously inferior tunes. Added to that, Harry is a cute man with a bittersweet sense of humor. He is Papa, he is quick-tempered, he is suspicious, and he is clannish. While I love him as a friend, I would hate to have him for an enemy.

Thirteen

Meanwhile, in Savannah, there were problems.

John's sister, Juliana, always called Julie, met a young man named Henry Gilbert Keith, known as Gil, who was working as a salesman at the time. The courtship was intense, and Juliana married him. He took her home to Detroit, where he found work in a bank. But before long, the Mercer family, especially Miss Lillian, persuaded them to return to Savannah, where Gil went to work in the Mercer family business.

Miss Lillian's behavior in the following weeks was reminiscent of her attempts to keep John from marrying Ginger. These events provide strong evidence that for all that John and Nancy adored her, she was underneath it all what a later generation would call a control freak. In his autobiographical manuscript John says not one word about his sister's marriage and its consequences, but the events are recorded in a series of letters from the Mercers to Gil Keith and his parents. The first of these, from Johnny's father, George A. Mercer, to Gil's mother, is dated June 5, 1940.

> *My Dear Mrs. Keith:*
> *I am writing you a little letter because I know how very sad and depressed you must be at Gil's leaving you. I know what a mother really means and I know what her love for her oldest boy is, as I was the oldest son of my mother.*
> *The great thing I am waiting for is that wonderful reunion in*

*the higher life where I know I will be in her arms again. God
always tries to make it merciful to a mother's heart and I expect
some day that when Gil is prosperous, which he will shortly be,
and owns his little home, that he will have you and his father
down to see him and you can spend many happy hours together.
He is a fine boy, and it must be quite a blow to him too to have to
leave his father and mother, but I somehow believe it was the
best in the end for all concerned. Certainly I have asked for
divine guidance and feel that I will get it. I have always felt that
way. Gil and Julie are now out looking for a little place of their
own, apartment or bungalow. It means so much to have my only
daughter with me in my declining years, and I believe that Gil
will be very happy in his new job. He has started in already
and will be a great help to me and my two sons. I firmly believe
divine guidance is in this whole affair, and that only happiness
and joy can come of it. I want you and Mr. Keith to feel the
same. Julie is ideally happy and loves Gil very dearly and misses
both of you too. With my sincerest love and best wishes,
devotedly yours,*

G.A. Mercer

Gil Keith went to work for George Mercer in the Mercer-Seiler Insurance Agency. "I showed rentals to people," he told me in October 2002. "I oversaw restoring some of the places that were damaged by hurricanes."

If John's father was affectionate toward his new son-in-law, his mother—Miss Lillian—was not.

"After the baby was born," Gil told me, "she treated me like a Southerner treats a Northerner. I don't know whether you can understand that."

I can. Hostility still bristles there in the Deep South. A simple example: Nancy Gerard (Gil's daughter, of course) and I were in a bank, cashing a check. I casually mentioned to her that the driving I had encountered in Connecticut a few days before was appalling. A clerk behind the counter intruded, "That's because they'uh Yankees." I took this at first for humor, but when I looked into his face, I saw no laughter at all. He *meant* it. And the insult was directed at me.

Gil said, "Lillian wanted me out of the family. I guess I'd done my job. I was the stud and Julie had the baby she wanted. I really don't know. She was a hard-minded lady. I lived in the house, but she told the cook not to feed me, and made it intolerable. I had to leave."

More to the point, Juliana had given Miss Lillian the baby *she* wanted, to replace the lost baby of long ago. And so the child was given the same name, Nancy.

(During this period, Gil had a conversation with John about, of all things, John's teeth. Gil recalled that Walter Rivers was present. John said he was thinking of having the gap between his incisors fixed. Gil advised against it: he said it would destroy John's hometown look. And John never did have that gap closed. Indeed, it became a sort of trademark. But when Nancy, who so startlingly resembles John, reached her adolescence, manifesting the same gap, John had her teeth straightened and paid for it.)

Within a month, George Mercer was dead. Gil Keith, having lost his protector, was dropped from the Mercer-Seiler agency. He went looking for a job in Savannah, but Miss Lillian put out the word against him, and the power of the Mercer name was more than enough to destroy him in the city.

"She killed me," he said. "I tried. I had one man who hired me. I lasted about three days, and he said, 'I have to let you go.' "

On January 3, 1941, when the new Nancy was two weeks old, Miss Lillian wrote this letter to Gil Keith's mother:

My Dear Becky:

I have been wanting to write to you for days, but I have been on a constant move between home and the hospital ever since the baby came. Of course Gil has described how beautiful she is. She really is lovely, just like a doll, and all who have seen her say she is really the prettiest baby they have seen in a long while. Juliana hasn't felt very well lately. Dr. Neville says the bladder condition she is suffering often-times follows a childbirth and should clear up in a few days. She wants to get home, and I can't blame her, although the old responsibility will start up once she learns that peaceful [illegible]. *You were very sweet to think of me at Christmas, and I appreciate so much* [illegible] *apron and* [illegible] *silk from you and Mr. Keith. I didn't bother about Christmas this year except for the children. This is only a line but I can't seem to settle down to long letter writing these days, and no doubt Gil has told you all the news of interest. He told me that his father had not been well and I hope by now he is himself again. Good-bye for now and thank you again for the lovely gifts. With love and best wishes for a happy New Year.*

As ever,
Lillian M.

On February 5, Walter Mercer, Johnny's half brother, wrote this letter on the stationery of Mercer-Seiler Insurance Agency, Savannah, Georgia:

To Mr. Gilbert Keith, Detroit, Michigan—
I'm glad to hear you arrived safely, as I am always worried about automobile trips these days. I haven't seen either Julie or Lillian since you left, so I know of nothing new. The only party I have talked to since I saw you was Walter Rivers, and he felt like I did about it. If anything new turns up, I certainly will write you immediately. I took the baby and Dorothy home last Saturday. Still have a practical nurse and everything's fine. Give my regards to your mother and father.

Sincerely yours,
Walter

The "baby and Dorothy" he speaks of are his own wife and newborn daughter, who was named Louise. Thus Amanda, Nancy Gerard, and Louise Mercer were all close in age. Nancy said: "So my father was already back home in Michigan. A lot had happened in four weeks."

On February 24, Walter's wife, Dorothy, known as Dot, wrote this letter:

Dear Gil:
We enjoyed so much hearing from you, and I think it is grand you found a job the first day. It must have been most heartening, after the struggle you had here trying to land one. It just shows what a one-horse town Savannah is. I haven't seen hide nor hair of Lillian or Julie since the day I left the hospital. They came that morning and brought gifts, which floored me. They must have been left over from the baby [illegible]. The baby cried every time I put her down. I still think [illegible]. Peter Batty came up last night and said he heard you had left. I said, yes, you were gone, and he said, Did he just walk out? And I said, 'Hell, no, he didn't walk out, he was invited out.' I understand that Lillian told Aunt Katherine to say you had gone away to look for a job. I decided I wasn't going to let people think that you walked out. That is why I said what I did to Peter.

Affectionately,
Dot

Portrait of Johnny

On March 4, on Mercer-Seiler stationery, Walter wrote this letter:

Dear Gil:

Please tell your mother how much Dorothy enjoyed her letter and I received yours in the same mail and was glad to hear from you. Dorothy also told me last night that she had heard Julie has retained the services of the attorney H. Paul Clark to file a divorce against you on the charge of mental cruelty. I don't know whether this is official or not, but presume that it is. As soon as I get some further dope, I will let you know. As Mrs Mercer and Julie avoid me, and I do the same to them, I never hear anything. However, they will have to notify you, and if you would like to write Clark, his address is care of Hester-Clark in the Commercial Building. I seriously doubt they are going to have the nerve to ask for alimony, but if they do, I certainly would fight it, as you can get a lot of the Mercer family to testify on your behalf. There is no other news at present.

Sincerely yours,
Walter

On March 6, Walter's wife, Dorothy, wrote this letter:

Dear Mrs. Keith:

We appreciated your letter so much. I do understand how you and Mr. Keith must feel. It is almost impossible to believe that some mothers can be so dumb and ignorant as Lillian has proved herself to be. Of course poor Julie doesn't have sense enough to think a thought for herself, as you probably found out when she was living with you. She is utterly spoiled, lazy, and useless. These might sound like very harsh words, but I have known her for years and I am not exaggerating. Gil probably thought that as soon as they were married she would take on responsibility as any other would do, but she failed, and she will continue to be the same kind of person she has always been: non compos mentis. I spoke very plainly to Gil when he came to tell me good-bye. He could never have a happy, full life with Julie. She isn't capable of it. Gil is well out of the whole mess. I do feel sorry for the baby. She will probably be raised as Julie was, just as useless. The whole family feels the same as we do so don't

*worry about the public thinking anything wrong about Gil. He
stood more than most people would have stood.*

Most cordially,
Dorothy

On March 30, Walter wrote:

Dear Gil:
*I noticed the divorce papers filed in the paper in the
Number 271 and I thought I looked them over carefully, but I
evidently missed seeing yours. I have never known positively
whether she had ever filed divorce action and was trying to find
out definitely so as to let you know. I am certainly glad that she is
not asking for any alimony. No doubt you would like to fight
that, and I would testify for your side. I would get in touch with
Lillian and Julie, and I might as well try to be as friendly as
possible with them. They are moving to Tybee for the summer on
June the first. Also the baby was christened last Sunday, and she
really looks wonderful, and cried all the way through the
christening. Elizabeth is one godmother and George and Bessie
stood for Johnny and Ginger, who are the other godparents.
Dorothy and myself have moved out of the house as we are
doing a lot of work on it. I am glad to hear you have gotten a
raise and hope you will continue to go forward with the
company. Business is all right, and everyone in the family is well.
Dorothy joins me in kindest regards to all your family and
yourself.*

Walter

Three weeks before the Japanese attack on Pearl Harbor, Walter
wrote:

Dear Gil:
*Sorry to hear you have got to go into the Army but it will
probably do you a lot of good from a health standpoint. Now
that you are a free man again, you need have no hesitancy about
making some dates. The final decree was granted some time
back, possibly a month or so ago. We are well. Drop me a line
when you get to the service. Maybe they will send you to the*

Portrait of Johnny

Savannah air base. Remember me to all of the family. Your baby is fine and has lots of personality.

Walter

It is quite apparent in those letters from Walter Mercer and his wife, Dorothy, that they considered Miss Lillian's treatment of Gil Keith reprehensible. As I said earlier, I spoke to Miss Lillian only once, and for all the Southern softness of her manner, I sensed a steely quality in her.

This is what she did: she took Julie's baby away from her and raised her as her own. Nancy adored her grandmother, and has always thought that her mother, Julie, was weak, flawed, incapable of taking care of herself—a view shared by Dorothy and Walter Mercer. But I cannot help speculating what would have happened in the evolution of Juliana's character had Lillian not destroyed her marriage, sent a loving husband packing, and taken Nancy to raise as her own child. Nancy excuses her, saying she thinks her grandmother foresaw many babies being born of a mother incapable of the responsibility of taking care of them and a husband.

"What did they tell you about these events?" I asked Nancy.

"No one ever, ever, ever said a word to me about all this."

"What did they say when you asked about your father?"

"My mother said, 'He was no good and he left us.' And by the way, Dot drank."

This was hardly novel for Savannah.

These events would bear tangled and curious consequences in the years ahead.

Ginger and I had the cutest little house just off Sunset Strip. The Strip was not shoddy then. The neighborhood was pretty, as was the little Cape Cod cottage that Ginger decorated in such good taste. It was small and friendly, with a little picket fence around it. I built the fence, Ginger painted it, and I gave her a mink coat as payment for the job.

This house was at 8218 De Longpre Avenue. Mandy's earliest memories are of that house. Johnny did a painting of it, which now hangs in her bedroom.

Given John's attachment to family and pride of ancestry, it was inevitable that he would want children. And he *liked* children and was good with them. Once, when he was visiting me in Toronto, I observed him with my nephew, who was then about two. The boy went immediately to John and crawled into his lap, and I remember the sweetness and interest with which John treated him. There is no question that John wanted to extend the family name into future generations.

Although the medical details are lost to time, it would appear from the scanty testimony we have that he and Ginger tried and failed to have children, so finally Johnny proposed that they adopt a baby. Again, by the testimony, and the pattern of her later behavior, Ginger did not want to do this; but John was determined and pressed ahead. Through an adoption court in Augusta, Georgia, he found a little girl born on May 12, 1939, in Harlem, Georgia. Her father's name was Otto Barnes; her mother's name was Smith. Little else is known about either of them. The baby was given the name Norma Clare Barnes, but Johnny changed this to Georgia Amanda Mercer. Although as she grew up, Mandy knew she was adopted, Ginger always told her that the adoption records had been lost.

After Johnny died, Ginger donated his papers to the Special Collections section at Georgia State University in Atlanta. One of the librarians found the birth certificate and adoption papers and sent them to Mandy, who hired a detective to learn more about her birth parents.

Mandy recalled: "My mom said that my records had been burned. I guess she didn't want me to know I was a hillbilly. My parents leased a section of a farm. They were cotton-pickers, sharecroppers. My father died at twenty-two from an allergic reaction to some medication he was given in a hospital. I wish I had known this earlier; my children and I are all allergic to certain penicillins.

"My mother was going to jail. We haven't been able to track down all the information. The paper only said she went to jail for 'revenue,' whatever that means. My father was already dead. And they were never married.

"My mother did come back to the court when I was about two years old and asked how the baby was doing. They told her she was doing fine and she was with a good family. She was told the family wanted the birth certificate. She had it and she gave it to them, and they were able to get my proper birthday. I have it now."

The adoption was in fact arranged by Paul Whiteman and his wife, who had previously adopted children and to whom John naturally turned for advice. They had dealt with the agency in Augusta, which had placed children with prominent families and celebrities. One of the agency's representatives, a Mrs. Hamilton, brought Mandy to the Whitemans' apartment in New York, and Johnny and Ginger went to see her there. Ginger's sister, Claire, told Mandy that Mrs. Whiteman had purchased clothes for the child.

Mandy said: "They brought me in and I had this little white dress and these little red shoes that Mrs. Whiteman had bought. Daddy had brought a little book with him, one of those baby books. They told me I started dancing around the room, trying to balance this book on my head, and singing. And I was apparently tiny, probably due to the lack of nutrition I'd had. I wasn't a year old yet. My daddy just thought I was great. Mom was a little nervous. Mrs. Whiteman said, 'If you don't adopt her, we will.' "

Johnny was smitten. He and Ginger took the little girl to Los Angeles and the house on De Longpre Avenue. It was there that John received a call from his mother, telling him his father was fading fast. John has written that his father's 1927 failure left him a broken, nervous, and harassed man. "It was no good to tell him," John said, "that his failure was due to the failure of other companies that *he* had trusted. He was never the same after that, and his ready laugh, the self-confidence, the erect bearing just seemed to disappear. He had gotten progressively older and weaker, and nothing my darling mother did could stop the inexorable process of time."

And now, his mother said, the end was near, and she wanted John to come home. Ginger told John the train would take too long to reach Savannah. John chose to fly. Air travel still was not commonplace; John had sinus troubles, like his father, and he suffered a severe attack on that flight, before the age of pressurized cabins. In any event, the flight took too long: by the time John reached Savannah, his father was gone. He died on December 14, 1940.

Sometimes I think funerals are for the living. You can't touch or reach the dead, can you? But I never cried like that before or since. I wasn't ashamed of it, it was the most natural, therapeutic thing imaginable. I simply let go and all the feeling I had held in and had not been able to reveal all those years were released that afternoon.

After his father's funeral, there is a notable silence about John's personal life, particularly his relations with his family in Savannah. He says nothing of it in his manuscript or in his surviving letters, and Nancy, who was still, shall we say, *in utero,* knows little about that time. There is some evidence that John liked Gil Keith, and he surely observed his mother's hostility toward Gil. Remembering, as he must have, her meddling in his courtship of and marriage to Ginger, he surely knew what Miss Lillian could do. We also know, from the letters written at the time of that court-ship, that occasionally, when he was driven to it, he was capable of stand-ing up to his mother, even showing her his anger.

After his father's funeral, an odd thing happened: John did not go back to Savannah for two years, the longest he had ever stayed away.

Fourteen

One of John's jobs on signing with Warner Bros. was a 1941 assignment to write, in collaboration with Harold Arlen, the songs for a film provisionally titled *Hot Nocturne.* It was intended to be an "authentic" film about jazz, but the elements in the story were those of just about every movie on the subject ever made: a jazz musician (played by Richard Whorf) torn between "real" jazz and the "commercial" version of it, with gangsters in the background, and the usual "good" girl in competition with the "bad" girl.

Arlen found Mercer's way of working a little disconcerting at first. "Our working habits were strange," Arlen said. "After we got a script and the spots for the songs were blocked out, we'd get together for an hour or so every day. While Johnny made himself comfortable on the couch, I'd play the tunes for him. He has a wonderfully retentive memory. After I would finish playing the songs, he'd just go away without a comment. I wouldn't hear from him for a couple of weeks, then he'd come around with the completed lyric."

This, of course, was long before the time of the tape recorder. John simply disappeared with the tunes fixed in his head. These habits also disconcerted Harry Warren and some others who wrote with him. John in fact did make some exceptions. Of Arlen he said, "Some guys bothered me. I couldn't write with them in the same room, but I could with Harold. He is probably our most original composer; he often uses very odd rhythms, which makes it difficult, and challenging, for the lyric writer."

An early scene in the film was set in a jail. The pianist-composer protagonist and a fellow musician are sitting in a cell when they hear a black man in a nearby cell singing a blues. This is the style in which they one day hope to play. Given this scene, Arlen sequestered himself in his studio—a converted garage filled with books, music, and his piano—and analyzed recordings of authentic blues, and began to experiment. When he hit on a tune that satisfied him, he played it first for his wife, Anya, then sent for Mercer. John listened and, for once, did not walk away. On the contrary, he began scribbling lyric ideas, four pages of them. When he showed them to Arlen, Harold made only one suggestion: he thought a line on the fourth page should be moved to the top of the song. The line was "My mama done tol' me . . ." John made the change. The song, of course, was "Blues in the Night." The lyric is undoubtedly inspired by his memory of the sound of train whistles at Five Mile Bend in Savannah ("Hear the train a-callin' / Whooee . . .").

When the producers heard the song, they changed the film's title from *Hot Nocturne* to *Blues in the Night*. It is the most memorable song from that score, although the picture also contained "This Time the Dream's on Me," of which John said to the BBC: "It's one of Harold's nicest tunes. It's kind of a poor lyric, I think. Built on the thing about 'the drink's on me.' I think it's too flip for that melody. I think it should be nicer. I was in a hurry. I remember the director didn't like it. I could have improved it, too. I really could. I wish I had. But, you know, we had a lot of songs to get out in a short amount of time, and we had another picture to do."

One of the admirers of the title song was Jerome Kern. Another was Oscar Hammerstein. "Blues in the Night" was nominated for an Academy Award, but in that time of sympathy for France under Nazi occupation, it lost out to Kern and Hammerstein's "The Last Time I Saw Paris." When the award was announced, Hammerstein whispered to a friend, "If you see Johnny Mercer, tell him he was robbed." "The Last Time I Saw Paris" had been interpolated into a picture called *Lady Be Good,* and after learning that "Paris" had won out over "Blues in the Night," Kern became the main force in changing Academy rules, which since 1941 have stipulated that a song must be written specifically for a film to be eligible.

That same year, John collaborated with Victor Schertzinger on the songs for a movie called *The Fleet's In,* with William Holden, Dorothy Lamour, and, making her screen debut, Betty Hutton. John said, "Victor

Schertzinger really was a movie director who played fiddle, or played a little piano for fun. Same thing with Edmund Goulding. He wrote two songs, 'Love, Your Magic Spell Is Everywhere' and 'Mam'selle.' "

There was a bit more to Schertzinger's musicianship than that. He played solo violin with the Victor Herbert Orchestra at the age of eight and studied at the University of Brussels School of Music. One of the songs that came out of his collaboration with Mercer was "I Remember You," one of John's most brilliant lyrics. John said, "I wrote it very fast, ten minutes, half an hour at the most. I wrote three songs that weekend." He and Schertzinger also wrote "Tangerine," "Not Mine," and "Arthur Murray Taught Me Dancing in a Hurry" for that picture, as well as a title song. Schertzinger directed the movie, which was released in 1942. He didn't, however, live to see it: he died in October 1941, at the age of fifty-one.

Shortly, Mercer would collaborate with Jerome Kern on a Fred Astaire film, *You Were Never Lovelier*, also released in 1942. Kern, born in New York City in 1885, was thirty-four years John's senior. And he was held in utter reverence by other songwriters, among them George Gershwin. John remembered: "I was absolutely awestruck when I walked into his house. And the first few conferences we had in his study, he played me a few tunes. He was terribly *shy*, and there was nothing to be so full of awe about, because he was awfully nice, and very paternal. And well bred. He couldn't have been nicer. He played me a few tunes I *wish* I could have written. One was 'Long Ago and Far Away.' " The lyricist for that one was Ira Gershwin.

John continued: "But he did play me this song [the tune that would become] 'I'm Old-Fashioned,' and I had an idea for it. I brought it in, and he played it over. And he got to that note '*stay* old-fashioned' and he got up and he *hugged* me. He called, 'Eva, Eva!'—he called his wife. She ran downstairs and he kissed me on the cheek and he said, 'Wait'll you hear this lyric!' Well, of course, you know, that makes you feel like a million dollars. It's just a fair lyric, but he was pleased."

Just a "fair" lyric?

I can't remember when I didn't love a Jerome Kern or Victor Herbert melody. To grow up with these tunes coloring my youth was one of the greatest gifts anyone could have. To have gone dancing in high school to "Who?" and "Make Believe," and to have all those tasteful melodies spread across those beautiful formative years is something I will be grateful for until I die. Just as I'm thankful every day of my life that I'm not

*crippled and am reasonably unretarded mentally, so do I also thank the
Lord that I am in a business I love.*

I once questioned John about his collaboration with Kern. Knowing
Kern's reputation among lyricists as difficult to work with, I asked John
what he was really like.

"Well," he said, "Mr. Kern was kind of the dean. He was the professor emeritus. He was the head man. And everybody respected him and
admired him because his tunes were so really far above the others. He was
new and yet he was classical in feeling. He had great melodic invention,
he had great harmonic things. So he was at home with the professional
composer. They respected him above all; he taught all of them something. The lyric writers liked him—if they could ever write with him.
Strangely enough, he wrote with about ten or fifteen lyric writers, more
than people think he did, although of course his biggest collaborator was
Hammerstein.

"I wrote one picture with him, and Dorothy Fields may have written
two or three. He was a fascinating guy. He was small. He wore glasses. He
had a prominent nose and a very quick, alert mind. He was terribly curious. Berlin has the same kind of mind. Porter too, although Porter's mind
was a little more sophisticated, more effete. Kern was terribly interested in
anything that went on around him. . . . He interested himself in the book
and in your lyrics and the costumes and the choreography just as much as
he did any other part of the show. And because he was good, he had a
kind of conceit about him. But he also, like most men of that much
stature, had a kind of modesty about him too. I liked him very much."

"Was he easy to work with or hard?" I asked.

"He was hard to work with because his standards were high. With
me, it was nothing at all, it was really fun, it was an enjoyable job. Of
course, I didn't work that long with him. I didn't have a fight with him. If
I'd had to write six or seven shows with him and he'd thrown his weight
around, I guess he could have been a son of a bitch. But he wasn't."

You Were Never Lovelier yielded six Kern-Mercer songs, three of
which remain classics: the title song, "Dearly Beloved," and "I'm Old-
Fashioned." John's output in that one year alone, 1942 (songs with Kern
and others), included "Tangerine," "The Fleet's In," "Arthur Murray
Taught Me Dancing in a Hurry," "If You Build a Better Mousetrap," "I
Remember You," "Not Mine," "Dearly Beloved," "You Were Never
Lovelier," "I'm Old-Fashioned," "That Old Black Magic," "Old Glory,"

John's grandfather, George Anderson Mercer. He married one of the Herndons of Virginia. *(Collection of Nancy Gerard)*

John's father, George Anderson Mercer, wearing a medal of either the St. Andrew's Society or the Sons of Cincinnatus. He was a member of both organizations. *(Collection of Nancy Gerard)*

John's mother, née Lillian Ciuchevich *(Collection of Nancy Gerard)*

Three generations: John with his father (standing) and grandfather. The photo is dated 1914; John was about to turn five. *(Collection of Georgia State University)*

John with his little sister Nancy. Her early death left a permanent scar on John's mother and on John, in the opinion of Nancy Keith Gerard, who was named after her. The photo is dated 1914. *(Collection of Nancy Gerard)*

John's sister Juliana, who married Gilbert Keith and gave birth to Nancy Keith, now Gerard. *(Collection of Georgia State University)*

Top: John, sitting on the ground, with the Woodberry Forest baseball team. *(Collection of Georgia State University) Bottom:* John in 1928. The photo was taken in November and may have been a birthday portrait for his mother. *(Collection of Nancy Gerard)*

To my mother with all my love —

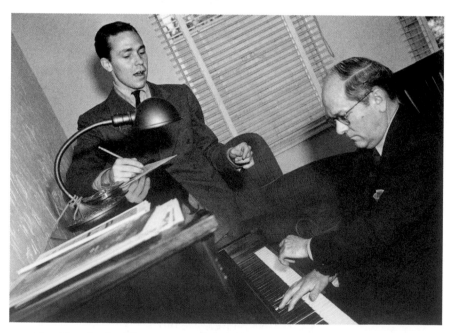

Top: Bing Crosby. The conventional dedication suggests that Ginger was not his paramount passion, although a few telegrams to her are frivolously flirtatious. She kept the photo all her life. *(Collection of Georgia State University) Bottom:* John, with composer Richard Whiting. They wrote "Hooray for Hollywood," "We're Working Our Way Through College," and "Too Marvelous for Words," among other songs. Whiting died in 1938 at forty-six. *(Collection of Georgia State University)*

Louis Armstrong, Maxine Sullivan, and John on the set of the
1938 film *Going Places*. It is a hokey, posed picture. For one
thing, John didn't play the piano. *(Collection of Georgia State
University)*

John with Jack Teagarden, recording "The Old
Music Master" with the Paul Whiteman
Orchestra, summer of 1942. *(Collection of
Georgia State University)*

Johnny, his mother, and Ginger
(Collection of Georgia State University)

Ginger and Mandy, spring 1941
(Collection of George State University)

"On the Swing Shift," "Hit the Road to Dreamland," and "Captains of the Clouds," and a number more that are now forgotten.

As the war ground on, Arlen and Mercer did a movie at Paramount, *Here Come the Waves*, with Bing Crosby and Betty Hutton. One of the several songs they wrote for it was "Let's Take the Long Way Home." About the genesis of another song from that movie John told the BBC: "When I was working with Benny Goodman back in '39, I had a publicity guy who told me he had been to hear Father Divine, and that was the subject of his sermon, 'Accentuate the positive and eliminate the negative.' Well, that amused me so, and it sounds so Southern and so funny that I wrote it down on a piece of paper. And this was, what, five years later? And Harold Arlen and I were riding home from the studio after a conference about getting a song for the sailors. The sailors wanted to put on a show on a big destroyer, and Bing Crosby and Sonny Tufts were going to sing a duet. And could we come up with something? And then Harold was singing me this little tune he had sung me before. Now, that's a strange thing about your subconscious, because here's a song that's kind of lying dormant in my subconscious for five years, and the minute he sang that tune, it jumped into my mind as if it dialed a phone number. Because it doesn't really *fit*. The accent is all different. I just think there's some kind of fate connected with it."

By the time Arlen and Mercer finished their drive, the song was all but completed. Arlen said later, "It must have really pleased John; it was the first time I ever saw him smile."

John said: "The song was a huge hit, and gave a phrase to the American language." It gave two phrases. The song opens:

> You've got to Ac-cent-tchu-ate the positive,
> ee-lim-i-nate the negative,
> latch on to the affirmative . . .

"Latch on to" seemed like an incredibly hip (or hep, as they said then) phrase. It is now so commonplace that it passes unremarked in our own time, turning up, for example, in such places as *New York Times* editorials.

In the next year, 1943, John had five songs on the *Hit Parade* in the same week—half its list.

John and Harold Arlen were engaged by Paramount to write songs for a frothy wartime musical called *Star Spangled Rhythm*. John recalled:

"We had to have a big song in a show. As a matter of fact, we had several songs in that movie.

"Harold had this tune and it impressed me as being a very elegant tune, a natural hit. It occurred to me that perhaps 'black magic' would be a good idea 'cause Cole Porter had written a song called 'You Do Something to Me,' and it went 'do do that voodoo that you do so well.' And I thought, gee, that's a great idea to be wasted on one word in a song. And I thought perhaps if I could incorporate that into a tune someday, it might work. Well, this tune just seemed to fill the bill. I wrote it up, with Harold. I remember working with Harold at his house in Beverly Hills. We wrote it in one afternoon. When we finished it, he drove me home and I said, 'You've got to come in and play it for Ginger.' Ginger was the first one to hear 'That Old Black Magic.' Ginger always says, 'I knew they had something good, because they come in and they stand around like little boys, and then they say, "Don't you want to hear what we wrote today?" And when they say that, you know they've got a big song.'

"We took it in to Paramount studios where they were making this movie, and it was assigned to Johnny Johnson. He sang it in his sleep and Vera Zorina danced it, and she was dressed all in black, and she did it against a snow scene. It was all black and white. It was a very effective piece of photography in the film, a marvelous dance, and, fortunately, as it happens, a great big hit song."

Also in that film was "Hit the Road to Dreamland."

At Paramount, Arlen and Mercer were assigned to come up with a title song for a James Cagney film about the Royal Canadian Air Force, *Captains of the Clouds.* Mercer said later, "We played it for some Canadians. They liked it." They more than liked it. The RCAF later adopted it as a march.

Their next job was at the RKO studio, a Fred Astaire film called *The Sky's the Limit.* They wrote two songs. "The funny thing about these two songs," Astaire said, "was that while the picture was in operation, neither of them registered as an immediate hit, but several months later 'My Shining Hour' became the number-one song of its day, and 'One for My Baby' has become a standard classic popular song and one of the best pieces of material that was written especially for me."

Arlen said "One for My Baby" was "a wandering song. Johnny took it and wrote it exactly the way it fell. Not only is it long—forty-eight bars—but it also changes key. Johnny made it work. I don't care what you give him, he'll find a way to save it, to help you."

John evaluated his relationship with Arlen: "Had Harold and I not separated to work with other collaborators, we might have become a very well-known team together. We had an affinity, not so much liking the same personal things but liking the same things in music and songs." And of one of their finest collaborations: "Everybody seemed to be enchanted with 'Blues in the Night.' To me, it was just another Southern song."

Fifteen

A songwriter earns money in royalties, and there are three kinds: those from sales of sheet music, which have in recent decades become so small as to be almost irrelevant; mechanical royalties; and performance royalties. Mechanical royalties derive their name from the player-piano rolls on which they were originally based under the Copyright Act of 1909, but the term was retained when the primary source of these funds became phonograph records, then LPs, prerecorded tapes, and CDs. A specified sum is paid by the record company to the publisher of a given song used in a recording, in whatever form. The executives of the record companies came in time to realize that they could establish publishing subsidiaries and pay this money to themselves. In the past, a publisher paid half this money to the writers of a song. The publisher got half, the lyricist got a quarter, and the melody writer got the other quarter. But many rock performers have had sufficient power to keep all the money for themselves.

There are so many ways for record companies and their distributors, and even retail outlets, to steal the true mechanical earnings. Howie Richmond estimates that only about forty percent of this money finds its way up through the pipe to the publisher. And if the publisher is dishonest, the writers get less than their correct share.

Johnny always felt frustrated by the mendacity of the entertainment industry, the dishonesty at so many levels of its component industries:

theft of record royalties at the retail and wholesale levels, theft by the record labels at the next level above that. It is hard to know when the idea for Capitol Records first came to him.

One of the most important artists on the young Capitol label was Jo Stafford, who was born in Coalinga, California, in 1920, and received extensive vocal training. She first worked professionally in Hollywood in a vocal group with her sisters, doing studio work. But she came to prominence in another vocal group called the Pied Pipers, which was hired to appear on a Tommy Dorsey radio program in 1938 and then joined the band on that program as a quartet.

"My first memory of Johnny was hearing him on the radio," Jo said. "I had been a fan of his singing from the Paul Whiteman days—he did some things with Jack Teagarden, such as 'Christmas Night in Harlem.' In 1936, my sisters and I used to frequent a place down on Vine Street called The Famous Door. It had jazz players. It got to be where we were there every night. We got to be the house singers, practically, the three of us. And one night, all of a sudden, there sits Johnny Mercer. I almost went out of my skull. I was such a fan. I went over and asked for his autograph, and he gave it to me. And at that time he didn't just sign his name. He had about a five-line sketch of himself that he did. And it looked just like him. He would draw this little caricature and sign his name. I still have it. It was awfully good.

"That was my first meeting. He was a big fan of the band and, as it turned out, of the Pied Pipers and me! And whenever we were in Hollywood at the Palladium, or wherever we were playing, he would always come in to hear us. And in New York at the Astor Hotel. I remember I met his mother there. He brought her in for dinner one night.

"He told me, 'If you ever leave the band and are free, a couple of other fellows and I are starting a record company out on the Coast. And we'd love to sign you as a solo singer and the Pipers as a group.'

"We were in Portland, Oregon, on the road. The guys had gone out on a party at someone's house. You know, people would come and see the band and take you to their house and feed you and get you loaded. And one of the Pipers had gotten real bombed. So now we have to catch this train at eight o'clock in the morning. So they're not feeling too hotsy-totsy, and I think Tommy was in the same shape. They all had terrible hangovers. Tommy ran into Chuck Lowry, one of the Pipers, in the station, and said, 'Where is our train?' Chuck gave him some directions to the siding where our train was, and told him wrong, and Tommy got lost.

We were all sitting on the train, waiting. When he finally found the train, he was fit to be tied. He lit into Chuck for giving him the wrong directions. And they got into a big fight, and Tommy said, 'You're fired.' And we walked off the train. We heard later that he said he had been real stupid about it. He said, 'I never intended to lose those kids. It was just dumb.' Of course, he could have come to us and said so, but that was not part of old Tom.

"And so when we left Tommy, we got in touch with Johnny, and that's when we went with Capitol Records. We not only made records, but we did radio shows with him a lot."

The "couple of other fellows" Johnny mentioned were Buddy DeSylva and Glenn Wallichs.

"I used to ask myself," Johnny told Hollywood journalist Lloyd Shearer in a 1944 interview, "what talented people around Hollywood did in between picture and radio jobs. I thought maybe I could organize them into some sort of cooperative and start a radio program. After talking with Glenn Wallichs, however, I decided to go into the recording business and use these people who weren't working steadily. I went to see Buddy DeSylva, a unit producer over at Paramount and a great lyric writer himself, and I asked him if he would let us sell our recordings in the lobby of the Paramount theaters. Buddy wasn't crazy about the idea but said he'd like to join the business with us. He supplied some of the dough and away we went."

Aside from the royalties from his songs, DeSylva had money from the sale of the publishing company he had owned, as well as his considerable salary at Paramount. The amount John told him they needed to start the record company was $25,000.

B. G. (Buddy) DeSylva was born in 1895 in Los Angeles and was educated at the University of Southern California. He made his first foray into New York as an accompanist to Al Jolson, later joining up with Lew Brown and Ray Henderson to form the lyric-writing and publishing team of DeSylva-Brown-Henderson. Whether in collaboration with Henderson and Brown, or with Jerome Kern, Victor Herbert, Richard Whiting, George Gershwin, or Vincent Youmans, he was the writer of many important songs, some of them now part of the collective American memory, among them "Look for the Silver Lining," "Avalon," "April Showers," "Somebody Loves Me," "California, Here I Come," "I'll Build a Stairway to Paradise," "If You Knew Susie," "When Day Is Done," "Alabama Bound," "The Best Things in Life Are Free," "Good News," "You're the

Cream in My Coffee," "Button Up Your Overcoat," "Sunny Side Up," and "I'm a Dreamer, Aren't We All." He cowrote a great many Broadway shows before signing a contract at Fox in 1929 and moving back to California, and by 1941, he was an executive producer at Paramount.

Johnny told me he first met Glenn Wallichs when Wallichs fixed his car radio. An excellent portrait of Glenn Wallichs was written by Dave Dexter, Jr., a former *Down Beat* writer and editor whom the three founders hired within months of Capitol's formation to create and edit a small magazine called *The Capitol News,* which the company distributed free to record stores all over America to publicize its artists. It was a clever publicity ploy. In 1972, Dexter wrote in *Billboard:* "The son of a railroad man, [Wallichs] ingeniously invented a tiny fixed-tuned radio set, when he was a twelve-year-old, that worked inside his mother's sewing thimble. The device brought him his first publicity in his home town. Moving with his family to North Hollywood in 1926, young Glenn overhauled a derelict Model T Ford and equipped it with a hand-held radio of his own design. It may have been the first receiver ever installed in a motor vehicle.

"Wallichs' skills led to a radio station job in Los Angeles, as a technician, and while working closely with KFWB's inordinately popular deejay, the late Al Jarvis, he learned about pop music and its makers. Later he opened his own radio repair shop in Hollywood. 'For a quarter,' he once reminisced, 'I'd promise to make any set work right. For a dollar I'd sell them a new set.'

"Somehow in the face of a despairing national economic depression his modest enterprise prospered. He then began to operate two small recording studios—and that was long before the era of demo disks and audition tapes. In 1940, only twenty-nine, Glenn leased the northwest corner of Sunset and Vine in the heart of Hollywood as the site of the first of a chain of Music City retail stores. . . .

"The success of the first Music City operation is now legendary in and outside the profession. Working virtually around the clock with never a complaint from his devoted wife, Dorothy, the ingratiating, untiring Nebraskan became the trusted confidant and pal of Hollywood's most renowned stars—singers, musicians and picture studio and radio luminaries. After two years on the frantic Hollywood corner, Wallichs collaborated with Johnny Mercer and George (Buddy) DeSylva in the founding of Capitol Records.

"DeSylva was a wealthy ex-songwriter and production boss at Paramount Pictures. Meeting at Lucey's restaurant, he wrote a check for

$10,000 and was allocated a one-third interest in the firm. Wallichs pocketed the check and, with Mercer in accord, warned DeSylva that it was a 'big, big risk trying to butt butts with Decca, RCA, and Columbia.'

" 'That ten grand,' Wallichs told us a few months later, when I signed on as a Capitol employee after moving west from New York, 'was the most money I'd ever handled. Buddy concentrated on making movies and left us alone. Mercer quickly signed Paul Whiteman's band—a flop—and Martha Tilton, Dennis Day, Tex Ritter, Bobby Sherwood's band, and pianist Freddie Slack.' "

But before the new company could issue record one, it had to find shellac. Shellac is a substance derived from a sticky resin secreted by the tiny lac insect and deposited on the twigs and young branches of certain trees, including the acacia, in India, Thailand, Burma, and other countries of southeast Asia, which during the years of World War II were controlled by the Japanese. From the earliest days, records had been pressed on shellac, and now you simply couldn't get the stuff. Where Capitol got its first supply—and from its first days, its records were pressed on better-quality shellac than the Big Three used—was always a mystery in the business. I have heard two or three stories about where Capitol got it, but the one I believe was the one both John and arranger Paul Weston, the company's first music director, told me.

Paul said, "Glenn found a guy down in San Diego who had a supply of shellac and who had a son who had an orchestra. So, it was a little deceptive, but we signed the son's orchestra, and the daddy came through with all the shellac, and the son made four sides, then disappeared, never to be heard from again. But meanwhile we had the shellac. It was sort of desperate."

Mercer decided to record one of his own songs, "Strip Polka," for the company's initial release. Paul Weston said, "Just by chance he asked me to arrange 'Strip Polka.' We went down with a bunch of guys and made this crazy record, not thinking that it was going to be a hit."

The other recording was "Cow Cow Boogie," which would sell a million copies. The two were released on July 1, 1942.

But there was fresh trouble ahead for Capitol. James Caesar Petrillo, the famously tyrannical head of the American Federation of Musicians, with ties to Al Capone, thought that recordings and radio threatened the livelihood of musicians. He was right in this perception but misguided in his attempt to solve the problem: on August 1, 1942, he ordered a ban on commercial recordings by instrumentalists, although musicians were allowed to make transcriptions for the V-discs distributed to the armed forces. Petrillo could not, however, control singers, who were not members of the musicians' union, and they continued to record, using choral groups as backup. For example, Frank Sinatra, on Columbia, recorded a number of songs in a cappella arrangements. Other singers made similar records. They were all rather syrupy, but they sold. And during the ban, these singers became immensely popular, and the public began to forget the great bands. Petrillo effectively contributed to the destruction of the big bands he was trying to protect.

The Nat King Cole Trio in its early days had recorded for the Decca label, mostly novelty tunes such as "I Like to Riff," "That Ain't Right," "Hit That Jive, Jack," "Scotchin' with the Soda," and "Early Morning Blues." The group built its reputation with an extended tour of major U.S. cities. When its Decca contract expired, Mercer signed Cole to Capitol, and bought a few sides the trio had made for the small Excelsior label, including "Vim Vom Veedle" and "All for You." Mercer and Wallichs also bought some sides Cole had recorded as transcriptions—sixteen-inch discs made specifically for radio play. They already had this material in hand when Petrillo called his strike, and were able to release it. Much of Capitol's success was built on Cole's sales. Cole, in turn, did *all* his recording for Capitol, except for those early sides and a few instrumentals for impresario Norman Granz. It was an incredibly lucrative partnership for both Cole and the company. He turned out hit after hit: "Straighten Up and Fly Right," "The Christmas Song," "Nature Boy," and, in due course, "Mona Lisa," which was written by Johnny's friends Jay Livingston and Ray Evans. Cole was one of the finest and most influential of all jazz pianists, but it was his husky and somewhat velvety singing that made him a star, a position he holds now, though he died in 1961. Capitol is still issuing his recordings, including those early ones produced by Johnny or Paul Weston.

Petrillo's record ban lasted nearly two years. Wallichs used that time to buy up 250 tons of scrap records at six cents a pound, which were melted down and used to press new records. Johnny used the time to scout talent. Capitol was the first label to reach an agreement with Petrillo, one that paid a royalty into a musician's trust fund. The ban ended for Capitol in November 1943, and when it did, Wallichs and Mercer were ready.

Martha Tilton had left the Benny Goodman band, and Johnny signed her. Pianist Freddie Slack, whom Johnny met when Slack was with Jimmy Dorsey, had left the Will Bradley band. The Stan Kenton band, playing a ballroom at Balboa Beach, California, was available, and Johnny signed them, along with Connie Haynes, Tex Ritter, Tennessee Ernie Ford

(Johnny liked good country music), Harry Owens, Dennis Day, Billy Butterfield, and Betty Hutton, whose frantic comedy songs "My Rocking Horse Ran Away" and "Doctor, Lawyer, Indian Chief" were huge hits. Capitol made many records that in their day were unprecedented. Johnny got an idea that children would enjoy hearing child star Margaret O'Brien reciting fairy tales, and they put out a "spoken-word" album. It was a big success and Capitol established a children's division. They put out records by the radio comedy team Fibber McGee and Molly (Marian and Jim Jordan in real life), as well as by comedian Jerry Colonna. They made records by Harold Perry, who in his radio incarnation was the dark-voiced Great Gildersleeve. They all sold.

Johnny's judgment of what and who would sell seemed infallible, with one exception: Paul Whiteman, whose career had faded and whom Johnny probably signed out of gratitude and loyalty. Whiteman never sold well for Capitol.

Meanwhile, the executives of the Big Three—Columbia, RCA Victor, and Decca—were aghast at the success of this upstart company. As Lloyd Shearer put it in his 1944 portrait of Johnny, "Executives of rival record companies began to sit up, puff angrily on their cigars, and sputter."

But it was a grand time for John:

Glenn was off to Washington, Scranton, New York, and even Europe, setting up distributorships, finding personnel, and doing all the organizational work his store and the presidency of the Junior Chamber of Commerce career had equipped him for, and I was writing and recording originals with any friend I could talk into it.

Bobby Sherwood wrote and played "Elk's Parade," sang "Harlem Butterfly" and "I Don't Know Why." I made "Strip Polka," and Freddie Slack, with the yeoman help of Don Raye and Gene De Paul, brought in their "Cow Cow Boogie" and "Mr. Five by Five," along with Ella Mae Morse and the Dinning Sisters.

When the publishers found there was actually money to be made with Capitol, we were really in. Harry Link sent "Candy" for me to record. As our activities snowballed, we signed Margaret Whiting, and from Paramount, Johnny Johnson, and all those people I thought could use a little honest work. Bobby Dolan contrived a tune, "Old Rob Roy," and recommended a former Tommy Dorsey arranger named Paul Weston, who soon became a mainstay of our fledgling firm. Everything seemed to work to our advantage. Sales were meteoric.

Sixteen

Born in Springfield, Massachusetts, in 1912, Paul Weston graduated Phi Beta Kappa from Dartmouth with a degree in economics, but finding in the depths of the Depression that there was no pressing demand for young economists, he began writing arrangements for the Rudy Vallee band, then went on to write for Tommy Dorsey. He settled in Los Angeles in the summer of 1940 to write for Dinah Shore, the Bob Crosby band, and movies. He worked at Paramount Pictures with Bing Crosby, Bob Hope, and Betty Hutton, and he was writing arrangements there for *Holiday Inn* when he met Mercer, working at the same studio on songs for *Star Spangled Rhythm*. Mercer made him Capitol's musical director.

He carried on in this executive position, producing such records as the early Nat King Cole Trio singles while turning out an incredible amount of writing for Mercer, Jo Stafford, Betty Hutton, Margaret Whiting, and, later, Gordon MacRae and Dean Martin. He also began to record a series of instrumental albums, the first of them being *Music for Dreaming,* all of which remain classics of elegant melodicism to this day.

Paul was an especially treasured friend of mine. A very funny man, he once described to me the atmosphere of the office in the early days of Capitol. Johnny, according to Paul, held the quaint—by later record-industry standards—idea that the music was everything. You should record music you liked, and never release a record you didn't like. By then Paul was Johnny's musical right hand. It was he who arranged Johnny's

"Dream," performed by the Pied Pipers, one of the few songs for which Mercer also wrote the music.

"When you write songs," John said, "and you wanna be a melody writer, but you write with great melody writers all the time, you're always trying to find some pretty song. It's easy to write a rhythm song, kinda like 'Something's Gotta Give' and 'I'm an Old Cowhand,' something like that, but a ballad is tough, and I was working on this song 'Dream.' I had a few chords. And I loved the sequence of the chords. I fool around on the piano. I don't play. So it's a real effort for me just to get *a chord,* and when I get two or three in a row, why that's like *composition.* So I had this thing going and I got these chords, and I was just in the middle of finishing the melody, and Paul Weston came out to the house to talk about the Chester-field program that we were going to go on. I was gonna be the singer and he had the band, and we were going to have the Pied Pipers. I said, 'By the way, I've got a tune that might be pretty good for the theme song.' I played it, and he said, 'That's wonderful,' and he took it down, and he wrote the lead sheet for me. He loved the chord sequences, so then I finished the lyric. But, y'know, I discovered later on after I'd written it and played it a long time that you can play it along with 'Whispering.' It's kind of 'Whispering' sideways."

On another occasion, John admitted to me that the fact that the program's sponsor was a cigarette maker did enter into his thinking as he polished the lyric for "Dream": "So with that thought in mind, I put in the line about the smoke rings. Otherwise it wouldn't have been in there."

Glenn Wallichs, who described himself as a "Nebraska square," never interfered with the artist. "I'm on the business end," he would say to the artists and repertoire people. "You guys concentrate on marrying the finest artists you can find with the best songs available. That's the toughest task in the business."

Dave Dexter, Jr., who moved from publishing *The Capitol News* to being "an A&R man," in the term of that era, wrote in *Billboard:*

"Wallichs was a non-smoker, and often he would remonstrate with an employee for courting lung cancer via the habit. He would drink as many as two cocktails if a situation was special. His dealings with artists, agents, and those who worked for Capitol were unfailingly fair. . . . Glenn loathed pretension and pompousness. He spoke and acted bluntly, directly, and candidly."

When they had completed a new record, Johnny would bring it back to the company's small office to listen to it. Paul Weston said: "Glenn Wallichs was on the telephone. Mercer and I were in the same room, listening to a record we had made a couple of nights before, and John liked to hear it at pretty good volume, and Glenn was hunched over, trying to make this phone call. Finally Glenn said, 'Can you guys turn it down a little bit?' And John said, 'We've gotta listen to these things. What are you doin', anyway?' And Glenn said, 'I'm trying to get a distributor in Pittsburgh,' and Mercer said, 'Ah, the hell with that. Don't worry about that kind of stuff. Let's listen to the music.' That was really John's attitude to the record company."

Margaret Whiting said:

"Johnny always saw every songwriter. He listened to every song. Because he wanted to pick the things for all of his artists individually.

"He said, 'We want to record you. I want you to do one of your father's songs and one of Buddy DeSylva's for luck. I've got an idea. You sing like a trumpet. And there's a great trumpet player, Billy Butterfield. I want you to do this record together.' I did 'My Ideal' and 'Without Love.' We used Les Brown's band. I sang the two songs. Two or three takes. The record did very well and we needed a follow-up. Johnny heard 'Moonlight in Vermont.' He said, 'That's for the kid.' He called me down and he sang the song, and Paul Weston was playing it. He said, 'What do you think?'

"I said, 'It's gorgeous.'

"So now I was beginning to sing, under the influence of my father and Johnny Mercer, and another great friend of my father's, Frank Loesser. He was such a vital, ballsy, different kind of guy from Johnny. Johnny was soft and funny and provocative.

"When Johnny found 'Moonlight in Vermont' for me, he never brought up the fact that it didn't rhyme, and I didn't think about it for many years."

(He also might have pointed out that the front strain of John Blackburn and Karl Suessdorf's 1944 hit does not contain a verb, nor do its two repeats; only the release contains verbs.)

"I never paid attention to it," Margaret said, "because Johnny said, 'I want you to think, what does Vermont mean to you?'

"I said, 'A calendar with a church in the snow.'

"He said, 'There are more images.'

"I said, 'Well, there's got to be summer, winter, fall. Fall. Everybody goes to see Vermont in the fall for the leaves.'

"He said, 'I want you to think of those pictures. I want you to think of the coming of spring. I want you to think of summer, people swimming and people walking, people having a lovely time outdoors.'

"So we go in and record it and I'm envisioning all these pictures. It gave me something to go on. That's what he taught me; and that's what Loesser taught me. Pick up that sheet music and look at those lyrics and make them mean something. Read the lyric aloud, over and over and over. Recite it until you get it. Your own natural instincts will tell you."

What John was teaching her, essentially, was the Stanislavsky method applied to singing.

"Capitol used to make maybe nine, ten different records a day with different people," Margaret continued. "Paul Weston would change his style in the arrangements. It got to be a very big thing, so they brought in other arrangers."

It was, Paul once told me, laughing at the memories, chaos.

Indeed, it must have been. One of John's best friends was Jerry Colonna, the onetime New York studio trombonist who had turned comedian and become famous as a regular on the Bob Hope radio show. Dave Dexter recounts in his autobiography that Colonna had a taste for marijuana and booze. John was producing a session with trumpeter Wingy Manone one afternoon when Colonna rode a big gray horse right into the studio. The animal, of course, decided to relieve itself amid Paul Weston's musicians.

Wingy told John, "This is the first record I ever made that I know won't sell. It stinks."

As the company prospered, it needed more employees. It added a music publishing division, and to run it, imported Michael (Mickey) Goldsen from New York. Known for his knowledge of music publishing and his scrupulous honesty, he would run their publishing division, Capitol Songs, as a partner with DeSylva, Wallichs, and Mercer, from 1943 to 1948.

Even while functioning as the head of a rapidly growing record company, Johnny sustained a formidable output of lyrics. The brilliantly witty "G.I. Jive" was a World War II equivalent of Berlin's World War I "Oh How I Hate to Get Up in the Morning." "G.I. Jive" contains one of Johnny's most felicitous rhymes—"duty" with "L.I.E.U.T." Another song of 1943, perhaps the most poignant of all the wartime songs, was "My Shining Hour," the work of Johnny and his friend Harold Arlen. It has a remarkably condensed lyric, evoking in the imagination what a young man might say to his girl on leaving for the war, possibly never to return. And note that it doesn't rhyme at the end, a trick Johnny occasionally used.

Portrait of Johnny

This will be my shining hour,
calm and happy and bright.
In my dreams your face will flower,
through the darkness of the night.

Like the lights of home before me,
or an angel watching o'er me,
this will be my shining hour
till I'm with you again.

Julius La Rosa, one of the best singers in the business, told me once that he always sang it "watching over me." "But, Julie," I said, "that antique contraction, *o'er,* makes it almost a prayer." To which he said, "I'll never change it again."

With the war at its peak, Johnny began to wonder what he could do to help his country. He made a trip to Washington to see Major Anatole Litvak, the Russian-born director of such films as *The Amazing Dr. Clitterhouse, Tovarich, The Sisters, All This and Heaven Too, City for Conquest, This Above All, The Snake Pit, Sorry Wrong Number,* and, most significantly for Johnny, *Blues in the Night.* In Washington, Litvak introduced Johnny to an army colonel in charge of strategic services, to whom he expressed his desire to do whatever he could for the war effort. He was urged to return to California, where he was at last advised that the army thought he should stay right where he was. Finally, Johnny said, "Could I do some shows for the army camps and naval bases? With our radio program and record company, we were all set up for it."

We had our arrangements with the Paul Weston band and our new material gathered for the radio show and the record company. Every weekend we were off to Camp Roberts, Port Hueneme, Fort MacArthur, or Camp Pendleton—you name it—to play a show for the enlisted men. We played nearly every hospital in Southern California and, during the week, when we weren't doing our national broadcasts, we would be recording for G.I. Journal *or* Command Performance *for the Armed Forces Radio. . . .*

Needless to say, it was gratifying to know you were doing your duty . . . and I was proud that I could bring a little cheer, even if on a small scale, just as Bob Hope was doing on a large scale, to the wounded men recuperating in California hospitals, as well as the men and women doing their training in the desert and oceanside camps.

I'll never forget the faces of the colored troops the first time they heard us do "Acc-cen-chu-ate the Positive." They must have been from the deepest part of Alabama or Mississippi, judging by their response. I don't think they had ever heard a white man sing like that. They beamed. Occasionally Nat Cole would come along and sing "Straighten Up and Fly Right," and, next to him, I think they enjoyed our arrangement of "Acc-Cent-Chu-Ate" as well as anything. As a matter of fact, a colored maid once said to me, "I am really surprised you are white, Mr. Mercer, we have always claimed you as one of our own." I received a postcard from the Abraham Lincoln Junior Boys Club of Chicago, upon which was written: "Dear Johnny Mercer: We have taken a vote and are pleased to inform you that you have been voted the most successful young colored singer of the year. Sincerely yours (signed) T.A.L.B.C. of C." I've still got it somewhere, and I wouldn't trade it for anything. Would you?

John also treasured a letter from the black Baltimore-born pianist and composer Eubie Blake, who wrote, among many other songs, "Memories of You" and "I'm Just Wild About Harry." He was seventy when he wrote the letter (which is in the Pullen Library) on November 21, 1953. (He lived to be a hundred years old.)

Dear Johnny

I saw and heard you on the Steve Allen show last night. Well first I want to tell you I am an old timer, and I've seen them all. Ophays, I mean. You are in my estimate the greatest Rhythm Singer of all Ophays I've ever heard. . . .

The term *ophay* was usually spelled *ofay*. It was black slang, purportedly the pig Latin for *foe*, meaning "white." But even by the 1940s, it had lost its aura of hostility and was used commonly by both black and white jazz musicians. It is nearly forgotten today, unknown even among most blacks.

Johnny continued his pace of songwriting, record producing, and running Capitol Records all through the war. In addition, he maintained a steady schedule of radio broadcasting, including *The Johnny Mercer Chesterfield Music Shop*. This show was on the air for fifteen minutes a night, five nights a week. Regulars on the show were Jo Stafford and the Pied Pipers, and the music director was Paul Weston. The show originated in NBC's Hollywood studio on Mondays through Thursdays, but on Fridays the show was done at such military installations as the U.S. Naval Hospital at Long Beach, California. The budget ran to about $14,000 a week (not so paltry a sum by the standards of the day), of which Johnny got $2,000, Paul Weston $1,640, and Jo Stafford $500.

These shows were all recorded for the Armed Forces Radio Service, and they still exist on tapes and CDs. They are remarkable on all levels, including the consistency of the performances—Johnny's own, and particularly those of Jo Stafford. Perhaps most striking of all is the performance of the band and the (for the time) almost avant-garde quality of the arrangements, many—but by no means all—of them by Paul Weston. Paul told me there was simply too much to be turned out each week for any one man to do. (One of the arrangers who wrote for him was Gil Evans.)

Many people remember those shows for the "Newsy Bluesies" Johnny would do. Right before the show someone would hand him the day's newspaper and he would improvise blues lyrics from the headlines. This was not a setup; he really hadn't seen the newspaper before going on the air.

Jo said, "I've been at parties where, after a couple of hours, he would start singing the blues about everybody in the room. He probably had been thinking a little bit ahead of time, but he couldn't have been too far ahead, because he didn't know who he was going to see."

It was a trick he could perform, as we shall see, to telling and cruel effect.

By 1944, Johnny's own records for Capitol had sold more than twelve million copies. He was now thirty-five, and Lloyd Shearer wrote of him at the time: "Above and behind his smiling eyes and button nose, he hides a trigger-like mind, an amazing memory, and a first-class intelligence. Despite the out-of-this-world impression he gives, he is really an exceptionally alert character."

Johnny denied to Shearer, however, that he had any business brains whatsoever. "I just rhyme a few words now and then," he told him. That's more of John's aw-shucks country-boy act. We see it again in a song Johnny wrote called "Little Old Tune," which purports to give advice on how to write a song. He recorded it on the last album he ever made, produced by Ken Barnes in England. "First you write a little old tune," he tells you, and then goes through the steps of the work. And when it's done and has become a success and you are being praised for it,

You act non-committal
and say, "Just a little
old tune."

John's habit of self-effacement may have been slightly disingenuous, but his habit of loyalty was anything but. As the *Savannah Evening Press* reported on December 20, 1945:

> Highlighting a lifelong friendship, Johnny Mercer, noted Savannah lyricist and composer, has just employed his hometown friend, Major Walter Rivers, as the press and public relations manager for Capitol Records Inc., recently formed phonograph recording company of which Mr. Mercer is president.
>
> This announcement was made here today by Mr. Mercer following his arrival last night. Both Mr. Mercer and Major Rivers are here to spend Christmas with their families. Accompanied by his wife, the former Cornelia McIntire, daughter of Mr. and Mrs. Frank McIntire, Major Rivers arrived earlier this month after battling the Japs on Saipan, Iwo Jima, and Okinawa. An officer in the United States Marines, Major Rivers spent a week in Japan after the occupation began. Major Rivers expects to take up his work with Mr. Mercer as soon as his terminal leave expires.
>
> It was recalled by an *Evening Press* reporter interviewing Messers Mercer and Rivers jointly today that the two Savannahians went to New York together a number of years ago to make their way in the show business. "Yes. Just say. 'Mercer made good and Rivers didn't' and I came back to Savannah to work in the bank," said Major Rivers.

The reporter didn't mention, and probably didn't know, that John and Walter Rivers were cousins.

Another returning veteran was a young man named Nicholas (Nick) Mamalakis, four years John's junior. When Johnny went home to Savannah in the summer of 1932, he found a new face in his brother Walter's office, that of Nick Mamalakis. His father had come to America from Greece and had gone into the restaurant business in Savannah. Nick graduated from Savannah High School in 1932, in the depth of the Depression, and went to work as a junior clerk for Walter Mercer, to whom he became utterly devoted, at the Mercer Insurance Agency. Nick recalled that whenever Johnny came home, he would drop by the office to say hello to his brother Walter and all the employees of Mercer Insurance.

As World War II approached, U.S. Naval Intelligence expanded, recruiting a Balkan-language division—Serbian, Bulgarian, Romanian, Albanian, and Greek. Nick spoke fluent Greek. He left Mercer Insurance and joined the navy.

He spent the last six months of his naval service in the U.S. Embassy in Athens. And then, like Walter Rivers, he came home. Walter Mercer called him into his office and handed him a check. He said he had been saving this money for Nick: the difference between his navy pay and what he would have earned in the office. He told Nick, "Now I want you to endorse this check over to me, and I'm going to sell you stock in the company."

Soon after that, the head of another insurance company approached Nick and offered him a half-interest partnership. "I turned him down flat," Nick told me. Long afterwards he described himself as the loving and honored slave of the Mercer family.

Later, Walter Mercer encouraged Nick to buy more stock in Mercer Insurance. Nick would spend fifty-five years with Mercer Insurance. After Walter retired, Nick was the majority shareholder and president of the company.

Seventeen

Ray Evans and Jay Livingston, both born in 1915, met at the University of Pennsylvania.

"I was taking banking and statistics at Wharton," Ray said. "I was playing clarinet and alto saxophone in the college band. Our piano player graduated. I recommended Jay and he auditioned for the job and got it. Then Jay became the bandleader. Alan Livingston, his brother, went into the band on saxophone.

"In those days, the eastern steamship lines used to hire college bands in the summer to play for dancers. In 1937 we had a sixty-day cruise into Russia on the Holland America Line. Nobody got to Russia in those days. But we did—Russia and Scandinavia. And then the next year we had a sixty-day cruise all around South America, down the west coast and up the east coast. We heard the tangos in Argentina and that wonderful Brazilian samba music. We had lots of cruises of the West Indies, including Cuba. We heard the sensational rumba music. Calypso in Jamaica. Coming up the Hudson River after one of the last trips, I said to Jay, being dumb, 'Let's stay in New York and write songs.' I did not realize how tough it was."

They had a 1941 hit with a song called "Good Bye Now," recorded by Martha Tilton. Jay was inducted into the army after Pearl Harbor, but spent most of his nine months there with asthma, after which he was given a medical discharge. Ray was kept out of service by a college football injury, which left him without cartilage in one knee. They resumed their writing.

"We came to California in 1944," Ray said. "We were struggling. Didn't know anybody here. It was really rough. We finally got a job doing a movie, with six songs in it. That had to be 1945. Martha Tilton was the star. She was recording for Capitol. She took us to meet Johnny Mercer so he could hear some songs we did for her and see if he wanted her to record any of them.

"He didn't record any of the songs. But Johnny had a radio show, *The Johnny Mercer Chesterfield Music Shop*. He wanted to do one of our songs, 'The Highway Polka.' Would we bring a copy down to Capitol Records? We couldn't get there fast enough. He performed the song on his show not once but two or three times. And he mentioned our names. 'A new song by Jay Livingston and Ray Evans.' My God! Maybe we were starting to break through. We got an idea: see if we could write some special songs for John. So we wrote a song called 'The Cat and the Canary,' the cat being a jazz musician and the canary being the singer in the band.

"We used to go to the little Capitol office on lower Vine Street, just off Sunset Boulevard, with a song in our pocket and ask the receptionist, 'Could we see Johnny Mercer?' Johnny was busy, and we got shuffled around a lot. Finally, one day she said to Johnny, 'These guys Jay and Ray have been out here two or three days. Could you listen to them?' We went in and we played the song for him. He said, 'I like it.' And once again, he did it on his radio show, and mentioned our names. We tried to write in the Mercer style, the kind of rhymes Johnny loved. We wrote a song called 'Band Baby,' about the kind of girl who hung around the bands. He did that several times and mentioned our names. Now people were starting to say, 'Who are these guys, writing songs for Johnny Mercer?'

"A few months later we get a call from Capitol, saying they were about to make a record with Betty Hutton. Do we have anything we'd like to submit for her? My God, now we're getting into the big leagues! We played them a song called 'Stuff Like That There.' She recorded it. It was on the charts for a few weeks.

"But we still weren't anywhere that was terribly important, and money was getting short. Jay and I were living in a five-dollars-a-week room in a home up in the Hollywood Hills and I was getting very discouraged. Then we got a call from Louis Lipstone, the head of the music department at Paramount Studios. He said, 'There's a movie we're making with Betty Hutton called *The Stork Club*.'

"Buddy DeSylva was producing it. He asked Johnny Mercer if he knew anybody who would write a song on speculation. Johnny recommended us. And we get this call in our little castle up in Hollywood Hills, living in one room. Did we want to try it? Over the weekend, we wrote three songs for Betty Hutton. Early the next week we go into Paramount and we played the three songs for Louis Lipstone.

"We went over and there we were, in a big producer's office, with the wonderful paneled walls and the soft lighting. Buddy DeSylva was such a nice man. He was kind of short, a round face. He liked one of the songs, 'I'm Just a Square in the Social Circle.' He said, 'I like it, I love it, I'll buy it.'

"About two weeks later we got a call from Louis Lipstone. He said, 'I'd like to see you in my office. We need someone to write songs for the shorts and things like that. We can't pay you very much, two hundred a week. But if you like it, it's a nine-to-five job.' We said, 'Of course!' He said, 'Okay, we'll give you a contract.' On the way out of his office, Jay said, 'Is it two hundred each or two hundred for both of us?' It was two hundred each.

"That was in August of 1946.

"The first thing we did for Paramount was a movie for Bob Hope. We were supposed to do songs for shorts and we start off doing a movie for Bob Hope called *Monsieur Beaucaire*. We did three songs.

"The biggest break came a few weeks later when there was a movie coming out called *To Each His Own*. It was a very obscure, abstruse title in those days. The publicity department called the music department and said, 'We're going to have a hard time selling this picture. Do you think you could get a song written to help us?' None of the top guys at Paramount would touch it. Victor Young, who wrote the score, said, 'I won't write a song with that dumb title.' So we did it without him. *Now* that phrase is part of the language, but it wasn't then.

"We said we could do it. It became the biggest hit of the whole decade of the 1940s, millions and millions of records. Several consecutive weeks, of the *Billboard* top-ten-selling records, *five* were different versions of 'To Each His Own.' The Ink Spots, Eddie Howard, Freddy Martin, Tony Martin, and the Modernaires. That's a *Guinness Book of Records* item.

"After that we were really in."

Livingston and Evans became enormously successful lyricists, though they also wrote music, collaborating with Henry Mancini, Victor Young, Percy Faith, Max Steiner, and many other composers. Their catalogue includes "Buttons and Bows," "Golden Earrings," "Que Será Será,"

"Never Let Me Go," "Tammy," "Dreamsville," "Mr. Lucky," "Dear Heart," "In the Arms of Love," and "Mona Lisa."

"And it all started with Johnny Mercer," Ray said. "Oh yes, by the way, the irony is that Johnny hated 'To Each His Own,' and Capitol was the only company that didn't record it. I'm told that when they'd have the executive sessions every week, they kept saying, 'Why didn't you record "To Each His Own"?' Johnny said, 'I don't like that song.' "

The number of careers Johnny started is beyond estimate. And his whole approach to producing records was to do the songs that *he* liked, with artists whom *he* liked and admired. Probably no record company in history was to such an extent the expression of the taste of one man. He was endlessly encouraging of other songwriters. Johnny told an interviewer for the ASCAP magazine:

"I'm crazy about songwriters. Harold Adamson says, 'I don't think there's anybody like songwriters,' and I kind of agree with him. They have this thing in common. They love songs. They're not a bit jealous of each other—once they've achieved some success of their own. I can remember being terribly jealous of a few writers when I was a young man, but after I got a few hits of my own, I didn't mind them at all. I've never been jealous since, of any writer. I love to hear a good song, no matter where it comes from."

One of the songwriters John encouraged was Peggy Lee, who in effect owed her career to Capitol Records. She had recorded with Benny Goodman, then married his guitarist, Dave Barbour, and retired to live quietly in Hollywood. Always agonizingly shy about performing, she decided to give it up entirely after the birth of her daughter, Nicki. Dave Dexter, by now a jazz producer at Capitol, planned a jazz album, to be issued on several 78 rpm records. It was unprecedented in jazz, and he asked her to be a part of it. Peg thought, "Well, I suppose I could get a babysitter and go down and sing a couple of songs."

On January 7, 1944, as World War II was grinding to a close, Peg recorded two songs, a blues called "Ain't Goin' No Place" and a standard by Lew Brown and Sammy Fain, "That Old Feeling." These two "sides" launched Peggy Lee's solo career, and her enormous record sales—at first singles, but then, with the arrival of the LP, albums—were, along with Nat Cole's sales, major factors in Capitol's success.

She had always tried her hand at lyrics—timidly, as she did most things. She showed some of them to Johnny. He was, she said, enormously encouraging and helpful, and in time she wrote (variously, with Victor

Young, Cy Coleman, Duke Ellington, and her husband, Dave Barbour) "It's a Good Day," "Mañana," "Goin' Fishin'," "I Don't Know Enough About You," "Where Can I Go Without You?", and "I Love Being Here with You," as well as a collection of brilliant lyrics for the Walt Disney film *Lady and the Tramp*.

It was just at that period when Capitol was first recording Peggy Lee that John wrote one of his most glorious lyrics, "Laura," one of his train songs: "And you see Laura / on the train that is passing through, / those eyes, how familiar they seem. . . ." The music was by David Raksin, one of the finest of all film composers. The melody was part of his score for the film *Laura* (in which Dana Andrews investigates the apparent murder of a beautiful girl, played by Gene Tierney).

Dave Raksin recalled: "When I was at Fox in 1944 I got assigned to *Laura* and I had to come up with a tune over the weekend, and I did. The tune turned out rather well. I've heard worse, and I've written worse. I suggested to the people at the studio that, judging by the response of the musicians and other people, it might be a good idea to put lyrics to it. They paid no attention at all. None. Until the picture was out and the letters started pouring in. I stopped counting when I had seventeen hundred in a profession where if you get six, that's a work of art. The stars, Gene Tierney and Dana Andrews and Judith Anderson and Vincent Price and Clifton Webb, and the director, Otto Preminger, and Darryl Zanuck all got letters. So the studio decided something should be done. Maybe they slipped word to the publisher, Jack Robbins. And Fox had a company with him.

"My wife was living in New York at the time. She played an acetate of the tune for my friend Dave Terry, a wonderful arranger. He played it for Oscar Hammerstein, who fell in love with the music and wanted to write a lyric to it. He got in touch with the publisher and they were about to let it go to him. All of a sudden Abe Olman, who was in charge of this part of the company, realized that if he let it go, it would go to Oscar's company, which would have been death for the song, since the other partner was Richard Rodgers, who was the scum of the earth, a swine. . . .

"Abe Olman sent me a lyric by a very famous lyricist whom I will not identify. It was a terrible lyric. A few days later Abe, whom I'd never met, called me and said, 'How'd you like the lyric?'

"I said, 'I don't.'

"He didn't know me, he thought I was some schmuck in Hollywood. He said, 'Who are you not to like it?'

"I said, 'The composer, Mr. Olman.'

"He turned out to be a wonderful guy, a dear man, and a good song-writer, by the way. He said, 'Who would you like to do it?'

"I said, 'Well, there's this guy out here I've never met. He's a marvelous lyricist, named Johnny Mercer.'

"He said, 'Okay, I'll send him around.'

"So Johnny came to see me. He said, 'Oh boy, what a great tune.' I gave him a copy of the tune and an acetate. He came back in a few days with the lyric. Somebody later said to me that I had changed the lyric. I said, 'I can just see myself changing Mercer's lyric!' It turned out that Johnny had two places where he had different words and couldn't choose and asked my opinion. I told him, 'I prefer this one,' 'I prefer that one.' And he accepted that. He said, 'You know, this kind of a tune needs a verse.' I made up a verse on the spur of the moment, and he wrote a lyric for it. It's very nice, but you never hear it.

"One time I had to play and sing it off the cuff at an ASCAP ceremony in a big theater in New York. I was so nervous that I didn't mention Johnny, which under ordinary circumstances I would have done. And Ginger sent me a nasty note. It made me think of how many times I've had to sit in audiences and read references in papers and books to Johnny Mercer's 'Laura.' "

John said of the song: "If a fellow plays me a melody that sounds like something, well, I try and fit the words to the sound of the melody. It has a mood, and if I can capture that mood, that's the way we go about it. *Laura* was that kind of a picture. It was predesigned, because Laura was a mystery. So I had to write 'Laura' with kind of a *misterioso* theme.

"That's hard, because there are so few notes. And because the intervals are tough, the key changes are strange. And at the time it came out, it was most strange. But since it has become so popular, it's easier now. But that kind of song is always difficult, because you have to write a lyric that's going to be a hit, and you don't have many notes to work with."

A hit the song surely was, and it remains a huge and important standard. Said Dave Raksin: "I'm told there are now well over four hundred recordings of 'Laura.' I haven't kept track of it. There is no way you can do it."

Meanwhile, Capitol seemed unable to do wrong. One day in 1947, Jo Stafford passed Country Washburn, talking with some of his cronies in a corridor at Capitol Records. "*There's* the girl who can do it," she heard him say. Washburn told her that he was planning a parody recording of

"Temptation" as it might be done by a hillbilly singer—the term in use in those days. He thought Jo could do it. Her mother, Anna York Stafford, was a Tennessean, a cousin of the World War I hero Sergeant Alvin York. And Jo really knew that music. So she made the record, under the pseudonym Cinderella Stump. Released as "Timtayshun," the record was a huge hit. The record industry, and the press, speculated over who Cinderella really was. Not even Jo's manager knew. When he found out, he was furious, and when he asked her what kind of deal she had made for herself, she told him there was no deal: she had made the record for fun, and for scale, and was receiving no royalty at all.

The label recorded "That Old Black Magic" with Johnny Johnson. Mercer had hits with "Accentuate the Positive," written with Harold Arlen, and "On the Atchison, Topeka and the Santa Fe," written with Harry Warren for the 1946 Judy Garland film *The Harvey Girls*. He had seen the name on the side of a railway car, and, as was his wont, made a note of it. He said, "I had penciled that title down in a book, and when I got that show, I had a song ready for it. I told Harry, 'This movie's about the railroad. Why don't we write a song called 'The Atchison, Topeka and the Santa Fe.' " Harry went to work. Later he said, "You never were in trouble with Johnny, no matter what you wrote. He never asked you to take a note out or said, 'I can't find a rhyme here.' " The song won the Academy Award that year, John's first of four. His own recording of the song became the biggest-selling record he ever had.

Jo Stafford had a hit with "Out of This World." Indeed, she had a seven-year run of hits on Capitol, ten of them duets with Gordon MacRae. (In the course of her career, including a post-Capitol period with Columbia Records, she had a total of 110 Top Forty hits, and was widely considered to be the preeminent female vocalist in the country.)

With the war's end, Capitol took on yet another new face, a young man whose influence on American culture (and, hence, world culture) is impossible to evaluate, for reasons we will see in due course. The young man was Alan Livingston, Jay Livingston's younger brother.

Alan recounted: "I came out of the service and said to myself, 'Before I settle down, I want to see what the West Coast is like.' I hitched a ride on an army plane, sitting on a bucket seat, hedgehopping across the country. I had no money, and I knew nobody. Capitol was the only West Coast label. It was very small, but they had some great records. Capitol was looking for a copywriter in the advertising department. An employment agency got me an appointment with the personnel director. I was still in uniform. He sent me over to see Jim Conkling. Jim had been at Dartmouth with Paul Weston.

"Jim was Johnny Mercer's assistant, but he was functioning as A and R head. Mercer was in New York, writing *St. Louis Woman*. Jim interviewed me. He was interested in me, but he said, 'The only thing we're looking for is someone to produce children's records. We're not in that field. It's very small.' "

Alan Livingston was hired at a hundred dollars a week and given a small office with a secretary. He recalled: "I said to myself, 'Children would like to hear funny sounds on records, funny voices. I'll have animals talking. Where would the animals be? The circus. Who's going to talk to the animals? A clown. I decided on a story format that became *Bozo at the Circus*. I wrote this album, but I did something that had never been done. I decided it should be done with a book. It was on four 78 rpm sides, two records. And Bozo said to the children, 'Every time I blow my whistle, you turn the page,' even though they couldn't read—they were three and four years old. But the text would be on one page, a picture on the other. I called it a Record Reader. Capitol released it, and it sold a million copies, which was unheard of. Capitol was delighted, and they wanted more. After that I wrote more of them, *Bozo in the Sea, Bozo and the Birds, Bozo on the Farm*. Billy May wrote the music. He was fabulous.

"I approached Warner Bros., who had no record company then, and got the exclusive rights to their cartoon characters, Bugs Bunny, Daffy Duck, Elmer Fudd. That helped launch Tweety Bird. Then I went to Walter Lantz and got the rights to Woody Woodpecker. He said, 'Every time I laugh, you turn the page.' Then I went to Disney and got the rights to original cast albums. Those were very successful.

"I built a Capitol children's library that became forty percent of Capitol's business."

This was an astounding achievement for a young man only two years out of the army who had never been in the record business before. Capitol then asked him to do other albums.

"Walter Rivers called me one day. He said, 'There's a woman here, a Peruvian Indian. She doesn't speak a word of English, but she has an unusual voice with a four-and-a-half octave range. Nobody knows what to do with her.' I heard her, we had a translator, and I went into the studio with her. That was Yma Sumac, and she was a big hit.

"And then Jim Conkling went to Columbia records, and Glenn Wallichs made me vice president in charge of A and R. I produced records with

Nat Cole, Stan Kenton. And I had other producers working under me, Lee Gillette, Dave Cavanaugh, Voyle Gilmore. I had a good career at Capitol, and I was in demand. RCA wanted me. They wanted me *out of Capitol* as much as they wanted me for themselves. I kept turning them down."

Dave Dexter recalled that by 1946 the little publication he had started and built, *The Capitol News,* had a monthly circulation of 800,000 worldwide. The company also marketed phonographs, needles, and other accoutrements. Capitol's promotion department was so aggressive that, according to Dexter, writing in *Billboard* in 1967, "it had inaugurated a system of supplying radio announcers with special vinylite pressings of all its new singles, which led to the lamentable dog-eat-dog radio exploitation system in effect today." Dexter said he and other executives would sit up nights typing labels that read, "This special pressing exclusively for Peter Potter," each one personalized for the intended announcer.

"With the end of World War II," Dexter wrote, "Capitol had accelerated its annual sales from a modest $200,000 in 1942 to $750,000 in 1943, then $2,250,000 in 1944 and a truly impressive $5,100,000 in 1945. That year Capitol marketed fourteen albums and forty-eight singles."

The Big Three of the recording industry, Dexter noted, had become the Big Four.

"Mercer was not only writing one hit after another as a lyricist, but his records as a vocalist were considered smashes. [And he] also kept a strong hand in signing and recording the talent he favored.

"Wallichs was tireless in guiding Capitol from the administrative and sales ends. He hit the road and set up company branches and indie distributors, and with the end of World War II he pioneered Capitol's entrenchment throughout Europe."

The war over, the company continued to expand. Its first public stock issue was offered on April 30, 1946. By 1948, artists were recording on tape rather than on acetate discs. Then the 45 rpm singles and 33⅓ rpm "long-playing" records began to replace the old 78s. Still the company continued its remarkable string of hits with Tex Williams's "Smoke, Smoke, Smoke," Peggy Lee's "Mañana," and Nat Cole's "Nature Boy."

Johnny signed a young man born in Los Angeles of Mexican parentage, a drummer who worked for Stan Kenton and sang extremely well. His real name was Andres Rabago. He recorded for Capitol a Latin tune titled "Bésame Mucho," and it sold half a million copies. By this time he was using the name Andy Russell. He did a number of these Latin tunes for the label, often one chorus in Spanish and one in English. Wallichs, a pioneer in the record industry for his attention to foreign markets, made sure Andy's records were released throughout Latin America. Later Andy told me that when he was going through a divorce and just wanted to get away, he took a trip to Mexico City. A huge crowd met his plane. He was astounded: he had no idea that he was so popular in the Spanish-speaking world. Still later, when his career in the United States faltered, he moved to Mexico City. In the 1950s and '60s, he was the biggest singing star in the entire Spanish-speaking world. And this was due to the aesthetics of Johnny Mercer and the business acumen of Glenn Wallichs.

"By 1950," Dave Dexter wrote in *Billboard*, "there were no more radio announcers. Now they were disc jockeys. Guys who didn't know a tenor sax from a tuba were spinning discs on three speeds and telling listeners what to buy. They were receiving hundreds of records a week from scores of companies. Payola became evident. More stress was being made on promoting, merchandising, and selling. The 'little' record shops began to fold."

Johnny would write of the rise of Capitol:

Busy, happy times; and a modern success story. It was unthinkable to compete with the big established record companies then, but we did, and succeeded. Nowadays everybody goes into business for themselves. Everybody seems to have his own recording company, and I wonder if it's good or not. Did we open Pandora's box or pave the way for independent enterprises? I suppose it depends on what you hear on the records. God knows, there are a lot of them I wish had never been made.

And through it all, the company maintained a reputation for unfailing honesty. "We were a bunch of Boy Scouts," Paul Weston said years later to Jo Stafford, by then his wife.

With the war over, Johnny mused:

Now it was all to be back to the swimming pools and business as usual. Or was it? Little did we all dream that seemingly every G.I. who had ever passed through California would return there to live, bringing his family and two or three cars. Little did we dream what a change the Second World War was to make upon our neighborly, friendly, and leisurely America, and on the sweet, orange-scented Los Angeles we had known.

There would be another change in John's life. With his company a huge success, he was determined to adopt another child. He returned to the same agency in Augusta, Georgia, through which they had adopted Mandy.

Mandy recalls that when she was eight, Ginger went to Augusta to receive the new child. "She came back on the train," Mandy recounted. "My dad said we were going to the station to pick up her and my new baby brother. It was the most exciting time of my life. I wanted a baby brother so badly. Actually I wanted a big brother, but a baby brother was all right, too. He was only a few weeks old. He was *tiny*."

Named John Jefferson Mercer, he would always be called Jeff.

Eighteen

At Judy Garland's funeral service in New York City in 1969, James Mason, her costar in *A Star Is Born,* said, "She was the most sympathetic, the funniest, the sharpest, and the most stimulating woman I ever knew."

Singer Mel Tormé wrote: "Had he added the adjectives 'frustrating, inspiring, devious, prank-loving, calculating,' he would have also hit the mark." This comment is found in his book *The Other Side of the Rainbow,* an account of his weeks as a special-material writer for her 1963 CBS television series *The Judy Garland Show,* an experience he found exhausting and frustrating. Tormé's image of himself was innocent of modesty, and that he should have collided with an ego like hers is hardly surprising. But Mel was not stupid, and he wrote, "Very few sacred cows can and did get away with some of the things Judy did throughout her later life. But she prevailed. She created a mystique that served her well through some incredibly troubled times: broken marriages, suicide attempts, canceled appearances. The world seemed perfectly willing to give her one more chance in perpetuity. After all, she was Dorothy. She had taken us all to Oz. . . ."

In her early days at MGM, Garland described herself as a "fat little frightening pig with pigtails," and Louis B. Mayer called her "my little hunchback." Tormé wrote, "She was short, high-waisted, small-breasted, with extremely bony wrists and arms and undistinguished legs. . . ." One of her biographers, Gerald Clarke, in his book *Get Happy,* refers to her "unfortunate proportions" and says, "Small—she was just under five feet in 1936—she had a disappearing neck, a big chest, a very short waist and long, long legs."

So much does our society value good looks in women that, whatever her other attributes—brains or talent or personality—it must be a cruel thing to grow up into a woman who isn't at least moderately pretty, especially for a woman in show business, who is always on display. Nothing brought this home to me as sharply as an incident in Dusseldorf in 1984. My friend Sarah Vaughan was onstage in the Tonhalle, rehearsing for a take on one of a number of songs I had written for her and making me almost gasp at her brilliance. As I stood beside her, coaching her, a German TV cameraman said to her, in the nicest way, "Is there anything I can do for you, Miss Vaughan?"

She said, "Yes. Make me look like Lena Horne."

I realized what a lifetime of pain infused that quick, sharp reply.

How must it have been for Garland, whose "friend" at MGM was the beautiful Lana Turner, always stealing men from her?

Though her *Wizard of Oz* image as Dorothy was one of innocence, Garland was sexually predatory. Gerald Clarke, after summarizing her early encounters with Freddie Bartholomew, Jackie Cooper, and Billy Halop, writes: "Who finally introduced her to the pleasures of sex, and where and when, is a question without an answer: what is certain is that Judy had lost her virginity by the age of fifteen. . . . Judy was a free spirit, unencumbered by guilt or inhibition. On occasion, indeed, she was almost breathtakingly bold and aggressive." At seventeen, she pursued pianist and wit Oscar Levant, who apparently kept their relationship platonic. She went after clarinetist and bandleader Artie Shaw, whom she met when she was fifteen. She told her mother she was in love with him. Shaw also kept it platonic, and his assertions to that effect are to be taken at face value: he never hesitated to name the flowers he had picked in Hollywood's garden.

Garland was born Frances Gumm in 1922 in Grand Rapids, Michigan, the daughter of a cold, ambitious, adulterous, manipulative show-business mother who didn't love her and a homosexual father who did. Her mother, Ethel Gumm, eventually estranged her daughter completely, and got a job at the Douglas Aircraft factory in Santa Monica, California, at the height of Garland's fame. Early in 1951, she dropped dead of a heart attack in the company parking lot. It was a bit of information Johnny Mercer stored in that filing cabinet memory of his for later retrieval, as we shall see.

Garland's father was Frank Gumm; he changed his last name to Garland after the youngest of his three daughters changed hers and became famous. Both parents were fringe performers in minor-league vaudeville, and at some points he ran movie theaters. He had to leave one town when the word got around that he was practicing his predilection on a couple of local high school boys in the back row of his movie house. It is scarcely surprising that many of the men in Garland's life were bisexual, as in the case of Tyrone Power, or homosexual, as was Vincente Minnelli, her director on the movie *The Clock,* whom she married. Some of the extras returned early from lunch one day to glimpse Garland and Minnelli in an alcove, where they thought they were unobserved. But the lighting men on the catwalk above had a perfect view of the performance, and the word spread rapidly among the cast and crew. "Is it true?" one of the extras was asked. "Was Judy really going down on Vincente Minnelli on the subway set?"

Yes, it was, and this seemed to be her primary and preferred method of sexual interaction throughout her life. After she married Minnelli, whose homosexuality was an open secret, and became pregnant, the noted orchestrator composer Conrad Sallinger said to André Previn, "On what? Spit?"

The daughter from that union, Liza Minnelli, shows the same leaning toward homosexual men.

When and where Garland met Johnny Mercer is unknown, but the show business world is a small one, almost a village, and two of his friends, Harold Arlen and Yip Harburg, had written the songs for *The Wizard of Oz.* It is almost impossible that he didn't meet her at about that time. And in 1940, when she was eighteen and he was thirty-one, she and John recorded a duet of Cole Porter's "Friendship," after which Mercer, according to Gerald Clarke, "wandered around in a lovesick daze."

No one knows when the relationship with Ginger turned cold. The evidence suggests that she didn't love John so much as she loved the status that went with being Mrs. Johnny Mercer; even her grandson said that. Furthermore, Ginger had not even a faint perception of the scope and character of John's artistic gifts. This became evident to me in conversations with her after his death. Finally, she never ceased to shove Bing Crosby in his face. She set up a rumor that she could have married Crosby, but this is unlikely, since it was Crosby who dumped her. Crosby's money and success were later waved in John's face, and it is likely that this began early, before John became truly wealthy.

It seems that everyone in the Hollywood world was aware of John's relationship with Garland, including Ginger—especially Ginger, who long afterwards told even Mandy's son, Jamie, about it. She would still be bitter about it more than forty years later.

Mickey Goldsen said, "Judy was a very attractive girl, and very kind of friendly-like, and Johnny fell madly in love with her. It was all over town."

Howie Richmond said, "Johnny was a very attractive human being. He was gentle with women, he was respectful of women, he was tender. I think she would have been the initiator."

"Oh, absolutely!" added Rose Gilbert.

One version of the story, still in circulation, holds that Johnny asked Ginger for a divorce, telling her he was in love with Garland and wanted to marry her. Supposedly, she told him he could have the divorce, since she had heard on the radio that morning that Garland had just eloped to Las Vegas with composer David Rose, and left John to the shock of finding out for himself. The story seems improbable—indeed impossible—since Garland's engagement to Rose had been announced in the press three days before a lavish June 1 engagement party on the lawn of Garland's home on Stone Canyon Road, with the Bobby Sherwood Orchestra from John's own Capitol Records providing the music. The six hundred guests included a spectacular collection of Hollywood luminaries, including James Stewart, Lana Turner, Joan Crawford, George Murphy, John Payne, Ann Shirley, and—according to Gerold Frank's biography *Judy*—Johnny and Ginger Mercer. So John was aware of the pending wedding to David Rose.

John once said: "I loved Judy Garland. She was marvelous when she was about seven years old, which is when I first saw her. She worked with her sisters and her mother played the piano. They had little dowdy black dresses on. And I think they were out of work. But she just knocked everybody right off their seats when she sang. Soon she was under contract to a picture company, and she was prominent by the time she was twelve. She made *Pigskin Parade,* I think, when she was about twelve."

The picture was released in 1936, by which time Garland was fourteen.

It will be recalled that one of the friends of John's childhood was Jimmy Downey, who had moved to New York at about the same time John did. He married a model and magazine editor named Betty McLaughlin, and adopted her two children, who thereby acquired the name Downey. One of these children is Robert Downey, the film director, whose son in turn is the actor Robert Downey, Jr.

Jean Bach quotes what she and her husband—writer and television producer Bob Bach—heard from Betty Downey: "Betty and Jimmy Downey had been very tight with Ginger and Johnny and would go and visit them in Hollywood when they were still living on De Longpre."

When Garland eloped with David Rose, MGM telephoned her in Las Vegas to tell her she must return immediately for work on the film *Babes on Broadway*. On their return, MGM gave them an elaborate wedding party at the Coconut Grove in Los Angeles.

Jean Bach continued: "At that party, Johnny was dancing with her. They were dancing closer and closer, getting drunker and drunker. They were both working on the same lot and she apparently asked him to have lunch with her the next day in her dressing room. They plighted their troth in her bungalow. And, Betty said, Johnny went home walking around the house in a lovesick haze. Apparently the passion was mutual. They were seeing each other every day, and Ginger was very put out.

"Betty Downey figured she had to put an end to this, so she took a cab to MGM, got on the lot, marched into Judy's bungalow, and said, 'This has got to stop. Johnny's walking around in a daze. You must do something about this.'

"Judy said, 'You're right. I've just gotten married.' So she agreed, and said it was affecting her, too, and they signed off."

Another witness to the affair is composer Hugh Martin, who with lyricist Ralph Blane wrote the score for the 1944 film *Meet Me in St. Louis,* one of Garland's most successful films (directed by Vincente Minnelli). That score contains, in addition to the title song, "The Boy Next Door," "The Trolley Song," and "Have Yourself a Merry Little Christmas." When the affair began, Hugh had been working as choral director on *I Walk with Music,* Mercer's first Broadway show, written with Hoagy Carmichael.

Hugh told me: "It was a little scandalous. I loved them both and I don't want to make them look bad. But they didn't behave very well. The night before Judy married David Rose, she had a wing-ding with Johnny in the garden of a friend. It caused quite a few raised eyebrows, and it was not very appropriate. As Hattie McDaniel says in *Gone with the Wind,* 'It ain't fittin'.'

"Judy was always fascinated by Johnny. When I met her, one of the first things she asked me to do was would I please teach her 'The Dixieland Band.' Which I did, and she sang it wonderfully. She said, 'Don't I sound square?' I said, 'I don't think so. I think Johnny would love it.' She always wanted his opinion. He was an icon to her, and of course she was to him.

"I saw them together at a party at Arthur Freed's house, and they misbehaved again. This was when I was at MGM, probably 1943 or '44." That, of course, was the period when Ralph Blane and Hugh were working on *Meet Me in St. Louis*.

"I just think they were always attracted to each other, and they couldn't resist. And neither of them had a very high moral account."

Garland's relationship with Mercer, then, began before her marriage to David Rose.

Rose Gilbert said, "Johnny really loved her. He truly did. That much I know."

And the affair went on for years, surviving Garland's marriage to Minnelli and her serial infidelities and bouts with pills and alcohol and suicide attempts. Whatever its hiatuses, the affair resumed at a party at Jean Bach's house in New York. Garland was about to open at the Palace Theater, with Hugh Martin as her accompanist and music director, after a triumphant series of performances in Europe. The date of the opening was October 16, 1951.

Jean Bach said, "Bob and I were then living at 50 Charles Street—the location of the original Nick's, when it was a speakeasy—and just starting out in life. You went up a few steps to a dining area and then French doors that opened onto a huge terrace with trees and chairs and gravel. It was great for parties, because people could get intoxicated and go out on the terrace and look at the town. It was a little chilly and I had already taken in the chair pads.

"The party was made up of people who were very suitable and sympathetic, including Willard Robison. We had one of those horrible little pianos with a truncated keyboard that had been used in a nightclub. Strayhorn and Ellington put 'Tonk' together on that piano. Betty and Jim Downey were there.

"The evening progressed. A lot of drinking. It was the Village. I had a low coffee table, a great huge thing in front of a sofa, and Judy sat down there and started to sing, and had everybody crying. She sang 'Over the Rainbow,' and she was sobbing, everybody was sobbing and clutching at their throats. And suddenly she stopped in mid-song and handed me her glass and said, 'Could I have about half a glass of bourbon, please?' I thought, *I don't want her for my best friend. She turns the tears off like that.* And I brought her the drink. She took a drink and went back to crying again. It was very funny. She had a great sense of drama. At one point she knelt down in front of Willard Robison, and said, 'You've always been pure. I so envy you and admire you.' And she was carrying on about how she had to make compromises.

"It got pretty late and people started leaving. Suddenly it was just Bob and me. We were pretty beat and had to get up in the morning. So I said, 'Don't empty any ashtrays, let's go straight to bed.' Our bedroom looked out over Charles Street. I peeked through the blinds and I saw a limo out in front. I said, 'I thought you said everybody's gone? Somebody forgot their car.' With that we went to bed.

"It turned out the next day that Johnny and Judy had gone out on that terrace. And, as I said, I had taken in all the chair pads. I had some army cots out there. They continued on until the dawn out there."

We are left to wonder whether Garland bothered to tell John that her current lover, actor Glenn Ford, was in New York with her. She had that capacity to carry on multiple affairs in a kind of counterpoint, but John presumably accepted it.

John's niece Nancy knew of their affair. She said: "He told my grandmother [Miss Lillian] everything, and *she* told *me* almost everything. She told me that he told her he was in love with Judy Garland, and that he and Ginger were going to get a divorce. I remember my grandmother didn't give advice but she tried in her way to discourage him. I think I was in the room and they were talking on the phone. And because I was in the room, I think that's why she told me about it. I was a teenager. I think it was in the house on Gwinnett Street. So that would mean it was before 1953."

Rose Gilbert said, "Johnny came to Ginger and asked for a divorce. That's what he told Wolfe and me." (This would make it at least the second such request.) "He told Ginger, 'You can have anything you want.' He told her he was going to marry Judy Garland.

"Ginger said, 'I would like to take my sister on a trip to China. We'll go by boat. When I come home, if you still feel the same way, you can have your divorce.' He thanked her, put her on the boat, sent her and her sister off first-class. Midway, I think it was, she got infectious hepatitis. They sent her home by plane. They put her in Cedars Sinai Hospital. I went to see her. You had to go in with a mask on. Very infectious. She seemed to be all right when I was there.

"Now this is hearsay from me; this is what my husband told me. Wolfe told me the doctor had told John that Ginger was going to die. And when John went in to see her, Ginger said, 'Will you stay with me? I'm really frightened.'

"He said, 'I'll stay with you as long as you live.'"

"And that cut off the divorce and anything else. Because Johnny was a man who would never break a promise."

An undated letter from John paints a less alarming picture. Since it refers to Mandy's family, and her son Jamie was born on November 19, 1961, we know that it was at least later than that date, possibly two or three years later. It reads:

> Mom:
>
> Hope all are well. Ginger arrived yesterday and went right to the hospital. Seems she picked up what looks like hepatitis on her trip. Will know tomorrow.
>
> Outside of looking yellow—she seems fine—and had as good a time as any two unescorted ladies can have, I imagine.
>
> Jeff doing pretty well in school. Mandy's family fine.
>
> Will write when there's time. Tell everybody to try and stay well, it gets too lonesome as we get older.
>
> Still on the wagon. Feel fine. Love to Big N.
>
> Kiss Ba-N.A.A. for me.
>
> Love you.
>
> [Signed in pencil] *Bubba.*

But that's not the way Mandy remembers that period.

"They fought all the time, mostly about money. She'd say, 'You're trusting this guy.' She said he would give money to any bum who asked for it. 'If you lend money to this hanger-on, you're never going to see it again, and we're never going to be like the Crosbys.' "

One sees in this a pattern of behavior John learned from his father—and his mother's insistence that he always be generous. And given Ginger's history with Crosby, one can understand that the references were intended to hurt.

"Of course they were both always loaded," Mandy said. "She was a terrible alcoholic. I used to talk to my dad about it and he told me it was none of my business. They were thinking of splitting up. My mother's sister's husband had just died of cancer, and so Mom and her sister went on a tour to the Orient on a ship. She got hepatitis and had to come back. She had to be quarantined when she came home. We had to wear masks to come and see her. And afterward the doctor told her, 'Don't drink.'

"So then she said to him, 'Please, it's so boring not drinking. I see everyone else drunk.' He said, 'Well, you can have a little wine, just to hold in your hand.' So we'd go out and she'd order a carafe of wine for the table. But she was the only one who drank it. She was always drinking her wine.

"She resented the money he sent to his family in Savannah. She even resented money he gave to her own sisters and her mother."

The late Jimmie Hancock, brother of Johnny's close childhood friend Dick Hancock, said, "Ginger and Savannah were not real hot for each other. There was some feeling in the family. I don't think anybody was really antagonistic toward her, but in some aspects some of the family didn't totally approve of Ginger from the beginning. I think in part it was because she was Jewish. And she was in show business and all kinds of terrible things like that. It just didn't rub the right way with Old Savannah."

I asked the late Steve Allen for his impressions of Ginger. Steve, a man who hardly ever said a harsh word about anyone, told me in 1998: "Although I found it easy enough to talk to John I cannot recall a single comfortable conversational exchange with Ginger. It wasn't that I disliked Ginger. My reaction to her could be more accurately described as blank. John, by contrast, was as he always was on the screen—cute, thoughtful, charming, naturally likeable."

Steve's impression of Ginger was in accord with that of many others. It was a sort of "Knock knock. Is anybody home?" You felt in her presence as if you were passing your hand through smoke. And she had a peculiar talent for making you uncomfortable. Jo Stafford said that during the Capitol years and the period of *The Johnny Mercer Chesterfield Music Shop,* Ginger was never part of their group, almost never attended a broadcast.

John was bitter about other aspects of their relationship. She had never wanted the children, and they knew it. John would say, "Can't we just go to church on Sunday and be a family?" She never did.

As the years went by, he visited Savannah—and New York—more and more frequently without her. If she didn't like Savannah (and she had reason not to) this could only have added to the alienation between them. A handwritten (in pencil) letter to his mother reveals his love for both her and his native city:

Mother, my darling:

In receipt (recipe) of your two letters, for which much thanks. A cause to stop, reflect and appreciate—the wonderful, warm and loving glow and effect they have given off for all these years—keeping us informed (in the most *entertaining way) about the "goings-on" at home, with all the chit-chat and gossip so* indigenous to a town the size of Savannah. Memories of one's boyhood are among the most dear one ever has, I suppose, and to be reminded of them in such an affectionate way, especially when one has had the great good luck to grow up in Savannah, is bliss unalloyed and a continuous source of pleasure of the highest order. If I seem extraordinary in my praise, it is only that I am hoping to thank you for keeping alive, in such a wise, appreciative way, all the old, gentle ways of life, through your letters to me. Oh, that I had saved them! You would probably be a literary genius right now, if you could spare the time from being such a charming, witty, attractive and beautiful woman and mother.

Don't be discouraged by the passing of time, darling; just hold on to all the nice, honest, tried-and-true old things and accept the good new ones as a blessing from the Almighty—from whom all blessings flow!

As indeed, they must. Else why would he single out a little "cracker" boy or strange people from all over the world to bring his benefits to it?

The inventors, doctors, artists, etc., all must have someone special to be so "gifted." Maybe mothers like you! You know someone said once, "God couldn't be everywhere—that's why he invented mothers."

Anyway, life is like a long link or chain of circumstances, and it's great when—primarily because of parents—you start out on the right road. The other one is so tough—and influences and help of friends made early helps continually to "stay on the right side, sister"!

Our old leisurely way of life has changed into a new concept—with more leisure time, but fewer places to enjoy it. Still any thinking person must try to keep as much beauty and love alive as he can, to affect all the "benefits" of super-markets, TV, and assembly line civilization.

Stay well, my dear mother, and think of us when you can.

I'm so anxious to have Mandy and Jeff see something of Savannah. It would do them so much good to know that way of life—and their family—with its philosophy of loyalty and the old Southern politeness and manners, which seem to be so fast going by the board in these money-grabbing, hard-drinking, war-like *times.* [The letter, as usual, is undated, but this reference suggests it was written during the Korean War.]

I love you. Don't be discouraged. Try and meet some of the nice young people. There are some. They'll restore your faith in human nature.

Love to my brothers, and all the family.

A big kiss for Julie and Nancy; and tell Nancy not to plug those things on the wrong kilocycle—she might find herself doing the hucklebuck in the automatic dishwasher.

Take it easy—
John

Hi, diddle dumpling
My son John
One shoe off, and one shoe on etc.
XXOOXXOOXXOOXX

(The reference to Nancy—or Big Nancy—is to the maid, not to John's niece.)

Mickey Goldsen told me a revealing story about John's sensitivity as a Southerner. It concerned the movie *Ruby Gentry*, released in 1953, in which Jennifer Jones plays a Southern woman of, as they used to say, easy virtue, who marries a wealthy man to spite the man who loves her.

Mickey said: "Johnny was very defensive about being a Southerner, and about the South.

"After Johnny and I had severed our business relationship as partners in Capitol's publishing—I published some of his songs later—Heinz Roemheld said to me, 'I wrote a theme for the movie I think is great. If you can get Johnny Mercer to write the lyrics, I'll give you the publishing.' We got a projection room, I brought Johnny. They rolled the movie. It had to do with unpleasant incidents and the overall picture didn't make the South look good.

"As we walked out, I said, 'That's a beautiful theme, Johnny.'

"He said, 'Yeah, but I won't do it. I don't like the way they treated the South.' The song—Mitchell Parish wrote the lyric—went on to be a big hit, called 'Ruby.' And I lost the publishing. Johnny was very serious."

All of these things, no doubt, contributed to John's abiding melancholy: the unhappy marriage to Ginger, the odd protracted love affair with Judy

Garland, his distance from the South and Savannah, his perpetual desire to go home; and we can speculate that these factors contributed to his drinking. What went on between John and Garland after that encounter at Jean Bach's party is unknown. Garland died of an overdose of sleeping pills on June 22, 1969. Nancy Gerard was with John in New York at the time.

Nancy said, "Any time I went to New York, it was because Johnny invited me. Johnny and I went a lot of places together. I met everyone with him. She had died, and he was very sad. We were walking somewhere. He said he wasn't feeling so copacetic, or something like that. I said that I know you're very sad about Judy Garland, and he thanked me for my solicitude. He acknowledged it. He was very different that week."

That is about as close as John ever came to discussing the affair with anyone. Despite its public character, he was silent about it. But I think his sense of discretion informs one of his greatest songs, "One for My Baby," published in 1943 and widely considered a memoir of the affair with Garland. The song contains the lines:

> *Could tell you a lot*
> *but that's not*
> *in a gentleman's code.*

It is also widely known that "That Old Black Magic," published in 1942, is about Garland, and in view of her proclivities, the sexual subtext is beyond doubting:

> *That old black magic has me in its spell,*
> *that old black magic that you weave so well,*
> *those icy fingers up and down my spine,*
> *the same old witchcraft when your eyes meet mine,*
> *the same old tingle that I feel inside,*
> *and then that elevator starts its ride,*
> *and down and down I go,*
> *round and round I go,*
> *like a leaf that's caught in the tide.*
> *I should stay away, but what can I do?*
> *I hear your name, and I'm aflame,*
> *aflame with such a burning desire*
> *that only your kiss can put out the fire;*
> *for you are the lover I have waited for,*

the mate that fate had me created for,
but every time your lips meet mine,
darling down and down I go,
round and round I go,
in a spin loving the spin that I'm in,
under that old black magic called love.

Sublimating personal experience into lyrics, Mercer had a capacity to wed passion with masterful craftsmanship, as is evident in this song. Excepting "When the World Was Young," which consists of many choruses, "That Old Black Magic" is probably the longest lyric Mercer ever wrote. And it comprises only two sentences and a question.

Amazing.

Nineteen

Everyone I interviewed who knew John well would begin his or her comments with some variant on: "Well, you know, John drank."

No kidding.

His friends exchanged stories about his drunken insults. One that I heard involved a prominent actor whom John insulted at (as usual) some party. He said, "You never could act! And, what's more, you're too short!" And he took a swing at the man, who, in response, gave him a push, sending Johnny sprawling. The next day, the actor, feeling remorse for the incident, called Johnny and apologized. John said, "Oh, it's all right. I thought you were Alan Ladd."

He once told Margaret Whiting, "You sing too fuckin' loud!"

His close companions during the period of *The Johnny Mercer Chesterfield Music Shop* were, of course, Paul Weston and Jo Stafford. Jo recalled: "We did *Chesterfield* and then we did a summer replacement show for Bob Hope for Pepsodent. And so we were together five days a week. We had no tape in those days, so we did two *Music Shop* shows a day, one at five o'clock for the East and one at eight o'clock for the West. We had some very entertaining eight o'clock shows, because the minute the five o'clock show was over, all the players would make a beeline for a place called the Tropics, which was right across the street. A South Seas bar with palm trees.

"But I never saw Johnny out of shape for a broadcast. He held back. We were on for twenty-six weeks at the end of 1944. The show did well, as far as ratings were concerned. The reason it went off, and I'd forgotten about this until recently because I just couldn't believe it, was because they said Johnny sounded too black.

"Paul always said that when we were doing that five-days-a-week radio show was the happiest time that he ever saw John. I guess five days a week, when John got up in the morning he knew exactly what he was going to do that day. And he loved being surrounded by all the musicians. The whole atmosphere was conducive to happiness. And it really was. But there was certainly melancholy there, all the time."

John listed a number of ailments he had suffered in his life, although he conspicuously failed to mention a hernia from which he suffered for years until he mustered the courage to get it repaired. He continued:

Despite all the occupational hazards, I would not have changed my career for any other under the sun. You'd think there'd be a few callouses from sliding off bar stools or dodging tomatoes and eggs. But no, the only two ailments I left out are the gout, which probably comes in a bottle, and a thrown-out back, which I got from the salubrious pastime of jogging. Forget it! I'm staying at my desk whether you like my songs or not. Whether they get recorded or not, I'm sticking to writing, even if it has to get lost in a lower drawer or some dusty attic. . . .

Oh yes, and there was a peaceful evening in the kitchen when I stuck an icepick through my thumb. . . .

You'll notice I haven't mentioned malaise du coeur, *a wounded psyche, nor any sadness of the spirit, but I've had them. You may find traces of them in my songs, but I hope it's the only place you do. I'm a private person and I never gossip. I don't approve of gossip. At least half of it's incorrect, and the poor object of the gossip winds up guilty by innuendo.*

A man's personal life should be his own unless, like some, he prefers to parade it in public for vanity or profit. I couldn't share my private ecstasies with anyone except the person who helped create them, no more than I would annoy anyone with my personal griefs. Memory to me is a secret treasure trove more exciting than any blue yonder—and just about the only privacy we have left.

In one of his letters to his mother, John wrote:

"You will be happy to know I haven't had a drink for over a month and a half, and expect to continue that course as long as I can—which may be from now on. I feel so much better, and from all indications, am so much nicer and easier to live with. Not just my family think so, but all my friends and acquaintances too."

In quite a number of letters he indicated that he had given up, or was trying to give up, drinking. And then he would go back to it and, with his gift for self-portraiture in the form of the lyric, write a song about it. "Drinking Again," of which there is an excellent recording by Frank Sinatra, is such a song. So is "I Wonder What Became of Me?", dropped from the *St. Louis Woman* score. Even the title of "This Times the Dream's on Me" derives from the expression "The drinks are on me."

The classic self-portrait, however, is "One for My Baby," written with Harold Arlen. It is one of his genuine masterpieces, a short story or even a one-man play in rhyme, keenly descriptive of drunks in general and John in particular. It shows the progression of a drunk's emotions late at night, from melancholy to maudlin through aggression to remorse.

> It's quarter to three,
> there's no one in the place except you and me,
> so set 'em up, Joe,
> I've got a little story you oughta know.

Why should Joe oughta know it? He's a tired, hardworking bartender at the end of his shift who just wants to go home.

> We're drinking, my friend,
> to the end of a brief episode.
> So make it one for my baby
> and one more for the road.

> I've got the routine,
> so drop another nickel in the machine.
> I'm feeling so bad,
> I wish you'd make the music dreamy and sad.

> Could tell you a lot,
> but that's not in a gentleman's code.
> So make it one for my baby
> and one more for the road.

Portrait of Johnny

At the start of the release, note the pugnacious tone that then softens:

> *You may not know it,*
> *but, buddy, I'm a kind of poet,*
> *and I've gotta lot of things to say.*
> *And when I'm gloomy,*
> *you simply gotta listen to me,*
> *until it's talked away.*

Now comes the apologetic remorse:

> *Well, that's how it goes,*
> *and Joe, I know you're getting anxious to close.*
> *So thanks for the cheer.*
> *I hope you didn't mind my bending your ear.*
> *This torch that I've found*
> *must be drowned or it soon might explode.*
> *Make it one for my baby*
> *and one more for the road,*
> *that long, long road.*

John often revised lyrics as the years went on. For a recording he did for the Pye label in London, the last he ever made, he eliminated the two lines about "this torch that I've found," substituting:

> *Don't let it be said*
> *old unsteady couldn't carry his load.*

It's a poignant line, and self-indicting.

As we have noted, one of John's best friends was the radio announcer and actor Bill Goodwin. Goodwin's son, also named Bill, became a musician, an outstanding drummer who has worked closely with saxophonist Phil Woods. And his sister Jill became Phil's wife. At one point I talked to Bill and Jill about life near the Mercers.

Bill said: "In the neighborhood where we lived, there were a lot of people in show business. Jack Carson lived right behind us. We shared a fence with his backyard. Gordon and Sheila MacRae and their kids were right down the street. Marian and Manny Klein were right across the street. The Bing Crosby family were three houses down. We were on Camarillo Street in Toluca Lake. The Mercers were regular visitors to the house. Johnny and Ginger and Dad and Mom were very close.

"Jill was born in '39, I was born in '42. Amanda was one of the kids we grew up with. We always had parties at our house, they had parties at their house. People had parties all the time. Birthday parties. Nancy Sinatra in her book has a list of who came to her first birthday party, and Jill is on the list. The Sinatras lived a mile away."

Mandy became aware of her father's status when she was in school: "The parents and the kids would come up to the car when he picked me up, and I realized he had to be somebody, or else they wouldn't do that. Later on, I remember saying to him, 'Well, you're famous to them.' And he got a kick out of that. And he was always on the radio.

"But I didn't realize how special he was until I was much older. Most of the children I knew, their parents were in the entertainment business. The Hope children, Linda and Tony, and of course Bing Crosby's boys, and the Goodwins, Jill and Bill. Jill was a good friend of mine. I think it was when I was a teenager that I said, '*Wait a minute!* These people *are* different; they *are* special.' But you don't realize it when you're growing up."

Bill Goodwin said: "I remember when we were kids going to parties at the Mercers', Amanda's birthday parties, and she would come to our parties. The MacRaes. Jack Carson's son John.

"I thought everybody was in that business. As a young child, I remember everything being great, these funny and entertaining people you knew from the radio used to come over."

Jill added: "And lots of musicians."

Bill said, "My dad and Benny Goodman were friends. I became friends with a lot of my dad's buddies, the out-of-work actors who would be hanging out, people over for dinner all the time, or hanging out at the pool, or out playing golf with Dad. It would always be like party time. Jackie Coogan, and Peter Leeds, the character actor. They played golf together, they drank together, and they probably smoked some pot together. Dad liked to hang out with musicians, and he liked to smoke some pot sometimes."

I asked Bill about the common hostility to Bing Crosby. He said, "Oh, my mother hated Bing. Mom always maintained Bing was responsible for his wife Dixie drinking herself to death. He was totally unfaithful and made no secret of it, and she, being a good Catholic, couldn't consider divorce, and so she drank. Mom said she was a saint. I worked with Gary

Crosby later on. Gary was an alcoholic. Probably had some of his father's characteristics.

"But in those days everybody was drinking as if there were no tomorrow and nobody even thought about whether they were alcoholic or not. You either drank or you were on the wagon. Of course we, being kids, could feel undercurrents, but didn't know much about it.

"It was just the neighborhood. I'd go out every day. I'd go by the Holdens', Bill Holden, Brenda Marshall, but Artis Weinberg was her real name. Very beautiful, and a really nice person. Their sons were Cub Scouts and I was, like, their Boy Scout adviser, and I used to go by to see them, supposedly, but I really wanted to hang out with her. I had a crush on her. Bill was out by the pool, hungover, every day. 'How are you, Mr. Holden?' 'I'm fine, Bill.' I was the social butterfly of the neighborhood. I would drop in on everybody. Gordon MacRae, another heavy drinker. A sweet guy. It was like a small town.

"Johnny was a real human being. My dad spent all the money. He was a big spender, a party guy. A lot of bad investments. When he died in 1958, my mom really wasn't in very good shape financially or otherwise. And a lot of so-called friends who had been at the house all the time kind of disappeared. The Mercers jumped in. They loaned her money. They gave her a place to stay, a little apartment in some property they owned. She lived there about six months and then got a place of her own and started working part-time. They really came through for her.

"Years later, I was in New York and ran into Jimmy Rowles in some bar. He was in New York with Mercer. They were doing a concert. He said that there was going to be a big party in Mercer's honor over at Bob and Jean Bach's house, in Greenwich Mews.

"It was a fantastic party. Everybody singing and playing the piano. Bob Dorough played and sang. Jimmy played and Mercer sang. Johnny'd had *so* much to drink. He was singing 'New Orleans' or one of those tunes. He was sitting down, holding on to the piano. He sounded absolutely marvelous. Everybody was totally loaded. He was so glad to see me, being really sweet. And then I said something, and he said, 'What the hell do you know about it?' And I thought, *Uh-oh, John's off,* and I said, 'Well, see you later, John.' "

Jimmy Rowles was one of John's favorite pianists. Jay Livingston witnessed an incident that he would never be able to get out of his mind. John was sitting in at some club, singing with Rowles. Ginger was at a front table. Johnny began singing a blues, improvising the lyrics, which were a scathing, vicious attack on Ginger. Jay described to me his torn emotions at this performance. He said that as a lyricist, he was in awe of John's brilliance. As a human being, he was horrified at the attack.

David Raksin said, "Everybody who knew Johnny knew about his Jekyll-and-Hyde quality. I didn't—until one evening my wife Jo and I were with Johnny and Ginger at some supper club in Hollywood. Johnny was drunk and he got onto Ginger. As I later found out, this was fairly common. He was being so terrible to her, really horrible.

"I said, 'Johnny, I want you to stop that right away.'

"He said, 'And if I don't?'

"I said, 'If you don't, I'm going to knock your fucking head off.'

"I've always had the feeling that part of this had to do with the fact that when he fell in love with Judy Garland and Judy with him, Ginger wouldn't let him go—which was a blessing in no disguise at all.

"He could turn on a dime. But with me he was always marvelous. It's sad. Ginger must in some way have understood that the root of this was some kind of crazy torment. I'm not excusing Johnny. But it had to be something terrible to make him say things like that.

"I think he was one of those guys from whom rage springs undiluted. All of a sudden it comes pouring out, and you've got to know it's hell in there. But otherwise, he was a darling man, I really loved him, he was wonderful. We worked together several times.

"In addition to his genius, there was a competence about that man. He was always cool. Whatever it was he could always handle it. He may have gone home and sweated blood, but you never knew it. It has something to do with being equal to impossible tasks."

Once in New York, at Charlie O's, a restaurant in Rockefeller Center that John particularly favored, we had a few drinks before ordering dinner. Johnny began to get nasty with the waitress, and I became very uncomfortable. I thought, more or less, *I can't put up with this. This friendship may end in the next few minutes, but I have to put a stop to this.*

The girl left to get more drinks. I said, "John, that is a hard-working young woman who has been perfectly nice to us. And you're behaving like a son of a bitch." He gave me a long look, and I concluded the friendship had ended.

But he said, "You're absolutely right." And when the girl returned he was courtly, charming as only he could be. I don't know how much money he put under an ashtray as we left, but it probably put her in shock.

You could stop John if you had the sand to do it. And the best stop ever put on him, at least that I ever heard of, came from Jo Stafford.

It was notorious that following a night of insulting friends and strangers alike, John, remorseful at what he had done, would not only apologize but send bundles of roses to whomever he had hurt or offended. Jo said he never insulted her, though one night he came close. As he started to sail into her, she held up a hand and said, "Please, John! I don't want any of your roses in the morning."

Alan Livingston said, "Johnny and I became friends, good friends— when he was sober. We used to go to dinner together. But when he drank, he became a monster. I was sitting next to him at a dinner party when he took his drink and poured it over Ginger's head.

"She took it. She always did." Alan thought she liked being Mrs. Johnny Mercer and all that went with it. "He never insulted me," Alan said.

Even his niece Nancy didn't escape his wrath entirely; he excoriated her when he found out she had voted for Richard Nixon.

One of the few persons who ever had the guts to ask Mercer directly about his drinking was Willis Conover, who on January 30, 1970, interviewed him for one of his Voice of America broadcasts. John said:

"I find that most people who drink, it eventually affects something, probably the liver, or the bile, or something, because most steady drinkers, as they get older, tend to get less friendly and more and more vitriolic. And I think it's a physical thing that your system just can't take any more. When you're young, you're happy and nobody gets mad, and you laugh, and you get sick. But when you get old and you've been drinking a lot, you don't get sick, it just sits there and you get mean. . . . I can say mean things and I don't mean them. I really don't. It's just the whiskey talking. I really like people. I harbor no grudges. I don't like to be taken advantage of, I don't think anybody does. But I essentially am an optimist and a very friendly man. I like almost everybody I meet. I don't mean like Will Rogers. But I genuinely want to like people. I hope that it's a happy comradeship or companionship."

There is, however, a dimension of rationalization there. His misbehavior did not begin as he grew older; it was there early on. Mickey Goldsen tells about an encounter with Glenn Wallichs. A songwriter had accused Mickey, as head of Capitol's publishing division, of an unethical practice, the details of which are not significant. Wallichs heard about it and called Mickey into his office. He said that Mickey and everyone else in the company had to be protective of Capitol's reputation.

At that time, Buddy DeSylva was involved in a paternity suit with his secretary, which she won in due course. Mickey told Wallichs: "Buddy DeSylva's got his secretary knocked up, and it's in the trade papers, and Johnny was just arrested for drunk driving and right now he's probably in the nearest bar, insulting everyone, and *I'm* compromising the company's reputation?"

Wallichs, to his credit, laughed.

Mickey said: "Johnny had three stages. First stage, he was happy and singing his songs. Second stage, he was insulting people. His best friends. And at the third stage, he would fall asleep in a corner.

"Having to go back to people and apologize may have affected his personality when he was sober. Because Johnny was a congenial guy, but he wasn't a jovial person by any means. He was very somber."

One of John's friends was the late Les Brown, who led one of the most tasteful dance-cum-jazz bands of the big-band era. Les, himself a gentleman, said: "I first knew Johnny in the early 1940s, when they were starting Capitol Records. We'd see each other at parties or jazz concerts. I always admired him immensely. To me, he was the consummate lyricist, and, as far as I'm concerned, the hippest.

"Also a wonderful man—when sober. After a few drinks he went from being the sweetest man in the world to a nasty one. You couldn't believe it.

"One time at our house, in Pacific Palisades, he started getting nasty. There were a lot of people there and he was spoiling the party. My wife took him by the ear and said, 'Johnny, follow me.' She took him right out into the driveway and put him in his car and said, 'When you want to be nice, you can come back.' He came back after a while. He'd got rid of his nastiness."

Singer Betty Bennett, who was the first wife of pianist and composer André Previn, said:

"John would be so darling, and then he'd get drunk and be nasty. And so those of us who knew him used to say, 'Well, has it happened to you yet?'

"Les Brown used to have a big Christmas party with a huge chorus that sang Christmas songs. André and I knew John very well. As we came in, John threw his arms around me and said, 'Oh, it's wonderful to see you, let's get together later; I'll see you later.'

"Some time passed and we decided to leave. And as we passed John he fixed this look at me and said, 'Good evening, Mrs. Previn, have *many* husbands.'

"I went to a fancy party at his house once. They had people to park the cars. When I got ready to leave, I was standing out there waiting for mine. Robert Mitchum was there with a couple of people. He had a little pipe. Everyone was having little tokes. He said, 'Would you care for this?' I said, 'No, thank you.' I got in the car and left. And the next day there was a blind item in the newspaper that said something about at this big party where somebody had marijuana and the host was outraged. And in truth, when Mercer found out about it, he was *furious*. I guess it was all right to fall down drunk but not to smoke marijuana."

The most amazing thing in all these stories is the extent of the tolerance extended to Johnny. He was immensely well liked. But not everybody was forgiving. Mickey Goldsen described an incident in New York:

"I had a date with Herb Hendler, who was head of A and R at RCA at the time. We were going to go to the Waldorf to see Xavier Cugat. The singer was Fran Warren. She and her manager were going to be at our table. I was with Johnny for dinner, and he started to drink. We went up to see Louis Armstrong, who was working on Broadway in one of those big, open, saloon-type places. And Johnny was kind of loaded and I wanted to get him the hell out of there. I wanted to get *away* from him. I said to Johnny, 'I've got a date at the Waldorf. I'll drop you off at your place.'

"He said, 'Why can't I go with you?' I said, 'Okay, fine.' I called up Herb Hendler. I said, 'Do you mind if I bring Johnny Mercer?'

"He said, 'Oh my God, he's my idol. Bring him!'

"So I brought Johnny. We had our table. They were playing a medley of songs, Gershwin, Victor Herbert. The first thing he said was, 'Why in the hell don't they play some of the *new* standards?' Then Fran Warren comes over to the table. He's introduced to her and he's introduced to her manager, a woman who looked not very feminine. Johnny looks at the two of them and says, 'Have you two got something going like Hilde-garde's got with *her* manager?'

"By this time, Herb's saying, 'I'm sorry you brought him.' He was just *obnoxious*, I mean it was just *terrible*. I can never forget that night. Herb said later, 'I'm sorry I ever met him.'

"I don't know why Johnny wanted to be with me. I didn't drink. Finally we got out of there alive, and I took him back to wherever the hell he was staying. He had an apartment somewhere.

"But I'll never forget that night. Oh! Oh!"

In 1962, Alan Livingston married the actress Nancy Olson, who looked like every young man's dream of the nice Midwestern girl. (She was indeed the daughter of a Milwaukee doctor.) She had made her mark in movies in *Sunset Boulevard,* among other pictures. In 1964, the year Capitol released its first Beatles record; the Livingstons had a party at their home in Beverly Hills, and Mercer of course was invited. He sat in an armchair, steadily drinking.

Alan recalled: "Nancy's mother was here from Milwaukee, a very nice and very bright woman, but not used to being around show-business people. She said, 'Oh, Mr. Mercer, I'm so happy to meet you. I want you to meet my son. He's a lawyer, David Olson.'

"And Johnny said, 'I don't want to meet your son, and I don't want to meet you either. You're a fuckin' pain in the ass.'

"The next day he called Nancy, all contrition. He said, 'I'd like to meet your brother again. I'd like him to write my will and do my legal work.'

"Nothing came of it, of course. But it was the kind of thing Johnny did to try to make amends."

It was widely known in the movie industry that relations between the actress sisters Joan Fontaine and Olivia de Havilland were strained and painful to both of them. Bill Harbach relates:

"Bob and Jean Bach gave great parties. You'd see Duke Ellington there, Lee Wiley, the whole world. One night when I was there, Ellington was there, Bobby Short was there, Harold Arlen was there, Johnny was there. And drunk. And in walked Joan Fontaine. And the first thing Johnny said was, 'I love your sister.'

"When he was drinking, he could turn a room into a garage. He could be mean as hell. In a Chinese restaurant on Third Avenue, he said, 'Hey, Squint, I want another drink.' In 1947, he would come up to our little apartment for dinner. My first wife and I weren't married yet. We would listen to records. And one night he got stoned and said to Ginger, 'God damn you, you little kike.' I couldn't believe it.

"ASCAP was having its board of directors' meeting. Afterwards they had dinner. Harold Adamson, the lyricist, called me and said, 'Bill, you've got to help us. Johnny's in the back room of our library here, and he's impossible. Will you come and get him?' I went over, and he was in the back room, all alone, sitting on a chair, looking down at his feet. I said, 'Johnny, let me take you home.'

"And he said, 'Listen, you son of a bitch, you've got no talent.' "

This was apparently a favorite jibe. He said it to Bill Harbach, Bill Goodwin, his niece Nancy, and, according to one report, he once (in Chasen's restaurant) even said it to Irving Berlin, whom he idolized. The next day he sent his customary bundles of roses and an apology. Berlin just laughed it off, and they remained close friends.

Bill Harbach related, "I said, 'Johnny, I know I don't have any talent.' Because I would never go for his bait.

"He said, 'Okay, take me home.'

"He loved me, but he would say things to me when he was drunk that I couldn't believe. Absolutely Jekyll and Hyde."

Jean Bach said: "He was two people. When he'd drink, he'd be the other person. He would remember the singing of the black people of the South, which he loved, and then he would be insulting to black people when he was drunk.

"There was this battle within him. I would have a lot of parties here. And I'd have musicians, and Johnny would always sing; he loved singing. And somebody was at the piano, a rather distinguished black jazz piano player. They picked a tune out, and he said, 'What key, Johnny?' And Johnny said, 'Oh, play it in a colored key.' I wouldn't have taken offense by it, but this guy, knowing Johnny's reputation, kind of bristled a little bit. He played, but reluctantly.

"Dorothy Davis, my maid, who was black, said that he started up with her a little bit, but she'd been through this before. I had a cat then named Seymour. Johnny said, 'What are you looking at? You're nothing but a cat.'

"And Dorothy said, 'Mr. Mercer, you can insult me, you can insult my madam, but *don't you pick on Seymour.*'

"And he would always be so contrite the next day. I kept all the notes he tucked into the flowers."

But the most harrowing of his assaults had Judy Garland as the victim. The story is recounted by the almost-legendary figure Irving Lazar, nicknamed "Swifty" by Humphrey Bogart for the speed with which he could make a business deal. He was the agent, at one time or another, for seemingly every major Hollywood actor, writer, or composer, including Cole Porter and Mercer. In his autobiography, *Swifty,* published posthumously in 1995, he describes a party he gave for Moss Hart, who had written the remake of *A Star Is Born,* which was about to go into production with Garland as the star. The guests included Lee and Ira Gershwin, the Oscar Levants, and Mercer. "Johnny had had a few drinks too many," Lazar wrote, and added by way of understatement, "That was never a good idea."

Garland arrived. And without even allowing her time to settle in, Johnny said, "Why did you let your mother die in a parking lot?"

She burst into tears. Lazar told her, "Go upstairs to the powder room, and pull yourself together. I'll ask Johnny to leave."

Eventually Lee Gershwin, a close friend of Garland's, noticed that Judy had been gone a long time and went looking for her. Garland had slashed her wrists and lay on the floor covered in blood. Lazar sent for an ambulance, and she was carried out on a stretcher.

"Naturally," Lazar wrote, "the incident was so macabre that everyone left."

Twenty

Big changes were coming to Capitol Records, and to Mercer's life. Although he was from the beginning the titular head of the company, its president, the actual function of that office had been discharged by the disciplined and highly organized Glenn Wallichs. John's most important function was as the de facto head of artists and repertoire, although that title was assigned to others. In 1947, John withdrew from the presidency of the company and Glenn Wallichs assumed that title.

The pace of his writing, however, was undiminished. He was writing songs with Hoagy Carmichael for a Bing Crosby film called *Here Comes the Groom,* directed by Frank Capra. Carmichael remembered:

"As I was driving down the highway, coming into Palm Springs, to join Johnny to write this score, I happened to think of an old old joke, not a very funny joke. But it was about a jackass. And it seemed that the king of the jungle, the lion, sent an emissary to the jackass to say, 'Jackass, are you coming to the king's big party?' And the jackass, sitting there with a pipe in his mouth and his legs crossed, said, 'Tell the king in the cool cool cool of the evening, I'll be there.' Well, I told this joke to Johnny Mercer and in two days we had the song, 'In the Cool, Cool, Cool of the Evening.'"

The film was released in 1951, and that song brought John his second Academy Award.

It is impossible to estimate how many of John's songs were written in cars, sometimes to melodies he heard on the radio. Such was the genesis of "Midnight Sun."

"I was riding in a car," he recalled, and I heard a radio announcer say, 'And now Lionel Hampton's new instrumental "Midnight Sun." ' So the title was already there. And the first thing I thought of with 'Midnight Sun' was 'aurora borealis.' So I heard it in the music. It fit the music. I thought, *Well, what rhymes with aurora borealis?* And I thought of 'chalice' and 'alabaster palace,' and that kind of started the song, and by the time I got to Los Angeles from Newport Beach, I had that lyric finished, in my car. So then I called up to find out who published it and if they had a lyric, and would they be interested if they didn't. And they didn't and they were."

That lyric was written in 1954. By then, plans were under way for a new office building for Capitol Records. Designed by architect Gordon Beck, it would be the first circular office building in the world, as well as the first air-conditioned high-rise in Hollywood. It would stand 150 feet tall at 1750 North Vine Street, not far up the street from the famous intersection of Hollywood and Vine, and it would be erected at the then-enormous cost of $2 million. Groundbreaking began on September 27, 1954.

It was widely reported at the time that the design was intended to resemble a stack of records on a turntable, an assertion the architect denied, giving among the reasons for the shape that it afforded maximum utilization of space. In fact, it does no such thing, since it loses the floor space of what would be its four corners. It remains a striking but oddly impractical building, whose floors and offices have a cramped and somewhat claustrophobic feeling. But it did contain two glorious recording studios, the first ever specifically designed for high-fidelity recording. They are still in use—though remodeled and repeatedly upgraded—and among the best on the West Coast.

The building remains a Hollywood landmark, long after its official grand opening on April 6, 1956. By that date, however, Mercer was gone from the company. The previous year, on January 15, 1955, Britain's giant Electric and Musical Industries (EMI) had purchased a controlling interest in Capitol for $8.5 million from Wallichs and Mercer and the widow of Buddy DeSylva. DeSylva had died in 1950. By the terms of the deal, Glenn Wallichs stayed on as president, and in April became a director. Alan Livingston said:

"Manny Sacks called me and said, 'How'd you like to be head of television for NBC?' That fascinated me. So I went to Glenn Wallichs, and he was very good about it. That was in 1955. I left on good terms and moved over to NBC."

That year, with sales of records by Frank Sinatra, Les Baxter, and Tennessee Ernie Ford, the little company Mercer, Wallichs, and DeSylva had started on $25,000 thirteen years earlier, in the midst of a World War II shellac shortage, grossed $20 million.

It was an astounding business achievement, and it was conceived by Johnny Mercer, who chose the right partners—Buddy DeSylva for funds and Glenn Wallichs for execution and business acumen—and then proved himself to be a more astute record producer than anyone else in America.

Northerners who move to the South sometimes learn that the slow speech of Dixie often conceals sharp and rapid thinking. This may be the result of the Southern experience during the carpetbagger exploitation of the Reconstruction period. I think Johnny was like that. Then, too, he may have absorbed some of it from blacks, for as one black friend of mine put it, "If you could convince the white-man boss that you were stupid, he didn't see you as a threat."

We should remember John's background. By diligent application, he made himself a typing champion. He grew up hearing the table talk of money and business from his father and his uncles. He worked in his father's business, and, before he established himself as a songwriter, was employed in a brokerage house in New York. Johnny knew something about money and investment.

And so when I see him, in printed interviews, dismissing his own abilities, saying that all he knew how to do was now and then write a li'l ol' song and put together a few rhymes, I recognize that he is being something less than ingenuous. Behind that soft Southern charm, John Herndon Mercer was one very shrewd cookie.

Dave Dexter wrote in *Playback*, his autobiography:

"Everything was coming up roses for Capitol in the early 1950s. . . . But there was a sad note as well. Johnny Mercer disappeared. There were no farewell parties, no ceremonies, no nothing. The founder and former president who had accomplished so much in Capitol's behalf in its early days simply walked away from our . . . executive offices and never came back. . . . Only Wallichs, of the three company founders, remained. The loss of . . . Mercer was difficult for me to accept.

"He was an inspirational boss who never, to my knowledge, pulled rank with employees. . . ."

"Capitol got too big," John told me later. "It wasn't fun anymore."

Dexter returned to the subject in 1980, in a liner note for a reissue of a group of songs Mercer had recorded for transcription. Dexter wrote that Mercer "abruptly walked away from Capitol, long before the company was sold to a British conglomerate and eight years before the firm moved into its circular building just north of Hollywood Boulevard.

"I stuck around Capitol for another quarter of a century, all the time deploring Mercer's absence and watching a covey of lawyers and Ivy League business majors take over the company's direction. In 1974, one of them called me into his office and informed me that he was placing me on a 'premature retirement' status. So be it. Capitol was no longer the innovative, exciting place it had been in its early days."

With Dexter gone, none of the label's pioneering figures was left.

Twenty-one

"Children don't really understand what fame is," Nancy Gerard said. "At least they didn't when I was young. We didn't have television; we just had radio. Children don't usually read newspapers. I just understood that my Uncle Johnny was a very special person. My grandmother adored him. There would be great excitement when we were supposed to tune in and hear him on the radio. And when he would come to Savannah, everything would stop. It would be all for Johnny. And he would just drop in. One day we were sitting there having dinner in the middle of the day, like Southerners do, at the big round mahogany table, and the front door opened, and he sang out, 'Oo-oo,' which is a sort of a thing that you do in the South, and my grandmother jumped up and said, 'Oh, Bubba, is that you?' He came in with his hat, his overcoat, and two bags. Unannounced.

"That was fairly typical. And so he was here, and everything stopped, and great excitement came, and we talked, and they'd go places. Sometimes he'd take my mother and my grandmother back to California with him, and I'd stay with a cousin.

"I spent an entire summer in California with Ginger and Johnny when I was twelve or thirteen years old. I think it was 1953. He took me to the MGM studio where he was working on *Seven Brides for Seven Brothers* with Gene De Paul. He said, 'I'm going to work with him for a couple of hours, and then we'll go to lunch.' I was thrilled to death.

"We went into this lovely studio with a big grand piano. I sat in a big easy chair. They were composing one of the songs, and they worked on it, and Gene would play a few notes, and Johnny would say, 'Okay, this is the word I want here, but how about doing this?' They collaborated like that, back and forth. After many hours, Johnny turned to me and said, 'I guess you want to go to lunch now.' And it was three o'clock. We'd gotten there about nine-thirty. He could focus like that and shut out the world."

De Paul was apparently one composer with whom John would work in direct confrontation. Harold Arlen was another. Ten years Johnny's junior, and not a conservatory-trained musician, De Paul had played piano in dance bands, written arrangements for vocal groups, and scored a few movies, including some of those featuring Abbott and Costello. He wrote "Mister Five by Five," "He's My Guy," "Milkman, Keep Those Bottles Quiet," "Cow Cow Boogie," "Star Eyes," "Teach Me Tonight," "You Don't Know What Love Is," and one of the most hauntingly beautiful of all American songs, the exquisite "I'll Remember April," with a brilliant lyric by Don Raye and Patricia Johnson.

Seven Brides for Seven Brothers was based on a Stephen Vincent Benét story that in turn was based on the Roman legend of the Rape of the Sabine Women. Howard Keel plays an Oregon farmer who decides to get himself a wife. He goes into town, which is twelve miles away, courts Jane Powell for approximately five minutes, and in that time persuades her to marry him—a coarse, buckskinned, loudmouthed, boastful lout of no discernible charm or virtue. She marries him immediately, as implausible as it may seem, and he takes her home, whereupon she discovers she is to be cook and maidservant to not one but seven bearded Neanderthals, Adam and his six brothers.

Seven Brides was being made at the same time as the Gene Kelly version of *Brigadoon,* and MGM, having little faith in it, diverted some of its funding to *Brigadoon.* It was therefore not shot on location, which at least might have lent it a visual grandeur, as director Stanley Donen had hoped it would have, and the painted backdrops and process shots and studio lighting are disconcertingly obvious throughout. The plot is silly at every turn, and the dialogue is appalling, a city slicker's idea of what them-there country folk must talk like: "if'n" and "off'n my mind" and "Don't let it fret you," and (a line that Russ Tamblyn seems particularly uncomfortable delivering) "You're the prettiest girl I ever acquainted." Indeed, the whole cast seems uncomfortable with the faux-bucolic terms.

The songs aren't particularly good, either. They're not the best by Gene De Paul, and certainly not the best by Mercer. One of them, "Spring Spring Spring," puts Mercer in company with Harold Rome's "Fanny

Fanny Fanny" and "Wish You Were Here, Wish You Were Here, Wish You Were Here" as an exercise in redundancy. As a celebration of nature it doesn't come close to Rodgers and Hammerstein's "Oh, What a Beautiful Mornin'," the John Latouche–Jerome Moross "Lazy Afternoon," or Lerner and Loewe's "The Heather on the Hill," prominent in *Brigadoon*.

"When You're In Love" has a trite lyric that says "your heart will tell you . . . ," which echoes a thousand other songs. And the music sounds like second-rate Friml. In fact, one day while the film was in preparation, Rudolf Friml was visiting John's friends Wolfe and Rose Gilbert in their Beverly Hills home when Gene De Paul dropped by. Rose remembered:

"Friml asked Gene De Paul, 'What do you do?' Gene said, 'I'm a composer.' Friml said, 'What do you compose?' 'Songs.' Friml said, 'Play me some of your songs.'

"Friml listened and then said, 'You steal. But you don't steal good.' "

One of the songs in *Seven Brides*, "June Bride," begins "Oh they say when you marry in June . . . ," which puts it squarely in a grouping I like to call "they say" songs, such as Berlin's "They say that falling in love is wonderful . . . so they tell me." How many times in your life has someone told you, "Falling in love is wonderful"? It can hardly be considered a profound or even intriguing observation. Likewise with "They tried to tell us we're too young." There are lots of these songs, and Mercer fell into this lazy trap here.

In the last eight bars of the song, Mercer writes:

> *By the light of the silvery moon,*
> *home you ride*
> *side by side*
> *with the echo of Mendelssohn's tune*
> *in your heart*
> *as you ride,*
> *for they say when you marry in June*
> *you will always be a bride.*

First of all, "By the light of the silvery moon" might be an acceptable line if the phrase could be considered current in the culture of the time, but, in fact, that is a song by Edward Madden and Gus Edwards, published in 1909. This makes the line baffling, because John was scrupulous in his efforts to avoid even the hint of lifting other people's ideas; and he could have fixed it: "velvety moon" or "friendly old moon" or "magical moon." The line is absolutely inexplicable.

In the reference to "Mendelssohn's tune," John has fallen into the trap of rhyme and his own cleverness. At his worst, he could be cute, and this is an example. Mendelssohn had been dead only three years at the time of the story of *Seven Brides*. More to the point, "Mendelssohn's tune" (i.e., the wedding march from his incidental music to *A Midsummer Night's Dream*) was never performed at a wedding until 1858, when Queen Victoria (who loved Mendelssohn) had it played at her daughter's wedding, after which it spread slowly throughout the English-speaking world. Thus the reference is an egregious anachronism. John should have known better.

The main theme of the picture, a hoedown-type tune titled "Bless Your Beautiful Hide," sounds like a lift from the score of every western you ever saw.

Meanwhile, *Brigadoon* contained such jewels as "Almost Like Being in Love," "Come to Me, Bend to Me," "The Heather on the Hill," "I'll Go Home with Bonnie Jean," and "There but for You Go I." Interestingly, though, *Brigadoon,* for which MGM had such high hopes, did only modestly well, and *Seven Brides for Seven Brothers* was a huge financial success. It was nominated for a best-picture Academy Award, and the score indeed won an Oscar. *Seven Brides* continues to get four-star recommendations in TV and video guides. Go figure, as they say in New York.

There is an interesting footnote to all this. Alan Bergman told me: "Johnny and Gene De Paul wrote some beautiful songs that were left out of that picture, including one called 'You Take After Your Mother.' A few years later, they decided to do *Brides* as a Broadway musical. The producer approached Marilyn and me to write some additional songs to fill it out. We told them that it was unnecessary, there was enough good material left over that could be used. But the producer got new songs in New York, and the stage version of it failed."

After *Seven Brides for Seven Brothers,* Johnny took up work on the Fred Astaire–Leslie Caron film *Daddy Long Legs.* Perhaps still hurting from the studio's exclusion of some of his songs from *Seven Brides,* he wrote a letter to his mother (postmarked Beverly Hills, October 8, 1954): "I'm finished with my job . . . and hope they make a nice picture out of it, and that some of the good songs are left in the picture."

Among the songs for the film is "Something's Gotta Give," one of his finest. He described how it was written: "I woke up one night with an idea for a song—'Something's Gotta Give,' that's another popular expression that everybody used. I got up and I wrote a kind of a sketch of it.

With Jimmy Van Heusen, with whom John wrote "I Thought About You" *(Collection of Georgia State University)*

With Dave Dexter, left, and Glenn Wallichs, a cofounder of Capitol Records, at the Capitol offices *(Collection of Georgia State University)*

With Frank Loesser, Betty Downey, Ginger, and an unidentified man and woman
(Collection of Georgia State University)

Jo Stafford and Paul Weston
(Photo courtesy of Jo Stafford Weston)

With Jeff
(Collection of Georgia State University)

John and Ginger in Hawaii
(Photographer unknown)

Henry Mancini and John
(Collection of Ginny Mancini)

Left to right: John, Artie Shaw, Woody Herman, George Simon, and Tommy Little-field. Tommy, now a songwriter and performer in Nashville, is Woody Herman's grandson. *(Collection of Georgia State University)*

Henry and Ginny Mancini, John, Ginger, and Mandy at an awards banquet
(Collection of Georgia State University)

Harry Warren, unknown officer, John, and Harold Arlen
(Collection of Harry Warren family)

Left: Johnny Mandel *(Photo by John Reeves)*
Right: Howie Richmond *(Photo by the author)*

John, after an interview at the New York Studio of the Canadian Broadcasting Corporation, circa 1968 *(Photo by the author)*

John's friend Jimmy Hancock, and his nephew, architect Hugh Mercer, standing in front of the house (the right half of the duplex) on Gwinnett Street where John grew up. Jimmy and Hugh are gone now. The photo is dated November 1998. *(Photo by the author)*

Rose Gilbert
(Photo by the author)

Nancy Gerard

Marc Cramer and Ginger on a ship en route to Europe
(Collection of Georgia State University)

Margaret Whiting and Ginger Mercer
(Collection of Georgia State University)

Like the bones, but not the full structure. I think the melody was a little different. . . ."

Shortly afterwards came the assignment for *Daddy Long Legs*.

"And I said, 'Well, this song would be perfect for the picture,' and it's the kind of song that Fred likes. You know, it sounds sophisticated, and it's got that kind of off-beat rhythm. But I had another ballad called 'I Never Knew'—I think it was called. There had been several songs called 'I Never Knew,' but mine was a *nice song*. I wrote both the music and the words for this picture, which I seldom do. And we went up one afternoon, the piano player and I, to play the songs for Fred, and we played a couple of dance songs, and the other ballad. And his face, I could see, he was really disappointed. I said, 'Oh, by the way, I've got another song that you might like better than that ballad.' So then I started to sing 'Something's Gotta Give' and a big smile came on his face, and before I finished the chorus, he was up on his feet, *dancing*. And he said, 'Oh, that's wonderful.' And I said, 'Why?' And he said, 'Well, don't you see? I'm forty or fifty years old, and I'm in love with a girl who's about eighteen or twenty, and it makes the whole thing believable. *When an old immovable object like me meets a . . .*' Whatever the words are, I've forgotten them right now. I was thrilled that he was thrilled" (BBC).

Daddy Long Legs, based on the famous children's book by Jean Webster, was released in 1955. It is a very bad movie, trite and long, in essence a cheesy knock-off of *An American in Paris*. The plot concerns a wealthy American (Astaire) who sponsors the education of a young French orphan (Leslie Caron) at an American university. The script is not in a class with the one Alan Jay Lerner wrote for *An American in Paris,* and it is imitative of that film even to the point of having Astaire dance a fantasy ballet with the girl. It's historically interesting only in that it is the sole film for which John wrote both words and music.

The ballet in *Daddy Long Legs,* in four segments (titled "Guardian Angel," "Carnival in Rio," "Daddy Long Legs," and "Hong Kong Cafe"), is itself a rather dreary knock-off of the ballet sequence that Gene Kelly choreographed and danced with Cyd Charisse in *Singin' in the Rain*. The ballet music was written by Alex North.

One good song is a recycled "Dream," by then more than ten years old, but the best song in the film is "Something's Gotta Give." It is a jewel, with a wonderful, natural jazz swing, and it was nominated for an Academy Award. John was always preoccupied with the passage of time and his own advancing age. This lyric is John himself:

When an irresistible force such as you
meets an old immovable object like me,
you can bet as sure as you live,
something's gotta give,
something's gotta give,
something's gotta give.

When an irrepressible smile such as yours
warms an old implacable heart such as mine,
don't say no, because I insist
somewhere, somehow, someone's gonna be kissed.

So, en garde,
who knows what the fates have in store,
from their vast mysterious sky?
I'll try hard
ignoring those lips I adore,
but how long can anyone try?

Fight, fight, fight, fight, fight it with all of your might.
Chances are, some heavily star-spangled night
we'll find out as sure as we live,
something's gotta give,
something's gotta give,
something's gotta give.

That is superb writing. Moreover, it is superb *song*writing. It is by far the best thing in the picture and lives on, while the film has achieved the comparative obscurity it deserves.

Capitol Records was sold to EMI in January of that year (1955). If Buddy DeSylva's share from the sale was $1.75 million, Johnny's presumably was the same. This came on top of the regular flow of his royalties, which even today amount to nearly $1.5 million a year. And this does not take into consideration his fees from film assignments. And in April, John did something that surprised all of Savannah.

After the liquidation of the G.A. Mercer Company in 1927, such was George Mercer's reputation that the Chatham Savings Bank made him a loan to set up Mercer Realty. His son, Walter—Johnny's older brother—bought into an insurance firm headed by a man named Otto Seiler. It became the Mercer-Seiler Insurance Agency, and the office that housed the Mercer business is still there. It is now a Tony Roma's restaurant, but except for the change in furnishings it has been left untouched. The dark-paneled walls are as they were. The big pane-glass windows face on Bay Street. Directly across the street is the bluff that overlooks the Savannah River; below that bluff is another street, paved with cobblestones, on which there is a long line of buildings housing restaurants, souvenir shops, and boutiques. These face directly on the water.

Immediately behind the Mercer-Seiler office, separated only by a service lane, is the Chatham Savings Bank, which faces on Bryan Street. When Walter Mercer or Nick Mamalakis had business at the bank, they would simply walk out their back door and into the bank's back door, and George W. Hunt, the president of the bank, would make that trip in reverse when he wanted to see them. Walter and Nick had a Friday afternoon custom: when the staff had gone home, they would hold a private prayer meeting. Nick Mamalakis told this story:

"One Friday afternoon, George Hunt knocked on our back door. And he came in, interrupting us. He said, 'Forgive me, but I got a letter from Johnny today. He wants to know what is the balance of his daddy's old account.'

"George said: 'Walter, he doesn't need to know. He has no obligation. This was a corporation. We have paid back eighty-two cents on the dollar, when every other son of a gun in those days was settling for ten and twenty cents on the dollar. And we still have enough to pay ten cents more. Walter, what should I do?'

"Walter said, 'Mr. Hunt, he just asked you to give him the balance. He didn't tell you what he wanted it for. The balance is public record, because this is in liquidation in a federal court. So give him the balance.'

"Two or three weeks later Walter and I were again having a meeting, and again there was a rap on the door. George Hunt came in and said, 'Walter, that brother of yours sent me a check for the figure I sent him.'

"And Walter said, 'Well, I thought he would.'

"And George Hunt said, 'Yes, but he didn't sign the damn check.'

"Walter said, 'Then send it back to him.'

"And George said, 'I don't know where he is, between going to Hollywood and New York and around, and the envelope didn't even have a return address. So I'll leave the check with you. Find out from his mother the best place to return the check for signature.'

"After George Hunt left, I said to Walter, 'I know how Johnny loved his parents, he loved his daddy. But I think Johnny would do better to take this money and set up some scholarships at some of the schools. That would be better than paying off four or five hundred people forty dollars apiece.'

"And Walter said, 'Nick, that's a damn good idea. You write him and tell him.'

"I said, 'Walter, he's your brother. You write him.'

"He said, 'Nick, you write a better letter. And besides, it's your idea.' So I wrote the letter to Johnny and almost in the return mail comes a signed check, for around three hundred twenty-five thousand dollars, and at the bottom of *my* letter he had penned these words—he said: 'Nick, you're talking with your head, and I'm speaking with my heart.' And it was signed 'J.' So, after that it was just a matter of paying off the people and folding up the tent."

When the now-signed check was presented to him, George Hunt stared at it for a time, then picked up the telephone and called Johnny's mother. "Miss Lillie," he said, "your son Johnny's just sent me a check for over three hundred thousand dollars for Mr. Mercer's certificate holders."

Johnny immediately made it clear to his brother, his mother, Nick, and George Hunt that he wanted all this kept secret, but it was impossible to keep the story contained. The *Savannah Morning News* soon got wind of it:

> For several days reports have been circulating that several hundred holders of certificates of deposit in the old G.A. Mercer Co. real estate and insurance firm are about to be paid in full, but it was not [known] until yesterday that the money is being put up by the noted songwriter [Johnny Mercer]. . . .
>
> Mr. Mercer was en route from New York to Hollywood yesterday and could not be reached for comment. Local speculation, however, is that he feels the wiping out of the debt would be a fitting tribute to his father's memory.

What the paper did not report is that Johnny Mercer, then forty-five, was fulfilling the pledge of a seventeen-year-old boy.

Nancy Gerard said: "My grandmother was so proud and so filled with love for him, and she was almost not surprised that he did that. Because he was always doing wonderful things for people. Our cook, Nancy Lee

Green, who came to us when I was about ten or eleven, she was a rather plump lady. She was called Big Nancy and I was Little Nancy. He put a roof on her church. He was always doing quiet things in that way."

Johnny's desire to leave his repayment of the debt unpublicized was doomed to even greater failure. The next year, *Reader's Digest* recapitulated the story in a five-page article. And every so often, one of the Georgia newspapers tells it yet again.

"Incidentally," Nick said, "there was some residue in the estate, property that hadn't been sold. When Johnny came back to Savannah to see his mother, George Hunt told him there was this residue, and Johnny said, 'What is residue?' And he pulled out an envelope and wrote on the back of it 'residue' and George said, 'You don't have to do that. We'll give you an accounting of everything.' Johnny said, 'I'm not worried about that. I'm just interested in the word. Someday I might want to use it in a lyric.' "

The "residue" amounted to $45,000. Johnny ordered that it be divided among three Savannah charities.

Johnny's attitude to money was very strange, and very contradictory. Mickey Goldsen said: "Johnny bought a house on Lido Isle at Newport Beach [California]. Lido Isle has waterfront homes on the bay, which are the expensive ones. He lived a few blocks from me. He bought a house three houses in from the water. He was at a party one night with some local people. Someone said, 'How come you live in a house in the interior, when you could be living right on the water?' He said, 'I can't afford it.'

"Everyone at Lido had a boat. He lived on Via Koron. There was a club dock. Johnny used to walk to the dock with an inner tube. He'd get in the water and sit in the tire and paddle around. Here is a wealthy man, the money's rolling in, and the guy sits in a goddamn rubber tube and that's his idea of pleasure. Why doesn't he own a boat? It's the strangest thing."

Other neighbors remember that children would come to the door and say to Ginger, "Can Johnny come out to play?" And Mercer would emerge with his inner tube and go down to the water and play with the children.

Alan Livingston said, "He lived very modestly. When I first knew him, he had a little house on De Longpre Avenue, in not the best section of town. He just never lived up to his income, or who he was, or his celebrity status.

"I never understood it. I never knew anyone like that."

To compound the mystery, John was notoriously cavalier about money. His friend James McIntire said, "He put the check he got for the sale of Capitol into his overcoat pocket and forgot about it. Six months later, he said, 'I wonder what the hell I did with that check?'

"His wife said, 'It's in your overcoat pocket.' "

Checks were left everywhere, in desk drawers and even in a flowerpot. One of his friends, composer Robert Emmett Dolan, said that the house looked as if a tornado had gone through a bank.

James McIntire's wife, Betty, said, "They used to come to our house on New Year's Eve. I always had a New Year's Eve party. And of course we were all pretty drunk. I went over and started talking to Ginger, and I said, 'Oh, it's so wonderful to have you in Savannah, blah blah blah.' And she was just crying! I said, 'Ginger, for heaven's sake, what's the matter?'

" 'Oh,' she said, 'Johnny is so rich and I just don't know what to do with all this money.' She had on a dress that must have cost even in those days maybe two thousand dollars. She started to wipe her eyes with this exquisite dress, and I said, 'Pull yourself together, girl. I'll help you spend it.' "

Twenty-two

Legend surrounds the writing of one of John's most affecting lyrics. I had heard sufficient variations on the story that all I could do was ask the man who knew it best—Mickey Goldsen, who, as the head of Capitol's publishing division, took a French song to Johnny. Mickey told me:

"A guy named Serge Glickson, a French musician, was like a liaison for Capitol Records in Europe. He sent me a batch of records of French songs. I came across this song called '*Les Feuilles Mortes,*' which had been recorded by Edith Piaf. I got ahold of the publisher through Serge. He wanted a $600 advance and he wanted a lyric within three months. I went to Jim Conkling, who by then was running Capitol. He said, 'If you think it's good, we'll give him the money.' I went to Johnny Mercer and said, 'Johnny, I've got a killer song for you.'

"He listened and said, 'That's a good song, Mickey.'

"I said, 'Get me a lyric for it.'

"This was 1951. I waited a couple of months. Finally it had, like, three weeks to go, and no lyric. I said, 'Hey, John, I've only got three weeks to go and I lose the song.'

"He said, 'I'm going to New York on Friday. I'll write it on the train and send it to you from New York. You'll have it within a week. Pick me up and take me to the train station.' They lived on De Longpre.

"I was delayed. I was fifteen minutes late, but we had time. I saw

Johnny on the porch, and he's nailing something to the door. I said, 'Hey, John, I'm sorry I'm late, but we've got plenty of time.'

"He said, 'I thought maybe you had an emergency. While I was waiting, I wrote the lyric.'

"We got into the car and he read me the lyric. Tears came to my eyes. Everybody I played that song for flipped out. It was 'Autumn Leaves.'

"Later I brought him a French song. I first showed the song to Carl Sigman, who was then living in Palm Springs. It had three sixteen-bar verses and three eighteen-bar choruses. Carl wrote lyrics only to one eighteen-bar chorus. I was terribly disappointed in his work. He ignored the dramatic verses, ignored the original story of the song, and came up with a light, romantic, workmanlike Tin Pan Alley ballad. I called him up and said that his lyric did not make the song important. By ignoring the verses, he robbed it of its dramatic strength. I had to be frank with him or I did not deserve to call myself a publisher.

"He took umbrage. He said, 'If you want an important lyric, then get an important writer.' So I did. I went to Johnny, and he fell in love with it and wrote three verses and three choruses in three days. It became 'When the World Was Young.' Carl didn't hold a grudge.

" 'Autumn Leaves' is, like, eighteen bars, and took him three months, and *this* song went on and on and took him three days.

"Johnny said to me later on, 'You know, Mickey, I've made more money on "Autumn Leaves" than any other song I ever wrote.' He had hundreds of records on it."

Everyone who knew John well was astounded at his technical facility and how rapidly he wrote—qualities he shared with Lorenz Hart, by the way. Betty Bennett recalled:

"When I was singing with the Alvino Rey band, we had a vocal group called the Blue Reys. Because we recorded for Capitol, Johnny was going to do a tune with us. He was writing special lyrics to 'Glow-Worm.' We met with him and rehearsed the tune, the first two choruses. But there was a chorus missing. So he said, 'Wait a minute, I'll run down to my office, I think it's on my desk.' So he was gone fifteen minutes and came back with a wonderful lyric—having just written it."

But John could also worry a tune, revising it endlessly, as I suspect was the case with "Skylark." André Previn remembered: "One weekend when we got together, he handed me this beautiful lyric to one of my tunes. The next weekend, he'd rewritten it. And the next weekend, he'd rewritten it again. I said, 'Johnny, why are you rewriting these? They're perfectly beautiful.' And Johnny said, 'Hell, I'm still rewriting "Goody Goody." ' "

By the time he completed work on *Seven Brides for Seven Brothers,* Johnny had been writing songs for movies for twenty years, not counting an abortive foray in 1933 and a picture called *College Coach,* from which no individual songs seem to have survived. He was the preeminent film lyricist, in constant demand and not only respected but even revered by other lyricists.

Since 1934, he had written songs for one picture a year at minimum, and if not all of them were classics, a large number were. The following is by no means a complete list, nor have I noted every song in a given picture, only the best of the work:

1934　"I'm Building Up to an Awful Let-Down" (from *Fools Rush In*), music by Fred Astaire

1935　"Comes the Revolution, Baby" (from *Old Man Rhythm,* with Betty Grable and Buddy Rogers), music by Lewis E. Gensler

1936　"I'm an Old Cowhand" (from the Bing Crosby film *Rhythm on the Range*), music by Johnny Mercer

1937　"Too Marvelous for Words" (from *Ready, Willing and Able*), music by Richard Whiting
　　　"We're Working Our Way Through College" (from *Varsity Show*), music by Richard Whiting
　　　"Hooray for Hollywood," "Bob White," and "Have You Got Any Castles, Baby?" (from *Hollywood Hotel,* with Dick Powell), music by Richard Whiting

1938　"Ride, Tenderfoot, Ride" (from *Cowboy from Brooklyn,* with Dick Powell and Ann Sheridan), music by Richard Whiting
　　　"The Girl Friend of the Whirling Dervish" (from *Garden of the Moon,* with John Payne), music by Harry Warren
　　　"Jeepers Creepers" (from *Going Places,* with Dick Powell, Anita Louise, and Ronald Reagan), music by Harry Warren

"You Must Have Been a Beautiful Baby" (from *Hard to Get,* with Dick Powell and Olivia de Havilland), music by Harry Warren

1940 "I'd Know You Anywhere," "Like the Fellow Once Said," and "You've Got Me This Way" (from *You'll Find Out*), music by Jimmy McHugh

1941 "Blues in the Night," "This Time the Dream's on Me," and "Says Who? Says You, Says I" (from *Blues in the Night,* with Richard Whorf and Priscilla Lane), music by Harold Arlen

1942 "Tangerine," "Arthur Murray Taught Me Dancing in a Hurry," "If You Build a Better Mouse Trap," "Not Mine," and "I Remember You" (from *The Fleet's In,* with William Holden, Dorothy Lamour, Betty Hutton, and the Jimmy Dorsey band), music by Victor Schertzinger

"Dearly Beloved," "You Were Never Lovelier," and "I'm Old-Fashioned" (from *You Were Never Lovelier,* with Fred Astaire, Rita Hayworth, Larry Parks, and the Xavier Cugat orchestra), music by Jerome Kern

"That Old Black Magic" and "Hit the Road to Dreamland" (from *Star Spangled Rhythm,* with Bing Crosby, Bob Hope, and Dick Powell), music by Harold Arlen

"Captains of the Clouds" (from *Captains of the Clouds,* with James Cagney), music by Harold Arlen

1943 "My Shining Hour" and "One for My Baby (and One More for the Road)" (from *The Sky's the Limit,* with Fred Astaire and Joan Leslie), music by Harold Arlen

1944 "Accentuate the Positive" and "Let's Take the Long Way Home" (from *Here Come the Waves,* with Bing Crosby and Betty Hutton), music by Harold Arlen

1945 "How Little We Know" (from *To Have and Have Not,* with Humphrey Bogart and Lauren Bacall), music by Hoagy Carmichael

"Laura" (from *Laura,* with Dana Andrews, Gene

Tierney, and Clifton Webb), music by David Raksin

"Out of This World" (from *Out of This World,* with Eddie Bracken), music by Harold Arlen

1946   "On the Atchison, Topeka and the Santa Fe" (from *The Harvey Girls,* with Judy Garland, John Hodiak, Kenny Baker, and Cyd Charisse), music by Harry Warren

1951   "In the Cool, Cool, Cool of the Evening" (from *Here Comes the Groom,* with Bing Crosby and Jane Wyman), music by Hoagy Carmichael

1955   "Something's Gotta Give" (from *Daddy Long Legs,* with Fred Astaire and Leslie Caron), music by Johnny Mercer

But by the 1950s, John's output of great songs almost dries up. Bill Haley and the Comets had a 1953 hit called "Crazy, Man, Crazy," and then a succession of hits, including "Shake, Rattle and Roll," in 1954. "Rock Around the Clock," which became a hit in 1955, ultimately sold 22 million copies. The age of rock had come, and if John did not foresee the scope of social and musical change that was under way, well, neither did anyone else.

John was a product of the big-band age. By the time he was fifteen, the Paul Whiteman band was in its ascendancy. And there was the Jean Goldkette band. When he entered his early twenties, the big-band era was in gestation. The Casa Loma Orchestra with Glen Gray, which Artie Shaw always insisted was the first swing band, made its first recording for the Okeh label in 1929. The Benny Goodman band was launched in 1934, when John was twenty-four, and then the band era was upon North America, with "sweet" bands and "swing" bands by the scores and even hundreds touring the continent, not to mention all the "territory bands" that were successful in their own regions, though not nationally.

The big bands flourished in symbiosis with a host of other social phenomena: the newly formed radio networks, the Broadway musical theater and Hollywood musical movies, the country's countless dance pavilions, and—an item generally overlooked in analyses of the era—the interurban electric railways. These railways, more than six hundred miles of them in Los Angeles County alone in the 1920s, carried young dancers to the dance pavilions, where they heard songs from Broadway and Hollywood made famous on the radio networks and played by the bands. The big broadcasting networks employed enormous numbers of musicians on their variety shows and "light classical" broadcasts, and both NBC and CBS maintained their own symphony orchestras. (The NBC Radio Orchestra was led by Arturo Toscanini.) Furthermore, they carried late-night "remote" broadcasts of big bands from such places as the Palomar Ballroom, the Glen Island Casino, and Frank Dailey's Meadowbrook, all of which became household names. These networks *made* the bands and the songs famous, and the bands made their singers famous: Frank Sinatra, Dick Haymes, Perry Como, Doris Day, Jo Stafford, Kay Starr, and many more.

But with the end of World War II, conditions changed once more, and just as rapidly. The young men who used to take their girls dancing were now getting married, starting families, and staying home, where they watched a medium whose development had been slowed by the war: television. Not only did attendance at dances drop, movie attendance fell to a new low. And in any case, it was becoming increasingly difficult to get to the dance pavilions in suburban entertainment parks. Various interests with an eye toward the development of the automobile and the highways bought up the street railways and interurban trolleys, reduced their schedules, and eventually dismantled them. And, observing the extraordinary power of television—and its potential as a source of advertising revenues—the networks gradually withdrew from radio broadcasting. One result was that local radio stations were increasingly left to their own resources, and the stations began to turn programming over to a new figure in America's cultural life: the disc jockey. These local stations soon found it profitable to cater to a progressively lower and lower common denominator of public musical taste.

The 1920s, '30s, and '40s produced songs of extraordinary quality and literacy. Perhaps the most respected study of the subject is *American Popular Song: The Great Innovators, 1900–1950,* by Alec Wilder in collaboration with James T. Maher. For Wilder, 1950 was the last year of the great song era. That was the year of Frank Loesser's brilliant virtuoso turn *Guys and Dolls.* The Lerner and Loewe masterpiece *My Fair Lady* and Frank Loesser's too-often-overlooked *The Most Happy Fella* were both produced in 1956, and Stephen Sondheim and Jule Styne's *Gypsy* appeared in 1959. But, given the fact that eras do not have convenient beginning and end years, in general Alec was right. And if you examine the hit lists of the 1950s, you can see the quality of songs dropping. If the young men who went off to World War II wrote literate letters home—and you can hear them in television documentaries about that war—it is in part because the communal ear had been informed and educated by the pervasive effect of song, with literate and clever lyrics by the likes of Johnny Mercer, Cole Porter, Dorothy Fields, Lorenz Hart, Oscar Hammerstein, Al Dubin, Harold Adamson, Leo Robin, Irving Berlin, Frank Loesser, and the breathtakingly clever Howard Dietz.

By 1955, the year Capitol was acquired by EMI, the first Elvis Presley records were reaching the market, and the next year his career would produce a seismic shock in popular music with his first records on the RCA Victor label. For a time, "quality" popular music coexisted with the rising tide of the meretricious, but nobody could foresee the scope of the change ahead.

Twenty-three

Most of us like to forget our failures; Johnny dwelled on his. He had a list of them on the wall of his studio, next to a quote from Hilaire Belloc: "It is the best of all trades to sing songs and the second best to write them." Once, as we walked down Central Park West in New York from my apartment, he had me almost hanging on lampposts with laughter as he sang me a medley of his flops.

He turned fifty in 1959. The range of his accomplishments by that age was astounding. He, with two colleagues, had built one of the world's major record companies from nothing but an idea, and against daunting odds. That Glenn Wallichs was a brilliant and indispensable executive is undeniable, but the creative musical force of that company was John Herndon Mercer. He had by now written probably a thousand lyrics, dozens of which are among the finest in the English language.

Aside from his huge output of classic songs, he had been an immensely successful singer, although to the end of his life he didn't think so.

He had twenty-seven hit vocal records between 1938 and 1952, sometimes two in the same month; once, he had four hit records at the same time. They are, including the dates and their positions on the Hit Parade:

| August 1938 | "Mr. Gallagher and Mr. Shean" | 7 |
| | "Small Fry" | 3 |

July 1940	"Mister Meadowlark"	18
August 1942	"Strip Polka"	7
January 1943	"I Lost My Sugar in Salt Lake City"	18
	"G.I. Jive"	11
April 1944	"San Fernando Valley"	21
September 1944	"Sam's Got Him"	24
January 1945	"Accentuate the Positive"	1
	"Candy"	1
	"I'm Gonna See My Baby"	12
July 1945	"On the Atchison, Topeka	1
	and the Santa Fe"	(for eight weeks)
November 1945	"Surprise Party"	5
January 1946	"Personality"	1
	"My Sugar Is So Refined"	11
	"Ugly Chile"	22
December 1946	"Zip-a-Dee-Do-Dah"	8
	"A Gal in Calico"	5
	"Winter Wonderland"	4
January 1947	"Hugging and A-Chalkin' "	8
April 1947	"I Do Do Do Like You"	13
	"Moon Faced, Starry-Eyed"	21
September 1947	"Sugar Blues"	4
October 1947	"Save the Bones for Henry Jones"	12
	"Harmony"	12
February 1948	"The Thousand Islands Song"	28
	"Hooray for Love"	25
	"Baby It's Cold Outside"	3
	"Glow-Worm"	30

He didn't write all of them, but most of them are humorous, or at least carefree, songs. He sang with a wonderful, rough exuberance, a countrified quality all his own infused with the black vocal influences of his youth, and a distinctive rapid vibrato. He did *not* record his ballads because—I came to realize in a conversation with him—he didn't think he was good enough. A failure as a singer, however, he assuredly was not.

All the while, his unhappiness with Ginger continued.

"He was mad at her. *Always,*" Mandy said. "I thought she was just aloof. And then my brother told me how angry she was. I'd hear the fighting and thought it was both of them. And then Jeff said, 'No, it's Mom. She's just got a burr up her ass all the time.'

"They used to fight *all* the time. My brother and I used to pray they would break up. I used to dream we lived on an island, and there was a big flash flood and it covered the whole house, and I was able to grab Jeff and the dog and we swam away and they drowned and I'd take care of my little brother and we'd be okay."

And yet, in spite of this, Mandy has happy memories of that period: "When we'd drive to Palm Springs, we'd sing all the way. And he'd tell us to watch for the big trucks, and when we passed we were supposed to wave and blow kisses."

Jeff, too, has some good memories. Johnny indulged him constantly, even to the extent of letting him have (for a short time) a pet lion. Jeff loved to go on trips with him, and remembers with warmth the train journeys to New York. All the black porters knew and revered Mercer.

But Jeff also remembers the drinking, Ginger's as well as John's:

"I was with him when he got a little out of control—when I was older. It was the booze talking. He had a friend named Matt Ober. He was a lieutenant colonel in the military. He lived on Lido Island. It was kind of strange, my father on one side of the wall, and a military man on the other side. The kids got together, myself and Mike Ober. I was six or seven years old. My dad and Mike Ober were really tight, very good friends. Because they were so opposite, there was no challenge there. My dad was basically a pacifist and this guy was in the military. They didn't have anything to confront each other with. My father didn't feel he had to put up a front, and neither did Matt.

"Matt had been decorated in the Korean War. He'd been in hand-to-hand combat with the North Koreans. He had some battle scars he loved to show.

"My dad went to a place called The Stuffed Shirt. He got drunk and started to pick a fight with some people. And Matt was a trained killer, not that he'd do anything. Matt told everybody to bunk out. He told them, 'You don't want to tangle with me.' And he got my dad out of there.

"Probably time-wise, my memories are not too accurate. It's hard, chronologically, sometimes, to place it. I think my father and Mandy fought a lot when I was really young. He never fought with me. He just thought I was a little boy. As long as he spoiled me, no problem. But Mandy, being a girl, he was really protective. If you're the father of a daughter, you're going to be a little different than if you're the father of a son. A son, you can look the other way and let him get away with something. Your daughter, you're really on top of it.

"Our family fought a lot. My mother was an alcoholic, and she was an alcoholic for a long time. I wasn't aware of it until later. I thought it was just something adults did—the liquor cabinet. The cocktail hour wasn't an hour, it was six or seven hours. I grew up with that. Everybody was drinking all the time. And driving. That was just a normal thing. You got a citation for driving drunk. Now you go to jail. They just haul you away. The whole thing has changed.

"The liquor cabinet was kind of a focus. By the time I got old enough to get interested, I'd swipe a bottle for myself and my friends, and I caught hell. Not so much from my dad as from my mom. I came home from high school once and she was gone—she was passed out. This was in L.A. Usually my mom would pick me up from school. But one day my dad picked me up, and I said, 'How come Mom didn't pick me up? I thought you were busy.' He said, 'I got a call because your mom isn't feeling too well.' When we got home, she was passed out on the stairs with her head facing downward. My dad didn't even bother with her. He stepped over her."

Mandy, like her friends Jill and Bill Goodwin, was very attracted to jazz. She began dating a young jazz pianist named Bob Corwin, and in 1960, she married him. "I liked Bob," Mandy said. "And I admired him. Bob had a darling son who I just adored. And it was the thing to do in those days. Girls of twenty, twenty-one years old got married, that's all there was to it. I loved running around with him and not being Johnny Mercer's daughter. I was his wife. We'd go and hang out with all these jazz musicians like Phil Woods. He worked with these guys, and I liked hanging around with him. I knew Bill Evans. I knew Daddy's friends and then I got to know Bobby's friends. I always loved that music. Daddy would play it for me, and Bob would take me out on dates to listen to it."

I asked Mandy if she married Bob because she loved him or just to get out of that house.

"Maybe a little of both," she said with a laugh. "When I got married, I used to talk to my husband about it. I said, 'I've got to adopt Jeff, if I could just get custody of him!' Bob said, 'Yeah, you're gonna get custody away from Johnny Mercer, right? Dream on.' Later, as Jeff and I got to be friends when we got older, he said he was put out with me for leaving him there. We're really good friends now."

When Mandy was dating Bob Corwin, she got letters from Miss Lillian much like those John received from her when he was courting Ginger: "She said she didn't want another Jew in the family and I should marry some nice Southern boy."

John was delighted when Bob and Mandy presented him with a grandson, Jamie, and took a deep interest in him. Jamie said, "I think he was probably a better grandfather than he was a father."

When Jamie joined the Cub Scouts, John wrote a song for them. Jamie can still sing it. He said:

"I was nine. Johnny rehearsed us and conducted us for a pack meeting:

> *We're men of the Werewolf Den.*
> *We're fearless, brave and true.*
> *We're men of the Werewolf Den,*
> *and this is what we do.*
>
> *Our nails are trimmed,*
> *our hair is neat.*
> *We help old ladies*
> *across the street.*
>
> *We're men of the Werewolf Den.*
> *Ah-oooo, ah-oooo.*

"He used to take my friends to the circus. He'd get a box of seats. Or he'd take them to a toy store and let them pick any toy in the store."

When Howie Richmond told me in 1997 that Mandy wanted me to write a biography of Johnny, and that Johnny had also told Howie that he wanted me to do it, Howie set up a luncheon with Bob Corwin. Bob had sketched some notes on what he wanted to say, and since he was highly organized, and almost terrifyingly honest, I'd like to lay his observations on you—as John would say—intact.

> Johnny was a very, very complex man. Your categories would be talent, generosity, frailties, ethics, quirks.
> I loved him—especially now. During the time I was married to his daughter, I was involved in drugs, and my mind was all screwed up. Now that I see a clear picture of him, he was a fabulously wonderful person. If I was able to see him now, I would thank him for all the things he tried to do for me, and apologize to

him for how little I appreciated it. He did everything in his power to make me a success. I believe he liked me. In a period of eighteen years he gave me a Camaro station wagon, he bought me a brand new Mustang. He bought Mandy a Volvo station wagon. He bought two houses for us.

He would ask me, "What do you want to do? Don't you want to be more successful? Do you want a band? I'll get a band for you." He was desperately trying to make me successful, and unfortunately I didn't care. I was only into: When can I get my next prescription?

As a father-in-law trying to help a son-in-law, you couldn't find anybody better in the world than he was. You want clothes? He bought me clothes. I didn't ask him for a lot of money, but some of the money he gave me I really didn't deserve. He put me on salary and I worked for him for a number of years.

He wanted me to be a successful songwriter. He paid me to just sit in a studio and write songs. I don't think I had a natural gift. I'm not trying to put myself down. I'm a very good piano player, but that didn't make a songwriter. He encouraged me to write melodies, and when I wrote them, he put lyrics to them. I wrote about ten songs with him. In the depths of depression, I threw them in a Dumpster in Calabasas. I don't have any of the songs. I remember a couple of the titles. "Where Does a Lover Go to Surrender?" "Little Miss Heartbreak."

There was a movie called *Strange Bedfellows*. He was called to write the title for the movie. He called me up and said, "We have to go over to Panama and Frank [the screenplay-writing team of Norman Panama and Melvin Frank]. I have this song I want to play for them." And he asked me to play the piano for him. We got to their office and he said, "I know you want a song called 'Strange Bedfellows.' It's not a good title, and I can't write a song with that title. But I have a song that I wrote that, I think, would be a perfect title song. It's called 'I Want to Be in Love Again.' " I played and he sang the song. They said, "Perfect. We love it. We're going to use it for the title song. We'll give you $25,000 for the song."

He said, "I don't want the $25,000. I just want the publishing rights to the song."

They said, "We can't give you the publishing rights."

He said, "No." And he turned around and walked out.

"It's a song that was eventually recorded by Jackie and Roy, and to this day I don't think the song made $25,000."

I was a flake. He was writing *Foxy* with Bobby Dolan. Bobby Dolan flew out here. I worked this job with Anita O'Day in Santa Barbara. I was driving home and my car broke down, and I ended up in the San Fernando Valley, at Fallbrook and Ventura Boulevard. I had to take a taxi home. We lived in Brentwood. Johnny was over in Bel Air, writing with Bobby Dolan. He called on the phone. I was going to take a bus out to get my car. He said, "I'll pick you up and drive you out there."

In the background, I heard Bobby Dolan, "What are you doing? We've got to write."

He came over. Bobby Dolan was with him. He drove me out to the Valley. And I'd forgotten my car keys. I couldn't get into the car. We drove all the way back to Brentwood. I got my car keys. I said, "I'll take a bus out. Or somebody else will drive me."

He said, "What do you mean? I'll drive you back."

Bobby Dolan was ready to kill me.

Johnny even paid for my psychiatrist.

One day he said, "Let's see what we can do with one of your songs. Andy Williams is looking for a song to do on his show. Let's show him one of the songs I wrote with you." That's when Andy Williams had a regular Sunday television show. We went up to Andy Williams's office, and Andy said, "I love it. I'll record it. If you'll change one line." It went:

> *We sit in bars,*
> *just getting loaded,*
> *drive fabulous cars,*
> *too soon outmoded.*
> *But looking at stars,*
> *that has become as square*
> *as a book or a walk or a prayer.*

Andy Williams said he didn't want to get into controversy or religion and asked if he would change it a little.

And Johnny said, "No."

It would have been an important recording for me.

He loved the state of Georgia and he loved Savannah. He was asked by the state legislature to write a state song. "Georgia on

My Mind" was written by Hoagy Carmichael. They wanted a song by a home-town boy. Johnny worked as hard on that song as any song he ever wrote. It was important to him. He asked me to write an arrangement for symphony orchestra. He performed it with the Savannah Symphony. Then it was played for the state legislature—and rejected. The reason it was rejected was that some legislator from the northern part of the state didn't approve it. I think it was a big heartbreak for him.

Johnny was a genius lyricist. We were making a demo for Howie Richmond of a song called "Star Sounds." We were in the studio, but now he was not the songwriter, he was the engineer. And he did not have a gift for that, in my opinion. Shelly Manne was playing drums. Every time we would do a take, he would come out and say to Shelly, "The drums are too loud. We need the drums softer."

Shelly came over to me and said, "I do whatever I'm told. If he wants me to play softer, I'm going to play softer. But this is supposed to be a bossa nova, and I am very experienced with recording. If you record the song the way he wants, you will not even hear the drums."

I went into the booth and told Johnny. Johnny said, "I don't care, just tell him to play softer." We recorded the thing, he mailed it to Howie, and Howie sent a telegram back to Johnny saying, "Loved your recording. What we need now is a bossa nova recording."

You couldn't hear the drums.

I wrote one lyric. I showed it to him, he said, "Ah, it sounds like Johnny Burke. Forget it." I thought it was a compliment. But I didn't write any more lyrics after that.

He got very strange when he drank. If he was drunk, and he was going to insult you, you had to be famous. He seemed to enjoy being creatively nasty to well-known people. I even saw him lace into Hoagy Carmichael.

One of my jobs was to get him out of places before he got punched.

There was a piano player who worked in Beverly Hills named Joe Marino. You couldn't stump him. Any song you could name, he could play. Johnny used to go in there. We were there and he was bombed and started insulting some people. I started really getting scared. Whoever it was, he was getting really mad. I'm not a good fighter. I went over to the bartender and said, "How do I get him outta here?" The bartender made a drink and said, "Give him this. Tell him somebody bought him a drink. He'll be outta here in five minutes."

We were gone, outta there in five minutes.

I once saw him get angry *at a curb*. He took a kick at the curb and broke his toe.

I remember one time we were in Chicago, getting on the Super Chief. The guy who takes the tickets said, "Excuse me, sir, do you have a ticket?" And Johnny said, "Yes I do," and kept on walking. And the guy came after him and said, "Could I see the ticket?" So he stopped and showed him the ticket.

He didn't fly. He picked me up one time. I was on the road. I came back by plane. He picked me up at the airport. He said, "How long did it take you to get here?" I said, "I don't know, couple of hours."

"Really?" he said. "Boy. One of these times I'm gonna fly. What time does the plane leave?"

I said, "Whadya mean, what time does the plane leave? What plane?"

He said, "Well, if you want to go to New York."

I said, "There's one every hour."

"Really?" he said. He thought there was one plane, like the Super Chief.

He was a fabulous cook. Fabulous. A gourmet cook. Ask Mandy. Some of the dishes he made, incredible. He loved to cook, and he was great at following a recipe. He would spend a whole day on a dish. He loved to go to church. He went to a little Episcopal church every Sunday, whenever he could.

Johnny liked to go to places that were either very expensive or places that nobody else could go. I asked him about it one time. He said, "That's one of the things that you enjoy about becoming successful: that you can go to places that other people can't go, because either they can't afford it or they're not invited because they're not famous enough." He *enjoyed* that.

I remember one time, my brain was out in left field. I said, "Johnny, I would never want to be famous. I can't even imagine what it's like to have people recognize you wherever you go. What is it like?"

He said, "It's the greatest feeling in the world!"

His ability to make up lyrics on the spot was amazing. One time I was working with Anita O'Day at the Lighthouse. He came in and he got up to sing. I said, "What are you going to sing?" He said, "Just play the blues."

He must have sung thirty choruses off the top of the head, with lyrics, on the blues. Unbelievable. Just made 'em up on the spot.

I was his stenographer. I took down the songs that he wrote the melody and the lyrics to. That was part of my job. He didn't read notes. He had his own way. If the next note meant it went from D to C, an arrow pointed down, and that meant it was the C below. If it pointed up, it meant the C above. He would give me these letters with arrows. Then he would sing you the rhythm. So now you'd have a melody. Now you got to the chords. The point that I'm getting at is one of the things I'm adamant about. Johnny *heard* songs. The fact that he was not a professional musician meant absolutely *nothing*. Johnny was a *songwriter*. He heard the melody, he heard the harmonies, he simply didn't know how to write them. As a musician, one of the things that infuriates me is musicians who say that when they take down songs for songwriters, the musician should get credit for writing the song. It is the biggest bunch of baloney.

I know guys that have actually conned songwriters into having them put their names on the music, saying, "You didn't know the chords. I wrote the chords."

Let me tell you how Johnny did it. After you got the melody down, and you'd play a chord, he'd say, "That's not it," and you'd play another chord, and he'd say, "That's not it." And then you'd play another one and he'd say, "That's it." He knew every single chord. Once in a while he'd say, "That's even nicer than what I was thinking."

Johnny always gave credit to others, and sometimes declined to take credit for his own contributions to the work of others (as in the case of Carl Sigman). In 1961, John recorded a duet album with Bobby Darin titled *Two of a Kind*. The title track was a song he had written years earlier, but when Darin contributed extra lyrics, John gave him full cowriter credit.

John said, "I was on a TV show with a very young man, who had written a couple of songs at the time, and he's written more since, and his name is Bobby Darin, and he said, 'Mr. Mercer, I'd like to make an album with you sometime.' Well, I couldn't have been more overjoyed, because I thought he was so talented, he had such a beat. He sings like a drum, he's wonderful. So we spent about six months trying to find tunes, and the one that we devised—because he and I wrote this—for the title, which opens the album and also closes it, was 'Two of a Kind.' And in many ways, we indeed are two of a kind."

There are a number of Mercer songs on the album, including a delightful version of "Bob White," which John had written in 1937 with Bernie Hanighen. Darin was an enormously talented singer, and, for all his success, an underappreciated one in his own lifetime. He was at the peak of his abilities, and so was Mercer at the time of the recording. And they had the advantage of exuberant Billy May arrangements.

But the classic case of Mercer sharing credit is the story of a Youngstown, Ohio, widow named Sadie Vimmerstedt. About the time the Darin album came out, she wrote Johnny a letter, suggesting an idea for a song: "I wanna be around to pick up the pieces when somebody breaks your heart." Mrs. Vimmerstedt later told William D. Laffler of the Associated Press, "Two years later he answered my letter and apologized for his tardiness."

In an interview published in the *Savannah News-Press Sunday Magazine* on January 2, 1977, she said: "The joy of hearing from this great man was overwhelming, and I felt this greatness coming through this humble letter.

"Not being schooled in the music business, and with no one to turn to, I wanted to assure him that the title was mine and that only he and I knew of it. It was his to do with what he wished. I never expected to be included in his plan, never expected any royalties.

"It was only then that I explained to my daughter what I had done. We mailed the answer to Johnny and were very pleased and grateful that such a marvelous composer would take time out to write to an unknown person like myself.

"After several months of correspondence, we became very close. A contract was signed where I would receive ten percent, Johnny to handle all the business end of it. After more correspondence, I received a letter from Johnny asking me to tear up the ten-percent contract, because he felt he had found himself a fine lady, and wanted to make me his partner. New contracts were set up which stand to this day where I am a fifty percent partner."

More years went by with nothing but silence from Mercer. Bob Corwin picks up the story:

"He thought 'I Wanna Be Around' stunk. But he thought Mrs. Vimmerstedt should have half the song because the title *is* half the song. The song was lying on a shelf when a fellow named Phil Zeller said, 'I would like to do some promotion work. Do you have any songs that haven't been recorded?'

"Johnny said, 'I've got tons of them. Why don't you go through them and pick whatever you think is any good?' Phil came up with only one song, 'I Wanna Be Around.' He said, 'I think I can do something with this song.'

"Johnny said, 'You've gotta be kidding. That's the worst song I ever wrote. You can't get arrested with that song.'

"Phil said, 'Could I try?'

"Johnny said, 'Okay.'

"Phil ran to the airport, went to Vegas. Tony Bennett was in Vegas. Phil Zeller could sell anything. He got in to see Tony Bennett, and played the song for him."

Mrs. Vimmerstedt told the *Savannah News-Press*:

"Four years went by and nobody recorded the song. Johnny would not do it himself. He said he wanted a good singer.

"Then one evening my daughter and I settled down to watch Johnny Carson's first *Tonight Show*. That was on October 1, 1962. Tony Bennett was one of his guests and sang 'I Left My Heart in San Francisco.'

"Johnny Carson questioned Tony on how he was going to follow up 'San Francisco.' Tony told him he felt he already had one. We were paying strict attention to Tony, with no thought of 'I Wanna' on our minds. We had no idea Tony Bennett had even seen the sheet music.

"Then Tony said, 'I would like to sing it here tonight, and if the audience approves, I will record it first thing in the morning.' "

Well, hardly. An arrangement had to be written, a studio booked, the orchestra hired. Presumably the record date was already set when Tony appeared on *The Tonight Show*.

Mrs. Vimmerstedt continued: "Johnny Carson asked, 'What is the name of the song?' and Tony said, 'I Wanna Be Around to Pick Up the Pieces.' Tony then sang the song and the audience approved.

"Of course, my daughter and I were in a state of shock and we still are. The people in Youngstown knew about the song and the phone began to ring. It hasn't stopped till this day. From the next day on my daughter and I began to realize what it was to become a celebrity overnight. And I still am."

Mrs. Vimmerstedt's husband had died a few months before she sent her first letter to Johnny, leaving her and her three daughters "just about enough money to bury him," as one of them, Joan Clarke, told me. Sadie took a job selling Elizabeth Arden cosmetics in a department store. Joan Clarke said: "A few months later, the royalties started to roll in, and have not stopped since. My mom received the bulk of the money when it was in the top ten. Since then it has been in *Midnight in the Garden of Good and Evil, The Scout, Love Boy, Pizza Man,* and other movies."

In Youngstown, people everywhere asked Mrs. Vimmerstedt for her autograph. She went to New York to appear on television shows, and to Hollywood to attend a Grammy Awards dinner. In time she found this very wearing, and wrote to John: "I'll tell you something. I'm getting tired of show business."

Joan Clarke said, "Thanks to Johnny's integrity and generosity, my mother's life was completely changed forever. She traveled around the world several times. My two sisters and I still receive checks from Warner Bros. and ASCAP. We met Johnny at an ASCAP meeting in New York, and you'd have thought Sadie was the celebrity. Johnny was *so* humble."

Mrs. Vimmerstedt said, "Every day there is a special joy in my life because of Johnny Mercer, the gentleman he was and the things he did for me. All the memories I have of him are very tender."

Tony Bennett also heard from Mrs. Vimmerstedt regularly. Tony told the BBC, "I got these cards for years from her. With the royalties from the money she had, from Greece, from Italy, from Britain, she just traveled with that money, and thanked me every time she sent me a card."

Twenty-four

Bob Corwin once put a question to John: "I asked Johnny what he would have liked to have done in his career that he didn't do. He told me that he would love to have had what he called a hit Broadway show. The other thing is that he would have liked to have written a hit Christmas song."

John wrote in 1953: "I don't know what it is about the theater and me, but I suppose it was love at first sight on my part. What started the infatuation, I don't remember exactly. Perhaps it was the blackface comedians in A. G. Fields Minstrels at the old Savannah Theater, or the old phonograph records of 'Evelyn, Oh Evelyn, Won't You Kindly Quit Your Devilin?' or 'When It's Apple Blossom Time in Normandie.' "

And although he was a conventionally religious Episcopalian, John said to me, "The theater is our modern church."

His first Broadway musical was *I Walk with Music,* written with Hoagy Carmichael in 1941. The choral arranger on that show was Hugh Martin. Hugh said, "It was originally called *Three After Three* and when they came into Broadway they changed the title to *I Walk with Music.* It wasn't a hit. But it was a delightful score. We traveled all over the Eastern Seaboard together. Hoagy was never there. He had other fish to fry. But Johnny was always there. I even wrote a song with Johnny on a train. It wasn't much of a song but it was very exciting for a neophyte like me to write with Johnny."

The show closed after fifty-five performances.

John's next musical came in 1946—*St. Louis Woman,* which he wrote with Harold Arlen. The project had originated with Arthur Freed, the former songwriter who headed what was known as the Freed Unit at MGM. Under his aegis the studio turned out *An American in Paris, Singin' in the Rain,* and many more of the best musicals of the era. *St. Louis Woman,* as it eventually came to be called, was based on a 1931 novel by Arna Bontemps (*God Sends Sunday*) and rendered into a play by the poet Countee Cullen. Bontemps and Cullen were among the more prominent lights in the Harlem Renaissance. The Broadway producer Edward Gross approached Freed about turning it into an all-black musical, and he wanted Arlen and Mercer to write the score. Freed and Sam Katz set up their own production company to back the show, planning to sell it to MGM once it had become the smash hit that seemed inevitable.

John had just finished work on *The Harvey Girls* with Harry Warren, and he was looking for a project—as if Capitol Records were not enough to keep him busy. He and Harold Arlen signed on, though they were unhappy with the script when they saw it. Arlen was living in Beverly Hills. When Johnny dropped by one day, Arlen played a little figure for him, a repeated note dropping a major third, then rising a minor third. It had something of a *recitativo* quality to it, and it elicited a phrase from John: "I'm gonna love you like nobody's loved you. . . ."

To which Arlen, always a witty man, said, "Come hell or high water."

"Of course!" John said, laughing. "Come rain or come shine." (Johnny, it will be recalled, had seen a play called *Rain or Shine* in his aspiring-actor days in New York.)

It was one of the first songs they wrote for the show, and it is one of the great classics to emerge from the collaboration of Arlen and Mercer.

Their work went well, but nothing else did. Walter White, secretary of the National Association for the Advancement of Colored People, said that the show "detracted from the dignity of the race." Whether he was basing this opinion on a copy of the script or the original Bontemps-Cullen play is unknown. But his comments soon circulated in the press. Lena Horne said that the show "sets the Negro back a hundred years," and she added, "It's full of gamblers, no-goods, et cetera, and I'll never play a part like that." The show had the backing of MGM's Freed, let us remember, and after that remark, Edward Jablonski notes in his authoritative biography *Harold Arlen: Rhythm, Rainbows and Blues,* "her career at MGM rapidly withered."

The story concerns a black jockey, Augie, who falls in love with Della Green (the St. Louis woman of the title), a lady of easy virtue who belongs to a saloon keeper. The saloon keeper is shot by an old mistress, but he thinks it's Augie who has done it and puts a dying curse on him. The superstitious Augie believes in it, and his winning streak at the track comes to an end. Edward Gross put together an excellent "all-Negro" cast, including a gifted but unknown young singer named Ruby Hill as Della, the distinguished actor Rex Ingram as the saloon keeper, and those superb tap dancers the Nicholas Brothers. Harold Nicholas played Augie, and his brother Fayard was cast as a competing jockey. Pearl Bailey would play opposite Fayard Nicholas as an employee in the saloon.

Arlen and Mercer remained unhappy with the structure of the show despite several rewrites, and when Countee Cullen, only forty-three years old, died, Arna Bontemps was left to struggle alone with the book. Rouben Mamoulian was brought in to replace Lemuel Ayers as the director. Mamoulian restructured the show into three acts, and fired the newcomer Ruby Hill from the role of Della, replacing her with a more experienced actress. He also tossed out of the show "I Wonder What Became of Me?", which would survive as one of the classics of the Arlen-Mercer catalogue. On Saturday, March 30, 1946, with the show set to open that evening, the cast, led by Pearl Bailey, went on strike. They told Mamoulian that if he did not rehire Ruby Hill, there would be no performance. He capitulated and the show opened.

The show got only two favorable reviews, and critic Louis Kronenberg savaged Arlen's music. Writing in the weekly *PM*, he said, "First-rate music might yet have turned the tide, but Harold Arlen's songs and orchestral tags and tidbits are second-rate even for him. They are most of them romantic or atmospheric enough, but they lack distinction, they lack melodic urgency, they lack the excitement and cohesive power that folk drama demands. It is an agreeable score, but nothing more than that."

Oh, really? "Come Rain or Come Shine," "Any Place I Hang My Hat Is Home," "Li'l Augie Is a Natural Man," and "Legalize My Name," among others, are second-rate?

The show closed after only 113 performances, one of the major disappointments of John's life, as he told me long afterwards. He recorded the score for Capitol a week after the opening. In 1993 it was rereleased in CD format, and if you can find a copy, you can judge for yourself what a classic score Mercer and Arlen had produced. And time has justified them. The show has been revived several times, including a "blues ballet" version by Dance Theater of Harlem. And *Variety* eventually referred to its "brilliant, enduring score."

The problem, as John knew even as he and Harold Arlen were at work on it, was the book. A strong book is essential to any musical, although occasionally good songs can overcome a weak book, as in the case of Lerner and Loewe's *Camelot*. What is surprising in the tepid reviews of *St. Louis Woman* is the number of critics who failed to perceive the originality of its distinctive songs.

The problem of a weak book also afflicted John's next musical, *Texas Li'l Darlin'*, in 1949. The idea was not without potential. A right-wing Republican publisher of a magazine called *Trends* (based not-so-loosely on Henry Luce, the publisher of *Time* and *Life* magazines) wants to elect as president his own man, "someone I can reach on the phone," and for his puppet he chooses a Texas politician named Hominy Smith. In view of the election of November 2000 and the subsequent scandals about business access to the White House, the idea now seems prophetic. But the book was the work of John Whedon and Sam Moore, whose previous experience was writing for radio, and it is clear that they had little knowledge of the structure of a stage musical. And satire is difficult to pull off in the theater, requiring a deft and secure touch that they obviously lacked.

The structure of a musical comedy is generally strict. Its principles are violated at risk, although it can be done, as in the case of *I Do, I Do*. It requires two plot lines revolving around the main characters. The secondary plot is, with rare exceptions, vital to the structure. In *The King and I*, for example, the main characters are the King and Anna Leonowens. The substory is about Tuptim and the boy she loves. The same structure can be seen in *Guys and Dolls*: Sky Masterson's affair with the Salvation Army Lady in the foreground, Nathan Detroit and Miss Adelaide as the second line. Ideally, the secondary plot uses comic characters. The reasons are practical: you have to be able to get your main characters offstage for a moment of rest and, when necessary, costume changes.

The alternation of dialogue and songs has to have a certain pace, a certain flow. And, furthermore, the songs themselves require balanced variation: ballads to bright songs, slow tempos to fast ones.

A two-act musical is, structurally, a three-act musical with the first intermission removed. I once asked Joshua Logan why this should be so. He said, "So you don't have to get the audience back into their seats twice."

Clearly, Whedon and Moore didn't know how to construct an effective book, and the critics caught them out.

The cast was good. Kenny Delmar, remembered at that time as the pompous puffing Senator Claghorn of the Fred Allen radio show, played Hominy Smith. Danny Scholl played his opponent. Mary Hatcher and

Fred Wayne provided the romantic second line of the story. All of them got good, even warmly enthusiastic reviews.

Brooks Atkinson wrote in the *New York Times:* "Most of the music is commonplace and most of the lyrics are in the same vein. But the book is the chief weakness. . . . It wastes the talents of some good performers."

Ward Morehouse wrote in the *New York Sun* on that same date: "Johnny Mercer's lyrics are sharp and frequently amusing, but the music is routine and the book of John Whedon and Sam Moore . . . is a plodding affair."

Howard Barnes in the *New York Herald-Tribune* praised the hard-working performers, adding, "They are given slight assistance by the John Whedon–Sam Moore libretto and the Robert Emmett Dolan score." A review by Robert Coleman on Saturday, November 26, was headlined CREAKY BOOK, DULL SCORE MAR 'TEXAS L'IL DARLIN'.

John came out of the show more or less unbruised. Richard Watts, Jr., wrote in the *New York Post,* "One of the most pleasant features of the new show are the lyrics of Johnny Mercer. The mocking quality . . . is expertly and even rather subtly managed, so that Mr. Mercer can write the words of a cowboy song that, for a terrifying moment, seems to belong to the horrible school of 'Ghost Riders in the Sky' until you realize with relief and pleasure that he is making fun of it. He has also devised a love song in which a young man courts his girl in the jargon known as Time-style and I think it is particularly good." ("Time-style" is a reference to the affected and artificial style extant at that period in *Time* magazine.)

But one review after another pointed to an awkward and unfocused book and routine music by Robert Emmett Dolan, who really took his lumps on that show (which brings us to a question we will take up later: Why was John so loyal to him?).

The show ran thirty-seven weeks and 293 performances at the Mark Hellinger Theater, whose owner, Anthony Brady Powell, had financed it entirely on his own. It was then sent on tour, and on October 17, 1950, *Variety* reported that it "folded here [in Chicago] after four weeks of a scheduled run. Despite fairly good reviews, the show never got off the ground, dropping about $10,000 a week during its three-week stay here and a bit more in a single week in Detroit previously.

" 'Texas,' which originally involved a cost of $100,000, had at one time during its . . . Broadway run earned back about $30,000, but subsequently lost that and an additional $10,000. The final deficit, including the tour, is figured to be around $150,000."

The show gave its last gasp a few months later, in Dallas, where it was presented with Jack Carson as Hominy Smith. The idea behind this production at the State Fair was apparently that Texans will wallow in anything that is about *them,* and the *Dallas Morning News,* in a dishonest story before the opening, referred to it as "the hit Broadway musical."

It was hardly that. In fact, it was a disaster, and after Dallas it was dead. Only two of its songs are remembered: "It's Great to Be Alive" and "Affable, Balding Me," and only the most devout Mercer devotees know them. Both songs are essentially autobiographical, and the lyrics of the former come directly out of a letter he wrote to his mother.

Work began on *Top Banana* before *Texas, Li'l Darlin'* drew its last breath. For this show, Mercer wrote both words and music. The book, by Hy Kraft, is about an egomaniacal knock-about vaudeville comedian who becomes a star in the burgeoning medium called television and is trying to hold on to his ratings. The model, obviously, was Milton Berle, and the lead was played by Phil Silvers, an old friend of John's. At the time of the show's opening, November 1, 1951, Silvers was not the star he would become on TV in the role of Master Sergeant Ernie Bilko on *The Phil Silvers Show: You'll Never Get Rich.* He was, rather, a serviceable supporting player in a long string of movies, notable for his horn-rimmed glasses, toothy smile, and trademark greeting "Gladda-seeya." *Top Banana* drew on his background in burlesque, and many of its best moments were derived from the routines of that style of theater. The bulk of the critical praise for the show went to Silvers. Walter Kerr, in his review for the *New York Herald-Tribune,* wrote, "Johnny Mercer's tunes are brisk and showy. His lyrics lean a little too heavily on a somewhat picky verbal humor, and he comes a-cropper with a second-act song called *A Word a Day.* But this is a minor qualification about a listenable score." Brooks Atkinson, in the *New York Times,* wrote, "Johnny Mercer's score is hackneyed. He has composed it as though he hoped it would not sound like music—successfully from this point of view." George Jean Nathan, in the *New York Journal-American,* refers to "Johnny Mercer's so-called songs which interrupt the proceedings," adding, "the music sounds like a juke box into which someone has poured a lot of coal," whatever that means. Richard Watts, Jr., in the *New York Post,* said that "the brilliant Johnny Mercer, who has written some of the best lyrics and composed some of the most memorable songs in American popular music, has provided a curiously commonplace score that didn't sound worthy of him. . . . In general the music of *Top Banana* struck me as amazingly uninteresting, particularly considering its source." A few of the lesser critics offered tepid praise for the music, and William Hawkins in the *New York World-Telegram* said, "The score of Johnny Mercer's is wonderfully rhythmic and gay." But most of the reviews were bad, and reading them, all these years later, I can only imagine how hurt John was by them at the time. The show ran 350 performances.

John would have somewhat better luck with his next Broadway musical, presented five years later. It was *Li'l Abner,* derived from the Al Capp comic strip of that name. The strip ran from 1934 until 1977, and at its peak of popularity appeared in newspapers with a total circulation of sixty million. It was admired by Charlie Chaplin, John Updike, and John Kenneth Galbraith. John Steinbeck called Capp "the best writer in the world."

The setting of the strip was a mythical town called Dogpatch, and its principal characters were hillbillies—the big, muscular, and simple-hearted young man of the title; his parents, Mammy and Pappy Yokum; and Daisy Mae, the blond beauty who pursues a reluctant Abner. All of them, and most of the other characters, are dressed in rags, and the comic strip in its early days touched an immediate chord with a public suffering through the depths of the Depression. But it was Capp's sure sense of satire that made the strip a favorite of both the general public and of more than a few intellectuals, who followed it avidly. Nothing in the culture was safe from Capp's mordant wit. Capp had a flair for names comparable to that of Dickens, and the strip's characters included the beautiful Stupefyin' Jones, the also beautiful Moonbeam McSwine (who preferred the company of pigs to that of men), Earthquake McGoon, Mayor Dawgmeat, Hairless Joe (who was anything but hairless), Senator Jack S. Phogbound, the wicked magician Evil Eye Fleagle, the heartless capitalist General Bullmoose, the country preacher Marryin' Sam, and Appassionata von Climax. There were many more, but these are the characters who turned up in the musical.

Attempts had been made, with little success, to put comic-strip characters on the stage. This time Mercer had book writers who knew what they were doing—the team of Norman Panama and Melvin Frank—and the show, which opened November 15, 1956, at the St. James Theater, was immediately and widely well received, in part for its fidelity to the Al Capp original. Whitney Bolton said in the *Morning Telegraph* that "it is all there complete with the characters, the nonsense, the amiable vulgarity, and, most important and intact, the wonderful, searing, wise satire Mr. Capp injects into his strip. Mr. Capp's unwashed mountaineers may be creatures of sloth and squalor, but they are also magnificent commentators on the foolishness of our times."

It was Johnny's natural territory. He had written satirically of America's evolving society for years, in such songs as "I'm an Old Cowhand" and "Hooray for Hollywood," always with a sure ear for the American vernacular, and to take Capp's biting satire into the world of rhyme and melody was easy for him. In consequence, Bolton would write, "Johnny Mercer has given them fabulously sound lyrics, with such engaging couplets as 'They wuz vile lookin' varmints wearin' vile lookin' garmints' sprinkled along the way. And Gene De Paul's score combines satire, romance and general orneriness in nice balance."

Abner was played by a newcomer just out of the army, Peter Palmer, and he got good reviews. Stubby Kaye played Marryin' Sam. Stupefyin' Jones was played by the stupefying Julie Newmar, and Appassionata von Climax was played by Tina Louise. Michael Kidd, who produced the show along with Panama and Frank, was also its director and choreographer. The songs included "Namely You," "Love in a Home," "If I Had My Druthers," and the satiric "The Country's in the Very Best of Hands."

The plot entailed a government plan to evacuate Dogpatch and use the site for A-bomb testing—and the efforts of General Bullmoose to make a huge profit on the deal. *Variety,* which seemed unable to make up its mind about the show, said, "There will probably be some objection to the caustic flavor of the show, mostly pin-sticking politics, but with extra barbs at big business, science, society, and contemporary mores. But that, added to the zing of the outlandish characters, tends to give the show its unusual point of view and, in a curious way, some substance. Without the satirical zing, 'Li'l Abner' would tend to be a tame antic." But of course, that was exactly the point of it: satirical zing. It was not an added ingredient, it was the essence of the show.

Li'l Abner, which ran 693 performances, was one of John's happier experiences of Broadway, but it would probably be difficult to revive, since mostly only older people remember the comic strip it celebrated.

"Hollywood was a desert in 1959 for the songwriter," Edward Jablonski wrote in his biography of Harold Arlen, so Arlen decided to take on a musical based on a sprawling novel, *Saratoga Trunk,* by Edna Ferber, whose *Show Boat* had been turned into a classic musical. Arlen persuaded Mercer that he should do the lyrics, although John had reservations about the show from the beginning, remarking, "If you're going to do *Show Boat,* you're thirty years too late." Arlen convinced Mercer that their asset in the project was Morton Da Costa, who was writing the adaptation and would direct the show as well. As a director, he'd had in a five-year period hits with *Plain and Fancy, No Time for Sergeants, Auntie Mame,* and *The Music Man.*

Arlen moved his family to Beverly Hills. The Mercers, by then, had the house at 108 Via Karon in Lido Isle at Newport Beach. John would make the drive, which took a little under two hours, up from Newport, spend some time with Arlen, then drive home with tapes of the tunes they were working on. The work went smoothly and quickly. "As to my work with John," Arlen said in a note to a friend, "I have a hunch we might come down to the finish line by middle of July or thereabouts." Arlen made an interesting observation in that note: "I don't think an audience nor the critics realize (alas why should they) how much is taken from a writer every time he goes to bat." By the end of July, Arlen and Mercer were not quite finished, but casting began in August with Howard Keel and Carol Lawrence in the lead roles. Keel played the professional gambler Clint Maroon and Lawrence played Clio Dulaine, a Creole fortune-hunter from New Orleans. The show was huge, with more than thirty speaking roles, plus singing and dancing chorus parts, and very elaborate costumes and settings in New Orleans, Paris, and Saratoga. Its financial burden was daunting.

"Arlen," Jablonski wrote, "was certain that 'Tec' (pronounced 'Teek,' from the director's original surname, Tecosky) could bring it off, as elephantine as it had become. Mercer, however, continued to sense that the elephant would be rendered whiter as time went by. The book was too unwieldy. . . .

"Tec had not stinted on his book, and Arlen and Mercer had followed his lead: a great deal of song had been poured into a show that ran for over three hours. Mercer, resigned to problems, took it all lightly, but Arlen began to worry. When he and [his wife] Anya, with a joking Mercer, left an afternoon's rehearsal, Arlen laughed at Mercer's impression of their director, but not heartily."

Mercer, as I came to realize over the years, was a shrewd observer of people, although he tended to keep his impressions from public sight. He could be prudent, to say the least, when he gave interviews.

Saratoga opened at the Shubert Theater in Philadelphia on October 26, 1959, to faint praise. *Variety* noted that Da Costa would have to do some "vital revamping." Da Costa brought Arthur Laurents in to help him with the task.

In its five weeks in Philadelphia, the show underwent extensive rewriting. Jablonski writes: "It was frustrating to Arlen, who never knew which Da Costa he was confronting, the director or the writer of the book, when songs were eliminated and new ones called for. It was wearing him out; he was tired of the freneticism and worried about Anya, suffering from a cold. Mercer was the picture of imperturbability, serenely ready for whatever came from day to day. Besides, he had never cared for the show anyway."

Anya Arlen took to bed in their Manhattan apartment and Harold Arlen checked into New York's Mount Sinai Hospital to rest and recover. This left Mercer to write the music as well as the lyrics of whatever new songs were required. He wrote the music for three, without claiming credit. This is an echo of his experience with Hoagy Carmichael in *I Walk with Music,* and I think this is an interesting insight into John. He seems *always* to have been unshakably professional and reliable.

In an interview Andrew Velez did for the 2000 CD issue of the *Saratoga* score, Howard Keel said, "Catastrophe! I felt when it started that the score wasn't there yet, but I was very naïve about theater in New York. I thought it would be corrected. I had a big number early on, and that was the first thing that was cut. We opened in Philadelphia, and [the critics] ripped us to shreds. And everyone left us. Johnny came back and worked with both words and music. He was the only one who really tried. Harold Arlen never showed up again. We didn't see Da Costa again for three weeks. Everyone went into a trauma. . . .

"Carol was wonderful in it and very brave. She'd attack anything. It's a very complex story and sometimes things just don't work. I don't think the story was really there. . . . Johnny and Harold were two great artists. I think Johnny Mercer was one of the greatest poets we ever had."

Given his lack of faith in the show, Mercer was asked why he had taken it on, to which he replied, "I'm always doing jobs I don't want." That has the ring of truth, without telling the full story. I think the reason John took on *Saratoga* is quite simple: his immense respect and love for Arlen. I think that John would have done anything Harold wanted him to do, and if Harold wanted to do *Saratoga,* then so be it. The big problem was Da Costa. After the New York opening, the critics gave it, according to a box score in the *New York World Telegram,* "six nays, two qualified yeas, and a definite yea." "While Da Costa suffered the most," Edward Jablonski wrote, "Arlen and Mercer, too, were surprisingly, and none too fairly, mauled."

One of the problems with Da Costa is one not uncommon in directors, perhaps in theater even more than in film. Because they contribute ideas on how to stage the show—which, after all, is what they are hired for—they leap to the conclusion that they contributed to the writing, and if they have big enough names, they demand and get writing credits (and part of the attendant royalties). In his previous shows, Da Costa had good scripts to work with. Carol Lawrence said, "In truth, Morton had never felt validated in what he contributed to shows. He thought, *Now I'm going to do all these things and they'll realize how much I did*. Well, he put himself in the hospital.

"I loved both Johnny and Harold. They were both so dear. Unfortunately, Harold became ill, so we had both of them in the hospital. All the changes fell to Johnny to make. We were floundering without any kind of experience or guidance."

'SARATOGA' PRETTY AS A PICTURE BUT OLD FASHIONED, read the headline in *Women's Wear Daily*, and pretty indeed it should have been, with sets and costumes designed by Cecil Beaton. (This brings to mind the old theater wheeze that the audience left humming the scenery.) A HANDSOME MUSICAL PLAY SUFFERS FROM BOOK TROUBLE, ran the headline of a review by Richard Watts, Jr., in the *New York Post*.

The show's credits in the program declared somewhat pompously that it was "dramatized and directed by Morton Da Costa." From this, a review in *Newsday* read on December 16, 1959, "it can be fairly assumed that Mr. Da Costa is largely responsible for the proceedings that are current at the Winter Garden. . . .

"The result is little short of disastrous, for in *Saratoga* Mr. Da Costa has taken Edna Ferber's novel *Saratoga Trunk* and truncated not only the title but the spirit and the quality."

Walter Kerr, in the *New York Herald-Tribune*, said that "the really distressing thing about *Saratoga* was the quality of the Da Costa book." John Chapman in the New York *Daily News* said it had "the most complicated music-show plot since Richard Wagner wrote *Siegfried*." *Variety* called it "shockingly lackluster" and Kenneth Tynan in *The New Yorker* used the same word, referring to the songs as "lackluster."

Variety reported that the show had cost $480,000, and lost $400,000, a huge figure in 1959. It would have to take in $40,000 a week to break even. "There's little likelihood of a film sale," the trade paper observed, thereby delivering the coup de grâce.

There is a strongly ironic line (intentionally?) in the Jablonski biography: "Had *Saratoga* been a ship, it was destined for the bottom." Nobody seems to have noticed its opening date: December 7. And it got bombed almost as badly as Pearl Harbor.

Saratoga survived for ten weeks, eighty performances, closing in early 1960, just before Arlen's birthday on February 15. Arlen was in Mount

Sinai Hospital, suffering from exhaustion. Da Costa, after attempts to salvage the mess, left for Europe.

Howard Keel said: "It was not a happy event and it took me months to get over it. But that's what show business is. You just keep going."

Carol Lawrence said, "I believe, in my heart, if Morton Da Costa had allowed Lillian Hellman to cowrite with him, that it would have been a better show."

Andrew Velez wrote: "At their only meeting, not one to mince words, Hellman reportedly told Da Costa, 'It's very obvious you can't write.' "

Sometime later, in the 1960s, Da Costa wanted to do a musical based on the 1951 Alec Guinness movie *The Man in the White Suit,* with composer Albert Hague, who had written the music for *Plain and Fancy.* Da Costa himself wrote the book. I was brought in to write the lyrics, and in just one read-through of the book, I found an enormous number of flaws—cracks in the logic. Furthermore, I found Da Costa to be a man of towering self-admiration, impervious to suggestions. After about a week of shapeless meetings, I walked out on the project, thinking it could never be made to work. It never got into production.

The memory of that experience gives me some idea of what John was dealing with.

But John always put the blame for the failure of those shows on himself. He said, "I'm just not a good show writer."

Well, that's hard to say. I remember something Josh Logan told me: "A musical is an incredibly complicated piece of machinery. You can have all the elements, the right songs, the right book, the right cast, the right director, the right costume designer—and the lighting man can screw it up."

Twenty-five

For some time, Harold Arlen had hoped to resurrect the score of *St. Louis Woman* with a revised book by Robert Breen, who would direct it, and with Breen's wife. It was to be presented in Europe, although the logic of doing a musical in English on the Continent has always been a little obscure. Retitled *Free and Easy,* from the opening line of Mercer's lyric for "Any Place I Hang My Hat Is Home," it opened in Brussels. The producer, Stanley Chase, and director Breen had been feuding and the show was in disarray. The music was reorchestrated for a full-scale jazz band led by Quincy Jones, performing not in the pit but onstage. Every change in the show, of course, required new arrangements. Quincy Jones would sketch them and trombonist Billy Byers, a brilliant arranger and composer, would complete the orchestrations. The band included some of the finest jazz musicians of America and Europe, among them alto saxophonist Phil Woods.

Woods recalled: "The show was a mess. We were never blocked properly. Robert Breen did not know what to do with the big band. Breen was fired and Donny McHale, the choreographer, took over. I think it was planned to rewrite the show from the git-go."

Worse, songs were being inserted that Mercer had no hand in, songs Arlen had written in earlier times with Ted Koehler, including "Ill Wind," which dates from 1934, and "I Gotta Right to Sing the Blues," from 1932. These and other interpolations offended Mercer deeply, and he wrote an angry letter to Arlen for allowing this to happen. The show was, in Jablonski's phrase, "a dramatic and musical mess." Almost everyone who had anything to do with the show or who saw it thought the jazz orchestrations were wrong for Arlen's music, though the band and the music were, in Phil Woods's words, "fantastic, absolutely gorgeous."

The show opened in Paris on January 14, 1960, and closed nine days later, leaving the cast—and the band—stranded. Quincy Jones hastily arranged a tour of Europe by the band to raise the money to get the musicians home. When they got back to New York, they held a party—or perhaps *wake* is the better term—for the show in the apartment of saxophonist Jerome Richardson.

Free and Easy and *Saratoga* were the second and third major defeats for Mercer and Arlen, the first being the original *St. Louis Woman*. They would never write another show; indeed, Arlen would never write for Broadway again. John told me, "Harold and I did two shows together, *St. Louis Woman* and *Saratoga,* which is kind of a quiet score. Not many people know it and not many people have heard it. Maybe that's because it isn't too good. It wasn't a hit."

In the summer of 1969, Arlen's beloved wife, Anya, finally surrendered to his entreaties that she see a doctor to discuss her deteriorating nervous condition. She was diagnosed with a brain tumor. She underwent surgery, but the location of the tumor was such that not all of it could be removed, and Arlen was reminded of the time he and Anya and Yip Harburg had visited George Gershwin, who looked dreadful. Gershwin died within days of being diagnosed with a brain tumor. On March 9, 1970, Anya Arlen died.

Not long after that, John said to me, "Harold Arlen is a *genius*. I don't know what to say about him, except he doesn't write enough [anymore]. He's been bothered by illnesses and the various mundane things of this world. But if he were writing like he wrote twenty years ago, I don't think you could catch up to his catalogue. I think he's been inactive so long that people have sort of forgotten about him. He's wonderful. I think he'd *like* to write. I think he probably *needs* to write, for his spirit, for his heart. He's a very tender, very sensitive man, and he writes so beautifully. It's easy for him. It sounds terribly inventive to us, terribly difficult, what he does, but not to him. It's like turning on a tap. It just flows out of him.

"We did about ten movies at Paramount. The songs that came out of them were songs like 'Out of this World,' 'Old Black Magic,' 'Acc-Cent-Tchu-Ate,' 'Come Rain or Come Shine.' We had a lot of songs that are people's favorites that you don't hear much, like 'Hit the Road to Dreamland,' 'This Time the Dream's on Me.' 'Blues in the Night' is probably our best-known song."

John wanted me to meet Arlen. I demurred, saying I understood he had become a recluse since the death of his wife. John said, "That's right. That's why I want you to meet him. I think it would be good for him."

John telephoned Arlen and arranged an appointment with him for me. I visited Arlen in his apartment on Central Park West, and there—watched by the quite remarkable oil portrait George Gershwin had painted of Jerome Kern—I asked him a question that, to judge from his air of slight surprise, had never been put to him before.

I said, "Mr. Arlen, when you and George Gershwin and Rodgers and Hart and the others were writing for the theater in the thirties, were you consciously aware that what you were writing was art music?"

He looked at me for what seems in memory a long moment and then said, softly, "Yes."

I stayed only a short while, then took my leave. He died quietly in bed in that apartment on the morning of April 23, 1986.

Mercer's next musical, *Foxy,* a loose adaptation of Ben Jonson's 1605 satire *Volpone,* starred Bert Lahr. Its book, by Ian McLellan Hunter and Ring Lardner, Jr., moved the story from Venice to the Yukon Territory during the Klondike gold rush. (It will be recalled that in his days as a young actor, John appeared in a production of *Volpone.*)

The project was odd from its instigation. *Volpone* itself is, from the perspective of our own time, a peculiar play, a satire on avarice with the kind of convoluted plot popular in its time but now incomprehensibly creaky. It is about a man who holds out the promise of his inheritance to "friends" who then court his favor and in the process let him cheat them of their money.

The transplantation of its story to the Yukon may well have been because its first producer, Robert Whitehead, a Canadian from Montreal, obtained subsidization for the production from the Canadian government, which was trying to attract tourists to Dawson City and its surrounding countryside. In 1899, at the height of the Klondike gold rush, Dawson had a population of ten thousand, but by 1921, it had dwindled to under a thousand. Its nightless summer is very brief, and its winter deep and bitter, with a January average temperature of twenty below zero Fahrenheit and extremes of fifty below.

Mercer's trip was circuitous. Fortunately, we have a witness to it: his son Jeff. Said Jeff: "Well, you know he wouldn't fly. We took the train up to Vancouver, Canada, and then we took a boat up the Inside Passage. We then took a little narrow-gauge train to White Horse. And then we rented a car and drove, like, three hundred miles up to Dawson City. He let me drive. I was underage, but it was a big double-wide dirt road. It was kept up. They didn't pave up there because the frost would just buckle it. They keep grading a dirt road. It was a nice road, but we were going sixty or seventy. The person in back of you would have caught a lot of dust. But there was nobody on the thing, and there were no potholes. It was pretty straight, but the scenery was quite bleak. This was during the summer, of course—August. You drive and drive and drive, and then you're in Dawson City, which just pops up out of nowhere.

"They had brand-new structures built to look old-fashioned, but you could tell because the wood was brand-new. The town was there, but they just cherried it out for that event. It was a dirt street, with boardwalks. It was built to withstand winter and the summer thaws. And the stage they did for opening night of *Foxy* was built from scratch. It was clean, new wood. They'd just stripped the bark off and used the bigger planks. But *Foxy* was about the gold rush, so they thought that would be a cool way to promote it. It was, too. Of course I don't know how much attendance they had.

"We went out fishing. This is the one time he *did* get in a plane. We took a little seaplane, single prop—my dad, myself, and this other fellow—and flew over to a lake. It was pretty close, maybe ten or fifteen minutes away. I'm amazed that he got into it. The flight was close to the ground. We had a little skiff tied underneath the plane. I think he wanted me to have some fun. I shouldn't even have been there; I was bored sick. I caught a big steelhead trout, about twenty pounds. I remember the water was so cold you couldn't even put your finger in it. It was worse than touching ice. It was a milky color, from glacier runoff. It didn't bother the fish any, because they were huge. That's about the only thing we did, other than waiting for the opening night."

Foxy was staged in Dawson City during the city's summer festival of 1962. Lahr, like Mercer, would not fly. In a remarkably objective biography of his father, *Notes on a Cowardly Lion*, published in 1969, John Lahr, who was to become a prominent drama critic, wrote, "For a man nearing seventy, the trip to the Yukon was a physical risk. The journey was one day's travel by plane, but ten days by Lahr's route of train, bus, and boat. He packed his medicines, his fishing tackle, his rabbit's foot." The book recounts:

"The play was intended to reopen the city as a resort, but Lahr immediately saw the drawback. There were seven hundred people in the town, half of them Indians. There was only one road. The only convenient way to get to Dawson City was to fly from Fairbanks, Alaska. Lahr, an inveterate box-office watcher, tabulated the result. Weekends were the only days the four-hundred-seat playhouse would be full. . . . Many a performance would play to an empty house; and Lahr's city clowning was lost on faces cracked from facing into the wind.

"In the theater, Lahr found himself with variables he had never considered. The old star came up against a new breed of actor who shared few of his traditions or concepts of the stage. The 'book musical' was still as clumsy and simplified as it had been twenty years before; the audience had changed more drastically than their stage entertainment. When Lahr applied his axioms to comedy, forcing attention back toward himself, he could still dominate the stage, but this very power ultimately dispelled the musical's total force. Lahr spoke with fifty years of experience—and he began to realize that nobody in *Foxy* shared those insights or understood him; they had come from another generation—one that never geared itself to the demands of his comedy. The director, Robert Lewis, could not help Lahr; his suggestions and his unwillingness to allow him to improvise reinforced the fact that Lahr was on his own. Lewis, a director responsible for such Broadway standards as *Teahouse of the August Moon, Brigadoon,* and *Jamaica,* did not know how to cope with Lahr. Ring Lardner, Jr., and Ian McLellan Hunter had never written a Broadway musical; yet in their first play they wanted to retain both the theme of *Volpone* and their lines exactly as they had written them. The show was not social satire; written with Lahr in mind, it was a farcical entertainment that encompassed his broad, loose playing. The problem was simple. Without Lahr's laughter, the show had very little to offer—a mediocre book, fair songs, and choreography that rarely kicked an original leg. His laughter and his improvisations gave it a chance; and yet the authors bridled him with language that was not funny and scenes that did not build to a comic climax.

"Lahr raged with a venom he usually reserved for liberals. 'I'm Bert Lahr. Bert Lahr. . . . Don't try to be funny. You be real. I'll be funny,' he'd call down to the authors. . . .

" 'The authors were stubborn,' recalls Larry Blyden. 'They indulged Bert in all the things he must not be indulged in: hogging of time, temper tantrums, willfulness, trying to dictate everything to be done in his own self-interest. On the other hand, they never once allowed him to be brilliant. There was no other actor alive who could do what Lahr could on stage. They wouldn't have it. He would say things to them in analyzing a scene that would be so perceptive and so precise that there was no arguing with him. Sometimes he might have been injured, although I doubt it, because Bert is never injured by anything he suggests. But certainly the scene would have worked better. They had their little idea of what was theatrical and what was honest; and they were all wrong.' "

John Lahr is not unfair in these passages. The songs, indeed, are only fair. And Mercer was once again saddled with a mediocre book, not to mention a mediocre composer. The show played out its time in Dawson City, closing after eight weeks.

After they had returned to New York, Robert Whitehead told Lahr that David Merrick was interested in producing it for Broadway. Lahr foresaw that the writers, Lardner and Hunter, would continue to be a problem. He told Whitehead, "I think I'm going to have a lot of trouble with these guys, they think they've written Ibsen's *A Doll's House*." And he was right: he continued to clash with the book writers. John Lahr wrote: "Merrick pacified him; but Lahr still had to contend with an unfunny script and adamant authors."

The show opened early in 1964. Nancy Gerard was there for the opening night. Afterwards John took her to Luchow's, the German restaurant where writers and actors, by long tradition, often waited for the first reviews.

"I don't know why Ginger wasn't there," Nancy said. "He had a pretty good idea what the reviews were going to be like."

Without exception they concentrated on the genius of Lahr and his fathomless talent for mime and mugging. Generally, Mercer came off better than Dolan in the reviews. Walter Kerr wrote in the *Herald-Tribune* that "Robert Emmett Dolan's score is on the whole conventionally pleasant, with a particularly appealing pop ballad in 'Talk to Me, Baby.' " He especially admired "the articulate intricacy of Johnny Mercer's lyrics." Whitney Bolton wrote: "Libretto, lyrics and music serve, but without detonation." Howard Taubman wrote in the *New York Times,* "The lyrics by Johnny Mercer are often bright, and Robert Emmett Dolan's tunes are bouncing and graceful in a way reminiscent of the self-assured twenties."

On February 2, Lahr received two letters in his dressing room. One was from Johnny Mercer. It read:

Dear Bert
. . . This is the first time I've ever seen a performer do my material better than I meant it. Usually we're happy with 75% or

*80% of what we would like—but you find laughs where the
laughs aren't even there! You're just marvelous and I love you.*

The other letter was from Merrick, who had nine other shows on
Broadway and two more on the road. He was withdrawing financial support from the show. For a time he changed his mind, but eventually he
withdrew it again, and *Foxy* closed after eighty-five Broadway performances. "When the final curtain fell at the Ziegfeld Theater," John Lahr
noted, "the house was full." Bert Lahr's career on the New York stage
was over.

So was Johnny Mercer's. He would write only one more show, *Good
Companions,* this one not for New York but for London, and it would be
near the end of his life.

Viewed in retrospect, the main problem with the Mercer stage musicals
lay with the libretti. But a secondary problem was the weakness of the
composers, the exception being Arlen. Frederick Loewe used to say that
he was not a songwriter but a dramatic composer, and when you observe
the way his compositions worked in the collaborations with Alan Jay
Lerner, you see that his evaluation of himself was astute. He knew how to
use music to build or underline the dramatic line. He was terribly good
at it.

The ability to write melody, supreme soaring melody, is uncommon.
Musical training will not confer it; lack of training will not preclude it.
Irving Berlin had virtually no musical training, and he could play piano in
only one key, F-sharp, which is why he used a transposing piano. (Contrary to legend, it was not built for him. Such pianos were common in the
offices of publishers in the 1920s and '30s.) Schubert had a supreme gift
for melody. So did Tchaikovsky. So did Frank Loesser, who began as a
lyricist and then started writing music without formal music training. I
think John had it, too, as witness some of the songs for which he also
wrote music, especially "I'm an Old Cowhand" and "Something's Gotta
Give." He simply had no confidence in it.

Alan Livingston thought that John wrote with too many composers who didn't have it. He mentioned, without naming him, a trained
arranger and conductor who lacked the gift.

"Robert Emmett Dolan," I said immediately.

"Right," Alan said, surprised that I had guessed.

I asked Johnny's daughter, Mandy, why John worked so much with
Bobby Dolan, who was not really a songwriter or dramatic composer at

all but, as Jo Stafford points out, an arranger and conductor. Mandy said, "Oh, I don't know. He was such a wonderful Irish leprechaun."

Robert Emmett Dolan was one of John's close friends. His background was extensive. He had studied composition with both Joseph Schillinger and Ernst Toch. He was a conductor of Broadway musicals and a music director at MGM. They wrote a lot of songs together, none of which is remembered today, and the two Broadway musicals, *Foxy* and *Texas, L'il Darling,* sank so far from sight that they are not even listed in *The Great Song Thesaurus* (published by Oxford University Press). I thought Bobby Dolan, as John affectionately referred to him, couldn't write an interesting tune to save his life. None of the songs from *Foxy* or *Texas, Li'l Darling* survive in the standard repertoire, with the single exception of the comparatively minor "Talk to Me, Baby."

"Johnny would write with the first person who approached him in the morning," Alan Livingston said. Paul Weston expressed the same sentiment almost verbatim.

I think John was to some extent aware of this weakness in himself. If you are a lyricist of any stature, you are constantly being approached by composers and jazz musicians who have "just written a tune I'd like you to look at," and often the underlying assumption is that there is nothing to writing a lyric. This can be annoying, and John and I talked about it once. He said, "Yeah. You get tired of being everybody's lyric boy." I thought that a wonderful turn of phrase.

Alan Livingston thought that John should have associated himself only with composers who had soaring talent, such as Jerome Kern (John's association with Kern was cut off by Kern's death in 1945 at the age of sixty), Richard Whiting (another association ended by a premature death), Harry Warren, and Harold Arlen.

The relationship with Harry Warren was prickly, owing in part to Harry's irascible and unpredictable nature.

His approval has always meant a great deal to a young writer. But he sometimes mistakes your motives. I'll give you an example. When I was recording for Capitol, my biggest record was "On the Atchison, Topeka and the Santa Fe," which Harry and I had written for the film The Harvey Girls. *The Capitol publicity department, unbeknownst to me, had issued a huge display card to be shown in music store windows that read "Johnny Mercer's 'On the Atchison, Topeka and the Santa Fe.' " Of course, they were referring to me as the singer, the performer, not as the writer. But never mind. Harry saw the sign in a Beverly Hills store, con-*

cluded I was claiming sole credit for the song, wrote me a nasty letter, and didn't speak to me for five years!

I love him, but I'd rather he'd thrown a plate of spaghetti at me than go through a long vendetta over something that wasn't even my fault.

How many good songs didn't get written during the five years of Mercer's estrangement from Warren?

Johnny had one more pet project to be written for Broadway. He told Howie Richmond that he wanted to write a musical version of *Gone with the Wind,* and do it in collaboration with Hoagy Carmichael, who would, he believed, be perfect for it. But the rights had to be cleared with the estate of Margaret Mitchell, who wrote the novel, and they were never obtained.

We are confronted with a question. Excepting those in *St. Louis Woman,* the songs in his six Broadway musicals are not John's best work. Far from it. None of them reaches the levels of soaring and often poignant lyricism and yearning found in "Skylark," "Autumn Leaves," "The Summer Wind," "One for My Baby," "Once Upon a Summertime," "My Shining Hour," "Laura," "When the World Was Young," "That Old Black Magic," "Moon River," "Let's Take the Long Way Home," "I Remember You," "Days of Wine and Roses," and so many more that are among the most inspired lyrics in the English language. Nor do they tap the wells of effervescent wit of which he was capable, as in "G.I. Jive," "Hooray for Hollywood," "Blues in the Night" (it's a dark wit, to be sure, but it's wit), and "Something's Gotta Give." Why is this so?

I don't think even John knew. I know only that he was disappointed with his forays into theater. I will, however, venture some speculation. I would like to preface this by relating that I once worked on a musical with Joshua Logan, a project that never went into production for convoluted legal reasons that have no place in this narrative. But I worked with Josh for the better part of a year, writing a full book and lyrics under his tutelage. (I got the job partly on Mercer's recommendation.)

Josh, of course, was one of our greatest directors. He was an incredibly generous man, both with his time and with his knowledge. At certain periods during that year, in Los Angeles and New York, I was with him all day every day and into the evenings. I listened raptly to his reminiscences, including talks about what he had learned from Konstantin Stanislavsky at the Moscow Art Theater.

Josh gave me a copy of an essay by Maxwell Anderson and urged that

I study it, which I did. Anderson set out to identify, through his studies of drama past and present, what makes a play work. I have read many studies of drama, including John Van Druten's wonderful *Playwright at Work*, but nothing as lucid and concise as that essay by Maxwell Anderson. Its essential point is that the play's protagonist must experience a self-revelation toward the end, an insight that redeems him or her. Alan Jay Lerner argued that the main cause of a play's failure was inconsistency of style, and I think that view has much to commend it, but the Maxwell Anderson insight, I believe, is of an even higher order. You can examine one great play after another, comedy or tragedy or musical, and you will find Anderson's theory verified.

Josh taught me that songs have certain specific functions in a musical. One of these is declamation. A second and very important function is that of the soliloquy, most obviously illustrated by the "Soliloquy" from *Carousel* and Loesser's "My Time of Day" in *Guys and Dolls*. And yet another is the duet, in which the two main characters can reveal themselves to each other. I told Josh that I personally loathe duets, to which he replied, "You may loathe them all you want, but they really *work* in the theater. Audiences love them," and he made me write several of them.

The ultimate masters of American musical theater were Rodgers and Hammerstein. I have certain reservations about their work, and so did Johnny. Their material is often saccharine, as in "I Whistle a Happy Tune" and the entire glutinous score of *The Sound of Music,* not to mention "You'll Never Walk Alone." But Hammerstein really understood book. He knew how to write one, and all of their shows are beautifully and solidly constructed. Furthermore, Hammerstein had the ability to get inside the characters in his plots, as, for example, with the rationalizations of a nymphomaniac in "I Cain't Say No" in *Oklahoma!* And consider "Ol' Man River" and "Why Do You Love Me?", written for *Show Boat,* long before his association with Richard Rodgers. (Indeed, I think Hammerstein's finest songs *qua* songs were written not with Rodgers but with Jerome Kern, as, for example, the *Show Boat* score and "The Folks Who Live on the Hill." But then, just about every classic lyricist, including Johnny, did some of their best work with Kern.)

Richard Rodgers once said that the *idea* was everything in a musical, adding that he and Hammerstein turned over and abandoned countless ideas before settling on one. And the shows in which John got involved were, for whatever reason, based on weak ideas about which he had reservations, and some of which he entered upon with grave doubts. Maybe he should simply have turned them down.

Portrait of Johnny

Nancy Gerard said: "He told me one time when I asked about the musicals that they never could seem to get all the right talent together at the right time. They would have Michael Kidd as choreographer but not the book writer or composer, or another combination of greats and not so greats. I guess the successful show producers had more acumen when it came to hiring the 'right' team."

Rereading the reviews of the shows by the New York critics, in some cases more than fifty years after their appearance, I am shocked by the insensitivity of most of them. Whatever they knew of drama, or thought they knew, their ignorance of music, and particularly American music, is dismaying. But ignorance breeds confidence, and they express their shaky opinions—particularly on the score of *St. Louis Woman*—with unshakable (one might even say unspeakable) aplomb.

And then the intransigence of the book writers, particularly Lardner and Hunter, is further ground for regret. What they did not seem to realize is that a musical is not about prose, it is about songs. As Josh Logan made abundantly clear to me, the emotional peaks in a musical *must* be expressed in the songs. The material in the book is what connects them, and while one may demand good writing, the purpose of the book is to get you from song to song. John was miserably served by book writers, above all Lardner and Hunter in *Foxy* and Da Costa in *Saratoga*.

Given the lack of good libretti, Johnny shines best in separate songs that are in some dimension autobiographical, as in "One for My Baby," "The Summer Wind," "Drinking Again," and the fabulous "Something's Gotta Give." He is most at home (excepting the comedy songs, of course) when he is dealing with the eternal aching themes of time and lost youth, as in "Laura" and "The Summer Wind," and with the desire to go home.

The form of the Broadway musical seemed to restrict him in a way that his contributions to individual scenes in movies did not. There his imagination could soar. Furthermore, the subject of his work—always—was America itself, and he chronicles its evolution from the comparative innocence of the early thirties in "Lazy Bones" through "I'm an Old Cowhand," when not only Texas but the nation was being transformed by technology, into the war years of "My Shining Hour" and "G.I. Jive," through to the paranoia of the McCarthy era in the deliciously witty "I'm Shadowing You." His true canvas was the country itself, and in painting his inner landscapes, he reflected it with precise social observation and an unerring feeling for its vernacular.

And of course there is, later on, yet another American portrait, "Moon River," one of his finest pieces of work.

. . .

At some point in the early 1970s I came out to California with my wife, and, as always, the first person I called was John. He said some people were coming to the house, and he invited us to join them, after which we could go somewhere for dinner. My wife grew up in northern Florida and New Orleans, and I noticed that whenever she and I were with John, after two or three glasses of wine, her Southern accent would come back. She really understood John and his background. By the time we got to the house, John was already fairly loaded, and went on drinking. His guests—who were mostly press, including the critic Leonard Feather—were gathered in the kitchen. Suddenly, with no provocation at all, John turned on Ginger, saying, "What are you? Just an ugly old woman who keeps hanging around." I remember the look of dismay on Leonard's face.

There was in the hallway of that house in Bel Air an exquisite little watercolor John had done, showing an old horse-and-shay, seen from the rear, making its way down a country lane. It was no doubt a memory of his childhood. (Jeff has it now.) My wife said, "Johnny, I'd like to talk to you about that painting in the hall." They left the room. In the hall, she told me later, she said, "Johnny, some of the people in there are press. They may not be your friends. And what would your mother think of you? Your family would be shocked to hear you talking like this. You're not behaving like the Southern gentleman you are."

"You're right," he said. They walked back to the kitchen and he became the perfect gentleman.

The party broke up, and John said, "Let's go to dinner." I drove. We went to Madame Woo's on Santa Monica Boulevard in Santa Monica, an exquisite Chinese restaurant that was one of his favorites. The transformation from malicious drunk to Southern gentleman was one of the damnedest things I ever saw. He could be transformed instantly in either direction, it seemed.

We had our usual chitchat about lyric writing, and he asked what I was working on, and then he began giving me avuncular advice. He told me I should be careful with whom I wrote. He said I should be sure I wasn't working with weak or second-rate composers.

Now I know that he was speaking from rueful experience.

Howie Richmond and Alan Bergman are among those who told me they never saw Johnny take a drink. But neither of them drinks, or at least not much, and John may have felt obligated to abstain in their presence. I did see him drink, and did a fair amount of drinking with him. Yet I never once saw the terrible despair that Alec Wilder, James Maher, Abe Olman, and others described. And I never saw him get nasty with anyone, except on that one occasion with the waitress in Charlie O's that I put a stop to, and that other incident with Ginger at his home that my wife put a stop to.

But I certainly heard about his attacks on Ginger from others, including David Raksin and Jay Livingston. And his family saw them. Jeff Mercer said:

"They threatened each other enough. My mom said, 'I'll get a divorce, and I'll take everything.' I was sitting there when she said that. So was my wife. We were having Thanksgiving dinner or something in Palm Springs. He got into the car, the Pinto, and drove up to visit some people he knew right above us, had a few more cocktails, and crashed the Pinto coming down the hill.

"He got a cab. We didn't see him for a day and a half. He came back and he was hungover."

Twenty-six

Network radio made the career of Johnny Mercer.

It is generally overlooked, and it is no coincidence, that the golden era of American song and the golden age of the big bands were exactly coeval with the great period of network radio. Radio could make a star, or a song, overnight. Records were secondary to the process. As John made clear in his memoir, the song-pluggers of the 1930s were seeking radio performances. Records were of secondary, even minor, interest to them. Records didn't make stars; stars made records. Indeed, in the early days, radio was barred from playing records on the air. In fact, during the Depression, record sales declined so fast and so far that the record industry came close to complete collapse.

Starting with an international conference in Berlin in 1903, nations entered into a series of agreements allocating radio broadcast frequencies. As broadcasting developed during the 1920s and, explosively, the 1930s, different countries took different ways to fund the emerging industry. Britain developed the BBC, owned by the government. Canada established a comparable Canadian Broadcasting Corporation. France, too, established a national, noncommercial broadcasting system, and Germany set up a series of government-owned regional systems, whose most spectacular immediate consequence was to permit Adolf Hitler to address all the people of a nation at the same time and impel them into adventures that would ultimately cost an estimated eighty million lives. In the United

States, Franklin Delano Roosevelt grasped the significance of the new medium and used it to inspired effect to help draw the nation out of the Depression, and later to unify it in the war that radio had helped launch in the first place. In England, Winston Churchill employed it for the same purpose. His broadcast speeches, and the Edward R. Murrow broadcasts from London during the worst of the German bombing raids, further galvanized the United States and Canada to a war effort that, seen in retrospect, is awesome.

Most histories of American broadcasting hold that it was born November 2, 1920, at KDKA in East Pittsburgh with the announcement of the results of the presidential election that put Warren G. Harding in the White House. In fact, North American broadcasting was born in late 1919, when the station known today as CFCF went on the air in Montreal. On May 20, 1920, CFCF broadcast a program by a full orchestra, although there were as yet few people with the equipment to receive it. In both countries, reaction to the new medium was quick and positive. The public rushed to buy radio receivers, even as the Marconi company was experimenting in Montreal with what would become television.

The United States did not develop a publicly owned and government-funded broadcasting system. On the contrary, it became the only major industrial nation to turn the AM (and later also the FM) broadcasting frequencies almost entirely over to private interests, assigning licenses to universities, labor unions, religious groups, and, above all, big business.

From the beginning, the problem of radio was how to pay for it. The idea of permitting it to be used as an advertising medium was not at first enthusiastically embraced in the United States. Herbert Hoover, who was then secretary of commerce, disliked the idea of broadcast advertising, and David Sarnoff was vociferously opposed to it. But the first commercial was broadcast on New York's WEAF (cost: $100) on August 28, 1922, and by 1925, Sarnoff had become a convert to this way of financing the medium; he was by then organizing NBC, which would evolve into two networks, the Red and the Blue. Large-scale broadcasting in the United States was from that time on funded by advertising revenues.

Executives of the record industry were frightened, and rightly so, by the new medium, and labels on the old 78 rpm recordings carried the inscription "Not licensed for radio broadcast." The newly emergent networks, and even many local stations, hired their own orchestras. NBC's Red Network employed a full symphony orchestra conducted by Arturo Toscanini, whose broadcasts made his a household name; CBS had a symphony orchestra conducted by Bruno Walter. Every comedy show had its own band or orchestra—directed by Skinnay Ennis and later Les Brown on the Bob Hope program; by Phil Harris on Jack Benny's show; by Billy Mills on *Fibber McGee and Molly.* Bing Crosby was the star of the *Kraft Music Hall,* with an orchestra directed by John Scott Trotter. Dinah Shore was heard with Paul Lavalle and the Chamber Music Society of Lower Basin Street.

Advertisers had little say in the content of early radio shows. The major broadcasting networks presented an astonishing amount of cultural material, some of it of a very high order. The power of the medium was unprecedented. The superb songs of Gershwin, Kern, Carmichael, Mercer, and their peers were launched nationally by radio. The medium proved to be the most powerful force for education in history. In time it would prove just as effective in disseminating ignorance.

Irving Berlin's 1911 song "Alexander's Ragtime Band" was a catalyst in a craze for dancing that would last for more than three decades in the United States. To cater to this new pastime, hundreds of ballrooms and dance pavilions sprang up across the country, many of them in amusement parks and at lakesides, and countless dance bands were formed to provide the music. The quality of songs in Broadway musicals was rising steadily, and radio made many of their best songs into hits. A three-way symbiosis emerged: movies and theater as a source of popular music; dance bands and their singers to perform it; and radio as a medium to present it nationally. The level of public musical taste throughout North America was lifted.

Broadcasts from the Cotton Club in New York established Duke Ellington as a major American musical figure before the 1930s began. When Ellington went on the road, Cab Calloway replaced him at the Cotton Club and on radio, and his band, too, became famous. A single radio broadcast in Chicago made the Guy Lombardo band a success: college students who heard it poured into the club where he was playing. One "remote" broadcast of the Benny Goodman band launched the band, and thus the swing era. The story is now legend.

NBC had a series of weekend *Dance Party* "remotes," usually broadcast live from New York or Chicago, starting at eleven p.m. and ending at one. But California time is three hours earlier than New York, two hours earlier than Chicago. Midnight in New York is nine p.m. in California. Goodman's broadcasts built up a following for the band on the West Coast, and when the band, whose fortunes were faltering in the East, played the Palomar in Los Angeles, the turnout of young fans almost caused a riot. Then other remotes established other bands, and soon there were scores of them, excellent bands, traveling the United States and Canada, packing the young people in at ballrooms and pavilions and hockey arenas. So important were these remote broadcasts that the pavilion and ballroom operators were willing to pay for the installation of the remote "wire" that connected them to the radio networks, and a band would play a location that had a wire for comparatively little money because of what the broadcasts could do for its reputation.

The networks aired a great many weekly programs devoted to "light classical" music, sponsored by Firestone, Bell Telephone, Cities Service, and others. If you turned on a network station and left it on, you got an education in music, from the Metropolitan Opera, heard on Saturday afternoons, to the Grand Ole Opry from Nashville. It was almost impossible not to know such names as John Charles Thomas, James Melton, Albert Spalding, Vivian Della Chiesa, Lily Pons, André Kostelanetz, Eugene Ormandy, Risë Stevens, Arturo Toscanini, Donald Voorhees, John Kirby, Woody Herman, Duke Ellington, Tommy Dorsey, and Glenn Miller. By the 1940s, most of the major bandleaders had regular network shows of their own. Radio was a potpourri that instilled Americans with astonishingly broad and eclectic tastes, and considerable sophistication.

And, as has been noted, Mildred Bailey sang "Lazy Bones" on a network radio broadcast and made the song a hit within a week. It was radio, then, that launched John's career as a songwriter, and sustained it, with his various radio engagements and then his own network radio show emanating from Los Angeles.

Harold Arlen, on that occasion when John sent me to meet him, produced a paper from his desk and read me a list of songs. Since nobody can remember a list like that, I later looked it up. It included:

"About a Quarter to Nine," "Begin the Beguine," "Bess, You Is My Woman Now," "Broadway Rhythm," "Cheek to Cheek," "East of the Sun and West of the Moon," "I Can't Get Started," "I Feel a Song Coming On," "I Got Plenty o' Nuttin'," "I Loves You, Porgy," "I Won't Dance," "I'm Gonna Sit Right Down and Write Myself a Letter," "I'm in the Mood for Love," "If I Should Lose You," "Isn't This a Lovely Day," "It Ain't Necessarily So," "It's Easy to Remember," "Just One of Those Things," "The Lady in Red," "Lovely to Look At," "Lullaby of Broadway," "Lulu's Back in Town," "Maybe," "Moon over Miami," "My Man's Gone Now," "My Romance," "Paris in the Spring," "The Piccolino," "Red Sails in the Sunset," "Stairway to the Stars," "Summertime,"

"These Foolish Things," "Top Hat, White Tie and Tails," "When I Grow Too Old to Dream," "Why Shouldn't I," "A Woman Is a Sometime Thing," and "You Are My Lucky Star."

He asked if I knew what it was. I could only say it was a list of great American songs. No, he said, it was a list of songs that came out in 1935 alone, most of them hits.

If you examine such annual lists of songs written in America in the twentieth century, you will note that they start to improve in the second decade, attain a higher quality in the 1920s, get still better in the '30s and '40s, and then begin to decline in the 1950s, increasingly crowded out by such material as "How Much Is That Doggy in the Window?", "Oh! My Pa-Pa," and "Vaya Con Dios," all from 1953. Yet Cole Porter was still hanging in there, and in that year produced "I Love Paris," "It's All Right with Me," and "From This Moment On."

Why the decline in quality of the American song? One of the factors was certainly television.

Television went on the air in New York City in 1928, though few people had the equipment to receive it. And with the advent of World War II, its development was postponed. But it came to the fore, and quite rapidly, at the end of the 1940s. When advertisers and their agencies saw the astonishing power of the new medium to sell merchandise, they diverted their interest from radio. The Jack Benny show ran on radio almost until the mid-1950s, and then even Benny made the transition to television, as he had previously made it from vaudeville to radio. So, too, Edgar Bergen and Charlie McCarthy. Astonishingly, even *Amos and Andy* moved on to television. Probably the last real network radio show was a one-hour Stan Freberg show, featuring the Billy May Orchestra, but it was not a success.

An illuminating testament to the process of change came in a 1989 conversation I had with the late Fred Hall, who began his career before the war not as an on-air personality but as an engineer, doing remote broadcasts of the big bands. Then he became a disc jockey, and later founded a series of radio stations across the country. He told me:

"When I got into radio, you just could not play records on the air. It was not allowed. There was a long argument about mechanical rights, and each record bore the inscription 'Not licensed for radio performance.' So they [i.e., bands, singers, orchestras] made radio transcriptions, big sixteen-inch discs produced especially for radio broadcast. They ran at 33⅓ rpm, and were therefore a predecessor of the LP.

"Then the broadcasting industry just began to ignore the prohibition of records. The station I was on in Washington, D.C., WWDC, was one of the first to let us play any record we felt like. The program director would set the tenor of the station. The stations, remember, were playing hits, but many of the hits were quality things. And so the disc jockeys—they weren't called disc jockeys yet, they were just called announcers—had a lot of leeway. They would pick their records from what was available, and what was available was often excellent material. A handful who were really good, such as Martin Block, were terribly influential in launching new records, a new band. There were no industry journals, such as *Billboard*, running elaborate lists of hits and governing the selection of music by the stations. There was the Hit Parade. It surveyed sheet-music sales in music stores. Sheet-music sales were still very important.

"Nobody was paying much attention to television after the war, or for that matter FM. In short order two or three thousand little radio stations went up all over the country, and many of them depended on the networks for news and drama, particularly the fifteen-minute daytime dramas. There were fewer remotes of the bands because there were fewer and fewer locations for them to play. These stations went right on playing hit records, and the hit records were for the most part still quality stuff. And gradually it began to go downhill. The networks withdrew, and withdrew, and withdrew, turning their attention to television, until all they were giving their affiliates was five minutes of news on the hour. And that left the stations to their own devices. But there were still many very innovative program directors who got deeply involved with local affairs, local programming, local news, local sports, to supplement the records they were playing."

And, of course, what the radio stations used to fill the airtime and sell their advertising was recordings. Gradually radio ceased to *produce* music at all; it simply appropriated the product of the record industry.

"Then," Fred continued, "as the small operations were bought up by large-scale operators—'group owners,' as they were called—the owners felt they had too little control over the stations that were far from their headquarters.

"So they turned to programmers. It began in the late 1950s, and by the mid-1970s, it was paramount, and today it is completely dominant."

In the 1940s and '50s and even into the mid-'60s there were an astonishing number of good singers in the United States, all with recording contracts, to whom John and other songwriters could present their material: David Allyn, Ed Ames, Ernestine Anderson, Betty Bennett, Tony Bennett, June Christy, Nat Cole, Perry Como, Chris Connor, Bing Crosby, Vic

Damone, Bobby Darin, Blossom Dearie (with whom John wrote "I'm Shadowing You"), Marge Dodson, Frank D'Rone, Billy Eckstine, Ethel Ennis, Ella Fitzgerald, Eydie Gorme, Johnny Hartman, Dick Haymes, Billie Holiday, Shirley Horn, Lurlean Hunter, Fran Jeffries, Herb Jeffries, Jack Jones, Kitty Kallen, Morgana King, Frankie Laine, Julius La Rosa, Steve Lawrence, Peggy Lee, Tommy Leonetti, Marilyn Maye, Carmen McRae, Helen Merrill, Matt Monro, Anita O'Day, Della Reese, Felicia Sanders, Sylvia Sims, Frank Sinatra, Dinah Shore, Carol Sloane, Keely Smith, Joannie Sommers, Jeri Southern, Jo Stafford, Kaye Starr, Teri Thornton, Mel Tormé, Dinah Washington, Andy Williams, Joe Williams, Nancy Wilson, and more, as well as such vocal groups as the Four Freshmen, Jackie and Roy, and the Hi-Los.

And there were many outstanding arrangers, working in New York and Los Angeles, turning out "charts" for these singers: Jack Andrews, Ralph Burns, Ralph Carmichael, Al Cohn, Frank Comstock, Don Costa, Frank de Vol, Marion Evans, Percy Faith, Robert Farnon in England, Gordon Jenkins, Joe Lipman, O. B. Masingil, Johnny Mandel, Peter Matz, Billy May, Claus Ogerman, Sy Oliver, Nick Perito, Nelson Riddle, Pete Rugolo, Paul Weston, Patrick Williams, Torrie Zito, and still more. Large orchestras were employed, including substantial string sections, and an enormous number of musicians were kept busy in the recording studios.

Most of these arrangers were conservatory trained, and all of them were steeped in two traditions, European classical music and jazz. The quality of the writing was extraordinary, and so was the performance level, and the great "standard" songs were revealed for what they were: works of art, worthy of comparison with (and in many cases superior to) European art songs.

When I first knew John, this was the world we knew. And when we would hang out and talk about songs, we assumed it would go on forever. We had no idea that Gresham's law operated not only in economics; it applied to the arts as well. Rock music had been rising steadily since the early 1950s and took a tremendous forward stride with Elvis Presley. It seemed that high-quality popular music could coexist with another kind of pop at the level of, as Dave Raksin puts it, finger painting. (In 2001, an English rock guitarist sought medical treatment for carpal tunnel syndrome, acquired, he said, from playing the same three chords for thirty years.)

Little did John, or I, or anyone else know that the most powerful blow to quality popular music would come from the very label he founded, and the group it signed under Alan Livingston, the Beatles. With the sale of

Beatles records on Capitol, the industry discovered just how much money could be made from records, and from then on it was interested in little else, and today is interested in *nothing* else.

One of the best record producers in New York was a former arranger from Holland named Joe René, who produced albums by Ethel Ennis and Marilyn Maye, among others. Joe told me: "They"—meaning the record executives, who were being displaced in their jobs by lawyers and accountants—"used to give me two, three, even four or five years to build a singer's name and career. Now they want a hit and a return on the money in a year."

In the mid-1950s, a man named Todd Storz, co-owner with his father of Storz Broadcasting, made the not particularly original observation that the public played the same few songs over and over on jukeboxes. He thought the same principle could be applied to radio, and applied it to the company's New Orleans station, WTIX. Thus, Top Forty radio was born. He then applied this principle to other stations the company acquired, including WHB in Kansas City in 1954, WDGY in Minneapolis–St. Paul in 1955, and WQAM in Miami in 1956. Gordon McLendon studied the Storz format at WHB in 1955 and applied it to his station KLIF in Dallas. Top Forty spread from there—in effect, a deliberate restriction of the music available to the public. And the music these stations played was not the best. American radio economics depends on what it calls "cost per thousand"—the cost charged the advertiser per thousand listeners—on which basis it can set its advertising rates, raising them for every additional thousand. Since bad taste is, and always has been, more common than good taste (which by definition is more selective), these stations sought a constantly lower common denominator in the music they played. There was no room in this for music by the likes of Kern and Porter and Mercer, much less Mozart and Duke Ellington. And in a remarkably few years it would be possible to drive a car across America and not hear a Johnny Mercer song on the radio, or those of any of the other songwriters justly revered by Dave Raksin.

Alexis de Tocqueville's *Democracy in America* was published in 1835, about 130 years before the rise of the Beatles. Though the book is often understood as a paean to American democracy, and in many ways it is, Tocqueville nonetheless feared what he saw as the tyranny of the majority. In Chapter 11 of the book, he writes:

"There are . . . in any democracy men whose fortunes are on the increase but whose desires increase much more quickly than their wealth, so that their eyes devour long before they can afford them. They are always on the lookout for shortcuts to these anticipated delights. These two elements always provide democracies with a crowd of citizens whose desires outrun their means and who will gladly agree to put up with an imperfect substitute rather than do without the object of their desire altogether.

"The craftsman easily understands this feeling, for he shares it. In aristocracies he charged very high prices to a few. He sees that he can now get rich quicker by selling cheaply to all.

"Now, there are only two ways of making a product cheaper.

"The first is to find better, quicker, more skillful ways of making it. The second is to make a great number of objects which are more or less the same but not so good. In a democracy every workman applies his wits to both these points.

"He seeks ways of working, not just better, but quicker and more cheaply, and if he cannot manage that, he economizes on the intrinsic quality of the thing he is making, without rendering it wholly unfit for its intended use. . . . In this way democracy . . . induces workmen to make shoddy things very quickly and consumers to put up with them."

And this phenomenon ultimately became evident in popular music.

One of the most bizarre stories of John's adventures when drinking involved the late Dick Gibson, an investment banker who founded and ran a festival called the Denver Jazz Party. Gibson was with John one night in Jim and Andy's, a musicians' bar on West Forty-eighth Street, just west of Sixth Avenue in New York. Both of them were loaded. Suddenly John got up and ran out of the place. Gibson, who was very portly, got up and tried to hurry after him. John headed east on Forty-eighth, with Gibson laboriously following. At last he caught up with John. John was sitting on a curb, sobbing, "Nobody gives a fuck, nobody cares!"

He was right.

The music scholar and historian James T. Maher, who collaborated with composer-songwriter Alec Wilder on the classic study *American Popular Song*, tells of an evening spent with John, Alec, and Abe Olman in New York.

"We started out at Charlie O's, a place that Johnny liked to hang around. He was walking up and down the bar being the hail good fellow, and all of a sudden there was this terrific shift. He said something very nasty, and I thought, *Wait a minute. Is this the same guy who for the last fifteen minutes has been so funny?* And then he switched back again. We walked over to Danny's Hideaway. We went into the back room where we had a big table. It was a wonderful evening, with lots and lots of talk.

"And then something happened that really bothered me, and I know it tortured Alec. Johnny got drunker and drunker and the mood got blacker and blacker and bleaker. And finally Johnny had his arms out on this big round table and his head down on the table, muttering. Alec and I leaned over, wondering, *What the hell is this guy murmuring?*

"And Johnny was saying, 'Why don't I die? Why don't I die?'

"And Abe Olman shook his head at us, indicating that we shouldn't get upset, because this was standard with Johnny, the progression into despair."

Twenty-seven

In 1958, MGM released the Danny Kaye film *Merry Andrew,* with songs by Saul Chaplin and John Mercer. They included "The Pipes of Pan," "The Square of the Hypotenuse," "Everything Is Tickety-Boo," and several others that never made it into the standard repertoire. After that, John's movie assignments grew scarce.

He was not alone. All his friends, including Jimmy Van Heusen, Jimmy McHugh, and Hoagy Carmichael, were experiencing the same malaise, the feeling of being passé. Richard Sudhalter, in his biography of Carmichael, notes:

"Hoagy kept writing songs, some of substantial quality. But to paraphrase one of his own titles, things had changed. By the early 1960s, according to pop historian Donald Clarke, the tastemakers of earlier times—bandleaders, songwriters, publishers—had simply abdicated, supplanted by a teenage generation 'encouraged to think that people with talent were kids just like them,' and uninterested in anything on the other side of the great divide.

"For Hoagy and his fellow songwriters, the most keenly felt loss was that of ready access to an immediate and accepting movie market. A new wave of young cinema composers, exhaustively skilled, had moved in; their scores, freely incorporating modern jazz and even more exotic elements, often included appealing individual themes easily converted into songs—which, in turn, took on lives of their own.

Portrait of Johnny

"The names of Johnny Mandel, Michel Legrand, Henry Mancini, Oliver Nelson, Lalo Schifrin, and others were appearing on more and more film credits and winning Oscars. They had displaced two discrete groups: such established, largely European-trained composers as Max Steiner, Franz Waxman, Miklos Rosza, and Dimitri Tiomkin, and the songwriters who had supplied individual tunes to complement their quasi-symphonic scores.

"Seemingly at a stroke, but actually over a decade, the new film scoring—evolving from such seminally 'modern' soundtracks as Elmer Bernstein's music for *The Man with the Golden Arm* (1955) and Mandel's no less powerful writing for the 1958 Susan Hayward melodrama *I Want to Live*—had rendered both the symphonic old guard and Carmichael's breed of songwriters obsolete."

In fact, these tastemakers did not abdicate. The bandleaders were put out of business by the disappearance of the ballrooms, by the retrenchment of the great radio networks (which had been their most powerful allies), and by the rise of television. As for the publishers, they were pushed to the side when the record companies expanded heavily into publishing, and by the commercially powerful new rock acts, many of which wrote their own material, setting up their own publishing firms. Johnny's friend Howie Richmond retired to the Palm Springs area, where John, too, had a home. They were often together, along with songwriter-turned-publisher Abe Olman, John's close friend, who wrote "Down Among the Sheltering Palms" and "Oh Johnny Oh."

As fate would have it, two of the "new" composers were the agents who extended John's Hollywood career—Henry Mancini and Johnny Mandel, both former big-band arrangers with whom I suspect John was comfortable. He wrote:

"Although my collaboration with Henry Mancini was pretty much a happenstance, it proved to be a happy one, and his great tunes have kept me going a little longer. I called him one day when I heard on the radio a melody he had titled 'Joanna.' He agreed to let me write a lyric."

We have noted that many highly trained composers cannot write compelling melody, while a few with no training at all, such as Irving Berlin, are inspired melodists. Mancini was one of those who had it all. He was a marvelous arranger and orchestrator who revolutionized film scoring. At the same time, he had a wondrous gift for writing soft, subtle, very beautiful and quite Italianate melodies.

Born in 1914, in Cleveland, Ohio, Henry Mancini was the only child of an immigrant father from the mountainous province of Italy called

Abruzzi. His father moved with his wife and son to West Aliquippa, Pennsylvania, when he obtained a steel-mill job there. Hank grew up there, learning flute from his father and studying arranging in nearby Pittsburgh with Max Adkins, who also trained Billy Strayhorn. He won admission to Juilliard and had barely begun his studies there when, in the early days of World War II, he received his draft notice and went into the Army Air Corps.

He went through the war as a musician, ending up in a band stationed at Nice. After the war, his old army master sergeant, Norman Leyden, was chief arranger for the Glenn Miller–Tex Beneke band, which Mancini joined as pianist and arranger.

He later settled in Los Angeles and, after a period of writing arrangements for radio, got a job in the scoring department of Universal Pictures, assembling music from previous scores for use in the company's cheap new pictures, but also occasionally writing scores or parts of scores for about 120 pictures, among them *Abbott and Costello Go to Mars, Veil of Baghdad, Creature from the Black Lagoon,* and *Ma and Pa Kettle at Home.* One may laugh at such titles, but those films often turn up on television, and the Mancini estate still receives royalties for the music Hank contributed to them. Hank never received screen credit for these films, but he did receive credit on the first important movie he scored, *The Glenn Miller Story.*

Among his friends was a rising young director named Blake Edwards. Edwards told him that he was about to start a private-eye series on television, to be called *Peter Gunn.* He wanted to know if Hank was interested in doing the music. He was indeed, and Hank went to work on music for the pilot. The story line of what became a long-running series involved the detective, Peter Gunn, who hangs out at a jazz club called Mother's. One of the songs Hank used in that pilot had a Mercer lyric.

Hank said, "Blake had cast Lola Albright for the role of Edie, Peter Gunn's girlfriend. Edie was to be a singer. Blake asked me to go over to Lola's house and set up a song for the pilot. We decided on the Rube Bloom–Johnny Mercer song 'Day In–Day Out.' "

Peter Gunn became an immediate success, and an album of the Mancini music derived from it became the biggest jazz hit in history, making Mancini a celebrity virtually overnight.

Then Edwards told Hank that he was going to do a picture at Paramount, from Truman Capote's *Breakfast at Tiffany's,* and he wanted Hank to do the score. Hank said:

"Blake was to direct it; Dick Shepherd and Marty Jurow were the producers, and the screenplay was by George Axelrod based on the Truman Capote novella. They had considered a number of actresses for the role of Holly Golightly, finally choosing Audrey Hepburn. . . .

"I went over to Paramount to have a meeting with Blake and the producers, Dick Shepherd and Marty Jurow, in their office. Dick and Marty felt that since the story had a New York location, they should hire a New York Broadway show writer to write the song that the script called for—a scene where Holly Golightly goes out on the fire escape and sings with her guitar. I would do the score, with someone else doing the song.

"My agent at MCA, Henry Alpert, said, 'You have a hell of a picture here with a great director and a great star; don't rock the boat. Let someone else do the song, you do the score.'

"But the albums, *Peter Gunn* and *Mr. Lucky,* were nothing if not a series of songs without words, and I knew I could write a tune. So I said to Blake, 'Give me a shot. Let me at least try something for that scene.' Blake took it up with Dick and Marty, who relented a little and agreed to let me try it.

"No decision had been made on who would [actually] sing the song. Audrey was not known as a singer. There was a question of whether she could handle it. Then, by chance, I was watching television one night when the movie *Funny Face* came on, with Fred Astaire and Audrey. It contains a scene in which Audrey sings 'How Long Has This Been Going On?' I thought, 'You can't buy that kind of thing, that kind of simplicity.' I went to the piano and played the song. It had a range of an octave and one, so I knew she could sing that. And I now felt strongly that she should be the one to sing the new song in our picture—the song I hadn't written yet.

"The song was one of the toughest I have ever had to write. It took me a month to think it through. What kind of song would this girl sing? What kind of melody was required? Should it be a jazz-flavored ballad? Would it be a blues? One night at home, I was relaxing after dinner. I went out to my studio off the garage, sat down at the piano, and all of a sudden I got the first three notes of a tune. It sounded attractive. I built the melody in a range of an octave and one. It was simple and completely diatonic: in the key of C. You can play it entirely on the white keys. It came quickly. It had taken me one month and a half hour to write that melody.

"I took it in and played it for Blake. He loved it. He said, 'Who would you like to do the lyrics?' I went for the best. I knew Johnny Mercer. Johnny was in the habit of writing lyrics for melodies he just happened to hear and like. He'd hear some music on his car radio and call the station to ask what it was; that was another of his habits. The tune was 'Joanna,' from the second *Peter Gunn* album. He wrote a lyric on it. Nothing came of it, but that was the start of my professional relationship with Johnny. We wanted to write together. So I called him.

"This was the low point of Johnny's artistic life. Illiterate songs were high on the charts, doo-wop groups were thriving. Johnny came to see me. He talked about the condition of the music business. We were almost ten years into the rock era, and he didn't have much hope for his kind of lyric or my kind of music. After I played him the melody, he said, 'Hank, who's going to record a waltz? We'll do it for the movie, but after that, it hasn't any future commercially.' I gave him a tape of the melody and he went home. . . .

"John called me one morning and said he had three lyrics to show me. That evening I was conducting the orchestra for a benefit dinner at the Beverly Wilshire Hotel. The rehearsal call was for four o'clock. I told John, 'Meet me in the ballroom of the Beverly Wilshire around noon.'

"I waited in the ballroom, which was deserted and dark but for a couple of bare-bulb work lights. John came in with an envelope full of papers. I sat down at the piano and started to play. The first lyric he sang was a personal one, about the girl, with the opening notes covered by the words 'I'm Holly.'

"John said, 'I don't know about that one.' Then he showed me another, quite different, and finally a third one. He said, 'I'm calling this one "Blue River." But it may change, because I went through the ASCAP archives and found that several of my friends have already written songs called "Blue River." ' There was nothing to prevent John using it: legally, you cannot copyright a title. But John was reluctant to use "Blue River." His kind of honesty has not caught on with many of the young songwriters today. They'll take the title of anything and use it. John wouldn't.

"John said, 'I have an optional word. "Moon River." ' And I said, 'You know, John, there used to be a radio show coming out of Cincinnati that had that title.'

" 'It wasn't a *song*, was it?'

" 'No, it was just a late-night show where a guy would talk in a deep voice about various things.'

" 'Okay,' he said.

"Sitting there on the bandstand in that deserted ballroom, I started to play the melody again, and he sang the third lyric. Every once in a while you hear something so right that it gives you chills. When he sang that 'huckleberry friend' line, I got them. I don't know whether he knew what effect those words had, or it was just something that came to him. But it was thrilling. It made you think of Mark Twain and Huckleberry Finn's trip down the Mississippi. It had such echoes of America. It was one of those remarkable lines that gives you a rush."

John remembered: "When I grew up in the South, by a river, there were always wild bushes, blackberries, strawberries, little wild strawberries, wild cherry trees, and huckleberries, and that coupled with the name Huckleberry Finn—and Mark Twain had written about the Mississippi, and this girl in *Breakfast at Tiffany's* was from around that neck of the woods, down there in the southwest United States, it just seemed to fit the need."

Mancini said: "A day or two later we played it for Blake, then for [the producers] Dick Shepherd and Marty Jurow. Everybody loved the song. And everybody was convinced that Audrey should do it. I taught it to her and we prerecorded.

"There have been more than a thousand recordings of 'Moon River.' Of all of them—and I am not overlooking the recordings by Andy Williams, Johnny Mathis, and Frank Sinatra—Audrey's performance was the definitive version. It transcended anything I had ever hoped for that song. . . .

"We recorded the song and scored the picture. Everyone was very high on it. Audrey, Mel Ferrer—who was then Audrey's husband—Blake, Ginny, Marty Rackin, who was head of Paramount, Dick Shepherd, Marty Jurow, and I went up to a preview near Stanford. The limousines took us back to our hotel in San Francisco, where Marty Rackin had a suite. The preview had gone very well. We continued to be excited about the song, no one more so than Blake, and we were elated about the picture as a whole, although we realized it was running long and would have to be cut. As is usual in those situations, everybody has different ideas about what should and should not go. It is a subjective process, with everyone trying to protect his or her own interests and involvement in the picture. We were all sitting around, nobody saying anything. Marty Rackin had his arm on the mantelpiece of the fireplace. He was very New York and personable, a tall, trim, and lovely man in his forties, with fine features.

"And the first thing Marty said was, 'Well, the fucking song has to go.'

"I looked over at Blake. I saw his face. The blood was rising to the top of his head, like a thermometer. He looked like he was going to burst.

Audrey made a move in her chair as if she were going to get up and say something. Everybody made a slight move toward Marty, as if they were thinking about lynching him.

"The song stayed in the picture.

"But I still wish I'd had Audrey do it on the album."

John would *never* take credit for anything but his own work, and he was even concerned about the title "Moon River." It's ironic that John thought the song had no commercial future; nominated for the 1961 Academy Award, it's one of the most recorded songs in history. Hank said:

"On Academy Award night, we hired a limousine and picked up Johnny and his wife, Ginger. They had a home, not really very large in view of Johnny's incredible catalogue of songs and his ASCAP rating, but beautifully decorated and charming. It seemed to be snuggled in a hollow among trees in Bel Air next to the golf course, and at the back of the property Johnny had a studio where he wrote. I guess the lyric to 'Moon River' was written there. . . .

"The limousine was moving slowly because of the traffic, and ours and all the other vehicles were surrounded by teenage girls, screaming when the movie stars arrived. They crowded around the cars and peered in the windows in search of celebrities. Movie composers did not fall into that category, and in the age of rock, Johnny—who had had a solid career as a singer—was not recognized either. I remember one little girl with a squeaky voice who stuck her head in our open window and inquired, 'Are you anybody?'

"We went in and found our places. Surprisingly, all they had for seating for all these people in tuxedos and evening gowns were hard folding chairs, set out on the floor of the auditorium. The longer you waited to see if your name would be called, the harder those chairs seemed to get. . . .

"The people in your own division vote on the nominations, whereas the full membership votes for the actual awards. Thus to be nominated for a score means your fellow composers have made the selection. I had grown up as an arranger, and to be nominated by my colleagues among such peers as Miklos Rosza and Dimitri Tiomkin made me feel as if I had arrived all of a sudden exactly at the end of the rainbow. But I didn't think I could win. . . .

"Those who have been nominated are always given aisle seats so they won't have to climb over a row of knees if they should win, so Johnny was seated on the aisle just in front of me. Johnny and I felt pretty good about 'Moon River''s chances. . . .

"As is the custom, all the nominated songs were sung in the course of the ceremony. . . . And of course Andy Williams, who had the big hit record of it—so much so that it has become for all practical purposes his theme song—sang 'Moon River.'

"They announced the nominations for the best score for a dramatic or comedy picture. Then I heard my name. I felt as if I'd been hit with a cattle prod. I jumped up and [my wife] Ginny looked at me and I looked at her and I think I gave her a kiss and I ran up to the stage, where somebody handed me an Oscar. I have no memory of what I said.

"The next category was best song. I was still in shock from winning for best score when I heard my name again, and Johnny grinned that impish smile of his, and we went up and picked up two Oscars.

"After the ceremony, we went to the Academy dinner ball at the Hilton and, as they say, danced the night away. Talk about highs!"

On the subject of "Moon River," Nick Mamalakis told me this:

"When Johnny bought this house on Back River, my wife and I would visit him from time to time and she would bake Greek sweets and take them to him and his wife—when she was there. When he won the Oscar for 'Moon River,' I had good friends on the Chatham County Commission. I went up to see them and said, 'Back River means nothing. Why don't we change the name of the river?' And they passed a resolution changing the name to Moon River.

"The main road through Wilmington Island was Highway 80. The area was building up. The state highway department created a bypass to avoid the stores and everything else on the way to Savannah Beach. The personnel director of Savannah was a friend of mine. He came to me and asked whether it would be all right with the Mercer family if they passed a resolution to change the name of old Highway 80 to Johnny Mercer Boulevard.

"And that's the name it has now."

Twenty-eight

Henry Mancini was a self-effacing man. He seemed most at ease when he was on the road with "my guys," as he called them, the rhythm section, lead trumpet player, and saxophonist he carried with him on concert tours. Then he was open and witty and down-to-earth. He always seemed to me a little uncomfortable in Hollywood, as if he were baffled by his success. And success he had. No other film composer had ever achieved the fame *for his music* that Henry Mancini did, able to fill concert halls everywhere for orchestral performances of his scores.

Mancini changed film scoring. Though he maintained that *Breakfast at Tiffany's* would probably not have won the Academy Award for the score were it not for the song, I'm not sure he was right. Watching that charming film again, one sees just how much he contributed to its mood and color. I, for one, cannot imagine it without his richly romantic and humorous music.

While it is true that Elmer Bernstein used jazz in the score of *The Man with the Golden Arm* and Johnny Mandel used it in *I'll Cry Tomorrow,* Mancini was the composer who opened the way to the use of jazz and elements of dance-based music—including Latin dance rhythms—in movie music. Indeed, the Americanization of film scoring, which up to that time had been strongly European and symphonic in style and tradition, starts with Henry Mancini.

He introduced all sorts of elements of orchestration, all sorts of sonorities, that had not been in use before: French horns voiced on top of low trombones, bass flutes (he was a flute player) in the bottom register to establish ominous moods, piccolo and high flutes in falling figures for a slight frightened feeling, and a particular way of using strings. Jimmy Rowles—his favorite pianist, and Mercer's as well—is often heard in his scores, and he used the finest of Los Angeles jazz musicians. It's small wonder that John was attracted to his music.

Howard Hawks was planning an African adventure film to be titled *Hatari,* the Swahili word for danger. At one point Hawks considered Hoagy Carmichael to write the music, but eventually settled on Mancini. Carmichael and Mercer, however, contributed a song to the picture, "Just for Tonight." That same year, Mancini was engaged to write a score for a new Blake Edwards movie to be called *Days of Wine and Roses.* It was to be a considerable departure for Edwards, known for his stylish detective show and *Breakfast at Tiffany's.* Adapted from a *Playhouse 90* television play, it is a very dark movie about alcoholism, with Jack Lemmon and Lee Remick, and it remains a stark film to this day.

Edwards and Mancini were in agreement that the film's title would serve well as the title line for its theme song. They agreed also to ask Johnny Mercer to write the lyric.

Hank told me:

"The title determined the melody—six words, seven syllables. I went to the piano and started on middle C and went up to A, 'The days . . .' The first phrase fell right into place. That theme was written in about half an hour. It just came, it rolled out. I played it for John on the piano at my house.

"By then he had one of the first cassette recorders, and he taped it. Like most lyricists, Johnny liked to hear the tune over and over again.

"I had learned something about John from 'Moon River'—that he will get back to you with a lyric. There was no point in prompting him. I made the mistake of calling him once and he let me know he wasn't ready. After that, I never made any moves until he called me. And before long he did. He said, 'Hank, I've got it, I've got the lyric.'

"I took the family down [the following] Sunday to Newport Beach. John and Ginger had a house there. Ginny and I arrived in the afternoon. I sat down at the piano, and John gave the first performance of 'Days of Wine and Roses.' There were no changes, but for one word. He had 'the golden face / that introduced me to . . . ,' and he changed *face* to *smile* and it was perfect.

"We were all elated with his lyric, which, like 'Moon River,' was unusual in that it was allegorical. I think 'Moon River' must have started his allegorical period. It was simply beautiful, and at that time Ginny and I were the only ones other than Ginger who heard it. I was a little envious of Ginger because she was the first one to hear Johnny's beautiful songs. . . . Her ears were always the first to hear all that great poetry that Johnny wrote. . . .

"I called [Blake] that evening and he made arrangements to hear it the following morning in a soundstage near where he was shooting the picture. Blake asked if Johnny and I minded if Jack Lemmon came along to hear the song. We said it was fine with us.

"Johnny and I went over to Warner Bros. next morning. We had an old upright piano in the middle of this huge soundstage. Those old soundstages have a haunted feeling. It won't do to call them barns: every one of them was big enough to hold ten barns. They were built of wood, and the rafters creaked, and they seemed filled with the ghosts of old movies, and they had a smell of the thousands of people who had worked there. Johnny Mercer was one of the finest demonstrators not only of his songs but anybody's songs. He had a captivating style. I sat down in that huge soundstage and played and Johnny sang 'Days of Wine and Roses' in his best bullfrog voice with a crack in it, and the jazz inflection that was always there somewhere.

"When I play songs for producers, I don't want to look at them. I have a tendency to get paranoid about halfway through. I was sitting with my shoulder toward Blake and Jack. Johnny of course was facing them. When we were through, there was a long, long, heavy, terrible silence. It probably lasted ten seconds, but it seemed like ten minutes. I kept staring into the keyboard. Finally I couldn't stand it, and I shifted myself around to look at Blake and Jack. And there was Jack with a tear coming down his cheek, and Blake was getting misty-eyed. We didn't have to ask them if they liked the song.

"In 1962, the song won Johnny and me another Academy Award."

Bob Corwin said:

"Johnny always wrote six, seven, eight, nine, ten lyrics, and then would filter through them and pick out the one. There was one lyric of 'Days of Wine and Roses' and only one. They asked him to change one line and he refused because, he said, it was the only song he wrote that only had one lyric, and he believed that God wrote 'Wine and Roses.' He said all he remembered was sitting down at the typewriter and the next thing he knew the song was done. He said, 'I'm not going to change that lyric, because I don't even think I wrote it.' "

Portrait of Johnny

And when columnist Earl Wilson asked John what lyric came to him most easily, he replied: "The easiest for me was 'Days of Wine and Roses.' I completed it in nine minutes. I had it all in my mind and couldn't get the words down fast enough."

> *The days of wine and roses*
> *laugh and run away,*
> *like a child at play,*
> *through the meadowland*
> *toward a closing door,*
> *a door marked "Nevermore"*
> *that wasn't there before.*
>
> *The lonely night discloses*
> *just a passing breeze*
> *filled with memories*
> *of the golden smile*
> *that introduced me to*
> *the days of wine and roses*
> *and you.*

John told a BBC interviewer: "Gene Lees did an article about me in a magazine. He noticed that that song was written with only two sentences. Well, that's true. But I didn't do it on purpose. I mean, it wasn't like a crossword puzzle or anything. I just followed where the melody went. As a matter of fact, I don't feel too responsible about this song, although it's one of my very favorites. Because Ernest Dowson [the English poet] wrote, 'They are not long, the days of wine and roses.' And that's where the picture title came from, and the television show, so I don't take too much credit for that. You know, I didn't want to write it, because I said it sounds like a French operetta, or the War of the Roses, or Sigmund Romberg, or Hammerstein and Kern, and you go in and you see two kids getting stoned out of their heads, and it's pretty depressing."

In 1963, Mancini and Mercer wrote another song together, this one for a Stanley Donen film, *Charade*, which featured Cary Grant and Audrey Hepburn and a Paris setting. Donen was then living in London. Hank said:

"Stanley wanted me to write the music there, so off I went to London, not knowing what I was facing. It seemed like a big commitment. I'd had some success but I didn't have a real body of work. I was then only thirty-nine. I got set up in a penthouse suite in the Mayfair Hotel, right off Berkeley Square. I rented a piano and went to work. I stayed for two months to write the score for *Charade,* developing a main-theme melody that I turned over to Johnny Mercer, who wrote yet another of his superb abstract lyrics for it. We were nominated for another Academy Award, though we lost out to [Jimmy Van Heusen and Sammy Cahn's] 'Call Me Irresponsible.' "

In 1963, John wrote a title song with Elmer Bernstein for the film *Love with the Proper Stranger.* Elmer had the same experience with him that so many others did. "He went away," Elmer said, "and I didn't hear from him for weeks. Then he called me and asked me to meet him at Paramount. He had seven pages of lyrics, and he said, 'Which one do you like?' He was an incredible writer."

That same year, Mercer got a call from Johnny Mandel. Born in New York City in 1925, Mandel, like Mancini, was a product of the big-band era. He had studied at Juilliard and the Manhattan School of Music, and later he studied (as did Mancini) with Mario Castelnuovo-Tedesco. He was a trombone player and arranger for the bands of Count Basie, Georgie Auld, Woody Herman, Boyd Raeburn, and Buddy Rich. Moving to Los Angeles, he worked as an album arranger for Peggy Lee and Frank Sinatra, among others, before breaking into film scoring. Warner Bros. assigned Mandel to the job of scoring the film *The Americanization of Emily,* a sardonic antiwar movie with a script by Paddy Chayefsky and starring James Garner and Julie Andrews.

Mandel said, "Warner Bros. wanted a lyric. They said, 'Who do you want for a lyricist?' I said, 'Can I have anyone I want?' 'Yeah,' they said. I said, 'We might as well start at the top. That's Johnny Mercer.' Johnny came in and put a wonderful lyric to it.

"It was an effortless type of collaboration. The song, 'Emily,' became a hit, with a lot of records, and I said, 'This is fun.' I've never looked back since. That's when I became a songwriter."

The question arises: Why, then, didn't John write the lyric to the melody Mandel used in *The Sandpiper*? I encountered two answers to that question, and they contradict each other irreconcilably. This is what John told me:

"Well, you know, the first six notes are the same as the opening of Hoagy Carmichael's 'New Orleans.' And I couldn't do it. Funny part is,

Hoagy asked me why I didn't write that lyric. I told him that the two songs had the same opening. Hoagy said, 'They do? I never noticed.' "

When I recounted this to Mandel, he said, "That's exactly how it happened. Johnny turned me down on that song for just that reason."

John told a BBC interviewer, however, that he *did* write a lyric for Mandel's melody. He said, "I wrote it for the movie with Elizabeth Taylor and Richard Burton and it was turned down and a fellow wrote 'The Shadow of Your Smile,' which got to be one of the biggest hits ever." (That lyric was written by Paul Francis Webster.)

Asked what his lyric was like, John recited the verse.

"My song was kinda nice, it was poetic, it fit the picture—

> *Today I saw a bird that broke its wing,*
> *which isn't in itself a tragic thing.*
> *Yet I had the feeling start*
> *I had seen my counterpart.*
> *And love would come and break my heart*
> *once again in spring.*

"I figured with 'the shadow of your smile' he was in love with a lady with a mustache."

You can take your choice of the two versions of the story.

There is a great subtlety at the end of "Emily." There is no true rhyme for that name, so John wrote an unfolding pattern of sound:

> *As my eyes visualize a family*
> *they see dreamily*
> *Emily too.*

But someone in the publishing division of Warner Bros. apparently didn't get it and changed it, and the sheet music went out with "they see Emily, / Emily too." A lot of singers have recorded it that way. John was everlastingly annoyed about it.

In 1965, Mancini scored *The Great Race,* a film starring Tony Curtis and Natalie Wood. He and John wrote a countrified waltz called "The Sweetheart Tree." Sung by a choral group, it pops up occasionally in reissues of Mancini music. That same year, he and Mancini wrote a lovely song called "Moment to Moment" for the score to a film of that name.

This one lingers on. That year John also wrote a song with Johnny Green titled "The World of the Heart" for a Robert Taylor movie called *Johnny Tiger,* but the song, like the picture, went down like a rock.

In 1966, he wrote two songs for a Tony Curtis comedy called *Not with My Wife You Don't.* The songs are "A Big Beautiful Ball" and "My Inamorata," and I doubt whether even the most ardent of Mercer admirers remember them. The composer was John Williams, at whose home Mancini introduced me to Mercer. In 1967, Mercer wrote a title lyric for the Robert Redford–Jane Fonda film *Barefoot in the Park,* but he was saddled with that title, which doesn't offer much scope for a lyric, and it, too, is forgotten. The music was by Neal Hefti. That same year John wrote something with Morton Stevens called "Tomorrow Never Comes" for a movie called *Cimarron Strip.*

And then came a project that aroused excitement in both Mancini and Mercer: *Darling Lili,* a movie for Paramount starring Rock Hudson and Julie Andrews, and directed by Blake Edwards.

"Johnny Mercer and I wrote the songs for it," Hank told me. "It was an appealing project, since the songs were to be performed in the story, not simply used in underscore, and we had a great singing star in Julie Andrews. It was a colorful period piece, set in World War I, with Julie in the role of a German spy who infiltrates the Allies and then falls in love with an American pilot played by Rock Hudson."

Unfortunately, the film ran into problems of all sorts—chief among them the ill will of Robert Evans, who was head of Paramount at the time—and never received the sort of studio support it needed.

The film critic and historian Leonard Maltin wrote of *Darling Lili* in the 1994 edition of his *Movie and Video Guide:* "Critically lambasted when first released, this entertaining spoof has Andrews and Hudson at their best, along with writer/director Blake Edwards, keeping tongue in cheek. . . . Great fun, good music, including Johnny Mercer and Henry Mancini's lovely 'Whistling Away the Dark.' "

Maltin is assuredly right about "Whistling Away the Dark." That title phrase, incidentally, never occurs in the song, and I don't know why it wasn't titled "Whistling in the Dark," the phrase as it appears in the song. The lyric expresses Mercer's perpetual regret about time and age and lost years. If you visit the house on Gwinnett Street in Savannah where he spent his childhood, then walk around the corner, you will come face-to-face with the park he refers to in the lyric. And James McIntire's recollection of the boys of the Gwinnett and Hall Street gangs ambushing and intimidating one of their members caught alone illumines the lyric. The lyric is about—there is no question in my mind about this—John's state of mind when he wrote it, but as so often, he was drawing on memories of Savannah to express it. The melody, which is in C minor, is quite dark, and so is the lyric. It goes:

> *Often I feel*
> *this sad old world*
> *is whistling in the dark,*
> *just like a child who,*
> *late from school,*
> *walks bravely home*
> *through the park.*
>
> *To keep their spirits soaring*
> *and keep the night at bay,*
> *never quite knowing*
> *which way they are going,*
> *they sing the shadows away.*
>
> *Often I think*
> *my poor old heart*
> *has given up for good.*
> *And then I see*
> *a brand-new face.*
> *I glimpse a new neighborhood.*
>
> *So walk me back home, my darling,*
> *Tell me dreams really come true.*
> *Whistling, whistling,*
> *here in the dark with you.*

After *Darling Lili*, John would write a song with Marvin Hamlisch for the film *Kotch*. Titled "Life Is What You Make It," it is a trivial song and is now forgotten.

With *Kotch*, John's career in film came to an end. The film was released in 1971. By then John was active as the founding president of the Songwriters Hall of Fame (he served from 1969 to 1973). The cofounders were his friends Abe Olman and Howie Richmond, who lived across the street from each other in Rancho Mirage, right across the Tamarisk Golf Course green from Frank Sinatra's compound, and not far from Johnny's Palm Springs home. "Johnny and Abe and I would go for walks and talk about the business," Howie said.

"In the 1960s, the old copyright law was running out. A lot of us were concerned because there was a lethargy on the part of Congress. We were trying to figure out how we could make the cultural contributions of song-writers more understandable both to the Congress and the people of the country. 'Alexander's Ragtime Band,' which was Irving Berlin's first important song, came out in 1909, and the copyright was expiring."

The arithmetic is simple. Under the old law, in America a copyright lasted for twenty-eight years and could be renewed for another twenty-eight, for a total of fifty-six years. This was primitive in comparison with European law, in which a copyright remained valid for fifty years after the death of the composer or lyricist; in the case of songs that were joint works, the copyright remained in place for fifty years after the death of the surviving partner. Berlin's fifty-four-year copyright was due to expire in 1963, while he was still very much alive. Congress legislated extensions for 'Alexander's Ragtime Band' while debating what a new copyright law should look like. The law has since been changed, and changed again, but it is still cluttered and confusing.

"So if Berlin had been a European and died at that time [i.e., 1963]," Howie Richmond continued, "the copyright would have existed world-wide for another fifty years.

"I told Abe Olman, '*You* know Irving Berlin. Why don't we get him on the *Ed Sullivan Show* and start some sort of celebration of songwriters, like the Baseball Hall of Fame?'

"Abe said, 'Howie, I like that. Yes, I know Irving. I'll talk to his lawyer.' We thought we'd honor all the older songwriters, like Stephen Foster, and the only living person at the start would be Irving Berlin. And we could publicize the whole issue of longevity of copyrights.

"But when Abe sat down with Berlin, Berlin said, 'Hey, I'm the only songwriter. The fellows who write lyrics are lyric-writers. The fellows who write music are composers. Outside of Cole Porter, I'm the only songwriter.' "

There were of course others he could have mentioned as writing both words and music, including Frank Loesser, Harold Rome, Noël Coward, and, looking further back, Paul Dresser and Stephen Foster. But Berlin was, in addition to everything else, a formidable egotist. "He said we couldn't call it the Songwriters Hall of Fame, and he didn't want to be connected with it," Howie said.

"Johnny said, 'I'll go to Irving. He likes me. He has complimented me a number of times.' Johnny talked to Berlin, and he, too, was refused. Again the three of us were talking, and Abe and I looked at him and we said, 'Johnny . . .'

"And he said, 'All right, I'll *do* it.'

"He accepted that he would take the leadership role. His personality was such that he could talk for everybody. More than Berlin—and much *better* than Berlin. . . .

"Immediately, everybody in the industry was interested in it. It was dedicated to picking up the history of songwriters and *identifying* them with their work. Berlin and Johnny and a few others had their histories already established. They were identified with their work. Most songwriters were *not*. We wanted to put the focus on how important their contributions actually were. Everybody who was a songwriter wanted to be in on it, but you had to be voted in.

"After about three or four years, bingo!, there were ten or fifteen writers, such as Sammy Cahn, saying to Johnny, 'How long do we have to wait to get in?' At the rate of about three a year, it could take forever. At one point, Johnny more or less legislated that they should be in. Their music was in the Hall of Fame, so why weren't they? One year a big group went in at one time."

Eventually, music publishers, artists' agents, and record producers were allowed membership, and the organization continues to this day. Even some wives of dead songwriters are now on the board of directors.

"Johnny," Howie said, "was very happy during those early days with the Songwriters Hall of Fame. All of those early dinners were in effect a sort of Algonquin round table of the most brilliant writers in the music business. To have Dorothy Fields, perhaps, at a table with Jimmy McHugh or Hoagy Carmichael, [this was] the inner sanctum of the profession."

The first dinner, in 1969 at the Waldorf-Astoria in New York, was produced by Oscar Brand, who is still the organization's curator, in company with Bill Harbach and Bob Bach. Bill Harbach remembers that Harold Arlen and Richard Rodgers attended that dinner, "and just about everyone else in the profession in New York." It was in honor of Rudolf Friml. Oscar said:

"Johnny was the emcee. As usual he was smooth, gracious. He wasn't a joke-teller onstage. He had a tremendous amount of respect for other people who wrote songs. In consequence, he was very careful not to say anything that would prove harmful or uncomfortable. He said that people knew songs without necessarily knowing who wrote them. Everybody knew 'The Star Spangled Banner,' but few people knew who wrote it. And that was the purpose of the organization—so that people who created songs that were milestones in people's lives are not forgotten. . . . Frank Sinatra made a speech that night. He said, 'I love you guys. If it weren't for you, I'd be pushing pencils in Hoboken.'

"Johnny was very devoted to the organization. His name was always around. When *Breakfast at Tiffany's* came out and 'Moon River' became a rage among people who cared about beautiful writing, they all knew who wrote it. I'd look at him, and think, *This man is one of the greatest writers the world has ever seen!*"

On the evening of March 14, 1971, Johnny and his work were featured in the "Lyrics and Lyricists" series produced at New York's Ninety-second Street YMHA by Maurice Levine. He sang a condensed medley covering much of his career, accompanied by pianist Richard Leonard. The results were released on an LP. It is available today (on CD) on GRP Records.

And it's astonishing. Hearing one after another of his works, in his own performance, one is blinded by the brilliance of his writing. He was everything other songwriters thought he was. The rich and often wildly funny ingenuity of his rhyming—and in our rhyme-poor language of English—will leave you with your mouth agape. Toward the end of the evening, Levine asked him about the songs of the current crop of young writers. This was during the time of the Vietnam War. John replied:

"I think it all springs from the war. They're all scared and they want to tell everybody what they know. They're really children philosophers. They're talking about . . . philosophically, they're trying to say to you what they want everybody to hear, and so they don't write any tunes. They write to the same tune, they have new words, and I just think it's appalling. But I think that out of it all there will come a lot of great writers, because there are so many young people writing. Almost everybody is a songwriter. There used to be maybe a hundred songwriters, or five hundred, now there are maybe fifty thousand or five million. Maybe eight, I don't know. But some of them are good. A few of them have a lot of integrity, like Jimmy Taylor. He's brand-new—he sings like he means it. The kid with Blood, Sweat and Tears—he's a marvelous singer. The writers I'm not so nutty about. I'm not so nutty about the Beatles. I think Stephen Sondheim is a wonderful writer. And I think some of these folk writers, the kids, are good, but there's nothing very new. Woody Guthrie wrote before that—before him, Vernon Dalhart used to sing 'The Death of Floyd Collins' and those narrative songs, 'The Wreck of the Old 97.' This whole folk bag is overdone. This is kind of a dull answer. When I get serious about things, it's dreary."

In the so-called folk field, he might have mentioned the superb songs of Gordon Lightfoot. But in general his evaluation is sound. Rock stripped popular music of any interesting harmony, and brought melody to a minimum, and today rap has eliminated melody altogether. And a lot of wonderful writers have *not* emerged. On the theory that an infinite number of monkeys at an infinite number of typewriters would *eventually* produce the plays of Shakespeare and the *Encyclopaedia Britannica,* rock and contemporary pop should have produced more good songs by sheer accident. Another point: John was inclined to be circumspect in public interviews. He may have publicly expressed respect for Stephen Sondheim's work, but personally he didn't like it. He thought it was cold. This was one of the few subjects on which John and I disagreed. We argued over Sondheim's *Company,* which he hated and I loved. And as for the Beatles, John simply *despised* them.

John's own era had passed, and he knew it, and the new directions of popular music only exacerbated his melancholia. John's constant awareness of time and its ravages is in so many of his songs. Paul Weston said, "John was worried about his age when he was twenty-eight."

Here is one of my most poignant memories of John:

John and Ginger were spending the better part of a week with my wife and me in Toronto in 1972 or '73. One afternoon after lunch, the four of us were walking along Yorkville Street, which is lined with boutiques and nice little restaurants. John and I were a little ahead. Two beautiful young girls came toward us, and passed, walking into their future and our past.

John said to me, "I'm still looking, but they're no longer looking back."

After that, since he wouldn't fly, he took a train all the way across Canada to Vancouver, then another one south to Los Angeles.

In his unfinished autobiography he wrote:

I am over sixty years old now. And when just the other day I heard Richard Frederick and Anna Moffo do a medley from Show Boat, *Jerry Kern's wonderful melodies, I pulled over to the side of the road, parked, and cried like a young boy.*

I sit here in California, writing these reminiscences in a heavy rain, thinking of the fires and the mud slides, and it does seem as if the magic sunny land I knew has been "struck," like the movie sets it built, and has disappeared overnight, all its genies gone back into bottles, leaving sky-scrapers where the orange blossoms used to scent the wind.

Twenty-nine

"A tune writer," John said to me in New York, "has to know how to build up a lyric so that the laughs come through, and the lyric writer has to know how to baby that tune, when he gets a good one, to search and search till he gets the right lyric to it. You can ruin great ideas if they're written improperly. I find that there's a very strange alchemy about working too little or too much on a tune. Sometimes if you work too much and you're *too* careful, you lose the whole thing. But if you get a fine fire going at the beginning, and you control it, you can rewrite enough without rewriting too much. That's the best way to write, I find."

I asked him, "What do you think of contemporary lyrics, as a whole?"

"I think in the main what we're going through right now is a lot of drivel. A lot of people who can't write are trying to write. And I think those who do write well are basing most of their stuff on a modern-day kind of hobo philosophy. It's a futility because of the war in Vietnam and because of crime and violence and everything. And it's built on Elizabethan structure, and hill music, which is also based on Elizabethan structure. And so a lot of these kids who are writing, like Simon and Garfunkel and Jimmy Webb and Johnny Hartford and the kids down in Nashville, take the guitar and try to philosophize to a hillbilly tune with chords that come from 'way 'way ago. That's the general picture. Of course, there are many exceptions, including a guy like Alan Jay Lerner. I think Webb is a superior writer; I didn't mean to classify him with the others. And Burt Bacharach is trying very hard to be different—too hard, as far as I'm concerned, although I think he's gifted. I don't know. What do you think?"

"I pretty much agree. I like Jimmy Webb's things, too. 'By the Time I Get to Phoenix' is a very good song. Why don't you record again?"

"I'd like to. I'm singing really not too badly, so they say. I think my voice is deeper. I think I know better how to sing in tune than I used to. I don't think anybody cares, that's the main thing."

"I think there would be considerable interest," I said. "You always did your humorous things. You never recorded your ballads. Why?"

"I can't sing well enough."

"I don't agree."

"I could try it now. I think I'm a little better than I used to be."

"I don't think," I said, "that I've ever heard a song of yours that didn't have a payoff in the last line."

"Well, I think that's kind of the way you approach writing; if you're brought up in that school, you don't even *begin* a song if you haven't got an ending of some kind."

"Have you ever started out when you didn't know what the ending was going to be?" I asked, and we both laughed.

"Yeah, I *have*. Sometimes I *wound up* without having an ending!"

"That's a desperate feeling!" I said.

"It is!"

"And particularly when you've got some good lines in there and you don't want to lose 'em, but you have to top 'em."

"That's right," John said, and we laughed some more.

We got talking about "Days of Wine and Roses."

"You see a thing in that song that I don't know if I see," John said.

"A quality of abstraction."

"Yeah," he said. "Well, I'm not so sure it's purposeful on my part. I don't know whether when Dalí painted his pictures, he did it purposefully or he just said, 'I've just got to say something I feel here, and this is the best way to say it.' I'm not sure it was all that intended."

"Oh, I'm not saying that it is or has to be intended. I'm just saying that things you wrote there and ways you wrote there would not have been acceptable or understandable to the public of the 1930s."

"Well, I'll tell you, maybe I give them more credit," John said. "Irving Berlin said a long time ago, 'Johnny gives everybody credit for knowing what he's talking about.' You don't write down to the ten-cent-store girl or anybody else. I don't. You certainly don't. And when I try to be literate, I just assume they know what I'm talking about. When I try to do what we're talking about right now, to get images—we did it in 'Charade,' in the middle part, where it goes, 'in the darkened wings, / the music box played on,' I assume they know what I'm talking about. I can't stop to say, 'You know, there's really not a music box, it's really the orchestra.' You take that to Andy Williams, who's really a fine, intelligent cat, and he says, 'There's always something in these songs I don't understand. But I'm gonna sing it anyway.' "

I took a photo of John that day. After he died, Ginger told me it was one of the few pictures of himself he ever liked. Maybe I caught him the way he saw himself. Or maybe—and this is more important—I saw him the way he saw himself. Or better yet, he let me see him as he was. It's in the eyes, and in the slight gentle smile. There is kindness in those eyes, and laughter, and sadness. It's John; at least it's the John Mercer I knew.

Not too long after that conversation, in 1974, John went to London and recorded two excellent LPs for the Pye label with producer Ken Barnes. (They are now available in the United States on a single CD on the DRG label.) Whether my urging had anything to do with it or not, I do not know, but he recorded some of his ballads, such as "The Summer Wind," to poignant effect. He did "Days of Wine and Roses," "Something's Gotta Give," "That Old Black Magic," "Come Rain or Come Shine," and the best reading of "One for My Baby" anyone has ever done. He was then sixty-five.

In his memoir, John muses on the songs that were popular in America in the early years of the twentieth century, and the various ethnic influences that went into creating this body of music. I find his reflections on the subject quite telling.

There was no television, no juke boxes, and radio hadn't even got started. So it took songs longer to get across the country, and they lasted longer. But today, and ever more so, we are exposed to all kinds of music, good, bad, and indifferent. We have to do our own screening. Lately more and more trash seems forced on us, so we are inclined to turn off the TV and radio and play the songs we prefer on phonographs.

John would have been surprised to know that in a short time, kids wouldn't know what you meant by "phonograph." Indeed, they wouldn't even know what you meant by LP, having never handled or even seen one. And soon the CD may suffer the same fate.

If you want to go back to Grandpa's Day, well, you can fiddle out "Pony Boy" or "The Great Speckled Bird"; a Hungarian csardas, a Greek dance, an Italian tarantella, or Lord knows what else, depending on who your grandfather was.

I used to listen with awe and wonder to every kind of music I could get my hands on. Gypsy airs on the accordion or zither, harmonica blues, gems from Broadway, the yodels of Jimmy Rodgers, cowboy songs from the prairies, all reached my ears and touched my heart. I was open and impartial, loving anything that had any kind of story and a pleasing air.

So when today's young people run back to their mother's arms and hide in the economic complaints of Woody Guthrie, or make a saint out of Hank Williams, they have a skeptical tartar in me. For I remember their betters—their daddies—and where they "borrowed" their inspirations from. . . .

When I remember talking to the old timers as a child, I know that the well of our folk music goes deeper than I or even my grandfather knew. The traditional songs that were brought over here in the holds of the immigrant boats and the slave traders, those that reached us via the islands, are only a drop in the bucket, so vast and deep is the reservoir that we have kept hidden in our heart.

After a man spent all day ploughing a field, or herding cattle, laboring on the docks or in the mills, poling the canals and picking cotton, he had no movies or phonograph to lighten his burden at the end of it. But he had his family, his jug and his banjo or mouth organ or concertina, and he could sing the old songs to escape and to remind himself of happier times and wonderful far-off places—'way over "The Big Rock Candy Mountains." These were the times when Mama and Pa and Grandpa and Uncle Silas forgot their troubles, forgot to be stern, and were as human as little kids.

That is a passage that never could have been written by Alan Jay Lerner, Cole Porter, Lorenz Hart, Dorothy Fields, or Howard Dietz, or even Yip Harburg or any of the other major lyricists John respected. It reveals his deep identification with the American people, the so-called common folk. Of all the sophisticated, literate lyricists, only John had this quality, which is why some people are inclined to think of his work as folk music, something it assuredly is not. But it draws from that well. He wrote this, remember, after watching the rise of Bob Dylan; Peter, Paul, and Mary; and others in that vein.

This resurgence of folk music is an ethnic, fearsome getting back to the womb for certain sections of America that don't want to lose the old days and "them good old boys from them good old hills and them pretty little valleys." So whether you were "a little bitty baby whose Mammy used to rock you in them old cotton fields down south" or you're "goin' to Kansas City—to get some o' them crazy little women there" or if you were born " 'way down yonder in the Indian Nation and make your home on the reservation, in those Oklahoma hills away back home," you are in a sense treading water, because, while you can't go back, you don't want to go forward; the prospect for forward today is not as pleasant as it was years ago. Then, "with someone like you, a pal good and true," you could go and find "a place that's known to God alone." But now you know wherever you go on this planet, you'll find more cars and more crowds. So while we wait for new planets and ways to get there, we are retreating into our past—our youth, where Mom and Dad made us secure—against the world, the bomb, the accidents, assassinations, and all the ugly things we are not correcting fast enough.

That was one of the reasons for the student rebellion. Those young people were looking for something honest that has gone out of our world, something to believe in, something "meaningful," to use their own word (one I can't abide, I must say). But I don't want to "just leave them alone and let them come home, wagging their tails behind them." I want to tell the young ones that we older writers were honest, too, and on a tougher basis, a harder pattern.

Our songs may not smell of sweat and the earth, but our rhymes, not just "time" and "mine," not just "wrong" and "alone" or "home," are pure. Sure, when a line is great, you can skip the rhyme. But how many lines are that great?

John would be horrified to see what is being taught today in most college courses on songwriting, courses that didn't exist in his time. The young people are being told to use what are called "slant rhymes" or "near rhymes," when often they don't even qualify as assonance. "Pure" rhyme, the kids are told, is corny. But in fact the very search for a perfect rhyme often leads to the discovery of a truly original idea. It should be noted that the teachers of such courses usually have never written professionally.

Writing the same old tune, and using imperfect rhymes, is a cop-out, and they know it.

No, they don't know it. The problem with people who don't know is that they don't know that they don't know.

I remember reading a copy of the magazine Popular Mechanics, *'way* back in the 1920s. It had a very advanced car on the cover and an article by Norman Bel Geddes inside. The car resembled today's Jaguar X-KE and looked as almost all cars are beginning to look. The article by Bel Geddes (father of the talented Barbara Bel Geddes) explained the shape of the car "being unavoidable in the future because it is dynamically right." Bel Geddes believed that things are beautiful in accordance with that functional principle, as a raindrop is beautiful and as a panther is beautiful. It is the shape nature evolved—in the case of the automobile, a shape to cope with wind pressure, air flow, gravity, and the other considerations.

So, partially, it is with music. What is right with it will evolve. And what is best.

But since music serves different purposes and moods, and a martial air and a love song will always be different, we will listen to what is palatable to our senses, not to what jars us continually. That is why there must be a future production of melodious, mellifluous tunes to soothe us, and, I suppose, new jazz to excite us. The lyrics can only be as witty as the men who produce them. But if we permit men of the intelligence of Gilbert, Hart, and Lerner to rise to the top, we'll get inventive, thought-provoking words set to music, most hopefully, by men like Kern and Van Heusen and Richard Rodgers.

We have such a rich heritage. It's also no wonder that it's so hard to be original, with all those songs to influence our writing. Someone said, "There are no original writers, just some who hide their sources better." But I don't believe that. I believe that a great composer can hear three pick-up notes and take you in twenty different directions with them, letting his heart and his knowledge lead the way. It's a gift, whether it is developed at Juilliard or on the porch of a ramshackle cabin in the hills when ev'ybody is just a-pickin'. Who cares? That's what the United States is all about. But I also believe that, though slow to catch on at times, we always see through the phonies and come around to the real men in our midst. It's something in the bone, brought more sharply into focus in the fierce competitive equality of this country.

Does your girl want to be a batoneer, a cheer leader, a stewardess, Miss America? If she's too poor to be a debutante, those alternatives are open to her. Have you no business to put your son into? He can get out of the mill or the mine, possibly, by being a football player, a pilot, a salesman, an arranger—or a songwriter.

That doesn't mean that he will necessarily be the best. But there is *room for an enormous number. It's remarkable how many can find a liv-ing in the worked-over ground of Nashville or Tin Pan Alley. So let 'em get in there and try.*

Oh, John, you have fallen into the trap of optimism. Since you died, popular music has only deteriorated further. In the age of Elvis, popular music dispensed with interesting and beautiful harmony. In the age of rap, it dispensed even with melody, beautiful or otherwise, developing a form of badly rhymed chant advocating mayhem, mutilation, and murder. It's truly ugly stuff. And radio evolved in such a way that it is impossible to find anything by Kern on the air, and jazz has disappeared from commer-cial radio broadcasting. Then, in 2002, National Public Radio also aban-doned it, canceling its jazz shows. The early fans of Elvis are now in their fifties and sixties, and their children and grandchildren have grown up completely ahistorical. You may not have liked *Hair* or the Beatles, and you may have resented their stealing a title from you, "P.S. I Love You," but compared with what is going on now, the songs of both seem like tow-ers of taste and intelligence. For that matter, Elvis Presley sounds pretty good these days. If you could hear the songs that are nominated for the Academy Award these years, you would be horrified. No, it wasn't going to get better, and it didn't.

Occasionally Shirley Horn or Natalie Cole will have a successful album of the great standards, and Diana Krall became a star singing them. But there is no circumstance to generate the creation of new songs in your tradition. I once played some songs with beautiful harmonies and me-lodic contours for a young rock musician. He said, "Oh, yes. M.O.R. [i.e., middle-of-the-road] changes." That was all he got out of it. And Broadway shows either have bad music or they are revivals of classic shows.

As for escaping the mills and the mines, these days countless out-of-work Americans wish they could escape *into* the mills and mines. Henry Mancini and I went to Aliquippa, Pennsylvania, and we were numbed into silence by the sight of the rusting fenced-in mills (including the one where his father had worked), filthy streets, broken glass, the boarded-up shop windows and abandoned houses with sagging porches and rotting steps.

And there is no more Tin Pan Alley.

You certainly did not foresee the media conglomerates. With record and movie companies merging with magazines and the Internet, with monstrous corporations devouring each other, I don't even know who holds the copyrights on your songs anymore. (Or on mine, for that matter.) Oh, I do know about one of them: after you left us, Paul McCartney acquired the copyright on your "Autumn Leaves." Eventually, he sold a half interest in the catalogue to Michael Jackson.

I *thought* that would thrill you.

Thirty

André Previn was born in Berlin in 1929. His father was a lawyer and former judge, but, with the rise of Hitler, Jews were expelled from such positions. His father was also a capable pianist. One day his secretary told him there was a Gestapo officer waiting in the outer office. He told her to show him in—what else could he do? The officer said something to this effect: "You don't remember me, do you? I came before you for a crime I didn't commit, and you believed me."

The officer told him to leave Berlin immediately, pretending he was going on vacation and taking only as much money as that would require; otherwise, he risked being noticed and detained. And so Judge Previn took his wife, daughter, and two sons to Paris. André was accepted at the Paris Conservatory by Marcel Dupré. When it became clear that Hitler was going to move against all of Europe, the Previn family managed to move to the United States, settling in Southern California, where they were part of a brilliant émigré community of musicians that included Rachmaninoff, Stravinsky, Joseph Szigetti, Ernst Krenek, Erich Wolfgang Korngold, Arnold Schoenberg, and Mario Castelnuovo-Tedesco.

Because of his hesitant English, André's father was unable to pass the bar exams, and so he taught piano to children. André felt compelled to help his family. When he was fourteen, he met Johnny Mercer, who was then thirty-four and had just founded Capitol Records. André was captivated by jazz from the time he arrived in America, and at sixteen made his first jazz piano album. He also began writing arrangements for Georgie Stoll at MGM, and at eighteen was working as a musical director for that company. When he was twenty he was nominated for an Academy Award for his score to the Fred Astaire–Red Skelton movie *Three Little Words,* a fanciful "biography" of the songwriting team of Burt Kalmar and Harry Ruby.

In 1950, when he was in the Army and stationed in San Francisco, André studied conducting with Pierre Monteux.

And he really distressed the jazz establishment—a film composer who dared to record jazz, and classical music as well. And in due course he wrote songs, such as "You're Gonna Hear from Me." Eventually he left Hollywood to become a symphony conductor.

André, like many composers and lyricists, wanted a Broadway show, and he wrote one with Alan Jay Lerner. Based on the life of the French fashion designer Coco Chanel, *Coco,* which starred Katharine Hepburn, opened in late 1969. Lerner's shows, with the exceptions of *My Fair Lady* and *Brigadoon,* tended to be overblown and grandiose, and *Coco* was no exception. André himself thought it was no good, complaining that it had grown too big, instead of maintaining a French musical intimacy. It lasted 332 performances in New York.

André said, "I had always wanted to write with Johnny. *Always.* I was in England and I wanted to write a West End musical. So I wrote to him and asked him if he would ever contemplate such a thing. He wrote back and said, 'Absolutely. And do you mind if I make a suggestion? I've always wanted to write, as a show, *Little Women.*' Now, I thought, *This has got to be a put-on.* I wrote back and I said, 'I'm not sure how to take this. Are you sure that's what you want to do with me?' And he said, 'Yes, I know it seems weird. But it's an immensely famous and very touching book.'

"So then I said, 'Okay, anything you want to write is all right with me. I only give you as an alternative suggestion the J. B. Priestley book *The Good Companions.*' He wrote me back and said, 'I can't believe you really said that. When I was a young man that was my single favorite book of the twentieth century. I would much rather do *The Good Companions.* Let's do it.' "

The Good Companions was published when John was twenty, and over the years the novel sold more than a million copies. Priestley and Edward Knobloch adapted it as a play, which opened in London in 1931 and ran for nine months. John went after the rights to do it as a musical, telling André in a letter dated September 5, 1972:

"Well, the wooing, screwing, and pursuing one has to do to get the rights to a musical play these days!

"But today, at long last, I have handed over a check for $2000, . . . and on your payment to me . . . of $1000, will be free to musicalize *The Good Companions* with a free mind, being the accredited owners of the option for 2 years minimum.

"I was disappointed by the news of your going to NYC, as I had hoped to have some sessions with you and [Ron] Harwood on my brief visit.

"I'm distressed at your reasons for leaving, but trust all will work out. I will be phoning you possibly before this letter arrives. Just thought you'd feel easier in your mind, as I do, now that the legalities are settled. Save some time for me in NYC. . . ."

This frustration at André's peripatetic activities—with new wife Mia Farrow and a busy symphony conducting schedule—continued, according to Rose Gilbert, throughout the writing of the show.

And then there is in a letter to André as ominous as the cello declamation in Bizet's opera *Carmen*:

"I trust this finds you well after a Merry Christmas, and Mia fully recovered. Ginger was in Mount Sinai a couple of months ago and we are trying to 'make it back' . . . she from her surgery, me from my dizzy spells!"

A peculiar thing happened in New York. Jeff Mercer and his wife Carrie went in to visit John. In his small apartment, they found paper bags of apricot pits. Apricot pits contain laetrile, which contains amygdalin, widely publicized at that time as a cure for cancer. The theory was that cancer was the consequence of a deficiency of vitamin B-17, which amygdalin was reputed to be. It was never shown to have any efficacy against cancer. (It is sometimes used today to alleviate the side effects of chemotherapy.) The fact that John had those apricot pits suggests that he suspected, or already knew, why he was getting dizzy spells. Perhaps he had seen a doctor who gave him a preliminary diagnosis.

About this time, John wrote a letter to Dave Dexter—who was still with Capitol—inquiring about the masters of some of his own recordings. In a letter dated October 31, 1973, which is now in the Pullen Library, Dexter wrote:

Dear John
A pleasure to receive your warm note. And nice to know that your creative juices are still flowing.

Along with several thousand other excellent packages, yours has long been deleted, I'm embarrassed to report. Our active catalogue is comprised almost exclusively these days of rock combos and Ken Nelson's country artists. A majority of the new LPs being issued are carried from six months to a year, then excised from activity. . . .

I'd obtain a quantity of them for you, Johnny, if any were available even in warehouses or branches, but in recent years deleted product—and I've never liked that term—has been destroyed. There just aren't any.

I should think working with Previn would be pleasurable. I knew him well back in the '40s, since then have followed his accomplishments with unusual interest. . . . I just can't listen to the radio any longer. Pop music is at its lowest level in my lifetime.

Capitol was never the same after you left. With Wallichs gone almost two years, it has changed even more. I'm elated if I recognize someone in the elevators once a week.

Best to you . . . and I regret I can't be of help on the albums.

Dave

Across the bottom of Dexter's letter, John had typed, in that odd cursive type of his little portable: "This is in answer to an inquiry about the 'Accentuate' album. Boy, our efforts are really written in water—or wind—aren't they. How come we can't get the masters?"

In any case, after the legal rights to the show were settled, André said, "We then made a date and he came over to England, and we worked together for maybe two months."

The book for the show was written by British playwright Ronald Harwood (who wrote *The Dresser* and the screenplay for the Roman Polanski film *The Pianist*), and the songs were completed in the spring of 1974. The show by then had, mysteriously, been retitled *Good Companions,* which doesn't work as well as *The Good Companions;* the former is too generic, while the original title refers specifically to the traveling theater group of the story. John had obvious reasons for being attracted to the story: one of its principals is a songwriter, who writes material for the theater company. In many ways, it's a standard show-business story, a struggling company that at last achieves a smash success in London, at which point its principals pair off and marry and everybody lives happily ever after.

André said, "Johnny was mind-boggling, the facility and the depth of his writing. I would send tapes to his flat near Grosvenor Square, and he would send me things and then we'd meet. And he was very generous and very sweet. When he got drunk occasionally, he got a little nasty. But he had warned me about that. He said, 'You know, we're going to start working, and sometimes I get drunk, and sometimes when I get drunk, I get very mean. If you know it now, you can avoid it. Just let's stop working or talking at that point. And I'm always over it a little later.' It did indeed come up, but only once, and I said, 'Let's quit for today.' And he went home and everything was fine, and it was never mentioned again.

"John would write overnight. It was unbelievable. I have a country house out in Surrey. He would come to my house and hand me a lyric. And I would then sit on the sofa and work on it. After a while I'd say, 'Okay, I've got it.' And I'd play it for him. He had never been with a composer before who could write a tune in absolute dead silence without trying it out on the piano. He thought it was a great parlor trick. He loved it.

"On the other hand, I would give him a tune and he would sit and have the lyric finished in half an hour. Then he would polish it for days and days and days, but basically it was done."

They both reveal an astute analytical grasp of the show, and of theater in general. John writes, in an undated letter, "I am worried about 'Balls.' It seems to want to go too fast and I think maybe the tune is at fault. Would you consider writing a more melodic tune that will perhaps slow it down . . . ? I find pretty tunes good for comedy songs anyway. For what it is worth I send you the one I wrote on your piano in the cottage. . . ."

There follows a tune in John's peculiar invented musical notation, with arrows pointing up and down toward the notes he wants.

He writes: "I realize that when the lyrics come first—it tends to lead to a more 'usual' pattern—not different enough . . . and that is why I *prefer* to write to your tunes. . . ."

And there is more, detailing his ideas about tunes, style, and the show as a whole. He concludes: "Now, having said all that . . . I will work on the tunes you sent me. I like them very much . . . if I can fit them into the play properly. . . ."

John had a ground-floor garden flat, close to the American embassy. On a floor above him lived the distinguished American television director Dwight Hemion, who directed the finest of the Frank Sinatra television specials and who earlier had been the director of the original Steve Allen *Tonight* show in New York. Hemion's wife and three sons were with him during this period. Dwight recalls that John was particularly close to his son, Peter, then six years old. "Our little guy would come home from school on the bus," Dwight recounted. "Every day, John was faithfully there to meet him and walk him home. Peter loved being with John. He would visit him and draw and paint while John worked on the lyrics of the show." Hemion is one of several people, Alan Bergman and Howie Richmond among them, who have said they never saw John take a drink.

"Johnny was great fun," André said. "He told endless stories—very funny, and very Southern. We went through the casting thing together, and rehearsals. We loved playing it. We played it out of town for two weeks or so in Manchester and then we brought it in to Her Majesty's Theater in London."

That summer of 1974, London was plagued by IRA terrorist attacks, and box office receipts were hampered. The show, which opened in July, closed after five months. It would be John's last work.

André said, "It was a nice little show. It didn't have much in the way of direction, and no choreography, but it did have Judi Dench and John Mills and an excellent cast. We wanted to bring it to America very badly. Alexander Cohen, the producer, came over to see it. But, he said, it is so relentlessly English that he wouldn't be able to get away with it. There were very few people in New York who knew about a traveling concert party around the seaside in England in the 1920s."

I have to disagree with André, and certainly with the late Alexander Cohen, in this evaluation. Although I never saw the show, I have read the score and heard it—it is available, if you can find it, on CD. André wrote some wonderfully felicitous and lovely melodies. And John produced what are, in my opinion, the best lyrics he ever wrote for a show, clever without being obvious about it, and graceful, and he demonstrated the miracle of his ear by producing lyrics in north-of-England dialect with enormous fidelity to the speech patterns of that region. I think the show could succeed in New York even now; to say that it's too English is like saying that *Fiddler on the Roof* is too Russian Jewish.

The show had a moderate London success. It produced no standards, but that is not the fault of the score: the record companies were moving farther away from good traditional songs, and certainly from good theatrical songs. Seeing the trend, Stephen Sondheim abandoned writing songs that could be extracted from the show and was by now writing lyrics and music *only* for the show.

I think it would still play on Broadway.

Thirty-one

During that time in England, André saw no signs of Mercer's looming illness.

"None," he said emphatically. "That came only at the end of our work. It was right after the show opened." But there is that reference, in a letter, to John's dizziness.

Ginger was in London with John, and Rose Gilbert came over for the opening with Abe and Peggy Olman.

John began taking falls. Dwight Hemion recalls seeing him with his head in bandages after one such incident: he had fallen off the back of a London bus. Rose Gilbert said, "We were going to get a piece of luggage. I needed an extra bag. John was going to help me. We walked down the street. He told me he had fallen the day before, or two days before, on the street, and they had taken him to the hospital. The doctor suggested he stay there for a few days and let them do some tests on him, and John said, 'No,' he wanted to go home. We felt that he should have stayed. Whatever there was wrong they probably could have corrected then. But Johnny was petrified of doctors. He hated them. He really did."

John's health continued to falter, and his friends (and the London doctor) urged him to return to America. Dwight Hemion was sufficiently concerned to telephone their mutual friend Bill Harbach in New York and tell him that John was "bouncing off the walls with dizziness." Finally John decided to return to America. Rose described what happened:

"We all went home by boat together, Ginger and Johnny, Peggy and Abe Olman, and me. We were sailing on the *Île de France*. We took the bus down to Southampton, and they told us on the bus that the ship was about to have a strike, the day before they were supposed to sail. When Johnny heard that, he was fit to be tied. He said, 'Well, that does it. We'll have to find another boat.'

"But there was nothing sailing that quickly. We said, 'Johnny, don't worry. You know Frenchmen, they'll settle it tomorrow and it'll be fine.'

"The bus driver said, 'All you who are supposed to go on the *Île de France,* if the boat doesn't leave tomorrow, you'll be put on an airline.' That's all John had to hear. He said, 'I'm not getting off the bus.' Abe and I convinced him he *had* to get off the bus. We said, 'Nothing's going to happen. We promise. We'll stay with you. We'll go back just the way we came.'

"Then next day they announced the strike was over. We got on the ship. It was lovely. He was fine, he loved it, though he did seem to have a little bit of a problem. We were having wine with dinner, and John looked as if he was inebriated, but he wasn't. He'd had only a couple of glasses of wine. In the old days, he could drink a bottle and still be fine. He was much more susceptible now, and his speech kept on slurring.

"We finally said to him, 'John, you have to see a doctor. When we get to New York or Los Angeles, you really, really *must*.' And he said, 'I thought you were my friends!' I said, 'John, we *are* your friends. That's why we're taking on like this. If we were your enemies, we wouldn't care.' "

The group arrived in New York. John decided he wanted to make a trip to Savannah to see his mother, who was by then in a nursing home. Ginger planned to go right on to Los Angeles, but she accompanied John and their son-in-law, Bob Corwin, to the railway station. Also present at the departure was John Corwin, Bob's son by his first marriage. John Corwin, now a real estate appraiser in Los Angeles, recalls that Ginger and John hugged each other. "It was very touching," he said. He added that it was one of the few times, perhaps the only time, he had ever seen any sign of affection between them. It sounds to me as if John had begun putting his house in order, even to the point of trying to reconcile his relationship with Ginger. Everything in his behavior from this time suggests that he had a pretty acute instinct about what lay ahead of him.

John and Bob went to Savannah, Ginger went home to Los Angeles. After seeing his mother, John wept. Bob said: "Somebody in Savannah said to me, 'You've got to get him to a hospital.' I said, 'Johnny, you've got to do something.' He said, 'I'm not gonna do anything.' He wasn't going to let them work on his head." When they returned to New York from Savannah, they had dinner with Bill Harbach.

Bill recalled: "Johnny called me up. At that time I was a bachelor. And I said, 'What are you doing for dinner?' And he said, 'I'm having it with you.'

"Bob Corwin was almost holding Johnny up. He had him sit down on a chair immediately. I said, 'Johnny, you've got to do something about this brain thing.'

"He said, 'Bill, I don't want to become a vegetable.'

"I said, 'Nobody wants to become a vegetable. But you're going down in flames now. You're not going to make day after tomorrow this way. You've got to do something about this.'

"He said, 'I guess you're right. Everybody's screaming at me, Ginger's crying on the phone.'

"I said, 'It's your life.' "

Bob Corwin said, "When Johnny went to the bathroom, I said to Bill, 'Everybody's trying to get him to have an operation. If there's anything you could do, I'd sure appreciate it.'

"Johnny came back. Bill Harbach went right straight ahead. He said, 'I understand you need an operation.' Johnny said, 'I'm not gonna do it.'

"Bill Harbach said, 'Why? Are you a coward? You're a coward.' He just humiliated Johnny, actually. He said, 'If you're a man, you'll go home and have the operation.' "

The confrontation worked. John said to Bill, "Will you call Ginger and tell her I'll okay the surgery?"

"I called Ginger on the phone in my library," Bill Harbach said. "She started crying with joy. And they talked. Then we went to have dinner. Later I played him the record Sinatra made with Antonio Carlos Jobim. He sat on my sofa with his head down, listening, and when the record was over he said, 'Oh God, why didn't the kids go this way?' Meaning, of course, instead of the rock-and-roll thing."

Had I been there that night, I could have offered John an answer to his question—or at least a hypothesis. I felt a distinct twinge when Bill told me that John was listening to that album, titled *Francis Albert Sinatra and Antonio Carlos Jobim*. (It was the first of two albums they made together.) For one thing, I was at those recording sessions with Jobim and the arranger Claus Ogerman, and, for another, that album contained one of my lyrics, *Quiet Nights of Quiet Stars*—indeed the first I wrote for Jobim, in early 1962 in Rio de Janeiro.

Popular art reflects the events and society around it with a rapidity and sensitivity not possible in more formal art. It took time for Tchaikovsky to write the 1812 Overture and see it through to its first symphony performance. When John F. Kennedy was assassinated, the Woody Herman band was in the midst of recording "A Taste of Honey" in New York City. Woody and the band were, like everyone in the country, shattered. Woody did one more take and called off the session. The melancholy the band was feeling is in that performance; you can hear it to this day. And the LP containing it was on the market within weeks, if not days.

Popular songs from the Depression era reflect their time: "Brother, Can You Spare a Dime?", "Let's Put Out the Lights and Go to Sleep" (opening line: "No more money in the bank"), "With Plenty of Money and You," "Pennies from Heaven," "Who Cares" ("Who cares what banks fail in Yonkers . . . ?"), "Side by Side" ("Though we ain't got a barrel of money, maybe we're ragged and funny . . ."), "I Found a Million Dollar Baby in a Five-and-Ten Cent Store," "Try a Little Tenderness" ("She may be weary; women do get weary, wearing the same shabby dress"), and many more.

The bossa nova movement in which Jobim was the salient composer evolved from the traditional Brazilian samba. Jobim, a highly trained musician, incorporated elements from other cultures into his work, primarily French—particularly Debussy—and American, especially jazz, though he was partial to Cole Porter, among others. It was music of astonishing sensuality and subtlety, both in harmony and melody, some of the most beautiful stuff ever to be inadequately described as popular music. And it had exquisite lyrics, wistful and witty, many of them by the diplomat, poet, and playwright Vinicius de Moraes. I tried to retain those characteristics in writing English adaptations of Jobim's songs.

Now, the bossa nova movement came into being in the years following the installation on January 1, 1956, of President Juscelino Kubitschek, under whose administration Brazil underwent a tremendous and rapid industrial development, with the building of Brasilia as its new capital the most visible symbol. And Brazil became a land of exuberant optimism. This was reflected in its extremely intelligent popular music, above all in bossa nova (which, by the way, merely means "new thing," "new gimmick").

Musicians around the world were deeply influenced by this new music from Brazil, and American rhythm sections began incorporating the music's patterns into their playing, at first awkwardly and then more and more proficiently. Jobim's songs were hits, and so were the recordings he made on piano and guitar in New York, by which time he and I were collaborating fairly frequently. It is not, in my opinion, coincidence that the United States was in a state of optimism not unlike that of Brazil. One country was under Kubitschek, the other under John F. Kennedy. With his youthful good looks and a beautiful young wife to set him off socially, Kennedy by his very example and wit put the country in a good mood, even as further trouble was brewing in Vietnam.

And then, on November 22, 1963, he was assassinated in Dallas. That killing shattered American idealism, with much of the country saying to itself, "they" killed him. Almost no one believed the Warren Commission report, and a large majority of Americans still don't. Lyndon Johnson took office and manufactured a pretext in the Gulf of Tonkin for launching the United States on a long, bloody, and almost genocidal war. Immediately, we heard highly politicized songs from folk and rock groups, and the snarling sound of guitar distortion became an element in American music that remains with us today. American popular music, which only two decades before had been at the level of Jerome Kern, descended to a harmonic infantilism—David Raksin compared it to children's finger painting—from which it has never recovered. America turned ugly, and its popular music reflected this.

That is why "the kids" did not go in the direction Jobim had come close to setting for us.

John told me once that he would like to write with Jobim. I told him it could easily be arranged. But it never happened. Whether they ever even met, I don't know, but John did not get to write with one of the finest melodists of the last hundred years.

Bob Corwin took John home to California.

Rose Gilbert said: "A group of us were at a meeting of the Songwriters Guild of America. John and I were sitting and talking. And all of a sudden he said, 'I don't feel well. I have to go outside.' Now, he hadn't been drinking. And somebody said, 'Oh, John's drunk again.' And I said, 'No, he *isn't!*' I was so angry! I helped him outside and he leaned against a tree and he stood there for about fifteen or twenty minutes and then we left."

About this time, Tony Bennett and Lena Horne did a concert at the Shubert Theater in Century City. Afterwards there was a reception. All sorts of movie people, including John's friend Fred Astaire, were at that party. I ran into John, whom I had not seen in a number of months, given his absence in England. I said, "Hey, John, how are you?"

He said, "I'm okay. I'm just falling down a lot."

I made the mistake of thinking he was talking about drinking.

As the party came to an end and everyone was leaving, John fell down. Ginger bent to help him up. I didn't know what to do. If he was loaded, and I helped him, I might embarrass him, and Ginger, too. And so I did nothing. She helped him to his feet, and we all left. I have felt guilty about that moment from that day to this. It was the last time I ever saw Johnny Mercer.

Rose Gilbert said, "I was around a lot then. Ginger seemed to need me. I don't know whether it was me, particularly; I think she would have latched on to anybody who was available, and I was the available one. I had just lost Wolfe. John really loved Wolfe.

"At night I would take Ginger out for dinner. I must tell you, she was not very quick with picking up a check, so I picked up the tabs. I didn't mind that, because I liked her, and what do you do for a friend? I thought, *She's in for a terrible time now with Johnny.*"

Ginger began a search for a neurosurgeon who would operate on John. Several—evidently as many as six—neurosurgeons declined, saying that the tumor was in a position that made surgery too dangerous. Finally she found one who agreed to operate, Theodore Kurze.

Kurze had an outstanding international reputation. Born in Brooklyn, he had received his degree from the Long Island University School of Medicine, was associated with the University of Southern California Medical Center for twenty-five years, and at the same time was director of neurological surgery at the Los Angeles County Medical Center. At one time he was a professor at the University of Pittsburgh School of Medicine and served on the American Board of Neurological Surgery. He also obtained degrees in philosophy and literature. He had all the credentials. Unfortunately, he also had a reputation as an aggressive and dramatic surgeon who played for the gallery.

On October 15, 1975, Mercer was admitted to Huntington Memorial Hospital in Pasadena.

"He had a tumor called astrocytoma of the cerebellum," Bob Corwin said. "The night before the operation, I went over to the house. He was sitting on a couch with his feet up. He said, 'I'm going to have this operation, but I'm not going to come out of it. This is probably the last time we'll be talking.' And that's exactly what happened."

Something else happened the night before he went to the hospital.

John had his son Jeff drive him to several banks in the Westwood area of Los Angeles, not far from the Mercer home on Chalon Road. "He wasn't driving at all by that time," Jeff said. "He quit driving before he got sick." Jeff was driving John's little brown Pinto. (Though he could have purchased any car he wanted, John kept that inexpensive Pinto for years.) John entered each bank, emptied his safe-deposit boxes, and came out carrying not money but papers. "I don't remember how many banks we went to," Jeff said. "He wanted to get the stuff out. Papers and stuff. I think it was love letters or some dang thing."

Jeff's wife Carrie remembers that, having extracted these papers, John had Jeff drive to various trash bins in the area, destroy the papers, and dispose of the remnants in the bins. No one can even guess what those papers were.

Bill Harbach recalled: "I went out to California to do two or three television shows and I had lunch with Johnny's doctor. The doctor said, 'He does not have cancer of the brain. It's a tumor, and we'll get it out, there's no problem.' And later, the doctor opened him up, and said, 'Oh Jesus Christ.' It *was* cancer."

The operation left John paralyzed and mute, the very condition he had predicted.

Rose Gilbert would drive Ginger to the hospital. She said, "Going down that driveway was—forget it!" She referred to the steep driveway down to John's house on Chalon Road in Bel Air, which was infamous among his friends. It was dangerous. "Going down it was bad and going up was worse," Rose said. "After I'd take her to the hospital, every night I would take her home, and then I'd drive home again. Every night I'd say, 'This is it! I'm not going to do this again.' And then, of course, I would do it the next day."

John was sent home from the hospital and installed in his studio at the back of the property, which had been transformed into a hospital room. Ginger engaged a radiation oncologist named Michael R. Kadin to give John treatments. In February 2004, Dr. Kadin told me:

"I did not see Mr. Mercer until after the surgery. But I understand that he had been functional in terms of time, place, position, and so on. He was alert, but after the surgery he was in pretty bad shape.

"I was asked to see him for radiation treatments. I remember it was a mixed glioma. And I had some reservations about treating him because of the poor quality of life. We call it a Karnofsky of performance status. And he was well below fifty percent, meaning that he was not able to take care of himself, to feed or clothe himself. He was below what I considered the standard for treatment. We started but we didn't give him more than something like five treatments and stopped.

"The main thing I look at is quality of life. You can live for six months or a year, but if you're in a vegetative state, you have no quality of life.

"Dr. Kurze was a very good doctor. He was an excellent surgeon. He was aggressive in going ahead and taking chances. He was more aggressive treating patients who were more at risk for damage. Tumors of the brain could be very small but located in critical areas where there was a risk of permanent brain damage when you went in there. A number of neurosurgeons had seen Johnny Mercer. I think they were all agreed that his prognosis was very guarded, very poor. I think Ginger had looked around quite a bit until Dr. Kurze told them he could operate and do Mr. Mercer some good. He was one of the few—or the only—neurosurgeons willing to take on the risk.

"At the time, in the 1970s, neurosurgeons were very aggressive. Neurologists, I think, have a tendency to look more at the quality of life and the potential damage done by surgery. They have a tendency to be more conservative, while neurosurgeons look at going in there and doing what they can do.

" 'Do no evil,' as they say."

I consulted several neurologists about this matter, because the operation, after all, was done on my friend.

Dr. Barry Little, a prominent Toronto neurologist for many years and associate professor of neurology at McMaster University, said:

"There are grades of glioma, but it is by definition a malignant tumor. Benignity depends on cell type, the histopathology, but also the location, particularly in [the] brain. It could have been a benign tumor to begin with. But it might not have been so benign because of its location. Not everything within the brain is operable, and certainly not in 1975. It has to be remembered—and I had a few years of experience with this—that a tumor under the microscope may be benign in one part and malignant in another. And some benign tumors turn malignant."

I also consulted Dr. Roméo Éthier, for twenty-five years chief neuro-radiologist at the Montreal Neurological Institute; a full professor of neurology, neurosurgery, and radiology at McGill University; and chairman of the Department of Radiology. He said unequivocally:

"That operation never should have been done. With the scanning techniques available even then, they'd have known that. Under such conditions, the patient is hanging on a last hope, and when somebody says they can operate, he says, 'Go ahead.' It's so sad. Spending so much time as a vegetable is a total loss of everything. He would have been better off dead.

"Some neurosurgeons think they are gods."

Kurze, however, has his defenders, among them Dr. Albert MacDade, a neurosurgeon in Forth Smith, Arkansas, trained at the Mayo Clinic in Rochester, Minnesota. He has reservations about the comments of neurologists on the field of neurosurgery, saying, "If you haven't been in the trenches, you don't know what it's like." He continued:

"Ted Kurze was a highly respected academic neurological surgeon with great technical and intellectual skills. He was appreciated by every resident I've ever spoken with, and also by staff academics who knew him well. He was an honest, forthright, gentle, ethical, and hard-working man. He was an excellent teacher of neurological surgeons. He impressed me during our one meeting with his bearing, his poise, and his dignity, not only toward himself but toward his residents and other doctors in the specialty, and also toward his patients. He was a crème de la crème sort of guy. Dr. Kurze was one of the early pioneers in bringing microsurgery to neurological surgery operating rooms. This was in 1957. He was using the operating microscope back in 1965.

"Johnny Mercer had a very malignant brain tumor. This tumor was in what we call the *posterior fossa,* Latin for *little hole.* It is that area of the cranial vault that is approximately from where the top of your ears go back to the bump on the back of your head down to where the spinal cord enters the brain case, at the very upper portion of the cervical spine. It's a very, very small area, with no available space, except for what is in there— for spinal fluid, which is there to buffer the brain from traumas. Dr. Kurze described the tumor Johnny Mercer had as a 'midline malignant glioma,' which had invaded the brain stem prior to the surgery.

"The general form of the tumor that occurs in the cerebellum, which is what Dr. Kurze is describing, is called an astrocytoma. These tumors arise out of astrocytes of the brain that for some reason go malignant. Many times this is a very benign tumor. Sometimes they can remain small and relatively asymptomatic, and then start growing after a long period of time. Even the so-called benign astrocytomas, or gliomas in this case, and we're using the terms synonymously, can have areas of what we call de-differentiation, or malignant transformation—small areas that are not always symptomatic clinically, but [have the] potential for turning into a big malignant tumor, which is very dangerous and difficult to handle. It's treacherous to handle anyway, in terms of its location at the back of the head and close to the brain stem. So this tumor is one that probably underwent malignant transformation after being there for a while. In a letter Ted Kurze wrote to other doctors, explaining Mr. Mercer's illness, [he] said that it had invaded the brain stem prior to the operation. That's perfectly plausible and perfectly correct, particularly if a guy of Dr. Kurze's intellect and experience said so."

I asked Dr. MacDade, "Would Johnny have lived very long without the operation?"

Without hesitation, he said, "No. He was falling so much and he probably had headaches. One can't predict, but Ted Kurze looked at all the data, and with the tumor he describes—I've not seen the pathology report or doctors' notes or radiology reports or looked at the films proper—I can say that it's unlikely Mr. Mercer would have lived more than a year. And I think that's generous at that. It would not have been a good quality of survival."

What about his comatose state? Dr. MacDade said:

"There are various kinds of coma. Coma is defined as unarousable un-responsiveness. That's the person who lies and can't be aroused under any circumstances, painful stimuli or medicines or anything. That's the strict definition, but it has a lot of twists to it, a lot of variations. There's a state call[ed] akinetic mutism, or *coma vigil*—those terms are synonymous—and it comes from various types of lesions. Some of them can be cerebel-lar, that is, a lesion in the cerebellum, which can cause unresponsiveness, which is a sort of mute state where a person does not respond to any stim-uli. Another form of coma is not strictly coma but a motor state, which we talk about as the locked-in state. It is a state in which the person is in a condition of alert wakefulness but can't respond—not only because the arms and legs are paralyzed, or very weak, but because it's impossible for the person to speak—and only has the ability to communicate by vertical eye movements, including blinking. That is because the lesion causes the person to have these deficits. They appear to be awake and their eyes are open but they are not capable of perceiving a lot of information as far as we can tell. They are in a quadriplegic state, although tetraplegic is proba-bly a better term.

"Those two forms of coma, akinetic mutism or the locked-in state, I can't tell with the information I have, but it appears to be one or the other of those."

In the end, I find myself thinking about the First Aphorism of Hip-pocrates: "Life is short, and the Art is long; opportunity fleeting; experi-ment dangerous; and judgment difficult."

Portrait of Johnny

. . .

Bill Harbach said: "They spent three hundred thousand dollars on nurses, Ginger told me. I would take Ginger out and then I would go and see Johnny. He was in a bed in his studio with a machine on and a nurse. He would see me and I would grab his hand and give it a squeeze and there would be that smile and then it would disappear. It was heartbreaking. I talked him into being a vegetable."

Ginger put a cordon of silence around John. Friends like Henry Mancini and Johnny Mandel would call to inquire about his condition, but couldn't get past the answering machine. We would call each other fairly regularly: Have you heard anything about John? No, have you? No, not a thing.

One of the few people who were able to get through and actually see John was Jamie Corwin, Bob and Mandy's son, Johnny's grandson, who is now corporate vice president of a hospital chain. Johnny lay there helpless, staring at the ceiling, Jamie said. Jamie, convinced that Johnny could understand whatever was said to him, would sit by the bed and talk to him, and sometimes tears would roll from John's eyes and down his temples, all in silence.

Rose Gilbert, too, was allowed to visit him. She said, "There were three round-the-clock nurses who took care of John. I don't think, in all the times I was there, that Ginger ever, ever went out to see how he was." John lingered for eight months after the surgery; he died on June 25, 1976.

I learned he was gone, as I suppose Hank Mancini and all his other friends did, from a television news broadcast. Ginger had kept his family as much in the dark as she did everyone else. "Do you know how my mother found out he was gone?" Nancy Gerard said. "She heard it on the radio."

John's ashes are buried in Savannah's Bonaventure Cemetery, close to his parents and many of his ancestral relatives. The cemetery is close to what used to be called Back River, renamed Moon River.

Barely a month after John's death, on July 22, at 11:30 a.m., Bill Harbach and another of John's friends, Bob Bach, produced a tribute to him at New York's Music Box Theater, owned by Irving Berlin. Berlin could not attend, but countless other famous show-business people were there. Harold Arlen was at the piano.

Producer Hal Kanter wrote a tribute to John that was read by Fred Astaire. Kanter, also a native of Savannah, wrote:

"From the day in 1928 when he left Savannah for New York, Johnny maintained that unique quality that is the essence of genius—a common touch he expressed in uncommon lyricism. No matter how far he went, he always found the time—and perhaps the need—to return home and refresh himself, reorient himself, to remind him who and what and where he was in this world.

"He's gone back to Savannah now to sleep beneath the Spanish moss dripping from the ancient oaks, hard by his beloved Moon River, but he has left us with the legacy of his simple truths, profound philosophies, his romantic, playful, witty, and eternal celebration of life."

When John's friend Alec Wilder—with whom, as far as I know, John wrote only one song, the lovely "The Sounds Around the House"—learned he was gone, he said: "John made me laugh, he made me cry. He made me almost patriotic. It's a scary world, and he made me feel safe."

Thirty-two

John's generosity had long been a cause of friction with Ginger, particularly his generosity to his mother, his sister, and his niece Nancy in Savannah. In 1953, he had moved them out of the house on Gwinnett Street to another at 110 East Forty-ninth Street. After his death, Ginger acted quickly to turn every asset she could into cash; furthermore, she gave away many of his lovely watercolors. Mandy has a few of them, which she was able to rescue from the house in Palm Springs. Among the things Ginger decided to liquidate was the house in Savannah.

Nancy said: "She thought the house belonged to Johnny, therefore now it belonged to her. But when Johnny bought it for my grandmother, he put it in her name. My grandmother by then was in the nursing home, and just my mother was living there. Ginger would have just sold it out from under her, and who knows where my mother would have gone? And then Ginger found out that she didn't own it."

My relations with Ginger had always been cordial; like Steve Allen, though, I was never comfortable with her. There was almost nothing you could talk about with her. After John's death, Ginger would often call my wife and me, and we would occasionally have lunch with her. I was always polite to her, for John's sake; I thought it was what he would want.

In due course, she brought me a manuscript John had written, an uncompleted autobiography; she asked me to read it and tell her what was wrong with it. For one thing, I found, it was chronologically incoherent.

John skipped all over the place, jumping, without warning, from one period of time to another. And I discovered, to my amazement, that this master of structure and form in the lyric had no sense of writing prose. Ginger asked if I could do anything with it, so I undertook to clarify it. I researched the periods of John's life when certain events occurred—checking copyright dates on songs, for example. I organized his text into discrete sections and then shuffled them into proper sequence. After that I ran the whole thing through my typewriter, producing a more coherent manuscript. The process took me about a month. Concerned that the manuscript be accurate, I sent copies of it to John's friends Jay Livingston, Paul Weston, and Jo Stafford. When Paul read it, he asked me to come to his home, where he had organized a meeting with Jay.

Jo made drinks. And then Paul, who was a gentle and humorous man, said with a sober adamancy of which I had not suspected he was capable, "Gene, if you have any influence at all with Ginger Mercer, tell her never to let this manuscript see the light of day."

Although there was much in it that was funny, it had an overall tone of darkness and despair, particularly toward the end, and Paul thought it should be suppressed. I felt otherwise. I gave a copy of my edited version of the manuscript to Ginger and kept one for myself. Ginger's copy eventually passed to Mandy, and I still have mine. It is from this edited version that I have drawn in this book.

One day Ginger called to say she wanted us to meet someone and invited us to dinner at the Beverly Hills Hotel. There she introduced us to a tall and quite handsome man of, I would say, about seventy, with gray-white hair and distinguished, even features. His name was Marc Cramer, and I got the feeling she was presenting him to us as if she were a girl bringing a potential fiancé home for parental approval. My cautious initial impression of him was favorable. She said he was an old friend of Johnny's, though it was apparent that she had met him only recently. I thought that was a little odd, but kept in mind that she hadn't associated much with John's friends. And I remembered Jo Stafford telling me that when she and John and Paul Weston were doing the *Johnny Mercer Chesterfield Music Shop* on network radio, Ginger never came to the rehearsals or broadcasts. I thought, too, of all the times John had come to New York alone.

There was a quite good piano trio in the restaurant, and I asked them if they would play some of Mercer's songs. I discussed some of the technical skills that had gone into the lyrics, including John's wonderful sense of euphony, the beautiful way his lyrics articulate, and the deceptive simplicity that concealed their complexity.

"Do you think Johnny knew any of that?" she said.

I was astonished by the question. Of course he knew these things; you just don't think about them when you're working. But the very question suggested what many of his friends suspected: she never really knew who he was. John was gone, however, and if she found companionship with this Marc Cramer fellow, good for her.

My wife and I moved up the coast from Los Angeles to a small town called Ojai, sequestered in the mountains about twelve miles inland from the ocean. Ginger and Marc drove up to see us on at least three occasions, and we spent a New Year's Eve with them at the Ojai Valley Inn and Country Club. And then, suddenly, they disappeared from our lives. Marc was by now living with her, and the word was out that he was separating her from all her friends so that he could take control of her life and considerable income. I learned later that John's will was twenty years out of date when he died. By its terms, Ginger was to receive all his assets, which were to pass at the time of her death to Jeff and Mandy.

But, as Jamie Corwin, Mandy's son, pointed out, "becoming a millionaire at the age of sixty doesn't do you a lot of good," and by agreement, Ginger allocated one quarter of John's royalties to Jeff, another quarter to Mandy, and retained half for herself. (In 2002 these royalties amounted to approximately $1,400,000 a year.)

So there was a great deal to capture Marc Cramer's interest: a lonely old lady with a big income, a lovely home in Bel Air, and a certain social status because of her husband's name—although that was soon to fade, partly because of Cramer himself. But it still bothered me that I had never heard of him. "If he was such a friend of Johnny's, how come none of us ever heard of him?" Paul Weston said.

Actually, some of John's friends *had* heard of him. One of them was Bill Harbach, who said: "I knew Red Cramer 'way before he knew Ginger. I knew him in New York. He escorted Jane Brant, Herbert Bayard Swope's daughter, as a walker—he'd take her to the horse races or something. He'd wear a derby, very dressed up. That's what he was: a walker. Taking rich women out. Taking them to 21 or El Morocco. And they'd pay for it.

"He tried to be an actor. He was in a couple of B pictures. And then he had a little radio show in New York at seven in the morning, called *Second Cup of Coffee,* that he did with another guy. One hour of chitchat and stuff like that. Red Cramer was a jack of no trades. He and Johnny *may* have met, but he didn't really know him at all."

"I was there when he first took up with Ginger," Rose Gilbert said. "He told her that he was a friend of Johnny's, that he had sent Johnny many articles and things, and Ginger *believed* him. And I said to her, 'I don't think he really knew John. It's too far from left field.' I'd never heard of him, never saw him. I was there when he told her that when he knew Johnny he had taken Mandy to the zoo. Mandy doesn't remember it. One reason I didn't like him is that he was a terrible liar. He found out names of men who had died, leaving wealthy widows. He would take them out for dinner, take them out for lunch. He never paid, period. And he pretended he wasn't Jewish. He said to me once, 'Ginger and I are going to a very important affair tonight.'

"I said, 'How nice.'

"He said, 'Yes, there's not going to be any of those kind of people there.'

"And I said, 'What kind of people?'

"He said, 'You know what kind of people.'

"I said, 'No, I live a very sheltered life.'

"He said, 'Well, you know—Jews. There are not going to be any Jews at the party.'

Rose, being Jewish, and quite sardonic, said, "Well, I know one who's going to be there. Ginger."

He replied, "Oh, Ginger gave up her faith so long ago it doesn't matter."

Rosie went on, "Ginger opened an account for him at a very exclusive men's shop at Rodeo Drive and Little Santa Monica. She opened a charge in the name of Johnny Mercer. He was a gigolo."

Jamie Corwin came to know him well. He said, "I hate to call Marc a gigolo, but that's the only thing that fits. He was a charming guy, very articulate, and very good-looking for his age. And he would get in with the crowd. He got free lodging almost always. He would hang out with people who had multiple homes or multiple living quarters in the same home. He would manage to get in there."

I told Jamie that Marc had told me he was a television producer, and had produced a children's TV show. Jamie said, "He was only a hired actor for the show. I think it ran for one season in 1951 and '52. He had some photos of himself on the show. He was your classic build-my-image kind of guy. He created a different image for each person he met. He had a military friend who at one point he led to believe he had some military background, a general in Colorado that he mooched off. Marc could be whatever you wanted him to be. He was a chameleon, and he was *good* at it.

"He never really earned a living. He managed to migrate to different places for anywhere from three months to several years. All his life was in filing cabinets in what had been Johnny's studio: Marc's bank records, his Rolodex, everything. When I began to realize what he was, I went through his files, tracing his life. He spent a period in Monte Carlo, living with some lady of royalty. He lived in Texas for a little while.

"He got to be close with Buddy Rogers. He actually helped put Mary Pickford's funeral together, helped eulogize her." (Pickford died in 1979; Rogers was her third husband.) "Marc lived with Buddy at Pickfair after she died." But Rogers tired of him and put him out.

Jamie continued: "He was living out of the Beverly Hills Hotel for about six months while he was wooing Ginger, until he convinced her to let him move into the guest house that had been Johnny's studio. Then he told her, 'It's cold out there, can I move into the house?' She and Johnny had separate bedrooms anyway. I think that house was forty-five hundred square feet, and the bedrooms were in the exact opposite corners. Johnny's room was right as he'd left it, and had all of his clothing in it. Marc had much as he could of those clothes retailored to fit him." (How any of the clothes of a man who stood five foot eight could be recut for a man six foot three I don't know, but Jamie and Rose Gilbert both attest to it.)

James (Jamie or Jim) Corwin was born November 19, 1961, one day after Johnny's birthday. Jamie said: "Johnny was part of Americana. He touched the average Joe. As for his drinking, it all depended on the environment. Drinking took Johnny to whatever emotion he was feeling. If he was angry, if he was happy, that's where the drinking took him.

"I called him Bee-bah. It was something I said when I was about two, and he liked it. By the time I was twelve to thirteen, when we would go over to the house in Bel Air, everything would start out nice and cordial. My father and he had music and sports in common. But then Johnny would start on, 'How are you raising the kids?' He didn't want us to grow up fatherless, because my father was always on the road. He told him, 'You work for me, I'll give you an eight-to-five job professionally and you can go home to your kids at night.' And my dad's going, 'Sounds good.

But that's not the challenge I want professionally. I don't want to be sitting here working for Johnny Mercer, trying to write music for Johnny Mercer lyrics.'

"Johnny probably hurt my father's career more than he helped it. My father was in Peggy Lee's band. Peggy Lee recorded 'Days of Wine and Roses.' It wasn't going to be released for six months. He knew Johnny would love it, so he got an early copy of it. He said, 'Johnny, this is going to come out in six months. Please don't make it public.' It was the greatest version of 'Days of Wine and Roses' I've ever heard. And two days later, my father was driving to a gig and he heard the record on the radio. Johnny had run to a radio station with the record, and my father lost his job with Peggy."

Jamie attended the University of Southern California. At one time he was having financial struggles, and he told Ginger he was about a thousand dollars in debt. She gave him seventy-five dollars. He graduated in 1988 with a B.S. in business administration. Ginger gave him fifty dollars as a graduation gift.

"I was living in an apartment in the San Fernando Valley," he said. "I held two jobs while I was in school. Then I got work for a radio group, Metropolitan Legacy Broadcasting, as a corporate accountant. They had offices on Sunset Boulevard. I wanted that job because it was in my area of interest. But I had been making twenty-seven thousand dollars and I had to step down to twenty-one thousand dollars to get into the industry.

"I went to visit Ginger. I hadn't seen her in a long time. I'd take her to lunch occasionally. She and Marc were starting to deteriorate pretty rapidly. I said, 'Gramma, why don't I move into the guest house?' Johnny's studio was being used for storage.

"Ginger was about eighty. She didn't feel she was losing her faculties, which she obviously was. I asked her to help me out. She said, 'Oh, I'd love you to come and live in the guest house. I understand from my accountant that it's worth about twelve hundred dollars a month.'

"I said, 'I can't afford that.'

"She said, 'Well, that's what it's worth. Sorry.'

"Bobby Rush was an interior decorator, a longtime friend of Ginger's. He decorated the Palm Springs house in its entirety and about half the Bel Air house. Johnny knew Bobby was gay, and he was Ginger's escort to a lot of events. Johnny loved her going out with him because he was harmless.

"Bobby felt a huge loyalty to Johnny and to Ginger. After Johnny passed, he spent a lot of time with her. He called me one time and said,

'Are you getting into the house? You've got to be there, the house is crumbling. Every time I go there I see something, alcohol bottles spilled all over the place, Ginger is incoherent, and this Argentine lady they have can't control the household. You can.' I said, 'Bobby, I'd love to go there, but Ginger wants to charge me twelve hundred dollars a month.' So Bobby intervened. He yelled at Ginger. He said, 'You're charging your grandson? This should be a zero charge. This is your family.'

"Ginger and Marc needed help. When they came back from lunch, they'd be drunk. Ginger would have Chardonnay and Marc would slam down Johnnie Walker Reds, and they'd be sloshed."

Jeff Mercer said of Ginger and Marc: "They were heavy lushes. He tried to treat me like I was something he had to discipline, and I was already in my twenties. I had to say, 'Look, Bud, stay away from me.' I never really liked the guy. And he knew it. That's all he did, was hang around widows. There were a couple of others, apparently, before my mom. He just moved right in. It wasn't my scene, it was hers, but I didn't have to like it."

Sometimes, when she was well into her cups, Ginger would express a deep bitterness about John's involvement with a certain movie star, never quite naming her. Finally she told Jamie it was Judy Garland.

"One time," Jamie said, "I arrived in the morning and Marc was already drunk and lying on the floor. He had a bad hip, so he couldn't get up. I helped get him up. We were going to lunch, but he was in no shape to go.

"The maid, Lydia Giovannini, was begging me to do something about the situation. She said she was going to quit. She was basically Gramma's caretaker.

"Sometimes when I got there, they'd both be on the floor, and Marc, more often than not, would be passed out. One time I came in and he was actually in a pool of urine. He'd pounded down, like, a bottle of Johnnie Walker Red. He used to be able to handle it, but now he was about seventy-one; he'd get drunk and right away he'd go down, and he was six foot three. And I started thinking, *Somebody needs to just keep an eye out here.* Certainly I'm no caretaker, but I thought, *She's got tons of money. I could bring people in to take care of them, and if I lived here, I could kind of oversee it. I'd feel a lot better.* She was now a little old lady. She still had a very mean streak in her, but it's hard to be mad at an eighty-year-old lady who's detached from her family.

"I think Marc just assessed who had his number. Because he needed the Jay Livingstons and Ray Evanses of the world to accept him. I could tell who he had poisoned her mind against. And some of it was her own poisoning.

"She said that the first year after Johnny died, she didn't get invited to Henry Mancini's New Year's party. That was a big slight to her. She would spew venom sometimes, and mostly toward Ginny Mancini. She felt that Ginny had a personal vendetta against Johnny because of a comment Ginger made one time in jest. She said, 'Hank's lucky that Johnny decided to write with him, so he could further his career and achieve an Academy Award. Because Johnny was famous, but Henry was not a national treasure.'

"She always talked about Marilyn Bergman as this kind of medium talent, this lady she had befriended. She said that Marilyn and Alan were lucky that she supported them and their career. So I do think there was animosity toward certain people before she even met Marc. She had cut off quite a string of people she didn't want to associate with. Marc whittled that down even further. And that's sort of where I came in. I sensed that Marc didn't like me initially, but she finally let me live in Johnny's studio for five hundred a month, and I moved in. I didn't know a lot about their relationship. I didn't know that everybody disliked him. After a while Marc realized he needed me. He had to have help. Ginger sort of stopped drinking three or four months after I moved in. I think she had developed an aversion to it.

"At least Johnny was with whatever environment he was in when he got drunk, whether he was happy or sad. But she turned mean instantly. She just went south. *Instantly.* When she was being polite and in a good mood, she masked. There were a very few people she had a sincerity to, a true kindness toward. I could see it, just by the way she talked. When she talked about Abe Olman, there was a warmth that came through. When she talked about Howie Richmond and Anita, there was a warmth. She reminisced about her whole life during those three or four years that I lived there. As soon as she would drink, the venom would come out— about her greedy children and all the losers who detached themselves from her once Johnny passed away, and how they were kind of low end or no talent."

During one of Ginger's visits with Marc to Ojai, she told my wife she had to do something about him. He had no job, and she was concerned about his dignity. She said she was thinking of forming a foundation, and making Marc a part of it.

The articles of incorporation of the Johnny Mercer Foundation were filed February 9, 1982, with the California Secretary of State's office in Sacramento. The charter states: "It is organized under the Nonprofit Public Benefit Corporation Law for charitable purposes."

Jamie said, "Marc Cramer became treasurer and a major officer of the foundation. She gave him expense accounts at locations like Mateo's, this wonderful Italian restaurant. Marc would go there every night and consume six to seven hundred dollars' worth of product, probably three-fifty of it in alcohol. He'd order another appetizer and take one bite out of it and order another one. There were certain clothing accounts that she paid for. She gave him fifty thousand dollars a year in salary. After twenty in taxes, he had about thirty thousand, and zero expenses. He was loading up the bank account he had in Denver. And he continually tried to get Ginger to marry him. He was trying to get the entire estate.

"Margaret Whiting had a close rapport with Ginger. Ginger wanted an entertainer, someone with a national name, to continue Johnny's name with the foundation. By then she had alienated all the links to anybody with a name. For lack of anyone else, she had Margaret. She thought someone who was a name could pull others into the foundation, people like Steve Allen."

I asked Jamie if they'd ever asked him to take a role in the foundation.

"No, they've never offered. And I haven't been depressed that they haven't."

Rose Gilbert said, "Red Cramer was charming for the first twenty minutes. He apparently got really nasty with Mandy two or three times."

Mandy, however, has a theory about that. She said that she believes Cramer was fulfilling Ginger's wishes, acting in effect as her hatchet man, and that when he got vicious with her on the telephone, he was acting on orders.

Howie Richmond recalled: "Marc got nasty with our dear friend Abe Olman. Abe was hesitant to accept him because he didn't have any credentials. But Abe was very cordial because of his long relationship with Ginger.

"After John passed on, Ginger said to Abe, 'I think we're going to do something at the Songwriters Hall of Fame.' If it weren't for Johnny, it wouldn't have happened, but Abe was behind it; Abe and Johnny made it happen. Ginger said something about making a charitable contribution. She said to Abe, 'What do you think I should give?' He said, 'Whatever you think.' And somehow a figure of ten thousand dollars came up and she gave it to him for the Songwriters Hall of Fame. And Marc shows up.

It suddenly appears that there is now a foundation that Ginger and Marc have set up. It was supposed to be something for children. Marc says to Abe, 'We now have a Johnny Mercer Foundation. You were a friend of Johnny's.' And one day Abe said, 'I am very upset. Marc sent a letter saying, 'You forced Ginger to give ten thousand dollars to your Songwriters Hall of Fame. Now you give ten thousand dollars to the Johnny Mercer Foundation.' Abe said, 'I don't like this letter.' He was very hurt.

"I said, 'Why don't you talk to Ginger?'

"He said, 'I can't do that. She had to know about this. He wouldn't dare write this letter without Ginger knowing.' "

Rose Gilbert said, "I think that Marc Cramer was a very, very bad man. And what happened was that our friendship with Ginger just went down the drain. He was a taker-over. His big talking point to her was, 'If it's not you, it's going to be one of these other ladies.' He would tell her about all the other women he could have. He was a tremendous manipulator. He was a name-dropper. He gave her this whole big line and she bought it.

"We went to Russia—Abe, I, and Ginger. Peggy Olman had died by then. Then we went to the Greek Islands. We bummed around Europe for two, three months. We always wound up in Mallorca, because we loved it. We went to New York. Marc came to New York, and met her there. Abe kept on buying theater tickets for the four of us. I said to him one day, 'Abe, why are you doing this?' He said, 'Well, Ginger's going to give it back to me.' The prices of tickets were prohibitive. I said, 'Lotsa luck.'

"We'd go out to shows, the four of us, and have dinner. One night Marc was making a tremendous scene about some restaurant we went to that he didn't like. You'd think he was picking up the check and paying for it, the way he carried on. He never picked up a check in his life. And I thought to myself, *What a chintzy guy.* And he was *drinking.* He drank three scotches to our one. But she kept on touting Marc, how wonderful he was, how great he was."

Jamie, meanwhile, was busy with his new job. "I was traveling a lot, installing software at radio stations. I would come back from trips and find accountants there. I'm an accountant myself. I saw the way the accountants billed her. They would take her monthly income and pay her bills. The invoice, coincidentally, was the balance. And all they did for her was taxes. They dabbled in investment of her money, which CPAs are discouraged from doing. The fee was always the excess of moneys she had. In the eighties she was probably receiving about fifty thousand dollars a month. Her excess was anywhere from eight thousand dollars to twenty-two thousand dollars. The accountants consistently took eight thousand dollars to twenty thousand dollars a month."

And all the while, Marc Cramer kept up his manipulations to separate Ginger from past friends. He told her he didn't want her to see Rose Gilbert anymore. He said that Rose was socially beneath her, and what's more, Rose was Jewish.

One day Jamie came home to find Marc passed out in the living room. An empty scotch bottle lay on his chest; the last of its contents had dribbled out onto him, soaking his clothes and the carpet. Jamie undressed him and put him to bed. He said Marc's torso was covered with brown lesions.

Then Cramer took seriously ill. "He had bad pneumonia," Jamie said, "the kind of infection you can't get rid of. He would not go to a doctor for three days. I could see that he was near death. I said, 'You have to go to the hospital.' I put clothes on him, and I put him in my car and took him to St. Vincent's Hospital in L.A. He had waited too long. He was stubborn. He had this false pride. He said, 'Don't put me on any life support.' I think he knew it was the beginning of the end. He died in late eighty-nine, as I remember."

I said, "If he died in a hospital under care, they did not by law have to do an autopsy. The lesions you described sound to me like Kaposi's sarcoma. And then there was the virulent pneumonia."

"I think the lesions were skin cancer," Jamie said. "It certainly was after the advent of AIDS. I wouldn't put it past Marc if he had been with prostitutes. He was Mister Testosterone. Or that was the image he put out."

"Did he have a homosexual relationship with that general?"

"I don't know. He corresponded with that gentleman."

"What happened to his remains?" I asked.

"He's buried in the Beverly Hills Mortuary on Glendon, where Marilyn Monroe is buried. He had no will, so the State of California impounded his assets. There was ten thousand bucks and a car."

But what happened to the money he had been sequestering in Denver? Who got it? Nobody knows.

"Ginger never once bothered with Johnny when he was out in that studio, sick," Rose Gilbert said. "She said she was grieving in her own way. And I believed that. But when Red Cramer died—oh, she carried on about him! She cried for three days. She called me up in the middle of the night and she said, 'Red is dead!' And I didn't know who the hell it was and I didn't know what she was talking about. Finally it dawned on me and I said,

'Oh, I'm sorry.' And she said, 'Didn't you hear me? Red is dead!' And I said, 'So what? We all have to go.'

"I don't think that placated her. She just got very angry and hung up on me."

Rose remained estranged from Ginger after Marc Cramer's death. She said, "We had stopped seeing each other. I was still angry with her over Cramer and the letter to Abe Olman. Then I saw her at an ASCAP memorial service for Jimmy Van Heusen. I said, 'Are you alone?' and she said, 'Yes.' Then she said, 'I miss you.' I said, 'I'm sorry, I live in Palm Springs now, and I'm going back in the morning. Do you have a lift home?' I was concerned about her. She said, 'Yes, I do.' She was thin and gaunt. Her words kept tumbling over each other, as if she didn't know what she was actually saying. I went back to Palm Springs.

"She called me one day and invited me to lunch. I was talking to Abe and he said, 'You might as well go. It's ridiculous to be angry after all this time. Red's dead now.' So we went to lunch at Cedar Creek Inn in Palm Springs. She was wearing her mink stole, and it was hot out. She had taken along a small radio, and she kept on saying that she had to get batteries for it. Mandy, who had driven her, said, 'Mom, we'll get the batteries after we have lunch.'

"Mandy said, 'Do you want a drink?' And I said, 'No, it's too early for me.' I said to Ginger, 'Are you going to have a drink?' And she said, 'No, I don't drink anymore.' But the next thing I knew there was a drink in front of her. Then she decided she wanted two. Mandy and I had salads but she wanted soup. The waitress brought her the soup, and she didn't eat it. She kept saying, 'I need batteries for the radio. It's not working.' I turned it on, and it went on.

"That was the last time I saw her. She was pretty far gone by then. She had deteriorated terribly."

The symptoms are fairly obvious. "For the last four years of her life," Jamie Corwin told me, "she had Alzheimer's. She had five stories that she just repeated. You could ask her questions and jog her memory. But if you didn't engage her, she just kept repeating her five stories."

During this period, with Marc Cramer dead under circumstances that are not entirely clear, Margaret Whiting was appointed president of the Johnny Mercer Foundation. Mandy said, "I don't think that Mom knew that she had given her control. She told me that she thought she was just giving Margaret permission to use some of his songs in her show." Whiting hoped to present a Johnny Mercer revue, starring herself, and eventually did so.

Ginger died October 21, 1994, at Cedars Sinai Hospital. She was eighty-five.

Ginger's attorney, Charles S. Tigerman, filed her will in Los Angeles Superior Court on October 24, 1994, three days after her death. It has six codicils. It distributes various sums to relatives, including $10,000 each to her sisters Debbie Burner and Claire Meltzer, both of Lehigh Acres, Florida, and $10,000 each to her grandchildren, James and Nickie Lee Corwin (Mandy's two children) and Teague Mercer (Jeff's son). Clause 11 of the sixth codicil specifies: "I give all original manuscripts of music compositions written or composed by my deceased husband, Johnny Mercer, together with all recordings, awards, and other memorabilia to the Georgia State University in Atlanta, Georgia, for use in the Johnny Mercer Room in the library of the Graduate School of Music."

The balance of her estate, roughly half of it, went to the Mercer Foundation. The royalties to the foundation amount to a substantial annual sum. For the period August 1, 2000, to July 31, 2001, the foundation received $752,607.74 in royalties, the largest sources being ASCAP ($118,357.23), ASCAP Foreign ($184,323.47), Warner Bros. ($111,855.60), and Warner Chappell ($127,029.33). The previous year, for the same fiscal period, the total was $829,624.36, with a similar proportion of sources. It is a comment on the state of American culture that more money came from foreign sources than from the United States—*and this for songs in the English language.*

Jamie Corwin said: "She made a million-dollar commitment over a ten-year period to the Mercer Collection at Georgia State. That will run to the year 2005. Some of the bequests were dictated by her will, and others were given by the board." The bequests are to various cultural foundations, charities, and hospitals.

Jamie continued:

"She made Margaret Whiting the president of the foundation in perpetuity. She gave the foundation her share of the royalties, which gave Margaret a lot of de facto authority."

Paragraph IV of the Articles of Incorporation of the Johnny Mercer Foundation states: "This corporation shall have not less than three (3) nor more than seven (7) directors." As of March 21, 2001, it had eighteen. They were Lewis M. Bachman, Alan Bergman, Alvin Deutsch, Ervin Drake, Ray Evans, Joseph Harris, Michael A. Kerker, Al Kohn, Patrick A. Lattore, Ginny Mancini, Robert Margolies, Nancy Rishagen, Charles S. Tigerman, George C. White, Margaret Whiting, Julia Marks Young, Don

Youpa, and Jack Wrangler, a former star of homosexual pornographic films who is now married to Whiting.

No member of the Mercer family—neither Mandy nor Jeff Mercer nor Jamie Corwin nor Nancy Gerard—is on the board of the Johnny Mercer Foundation. Nick Mamalakis was on it for a year, but he says that Whiting dropped him, telling him it was too expensive to fly him to California for board meetings.

Thirty-three

Three and a half years after John's death, Calvin Trillin wrote in the February 2, 1981, issue of *The New Yorker*:

"The Mercers have long been a prominent family in Savannah—a city particularly conscious of prominent families. In Atlanta, a successful businessman who wants to upgrade his background beyond simply awarding posthumous commissions to a few Civil War ancestors may allow his neighbors to infer that his family was originally from Savannah, Georgia's first settlement. The Mercers are the sort of family he would be trying to suggest—the sort of family whose discussions of military forebears tend to focus not on the Civil War but on the American Revolution. The Mercers are among the families that people in Savannah sometimes allow themselves to refer to as 'the bluebloods'—a phrase that would be difficult to utter without a smile in Atlanta, one of the Southern cities where the most powerful citizens in town used to be known as 'the big mules.' In Savannah, the bluebloods still have the sort of power that big mules might have in another city—partly because Savannah has not been the kind of place that attracts a lot of ambitious newcomers who might shoulder them aside. Until their family company, which manufactured Great Dane truck trailers, was bought up by a conglomerate several years ago, the Mercers were one of Savannah's major industrial employers. George Mercer III, who did not remain with Great Dane after the purchase, is the chairman of the board of Savannah's Memorial Hospital and a former member of the Chatham County Commission. Although no one named Mercer is a force in the business life of the city these days, the Mercers remain the Mercers—stalwarts of the Oglethorpe Club, the kind of family that can ordinarily sort out any difficulty with a telephone call."

The context of this comment was a report by Trillin on the kidnapping of George Mercer IV, whose father, George Mercer III, was John's nephew, son of one of his three half brothers. A newspaper photo, Trillin wrote, "showed a young man with the sort of thick mustache and blow-dried hair that makes a lot of twenty-two-year-olds look pretty much alike. . . ." A description of young Mercer in the newspapers gave his height as five feet eight, his weight as 155 pounds. He was, Trillin tells us, considering various get-rich-quick possibilities.

When he was a student at La Grange College, word circulated that he was a grandnephew of Johnny Mercer. He played guitar and wrote songs. For a while he sold vacuum cleaners. On January 29, 1980, he vanished. A police search was joined by the Federal Bureau of Investigation, whose agents believed he had been kidnapped. The family soon received ransom notes. Police began showing his photo in the boutiques, bars, and restaurants lodged in converted warehouses along cobblestoned River Street, below the bluff right across the street from the old Mercer family real estate office. FBI agents had no idea whether he was alive or dead, but thought they knew who might have written the notes and began showing not only Mercer's picture but also one of a young man named Michael Harper.

Harper was, by all accounts, smart and shrewd, accomplished in electronics and math, and a skilled scuba diver. At one point he had worked as a disc jockey, and he dreamed up a scheme to use a Savannah Police Department badge to cheat a couple of dealers out of some marijuana. Harper had gone to jail in 1974, at the age of seventeen, for trying to extort $4,500 from a former neighbor by threatening to kill him and his family. An FBI agent who had worked on the extortion case thought he recognized Harper's style in the disappearance of young Mercer.

Michael Harper left Savannah, but was unlucky enough to hitch a ride with a van that police stopped for speeding. A day later he was in jail for a probation violation, and the FBI charged him with trying to extort $42,000 from George Mercer III.

At last, toward the end of April, the police found George Mercer IV. He had been shot twice in the head and buried in a shallow grave on the grounds of Armstrong State University in Savannah. Harper was charged with the murder. He went on trial in the winter of 1980–81, pleading guilty to extortion but denying the murder charge. In his defense he said that he, young Mercer, and two others had tried to raise capital to start a stereo business by acquiring $40,000 worth of marijuana on credit for resale, but before they could unload it, it was stolen. After receiving death threats over the debt, they decided to try to extort the money from George Mercer III, and when the plot imploded, the four fled in sundry directions. The jury took four hours to convict him of murder.

With the death of George Mercer IV and the subsequent demise of his father from cancer, the story of the Mercers in Savannah, those descended from the Hugh Mercer of Aberdeen who was an aide to George Washington, comes to an end. Johnny Mercer's nephew, the architect Hugh Mercer, son of John's half brother Hugh, never married. He died not long after I interviewed him, a man frustrated by a defective memory, resulting from his stroke. Jimmie Hancock, John's friend and my first guide to Savannah, died in 2001. Jimmy McIntire, John's friend from childhood, a prominent business leader in Savannah, died in late 2002, at the age of ninety-two.

In time Nancy became determined to learn more about her father, having lived for years with nothing more to go on than her mother's terse "He was no good and he left us."

"I didn't even know if he'd survived the war," Nancy said.

He had gone into the Army as a second lieutenant in the Signal Corps, but because he had a background in photography he was assigned to photo reconnaissance, first with the Eighth Air Force and then the Ninth, serving in England and France, in charge of the photo lab.

After the war he worked for Title Insurance and Trust Company in Los Angeles. Steve Gerard at last tracked him down, working from his birth date and birthplace, which were listed on Nancy's birth certificate. Nancy was then twenty-nine.

Gil Keith said, "She had Steve call me first. He ascertained who I was."

"Were you shocked?" I asked.

"No," he said. "Because I had been planning to go back to Savannah and look for her. I guess Lillian told everyone that I was dead."

Nancy flew to Los Angeles with her eighteen-month-old daughter for her first meeting with her father, whom she had never so much as seen. And he was seeing her for the first time as well. "I had a hard time accepting it at first," he said. "It was very, very emotional," Nancy said. She learned that she had three half sisters and a half brother, and in the years since that reunion in 1971, they have all grown very close to her.

"My father is a quiet, sensitive man, and a reader," Nancy told me.

Gil Keith said, "I told Nancy that I forgave Lillian a long time ago." Now retired, he lives in Carlsbad, California.

Nancy is, of course, a direct descendant of Hugh Mercer of Aberdeen, and she has cousins. But they are all women, and none bears the Mercer name. And since John had no blood children of his own, the Mercer line in Savannah is extinct. No Mercer lives in the house at Vernon View, which had been renamed Moon River. Jeff sold it soon after Ginger's death.

When I stayed with Nancy and Steve in June 2001, she hauled out cartons of Mercer memorabilia. We spent days going through them, often sneezing from the rising dust. Nancy took me to various of John's haunts, including the house at Vernon View. And we went to Bonaventure Cemetery, where John is buried among ancestors. He lies under a horizontal slab of marble engraved JOHN HERNDON (JOHNNY) MERCER. AND THE ANGELS SING. That was yet another of his songs. I kissed my fingertips and touched them to the stone and said, "So long, John."

Someone had placed a little toy grand piano on the stone. Someone else had placed a little paper cutout of a grand piano beside it, weighted down by a small rock. Nearby were a number of coins (nickels and pennies) and inexpensive gems.

"The coins are always there," Nancy said. "We don't know who puts them there."

Ginger lies beside John under a slab engraved YOU MUST HAVE BEEN A BEAUTIFUL BABY. Nancy arranged for a stone bench to face the graves.

John Herndon Mercer's name is enormous in Savannah, of course. There is a Johnny Mercer Boulevard, and a small suburban district called Mercer's Place is where Nick Mamalakis lives; its streets, at his behest, were named after Mercer songs. Nick lives on Summer Wind Drive. Other streets bear the names Indian Summer and Autumn Leaves. There is now a Johnny Mercer Theater in central Savannah, and, as we have noted, Back River is now known as Moon River; younger people don't realize that it was ever anything else.

Mandy, long ago divorced from Bob Corwin, lives in Palm Desert, California. "I was a premature baby," she said, "and my birth mother was on the street with me in the first few weeks." The consequence was a respiratory ailment known as chronic obstructive pulmonary disease, COPD for short. And the medication to treat it has exacerbated her osteoporosis to the degree that she is a semi-invalid. She remains remarkably sunny of disposition, and close to her daughter and son and grandchildren. Her brother, Jeff, lives in Oregon with his wife. His son works for the forestry department. Jeff and Mandy are in constant communication.

Jeff has strong feelings about the adoption laws, and his own experience as an adopted child.

"The old laws are disgraceful," he said. "What right do people have, when they adopt a child, to exclusion? The child should have superseding rights to know the facts. There should be no such thing as closed adoptions. Everything should be public. The child has a right to the facts—first of all, for health reasons. You might be predisposed to getting a certain type of cancer. All that. All adopted people who don't know the facts are living on the edge.

"My mom had the information all the time and she finally, in a sarcastic way, gave it to me. My birth parents were from Georgia. My father was a pre-med student or something. It was out of wedlock. They were going to get married. They were real proper. And so they put me up for adoption. They probably got married and had three or four kids anyway. I never followed up. I just know that I'm Welsh—which isn't too far from being Scottish! Or Irish.

"It's a matter of your heritage. All my father was interested in was heritage, and you'd think he might have pushed for it for me. I think it was mainly my mother who didn't want to deal with it."

We are left to wonder why Johnny and Ginger never had children of their own. Was one or the other of them incapable of it? Or did Ginger just not want them? She left little evidence that she even wanted the two they adopted.

The Gerard house, part of a new development, is, as I said at the beginning, on one of the great salt marshes of Savannah. Steve has a splendid speedboat, and took us for a cruise of the waterways, past any number of places connected to John's youth. In the evenings, I would sometimes sit on their back terrace, overlooking the marsh and the waterway.

Several persons along the way asked me if I had figured out the cause of John's melancholy. Originally I would answer, "No." But now I think I have. On reading those pathetic (to my mind), pleading letters that he wrote to Ginger when he was twenty-one, his pleadings for affection, and her evident way of tantalizing him with mentions of other men—which apparently kept up, to judge by her evidently endless comparison of Mercer's position with the enormous success of Bing Crosby—it became painfully obvious.

Rose Gilbert said, "Maybe it was the result of being married to the wrong woman." If, as has often been postulated by psychiatrists, depression is anger turned inward, it is a tempting corollary that anger is depression turned outward. This theory fits John Herndon Mercer.

Since Ginger never really knew who John was, and certainly never understood the nature and scope of his towering talent, it is little wonder that he took up with someone who did: Judy Garland.

There is no question in my mind, though, after looking at the pictures of Ginger and John together, and particularly after reading his letters to Ginger and those to his mother in defense of her, that he truly loved her. Recalling their days in Brooklyn as aspiring young songwriters, Carl Sigman said, "They seemed to be very close. She sat through it very patiently as we worked. She never said a word. Very nice, quiet person. I thought they got along beautifully. Later on, who knows? Things happen. But they were terrific together then and I really enjoyed both of them."

In the end there is the puzzle of Johnny's relationship with his mother. His letters to her all have the same tone of almost obsequious subservience, an almost pathological adoration, endlessly catering to her.

Jamie Corwin knew Lillian from the time he was about eleven, and she was nearing the end of her life. He said: "I met Lillian probably in 1972. I spent a spring with her in the house at Palm Springs. She couldn't remember who I was, but she was lucid enough to have conversations. I was a baseball buff, and she had a lot of stories about the Yankees in the twenties. She could tell a story very well.

"She had a lot of authority over Johnny. She insisted on speaking Gullah with him. She'd slap his hand, a grown man in his early sixties. She'd tell him what to wear to Thanksgiving and Easter meals. One time she insisted he wear this Colonel Sanders–type suit at Easter. He came in wearing the white suit and white hat and black tie.

"He would get me to sit by her side to keep her off him.

"She was a tough lady. She was not a pushover, that's for sure.

"Ginger was not thrilled by the way Johnny treated either one of their mothers. She felt he was too accommodating to his own mother, and even more so to *her* mother. He would send her mother on trips with Ginger's sister Claire. She'd say, 'Why are you footing the bill on this one?' And he'd say, 'It's your *mother.*' "

Mickey Goldsen liked Ginger. After John's death, he and his wife would take her to dinner at restaurants such as Scandia. "Ginger and my wife were both born in Brooklyn, and they got along very well.

"Ginger and Johnny started out with nothing. She was a poor chorus girl and he was a beginning songwriter. They wanted fame and fortune, and they got what they were looking for.

"They found everything in the world but love."

Finally, I am left to contemplate the hideous way John died. Why was he not allowed, instead of undergoing that cruel and useless surgery, to go home to Georgia and, appropriately medicated, sit looking out over the saw grass and the wooden piers and the saltwater meanders and the seabirds and the great huge Georgia clouds and the rain coming in across the sea? All the things he loved and used to talk to me about. Why?

Jo Stafford asked me, "Now that you've really studied him, how do you feel about him?"

"I loved him, Jo," I said.

"So did I," she said.

Southern writing is more than Southern: it's Celtic—Irish and Scottish, which are of course of the same root stock. It has about it a quality of pathological sensitivity, an awareness often heightened by drugs or alcohol. Nor should we consider alcohol to be less mind-altering merely because of its general social acceptance. It is powerful and effective stuff. William Faulkner, Tennessee Williams, Thomas Wolfe, Edgar Allan Poe, and John Mercer were all drinkers, though of course the proclivity is hardly limited to Southern and Celtic writers. Hemingway, Steinbeck, Cheever, and London were all drinkers to the point of self-destructiveness. The affinity between writers and alcohol has been the subject of rumination among psychologists, who overlook one of the main reasons writers drink: because they can. They work alone, often at home, and there is nothing to prevent their starting in the morning. But I suspect two other factors as well. One is that alcohol (like other drugs) lowers the barrier between the left and right brain, allowing dreamy images and perceptions to be transmuted into the clear and analytical medium of structured words. The second factor is that it lowers self-awareness and therefore inhibition. It thereby enhances the flow. It also eases the loneliness of the task, of which psychologists have made much, though I think this is a minor factor. Artists love the loneliness, reveling in their essential solipsism.

At its extreme, these qualities in Southern writers—an extreme sensitivity, in many cases sourced in a Celtic self-pity—produced Poe and Faulkner, whose works are memorable above all for their flamboyant morbidity.

It is this ability to walk to the edge of the pit and step back from it with a good story that makes a great writer. In the case of lyric writing, this surefootedness is even more necessary, for the lament is one of the main forms of the art, and the ability to walk that wire of pathos without falling into the pit of bathos is an indispensable element of the craft. You cannot write tragedy without a sense of humor; the lack of it produces something turgid and dull. Wit must be the underpainting of all dark writing. There lies the secret of Larry Hart's brilliance, and indeed of all the great lyricists: think of Yip Harburg and Dorothy Fields and Cole Porter. There is laughter in John's tragic songs: self-mockery is the essence of "One for My Baby." And there is melancholy in his humor. And in all his writing there is that Southern vision, the marshes and dark oaks and the deep shadows of the pine woodlands, and everywhere, beautiful in its own strange way, the eternal haunting Spanish moss.

Walter Pater said to Oscar Wilde, during Wilde's early days, "Why do you always write poetry? Why do you not write prose? Prose is so much more difficult."

Yet the song lyric may be the most difficult literary form of all; at least it is when it is pursued to its highest level.

David Raksin, whose "Laura" (written with Mercer) is one of the great classics, said, "I write all kinds of music, including concert music. I think that our country's greatest musical gift to the world is not concert music, and not jazz—and I love jazz. Our greatest contribution is the American popular song. I'm talking about the songs of Jerome Kern, Harold Arlen, George Gershwin, Vernon Duke, Vincent Youmans, Richard Rodgers, Cole Porter, Arthur Schwartz, Stephen Sondheim. It is the most incredible flowering ever of that kind of music.

"When you listen to one of the great Kern or Arlen songs, you realize you are hearing the work of a genius. There is something Schubertian about a song like 'Look for the Silver Lining.' A tune like 'All the Things You Are' is an absolute marvel. Those people were wizards.

"In Vienna in the time of Lehar and those people, they wrote marvelous music, but nothing like what went on here in this country. Nothing like it has ever been done. Richard Rodgers was the best waltz composer of our time. It's amazing what went on, and it should be appreciated."

A BBC interviewer asked John for his evaluation of his legacy. Sternly realistic, in view of the direction in which American culture was tending, he replied: "I think some of my songs will maybe be noticed as individual pieces, but I think Gilbert, Hart, possibly [Ira] Gershwin—because of his brother, but mostly because of his wit, his sly sense of humor—and Berlin and Porter, going right on up into Lerner and Loesser, will be studied and taught in schools, and collected . . . and forgotten."

And, of course, Howard Dietz, Otto Harbach, Dorothy Fields, Carolyn Leigh, Leo Robin, Alan and Marilyn Bergman, Tom Adair, Oscar Hammerstein, and a few more.

Nancy brought one of John's friends over to meet me on one of those days when we were exploring her memorabilia. The man said, "Don't you think Johnny was more than a lyricist—he was a poet?"

"No," I said without hesitation, "he was more than a poet, he was a lyricist."

Bibliography

ASCAP Biographical Dictionary. New Providence, N.J.: R.R. Bowker, 1980.

Bach, Bob, and Ginger Mercer. *Our Huckleberry Friend: The Life, Times and Lyrics of Johnny Mercer.* New York: Citadel Press, 1982.

Dexter, Dave, Jr. *Playback.* New York: Billboard Publications, 1996.

Giddins, Gary. *Bing Crosby: A Pocketful of Dreams—The Early Years, 1903–1940.* New York: Little, Brown and Company, 2001.

Jablonski, Edward. *Harold Arlen: Rhythm, Rainbows and Blues.* Boston: Northeastern University Press, 1996.

Lahr, John. *Notes on a Cowardly Lion: The Biography of Bert Lahr.* New York: Alfred A. Knopf, 1969.

Lees, Gene. *The Modern Rhyming Dictionary: How to Write Lyrics.* New York: Cherry Lane Music Company, 1981.

———. *Singers and the Song.* New York: Oxford University Press, 1987.

Maltin, Leonard. *Movie Encyclopedia.* New York: Dutton, 1994.

Mancini, Henry, and Gene Lees (contributor). *Did They Mention the Music?* New York: St. Martin's Press, 1989.

Patton, Robert H. *The Pattons: A Personal History of an American Family.* New York: Crown, 1994.

Sudhalter, Richard M. *Stardust Melody: The Life and Music of Hoagy Carmichael.* New York: Oxford University Press, 2002.

Wilk, Max. *They're Playing Our Song.* New York: Atheneum, 1973.

Index

Index

Beatles, 266–7, 289, 297

Beaton, Cecil, 245

Beck, Gordon, 202

Beiderbecke, Bix, 38–9, 61, 92, 97

Bel Geddes, Norman, 296

Bennett, Betty, 3, 196, 216, 309

Bennett, Tony, 233, 234

Benny, Jack, 262, 264

Bergman, Alan, 5, 208, 258, 304, 329, 339

Bergman, Marilyn, 5, 324, 339

Berkeley, Busby, 117, 125

Berlin, Irving, 33, 47, 96, 116, 130, 144, 158, 198, 207, 221, 253, 262, 286–7, 292, 315, 338

Bernstein, Elmer, 271, 278, 282

Blackburn, John, 157

Blackie, Nell, 114

Blake, Eubie, 160

Blane, Ralph, 179, 180

Bleyer, Archie, 93–4, 95

Block, Martin, 265

Bloom, Rube, 113–14, 272

Blue Reys, 216

Blues in the Night (film), 141–2, 218

Bogart, Humphrey, 199, 218

Bolton, Whitney, 241, 252

Bontemps, Arna, 236, 237

Brand, Oscar, 287

Breakfast at Tiffany's (film), 272–6, 278, 279, 288

Breen, Robert, 247

Bregman, Jack, 110

Brown, Les, 157, 196, 262

Brown, Lew, 47, 150, 167

Brown, Tony, 54

Burke, Johnny, 229

Butterfield, Billy, 154, 157

Byers, Billy, 247

Caesar, Irving, 34, 51

Cagney, James, 146, 218

Cahn, Sammy, 282, 287

Calloway, Cab, 82, 262

Cantor, Eddie, 58

Capitol News, The, 151, 156, 172

Capitol Records

artists with, 4, 92, 152, 153–4, 165, 167, 170, 172–3, 216, 266–7

children's division, 154, 171

development of, 154, 155–7, 162, 167, 170–3

EMI's purchase of, 202, 210, 214, 221

in foreign markets, 173

founding of, 4, 47, 149–50, 151–4, 196, 203, 222, 299

initial public offering of, 172

integrity of, 89, 173

Johnny's records for, 161

Johnny's withdrawal from, 201, 202, 203–4

masters destroyed in, 301–2

and musician strike, 152–3

new office building of, 202

promotion department, 172

publishing division, 158, 195

spoken-word division, 154

and World War II, 160

Capitol Songs, 158

Capone, Al, 152

Capp, Al, 241–2

Capra, Frank, 201

Captains of the Clouds (film), 146, 218

344

Index

Index

Index

Index

Index

Index

Index

Index

Index

Index

Permissions Acknowledgments

A Note About the Author

Gene Lees is the author of fourteen books of jazz history and analysis, including *Cats of Any Color: Jazz, Black and White; You Can't Steal a Gift: Dizzy, Clark, Milt, and Nat; Leader of the Band: The Life of Woody Herman; Oscar Peterson: The Will to Swing;* and *The Modern Rhyming Dictionary: How to Write Lyrics,* a standard reference work. He has written for newspapers around the world, including the *Los Angeles Times,* the *New York Times,* and the *Globe and Mail* (Toronto). Also a renowned lyricist, he has written songs with Antonio Carlos Jobim, Bill Evans, Charles Aznavour, Gerry Mulligan, and Roger Kellaway, among others. His work has been recorded by many acclaimed singers, including Frank Sinatra, Tony Bennett, Peggy Lee, Carmen McRae, Joe Williams, Nancy Wilson, and Ella Fitzgerald. A three-time winner of the ASCAP–Deems Taylor Award, Lees writes and publishes the *Jazzletter,* P.O. Box 240, Ojai, Calif., 93024-0240.

A Note on the Type

The text of this book was set in Sabon, a typeface designed by Jan Tschichold (1902–1974), the well-known German typographer. Based loosely on the original designs by Claude Garamond (c. 1480–1561), Sabon is unique in that it was explicitly designed for hot metal composition on both the Monotype and Linotype machines as well as for film setting. Designed in 1966 in Frankfurt, Sabon was named for the famous Lyons punch-cutter Jacques Sabon, who is thought to have brought some of Garamond's matrices to Frankfurt.